MARVEL FIRSTS
THE 1990s
VOL. 1

MARVEL FIRSTS: THE 1990S VOL. 1. Contains material originally published in magazine form as GHOST RIDER #1, DEATHLOK #1, NEW WARRIORS #1, FOOLKILLER #1, DARKHAWK #1, SLEEPWALKER #1, X-FORCE #1, X-FACTOR #71, WARLOCK AND THE INFINITY WATCH #2, DEATH'S HEAD II #1, SILVER SABLE AND THE WILD PACK #1, TERROR INC. #1, NIGHT THRASHER: FOUR CONTROL #1, DARKHOLD: PAGES FROM THE BOOK OF SINS #1, CAPTAIN AMERICA ANNUAL #9 and SPIDER-MAN 2099 #1. First printing 2016. ISBN# 978-0-7851-9833-8. Published by MARVEL WORLDWIDE, INC., a subsidiary of MARVEL ENTERTAINMENT, LLC. OFFICE OF PUBLICATION: 135 West 50th Street, New York, NY 10020. **Printed in the U.S.A.** ALAN FINE, President, Marvel Entertainment; DAN BUCKLEY, President, TV, Publishing & Brand Management; JOE QUESADA, Chief Creative Officer; TOM BREVOORT, SVP of Publishing; DAVID BOGART, SVP of Business Affairs & Operations, Publishing & Partnership; C.B. CEBULSKI, VP of Brand Management & Development, Asia; DAVID GABRIEL, SVP of Sales & Marketing, Publishing; JEFF YOUNGQUIST, VP of Production & Special Projects; DAN CARR, Executive Director of Publishing Technology; ALEX MORALES, Director of Publishing Operations; SUSAN CRESPI, Production Manager; STAN LEE, Chairman Emeritus. For information regarding advertising in Marvel Comics or on Marvel.com, please contact Vit DeBellis, Integrated Sales Manager, at vdebellis@marvel.com. For Marvel subscription inquiries, please call 888-511-5480. **Manufactured between 2/26/2016 and 4/4/2016 by R.R. DONNELLEY, INC., SALEM, VA, USA.**

10 9 8 7 6 5 4 3 2 1

MARVEL FIRSTS THE 1990s

GHOST RIDER #1
"Life's Blood"
starring DAN KETCH
WRITER: **Howard Mackie**
PENCILER: **Javier Saltares**
INKER: **Mark Texeira**
COLORIST: **Gregory Wright**
LETTERER: **Michael Heisler**
EDITOR: **Bobbie Chase**

DEATHLOK #1
"Book One: The Brains of the Outfit"
starring MICHAEL COLLINS
WRITERS: **Dwayne McDuffie & Gregory Wright**
PENCILER: **Jackson Guice**
INKER: **Scott Williams**
COLORISTS: **Gregory Wright with Paul Mounts & Brad Vancata**
LETTERER: **Richard Starkings**
ASSISTANT EDITOR: **Tom Brevoort**
EDITOR: **Bob Budiansky**

NEW WARRIORS #1
"From the Ground Up!"
WRITER: **Fabian Nicieza**
PENCILER: **Mark Bagley**
INKER: **Al Williamson**
COLORIST: **Mike Rockwitz**
LETTERER: **Michael Heisler**
EDITOR: **Danny Fingeroth**

CAPTAIN AMERICA ANNUAL #9
"Walking the Line"
starring JACK MONROE: NOMAD
WRITER: **Fabian Nicieza**
PENCILER: **Don Hudson**
INKER: **Tom Morgan**
COLORIST: **Ed Lazellari**
LETTERER: **Pat Brosseau**
ASSISTANT EDITOR: **Michael Heisler**
EDITOR: **Ralph Macchio**

FOOLKILLER #1
"Mad...As In Angry"
WRITER: **Steve Gerber**
PENCILER: **J.J. Birch**
INKER: **Tony DeZuniga**
COLORIST: **Gregory Wright**
LETTERER: **Phil Felix**
EDITOR: **Craig Anderson**

DARKHAWK #1
"Dawn of the Darkhawk"
WRITER: **Danny Fingeroth**
ARTIST: **Mike Manley**
COLORIST: **Joe Rosas**
LETTERER: **Joe Rosen**
EDITOR: **Howard Mackie**

SLEEPWALKER #1
"To Sleep Perchance to Scream!"
WRITER & COLORIST: **Bob Budiansky**
ARTIST: **Bret Blevins**
LETTERER: **Tom Orzechowski**
EDITOR: **Don Daley**

X-FORCE #1
"A Force To Be Reckoned With"
PLOTTER & ARTIST: **Rob Liefeld**
SCRIPTER: **Fabian Nicieza**
COLORIST: **Brad Vancata**
LETTERER: **Chris Eliopoulos**
ASSISTANT EDITOR: **Suzanne Gaffney**
EDITOR: **Bob Harras**

X-FACTOR #71
"Cutting the Mustard"
starring THE ALL-NEW, ALL-DIFFERENT X-FACTOR
WRITER: **Peter David**
PENCILER: **Larry Stroman**
INKER: **Al Milgrom**
COLORIST: **Glynis Oliver**
LETTERER: **Michael Heisler**
ASSISTANT EDITOR: **Suzanne Gaffney**
EDITOR: **Bob Harras**

WARLOCK AND THE INFINITY WATCH #2
"Gathering the Watch!"
WRITER: **Jim Starlin**
PENCILER: **Angel Medina**
INKER: **Terry Austin**
COLORIST: **Ian Laughlin**
LETTERER: **Jack Morelli**
EDITOR: **Craig Anderson**

DEATH'S HEAD II #1
"The Wild Hunt, Part One: Mergers and Acquisitions"
WRITER: **Dan Abnett**
PENCILER: **Liam Sharp**
INKERS: **Andy Lanning**
& Bambos Georgiou
COLORIST: **Helen Stone**
LETTERER: **Peri Godbold**
EDITOR: **Steve White**

SILVER SABLE & THE WILD PACK #1
"Personal Stakes"
WRITER: **Gregory Wright**
PENCILER: **Steven Butler**
INKER: **Jim Sanders III**
COLORIST: **Joe Rosas**
LETTERER: **Jade Moede**
EDITOR: **Craig Anderson**

TERROR INC. #1
"Caveat Emptor"
WRITER: **D.G. Chichester**
ARTIST: **Jorge Zaffino**
COLORIST: **Steve Buccellato**
LETTERER: **Gaspar Saladino**
EDITOR: **Marcus McLaurin**

NIGHT THRASHER: FOUR CONTROL #1
"Four Control, One: Strength"
WRITER: **Fabian Nicieza**
ARTIST: **Dave Hoover**
COLORIST: **Brad Vancata**
LETTERER: **Chris Eliopoulos**
ASSISTANT EDITOR: **Eric Fein**
EDITOR: **Danny Fingeroth**

DARKHOLD: PAGES FROM THE BOOK OF SINS #1
"Rise of the Midnight Sons, Part 4: Black Letter"
starring **THE DARKHOLD REDEEMERS**
WRITER: **Chris Cooper**
PENCILER: **Richard Case**
INKER: **Mark McKenna**
COLORIST: **Glynis Oliver**
LETTERER: **Phil Felix**
EDITOR: **Bobbie Chase**
MANAGING EDITOR: **Kelly Corvese**

SPIDER-MAN 2099 #1
"Spider-Man 2099"
WRITER: **Peter David**
PENCILER: **Rick Leonardi**
INKER: **Al Williamson**
COLORIST: **Steve Buccellato**
LETTERER: **Rick Parker**
ASSISTANT EDITOR: **Sarra Mossoff**
EDITOR: **Joey Cavalieri**
COLORIST: **Steve Buccellato**
LETTERER: **Richard Starkings**
EDITOR: **Bob Harras**

COLLECTION EDITOR: **Mark D. Beazley**
ASSOCIATE EDITOR: **Sarah Brunstad**
ASSOCIATE MANAGER, DIGITAL ASSETS: **Joe Hochstein**
ASSOCIATE MANAGING EDITOR: **Alex Starbuck**
EDITOR, SPECIAL PROJECTS: **Jennifer Grünwald**
VP, PRODUCTION & SPECIAL PROJECTS: **Jeff Youngquist**
RESEARCH & LAYOUT: **Jeph York**
PRODUCTION & COLOR RECONSTRUCTION: **ColorTek, Ryan Devall, Jerron Quality Color, Romie Jeffers, Digikore & Joe Frontirre**
SVP PRINT, SALES & MARKETING: **David Gabriel**

EDITOR IN CHIEF: **Axel Alonso**
CHIEF CREATIVE OFFICER: **Joe Quesada**
PUBLISHER: **Dan Buckley**
EXECUTIVE PRODUCER: **Alan Fine**

Special Thanks to Jeremy Hall, Jess Harrold, Gregory Hecht, Gary Henderson, Daron Jensen, Rob London, Markus Raymond & Marc Riemer

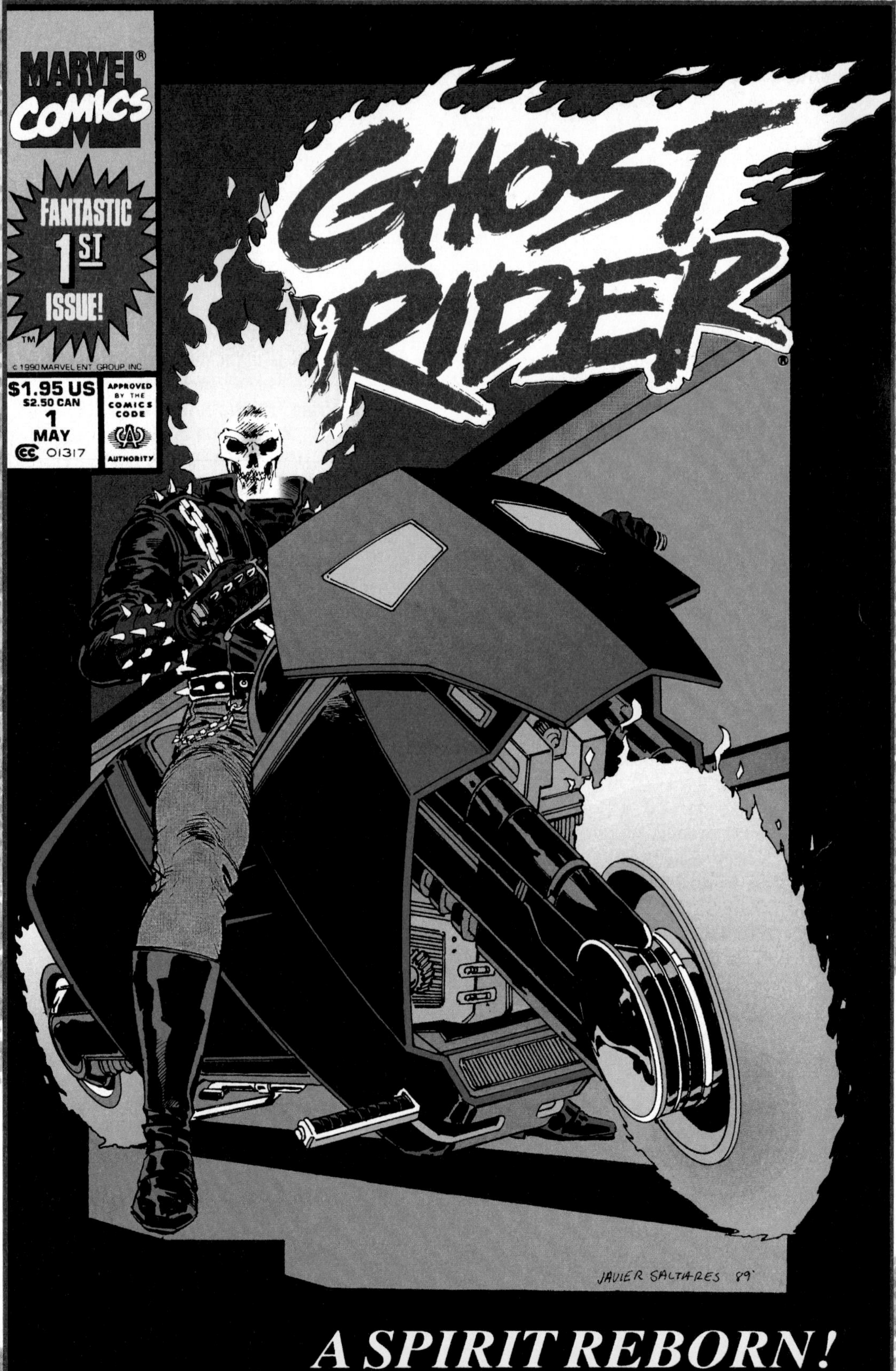
MARVEL COMICS
FANTASTIC 1ST ISSUE!
GHOST RIDER
© 1990 MARVEL ENT. GROUP, INC.
$1.95 US
$2.50 CAN
1
MAY
01317
APPROVED BY THE COMICS CODE AUTHORITY
JAVIER SALTARES '89
A SPIRIT REBORN!

GHOST RIDER #1, published in March 1990, began an ongoing series that revamped the 1970s character, introducing Dan Ketch as a new version of the flame-skulled, motorcycle-riding antihero.

WHEN INNOCENT BLOOD IS SPILLED, A SPIRIT OF VENGEANCE IS BORN, AND DANNY KETCH FINDS HIMSELF TRANSFORMED INTO THE

GHOST RIDER

STAN LEE PRESENTS:

LIFE'S BLOOD

writer: HOWARD MACKIE
penciler: JAVIER SALTARES
inker: MARK TEXEIRA
letterer: MICHAEL HEISLER
colorist: GREGORY WRIGHT
editor: BOBBIE CHASE
editor in chief: TOM DeFALCO

"Revenge proves its own executioner."

—John Ford

"I am the spirit of vengeance. Nothing will stop me from inflicting pain on all those who have inflicted it on innocent beings."

—Ghost Rider

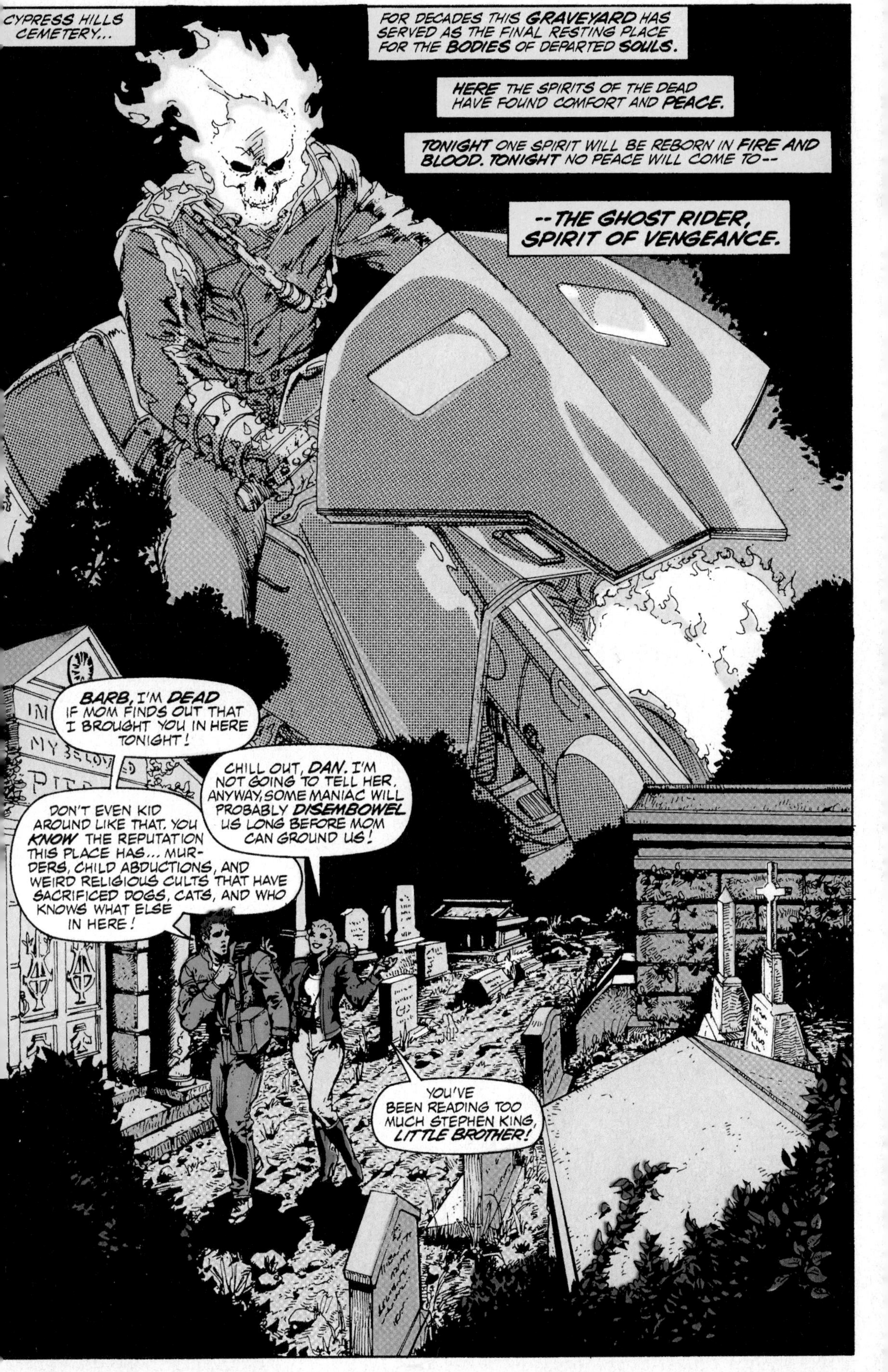
CYPRESS HILLS CEMETERY...
FOR DECADES THIS GRAVEYARD HAS SERVED AS THE FINAL RESTING PLACE FOR THE BODIES OF DEPARTED SOULS.
HERE THE SPIRITS OF THE DEAD HAVE FOUND COMFORT AND PEACE.
TONIGHT ONE SPIRIT WILL BE REBORN IN FIRE AND BLOOD. TONIGHT NO PEACE WILL COME TO--
--THE GHOST RIDER, SPIRIT OF VENGEANCE.
BARB, I'M DEAD IF MOM FINDS OUT THAT I BROUGHT YOU IN HERE TONIGHT!
CHILL OUT, DAN. I'M NOT GOING TO TELL HER. ANYWAY, SOME MANIAC WILL PROBABLY DISEMBOWEL US LONG BEFORE MOM CAN GROUND US!
DON'T EVEN KID AROUND LIKE THAT. YOU KNOW THE REPUTATION THIS PLACE HAS... MURDERS, CHILD ABDUCTIONS, AND WEIRD RELIGIOUS CULTS THAT HAVE SACRIFICED DOGS, CATS, AND WHO KNOWS WHAT ELSE IN HERE!
YOU'VE BEEN READING TOO MUCH STEPHEN KING, LITTLE BROTHER!

YOU PROMISED YOU'D TAKE ME TO SEE HOUDINI'S GRAVESITE ON HALLOWEEN EVE, AND YOU'RE NOT BACKING OUT.
I WANT TO GET SOME PICTURES OF THOSE ALLEGED PSYCHICS TRYING TO MAKE CONTACT WITH HIM ON THE OTHER SIDE.
RELAX. LET'S JUST HAVE SOME FUN. MONSTERS AREN'T WAITING FOR US AROUND EVERY CORNER--!
I HAVE A REAL BAD FEELING ABOUT THIS PLACE, BARB!
IT WAS JUST LAST HALLOWEEN THAT THOSE FIVE KIDS FROM RIDGEWOOD DISAPPEARED--
BOOOOOOO!
R-RUN!
NO, DAN, THEY'RE JUST KIDS--!
HA, HA, HA! LOOK AT THE BIG DOPE!
WHATTA YA AFRAID THAT THE BOGEYMAN IS GONNA GET YA?
HEY, CUTIE, WHAT'CHA GOT IN THIS PURSE OF YOURS?
HEY!
MAYBE A TREAT SO WE DON'T PLAY A TRICK ON YOU?!
HANDS OFF THE CAMERA BAG, YOU LITTLE BIMBO!
YEOW!
LET'S GET OUT OF HERE! THESE WIMPS AIN'T WORTH THE TIME OF THE CYPRESS POOL JOKERS!
LET'S GET TO THE GRAVESITE, MY BODYGUARD, BEFORE HOUDINI REALLY DOES COME BACK TO LIFE!
BARB, I'M SORRY I WASN'T MORE HELP. NEXT TIME...

A FEW MINUTES LATER...
BTOOM
RRRRR
WHAT'S THAT? IT SOUNDED LIKE A GUNSHOT AND A SCREAM!
PROBABLY JUST THOSE KIDS AGAIN--
--BUT IT COULD BE SOMETHING GOOD THAT I COULD GET ON FILM!
BARB, WAIT, IT ISN'T SAFE!
DON'T WORRY, DAN, THIS COULD BE EXCITING.
NOW SHUSH. I THINK THE NOISE CAME FROM RIGHT OVER HERE BY GALLAGHER'S JUNKYARD.
LOOKS LIKE WE'RE NOT THE ONLY CURIOUS ONES.
THEY'D BETTER GET OUT OF THERE, 'CAUSE FROM THE LOOKS OF THINGS--
CYPRESS POOL
JOKERS
--SOMETHING PRETTY UGLY IS ABOUT TO HAPPEN!
BACK OFF, YOU COSTUMED CLOWN! THIS HERE BELONGS TO THE KINGPIN!
SO WE'RE GONNA HAFTA BURN YOU FOR KILLING HIS COURIER.
NO OFFENSE.

SNAP
NONE TAKEN.
GLAD TO SEE YOU AIN'T GONNA PUT UP A FIGHT--
--WE DO HAVE YOU OUTNUMBERED FOUR TO ONE.
JUST STAND STILL AND WE'LL DO YOU AS QUICK AND PAINLESS AS POSSIBLE.
TONY?
FWIP
BKOOM
WHAT THE--? GURGH!
WHO... ARE... YOU?
I AM DEATHWATCH.
I AM YOUR DEATH!
KRAK

KERACK
NO!!!
UP THERE! THAT GIRL.
WHAT WAS THAT?
SHE'S SEEN MY FACE.
KILL HER.
HUHF!
WHOOSHMP
BARB!

TOO MANY PEOPLE ARE GETTIN' TRASHED HERE!
LET'S TAKE OFF.
C'MON, PAULIE, GET OUTTA THERE!
PAULIE!!
EVERYONE WANTED THIS SUITCASE PRETTY BAD. IT'S GOTTA BE FULL OF DRUGS OR MONEY OR SOMETHING.
AND SINCE IT AIN'T DOING THIS DEAD GUY NO GOOD--
--I MIGHT AS WELL HELP MYSELF TO IT!
WHAT?
THE CASE!
STOP THAT CHILD AND RETURN THE CASE AT ALL COSTS.
BE CAREFUL--
--ITS CONTENTS ARE MORE VALUABLE THAN ANY OF YOUR LIVES.
I AM LEAVING BEFORE I AM DISCOVERED AMONGST THIS HUMAN REFUSE.
DO NOT FAIL ME! AND LEAVE NO WITNESSES!

EARBY...
JUST HOLD ON, BARB, I'VE GOT YOU.
THEY'LL NEVER FIND US IN HERE.
I KNOW THIS PLACE LIKE THE BACK OF MY HAND!
WE'LL HIDE UNDER HERE UNTIL THEY LEAVE --
--THEN I'LL GET YOU TO A HOSPITAL.
YOU'RE GOING TO BE OKAY--!
OOMPH!
WHAT'S THAT GLOWING IN THE DARK? EYES?!
NO! NO MORE! GO AWAY!
THE BLOOD TRAIL ENDS HERE.
THEY COULD BE HIDING ANYWHERE IN ALL THIS WRECKAGE.
AND WE DON'T HAVE ALL NIGHT BEFORE THE AUTHORITIES APPEAR.
MY FRIEND, WE WANT TO HELP YOU! WE WANT TO HELP YOU AND THE GIRL. IT WAS ALL A TERRIBLE MISTAKE.
COME OUT AND LET US TAKE HER TO A DOCTOR.

DON'T WORRY, BARB. I'LL PROTECT YOU.
THEY WON'T HURT YOU ANY MORE.
LIGHTS IN THE DARK STILL GLOWING.
MORE THINGS TO HURT US?
NO.
A MOTORCYCLE.
SO NEW. IT SHOULDN'T BE HERE! NOT WITH ALL THIS JUNK.
CAN'T THINK ABOUT THAT NOW--
--HAVE TO TRY AND STOP THE BLEEDING.
SO MUCH BLOOD--
--ALL OVER ME.
ALL OVER EVERYTHING.
I'VE GOT THE GIRL AND THE CASE. LET'S GO!
DEATHWATCH WANTS NO WITNESSES AND WE HAVEN'T FOUND THE OTHER TWO YET.
WE DON'T HAVE THE TIME TO WASTE LOOKING FOR THEM--
HERE. THEN DESTROY IT ALL!
THERMITE GRENADES ARE SO ALL-ENCOMPASSING!

THIS IS IT, FRIEND. YOUR LAST CHANCE. COME OUT. LET US HELP YOU!
EVERYTHING'S GOING TO BE OKAY, BARB!
I WON'T LET THEM HURT YOU ANYMORE!
I'M GOING TO MAKE THE BLEEDING STOP.
BUT THERE'S TOO MUCH BLOOD! SO HOT AND STICKY ON MY HANDS.
I'D DO ANYTHING TO SAVE HER.
THE GAS CAP. GLOWING?!
THAT'S IT.
THE GIRL MUST'VE DIED.
USE THE GRENADE NOW. LEAVE NO EVIDENCE.
RRRMMMMBBBBLE
TCHANK
THE GROUND IS SHAKING-- THAT GLOW. WHAT IS IT?
WHO IS IT?!

I AM GHOST RIDER, THE SPIRIT OF VENGEANCE!

I DON'T KNOW WHO OR WHAT THAT THING IS, BUT IT HAS THE OTHER GIRL.
KILL THEM--
--KILL THEM ALL!
RELEASE HER OR DIE!
YOU'LL DIE FIRST, FREAK!
NO MORE INNOCENTS WILL BE HARMED HERE TODAY!
KA-BOW!

QUICKLY, KILL THE GIRL--I'LL TAKE CARE OF HIM!
BUT?!
TCHINK
WHAKRAK
YOU MUST SUFFER FOR THE PAIN YOU HAVE SOUGHT TO INFLICT--
--THE PAIN FELT BY THOUSANDS OF INNOCENT BEINGS!
N-NO! NO... NOOOO!
NOBODY MOVE!
WROOOO
THANKS FOR YOUR HELP, MISTER! 'BYE!

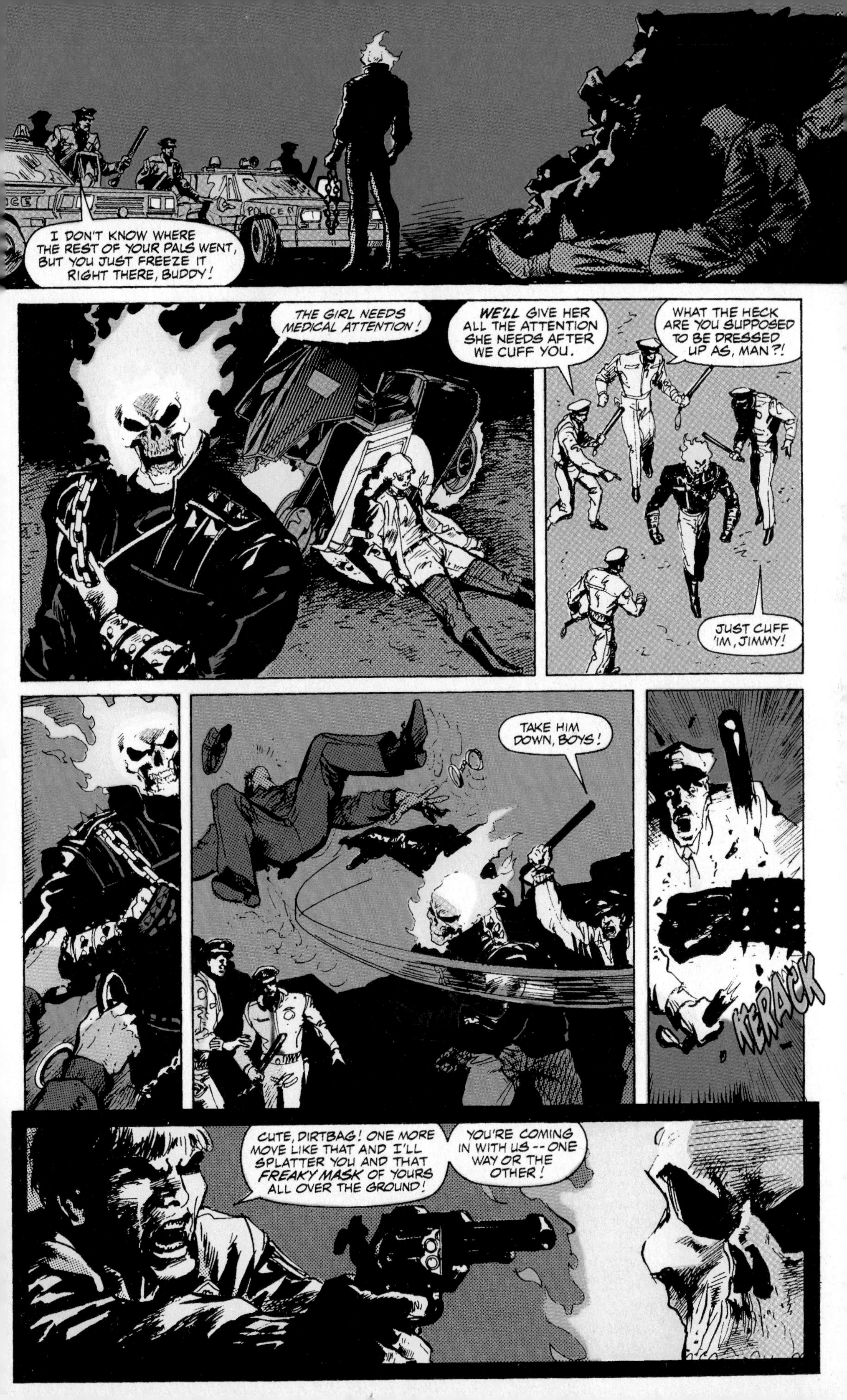
I DON'T KNOW WHERE THE REST OF YOUR PALS WENT, BUT YOU JUST FREEZE IT RIGHT THERE, BUDDY!
THE GIRL NEEDS MEDICAL ATTENTION!
WE'LL GIVE HER ALL THE ATTENTION SHE NEEDS AFTER WE CUFF YOU.
WHAT THE HECK ARE YOU SUPPOSED TO BE DRESSED UP AS, MAN?!
JUST CUFF 'IM, JIMMY!
TAKE HIM DOWN, BOYS!
KRACK
CUTE, DIRTBAG! ONE MORE MOVE LIKE THAT AND I'LL SPLATTER YOU AND THAT FREAKY MASK OF YOURS ALL OVER THE GROUND!
YOU'RE COMING IN WITH US -- ONE WAY OR THE OTHER!

SNOK!
THE INNOCENT BLOOD SPILLED HERE TONIGHT MUST BE AVENGED!
OOF!
IT IS MY SOLEMN DUTY.
DO HIM!
POLICE
POLICE

I CANNOT BE STOPPED.
SREE
I WILL NOT BE STOPPED.
FWAM
DO NOT TRY TO FOLLOW ME.
WHAT WAS THAT THING?
THIS WAS SUPPOSED TO BE A ROUTINE PUBLIC DISTURBANCE AND TRES-PASSING CALL!
WELL, IT TURNED OUT TO BE A WHOLE LOT MORE THAN THAT.
CALL FOR AN AMBULANCE AND SOME BACK-UP. THIS GIRL IS IN REAL BAD SHAPE. WHO KNOWS HOW MANY OTHER BODIES THAT FREAK LEFT BEHIND!

A FEW MINUTES LATER...
THAT'S GOTTA BE HIM. LET'S TAKE HIM.
WREOOOO
BLEVINS
YOU, ON THE BIKE! PULL OVER!!
CLIK
POLICE
FWOOSH
RRAWWW
I DON'T BELIEVE THAT.
ME NEITHER, BUT TWO UNITS HAVE HIM BOXED OFF AT THE END OF THE BLOCK.
POLICE

NITS 265 AND
, WE'VE GOT HIM
TWEEN US. THERE'S
NHERE FOR THE
REAK TO GO
NOW.
UH, I WOULDN'T SAY THAT.
DISPATCH, WE NEED MORE UNITS OUT HERE-- PRONTO!
I CAN LET NOTHING STOP ME FROM FINDING THOSE WHO HAVE SPILLED THE BLOOD OF THE INNOCENT.
NOTHING.
END OF THE LINE, BUDDY. PUT IT IN PARK BEFORE WE BLOW YOU AWAY.
NOTHING.
CLICK
FWAAAM
NOTHING!

GET ON THE HORN. I WANT EVERY AVAILABLE UNIT ON THAT GUY.
A FEW MINUTES LATER...
WE GOT HIM. WE GOT HIM!
DISPATCH. THIS IS UNIT 54. WE'VE GOT THE SUSPECT IN THE JUNKYARD ATTACK CORNERED ON 94TH STREET.
IT'S A DEAD END STREET.
THERE'S NOWHERE FOR HIM--
--TO...GO?
VROOOM!

ATER THAT NIGHT...
SALEM FIELDS
INNOCENT BLOOD HAS BEEN SPILLED TONIGHT--
--AWAKENING ME FROM MY LONG SLEEP.
VENGEANCE MUST BE DELIVERED.
VENGEANCE BY MY HANDS.
VENGEANCE BY MY--
--HANDS?
WHAT'S HAPPENED?
WHAT HAVE I DONE?
I HAVE TO FIND BARB!
I HAVE TO GET AWAY.

WALL STREET.
THE FINANCIAL CAPITAL OF THE WORLD.
HERE, IN THE SHADOW OF THE WORLD TRADE CENTER, FORTUNES ARE WON AND LOST EVERY DAY.
TONIGHT, MORE THAN MONEY HANGS IN THE BALANCE.
SEND THEM IN.
THE BRIEFCASE. WHERE IS IT?
WE WEREN'T ABLE TO GET IT BACK.
YEAH! SOME GUY ON A MOTORCYCL DID A NUMBE ON CARL AN THE KID TOO OFF WITH TH CASE.
AND YOU RETURNED TO ME ANYWAY?
SAY NO MORE.
I WILL LEARN OF YOUR FAILURE IN MY OWN WAY.
WITH THE SKILL OF A PSYCHIC SURGEON, DEATHWATCH PENETRATES THE ASSASSIN'S SKULL WITH HIS FINGERS.
RECENT MEMORIES ARE ABSORBED.
MEMORIES OF VIOLENCE AND--

--PAIN.
RR--ENOUGH!
YOU HAVE FAILED ME--
--AND YOU KNOW THE PENALTY FOR FAILURE.
NO! I'M NOT PLAYING ANY MORE OF YOUR SICK GAMES.
I'LL KILL YOU FIRST!
BLAM
HUUCKK
NICE OF YOU TO VOLUNTEER YOUR LIFE, SO THAT YOUR FRIENDS CAN CONTINUE LIVING.
THANK CARL, GENTLEMEN.
KRAK
THANKS, CARL.
FIND THE GIRL WITH THE SUITCASE.
I WANT IT, AND ITS CONTENTS, IN MY HANDS BEFORE THAT FAT, PETTY THUG HAS A CHANCE TO RECOVER IT.
DO NOT FAIL ME AGAIN.

THE FISK BUILDING IN MIDTOWN MANHATTAN.
WILSON FISK IS KNOWN TO MANY AS A RUTHLESS AND ACCOMPLISHED BUSINESSMAN.
TO OTHERS HE IS A COMMON CRIMINAL BENEATH CONTEMPT.
BUT TO THOSE WHO TRULY KNOW AND FEAR HIM HE IS--
--THE KINGPIN, POWERFUL OVERLORD OF EVERY CRIMINAL ACTIVITY IN NEW YORK CITY.
THE KINGPIN'S POWER IS NOT ONLY FIGURATIVE.
WHAK
SWAK
YOU CALL YOURSELVES MARTIAL ARTS MASTERS?
SLAM
SWOOSH
FINISH ME.

YOU RELY ON YOUR KATANA TOO MUCH, KENJI.
ANY WEAPON CAN BE TAKEN AWAY--
--AND DISABLED.
AH--EXCUSE ME, MR. FISK. I HAVE SOME BAD NEWS.
THE DELIVERY WE WERE EXPECTING THIS EVENING HAS BEEN WAYLAID.
ONE OF OUR COURIERS WAS ABLE TO PASS ON SOME INFORMATION REGARDING THE THEFT. I HAVE OUR PEOPLE SEARCHING FOR IT EVEN AS WE SPEAK.
THE CONTENTS OF THAT SUITCASE POSE A GREAT DANGER TO OUR ORGANIZATION. IT MUST NOT FALL INTO THE WRONG HANDS.
BRING ME THAT SUITCASE AND THE NAMES OF THE PEOPLE WHO DARE INTERFERE WITH ONE OF MY OPERATIONS.

SALEM FIELDS
MEANWHILE, IN ANOTHER PART OF THE CYPRESS HILLS CEMETERY...
I HOPE THEY AIN'T FOLLOWING ME!
THIS CASE HAS GOT TO BE PRETTY VALUABLE FOR ALL THOSE GUYS TO DIE FOR IT.
PROBABLY FULL OF DRUGS, OR BETTER YET--CASH!
ONLY ONE WAY TO FIND OUT. TAKE IT TO A NICE QUIET PLACE AND--
IN LOVING MEMORY
--OPEN IT!
YO, PAULIE, WE THOUGHT YOU WAS DEAD!
ALL RIGHT, YOU STILL GOT THE CASE!
BRING IT HERE AND I'LL POP THE LOCKS!
CLIK

DO IT QUICK, RALPHIE! I'VE GOT A GOOD FEELING ABOUT--
--THIS?!
WHERE'S THE MONEY? THE DRUGS?
IN THE BANK AND THE DRUG STORE, BABE!
LOOKS LIKE YOU ALMOST GOT YOURSELF KILLED FOR THREE CANS OF DEODORANT OR SOMETHING.
BUT THOSE GUYS IN THE CEMETERY... AND THE ONE THAT SAVED ME... HIS HEAD WAS ON FIRE!
SO'S YOUR BRAIN!
THERE'S GOT TO BE SOMETHING MORE!
WELL, IT AIN'T ANYTHING WE CAN USE!
SO WE'D BETTER GET RID OF THEM BEFORE THOSE GUYS FROM THE CEMETERY COME LOOKING FOR THEM!
THEN LET'S MAKE SURE WE PUT THEM WHERE THEY'LL NEVER FIND THEM!

EMERGENCY
EMERGENCY
OH, NO! MRS. KETCH, DAD--
--LOOK!
DANIEL?
STAY RIGHT THERE, BOY! EVERYTHING'S GOING TO BE FINE.
NOT MY SON, TOO!
DAN! IT'S CAPTAIN DOLAN. JUST HANG ON!
SOMEONE GET A DOCTOR-- QUICK!

NEXT DAY...
YOU GAVE US QUITE A SCARE, BOY!
BUT YOU DON'T SEEM TO BE TOO MUCH THE WORSE FOR WEAR!
OHN'S HOSPIT
WE REALLY COULD USE YOUR HELP IN FIGURING OUT WHAT HAPPENED IN THE CEMETERY.
YOU'RE GOING TO HAVE TO TRY IF WE'RE GOING TO CATCH THE GUY WHO HURT YOUR SISTER.
I REALLY DON'T REMEMBER TOO MUCH.
DADDY, BACK OFF A LITTLE!
DANIEL, THANK THE LORD YOU'RE ALL RIGHT. I KNOW THIS IS A SIGN THAT BARB IS GOING TO GET BETTER AS WELL.
MRS. KETCH? I NEED TO TALK TO YOU ABOUT YOUR DAUGHTER.
BARB? IS SHE ALL RIGHT? CAN I SEE HER?
SHE'S STILL IN SERIOUS CONDITION, BUT I SUPPOSE YOU CAN SEE HER FOR FIVE MINUTES!
DOCTOR, I'D LIKE TO SEE MY DAUGHTER AS WELL.
I'D RATHER TALK TO YOU ABOUT HER CONDITION IN MY OFFICE.
DANIEL, GIVE YOUR SISTER MY LOVE. I'LL BE THERE AS SOON AS I CAN.
YEAH, MOM.
DON'T WORRY, DAN, I'LL STAY WITH YOUR MOM. EVERYTHING'S GOING TO BE OKAY. YOU'LL SEE.
BARB?

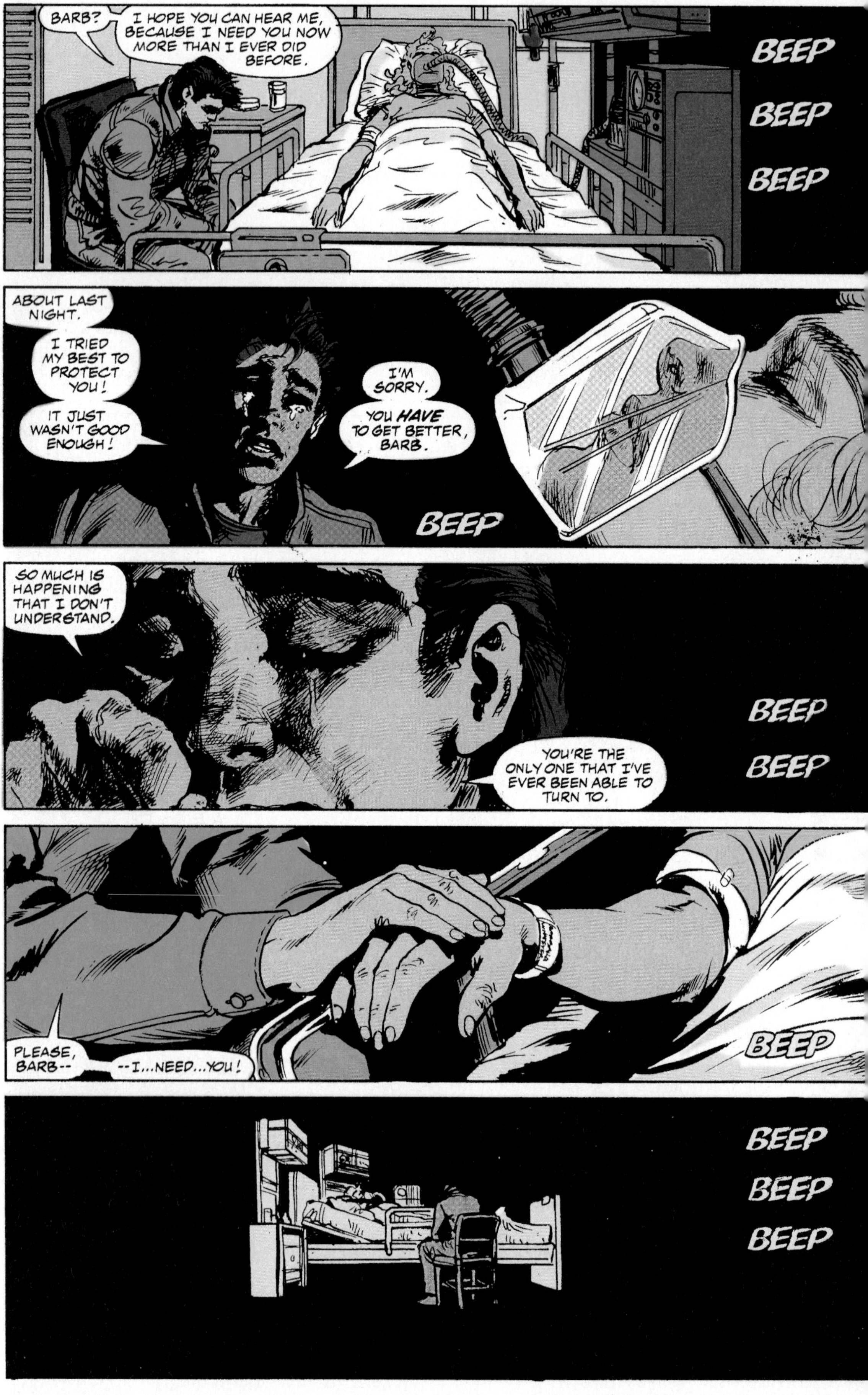

BARB?
I HOPE YOU CAN HEAR ME, BECAUSE I NEED YOU NOW MORE THAN I EVER DID BEFORE.
BEEP
BEEP
BEEP
ABOUT LAST NIGHT.
I TRIED MY BEST TO PROTECT YOU!
IT JUST WASN'T GOOD ENOUGH!
I'M SORRY.
YOU HAVE TO GET BETTER, BARB.
BEEP
SO MUCH IS HAPPENING THAT I DON'T UNDERSTAND.
BEEP
BEEP
YOU'RE THE ONLY ONE THAT I'VE EVER BEEN ABLE TO TURN TO.
PLEASE, BARB--
--I...NEED...YOU!
BEEP
BEEP
BEEP
BEEP

FEW HOURS LATER...
HE DOCTOR SAYS THAT
ARB'S CONDITION HAS
TABILIZED TEMPORARILY.
HE'S GOT TO GET
ETTER SO SHE CAN
ELP ME FIGURE OUT
WHAT'S GOING ON.
TALKING TO BARB MADE ME REALIZE THAT ONLY ONE THING HOLDS ANY ANSWERS FOR ME.
BARB ALWAYS TOLD ME TO CONFRONT THE UNKNOWN HEAD ON.
WELL, HERE GOES!
VROOMM
WITH ANY LUCK THE MAGIC, OR WHATEVER IT IS THAT'S IN THIS THING, WILL HELP ME HEAL BARB.

HALF A MILE AWAY ON JAMAICA AVENUE...
KEEESH
AW, PAULIE, LOOK WHAT YOU MADE ME DO!
NICE MOVE, JOHNNY! NOW THE LADY'S OREOS ARE TRASHED.
SCREEEE
YO, JOKERS, HEADS UP!
DON'T GET SCARED, KIDS. I JUST WANT TO TALK TO YOU ABOUT THE BRIEFCASE YOU LIFTED LAST NIGHT.
TELL US WHERE WE CAN FIND IT AND WE'RE OUT OF HERE. TRUST ME, THERE'S NOTHING IN IT THAT'S WORTH ANYTHING TO YOU!
WE DON'T KNOW WHAT YOU'RE TALKING ABOUT! WHY DON'T YOU GET YOUR TAIL OFF OUR STREET?
NICE MOUTH, PUNK.
YOU'RE GOING TO HAVE ANOTHER ONE IN THE BACK OF YOUR HEAD IF SOMEBODY DOESN'T HAND OVER THE SUITCASE NOW!
I-I-I...
ARRGPH!
WHO THE--?

BACK OFF! THE KIDS ARE OURS!
IT'S DEATHWATCH'S MEN AGAIN!
THIS TIME WE'RE READY FOR THE PAJAMA WEARING CREEPS!
DO 'EM!
BRAAAP
KILL THEM ALL, BUT DON'T LET THE KIDS GET AWAY!
BUDDA
UNGHARG!

BUDDA BUDDA
BRAAAP
PAULIE, GET DOWN!
PTNG
NO! WE'VE GOT TO GET AWAY! COME ON, RALPHIE, GET UP! WE'VE GOTTA RUN!
PTING
THERE DOESN'T SEEM TO BE ANYTHING WEIRD ABOUT THIS BIKE!
I WONDER IF I IMAGINED THE WHOLE THING AFTER BARB GOT HURT?
AIEEEEE!
BUDDA BUDDA
BRAAAP
SOMETHING'S GOING ON DOWN NEAR THE EL!
NO... NOT AGAIN!
BUDDA BUDDA
BRAAAP

I TOUCH IT I
IGHT TURN INTO
HAT THING
GAIN -- THAT
MONSTER!
NO, I CAN'T.
I WON'T!
AS HIS HAND MAKES CONTACT WITH THE GLOWING GAS CAP, DAN'S BODY IS ENGULFED BY MYSTICAL FUMES.
NO.
THE FUMES IGNITE INTO HELLFIRE...
NO!
NSTANTANEOUSLY HE
S TRANSFORMED INTO--
FWOOSH

--THE GHOST RIDER, SPIRIT OF VENGEANCE!
THOSE WHO LOOK ON CANNOT BELIEVE THEIR EYES.
THE MORNING NEWS-PAPERS WILL BE FULL OF THEIR DISBELIEF.
N.Y. SALTARES• TEXEIRA

WE'RE DEAD, MAN! WE'RE DEAD! NO MATTER WHO WINS WE'RE GONNA GET KILLED! ALL BECAUSE OF THAT STUPID SUITCASE.
SHUT UP, ANGEL!
YA GOTTA GET BEHIND SOMETHING, PAULIE.
BUT--RALPHIE...
WASTE THEM! WASTE THEM ALL-- OR THE KINGPIN IS GONNA HAVE OUR BUTTS!
YO, VIC, BEHIND US... SOMETHING WEIRD!
OH, @#☆$&%!
IT'S THE GUY WITH THE WEIRD HELMET WHO SCREWED UP LAST NIGHT'S OPERATION!
HE'S CORRECT. IT'S THE ONE DEATHWATCH WANTS DEAD. SO DO IT--NOW!
BUDDA BUDDA

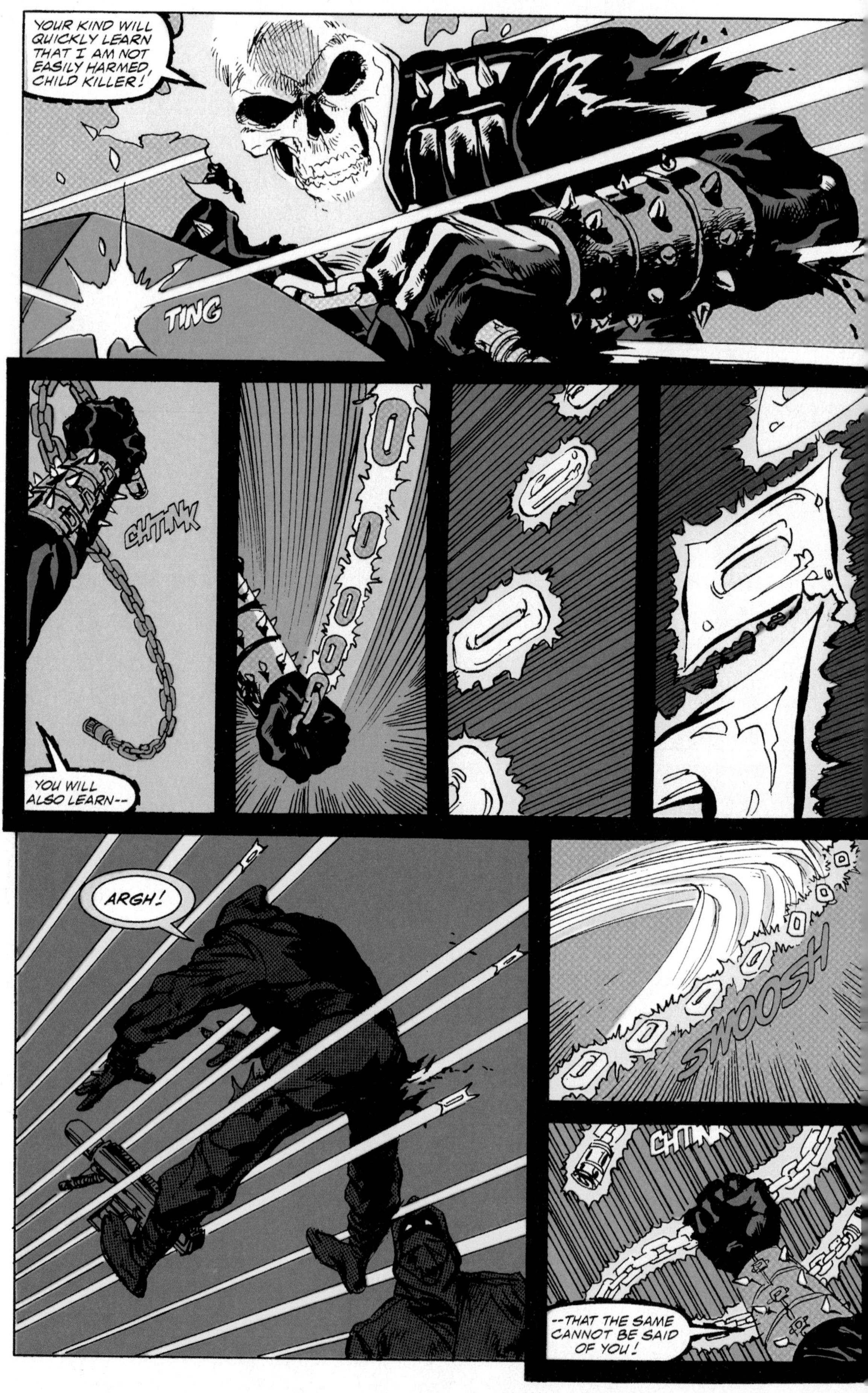
YOUR KIND WILL QUICKLY LEARN THAT I AM NOT EASILY HARMED, CHILD KILLER!
TING
CHTINK
YOU WILL ALSO LEARN--
ARGH!
SWOOSH
CHTINK
--THAT THE SAME CANNOT BE SAID OF YOU!

CHILDREN, I MEAN YOU NO HARM!
COME. I WILL SEE THAT YOU ARE SAFE!
MY EYES DISSIN' ME OR WHAT?
SHWOOSH
YOU AREN'T THE ONLY ONE WHO CAN USE A CHAIN, BIKER!
THOUGH I APPRECIATE YOU GETTING RID OF ANOTHER ONE OF DEATHWATCH'S MEN.
THIS WEAPON WILL PROVE EVEN LESS EFFECTIVE THAN THE LAST.
HOLY--!
WHOMP

I'M DONE PLAYING AROUND WITH YOU, MAN.
THE KINGPIN GAVE ME A JOB TO DO AND I'M NOT GOING TO LET YOU STOP ME!
YOU'RE WASTED.
THAT'S A HEAVY DUTY PIECE HE'S GOT. LET'S GET OUT OF HERE BEFORE THE WHOLE BLOCK GETS TRASHED.
EAT THIS, JERK!
SHTKOOM

OH, NO! RALPHIE, HE WAS OUR ONLY CHANCE!
PAULIE, YOU GOT TO GET AWAY.
TOOK CARE OF THAT PAIN IN THE BUTT-- FOR GOOD.
LOOKS LIKE IT'S JUST--
--THE TWO OF US LEFT!
IT APPEARS WE HAVE A STAND-OFF.
WHY NOT CALL A TRUCE UNTIL WE GET THE INFORMATION WE BOTH SEEM TO REQUIRE FROM THE GIRL--
--ONCE WE GET IT WE CAN THEN SETTLE BETWEEN OURSELVES.
YOU GOT IT!
THIS SHOULD DISTRACT HIM LONG ENOUGH TO LET ME GET THE DROP ON HIM!
LEAVE ME ALONE--I'VE GOT TO HELP RALPHIE!
OKAY, BABE, YOU DON'T TELL ME WHERE THE CANNISTERS ARE AND YOUR BRAINS ARE GOING TO BE LAYING NEXT TO YOUR FRIEND'S GUTS.
TELL ME WHERE THEY ARE, AND MAYBE WE'LL GET YOUR FRIEND SOME HELP.
THEY'RE IN THE CEMETERY IN THREE DIFFERENT MAUSOLEUMS. I DON'T REMEMBER WHERE. I ONLY HID ONE. RALPHIE HID ANOTHER AND JOHNNY THE LAST.
I JUST DON'T REMEMBER.
SHE'S NOT GOING TO BE ABLE TO GIVE US ANY MORE, SITTING HERE.
I'LL TAKE HER TO MY BOSS--HE'S GOT PEOPLE WHO CAN HELP HER REMEMBER THINGS.
I THINK--

--NOT!
THE TRUCE IS OVER.
DEATHWATCH CAN EXTRACT THE INFORMATION STRAIGHT FROM HER MIND. KILL THE KID QUICKLY FOR ME. YOU WILL JOIN HER MOMENTARILY.
LOOKS LIKE OUR DEMON FRIEND HAS OTHER PLANS!
IT'S HIM!
WHAT?
CHTINK
SKRAK
CHTINK
DO NOT BE AFRAID.

ST. JOHN'S HOSPITAL
THIS BOY NEEDS HELP. BRING A DOCTOR.
EMERGENCY
KEEP GOIN' INSIDE.
WHAT THE--?
JUST WHAT DO YOU THINK YOU'RE DOING?
NO QUESTIONS! THE BOY NEEDS MEDICAL ATTENTION--
--NOW!
MISTER, YOU SAVED HIS LIFE--
--YOU SAVED BOTH OUR LIVES!
THANKS.
HEY! YOU CAN'T JUST STROLL IN HERE, DROP OFF A BODY AND... ER... WELL I GUESS YOU CAN!

BY DAY'S END, THE CITY IS IN AN UPROAR OVER THE SMALL WAR THAT WAS WAGED IN BROOKLYN THE NIGHT BEFORE.
LOCAL NEWSPAPERS ARE FULL OF REPORTS OF THE DEMONIC GHOST RIDER IN THE MIDDLE OF THE DEATH AND DESTRUCTION.
I KNEW THE FREAK WITH THE FLAMING HEAD WAS BEHIND EVERYTHING ALL ALONG.
HE'S THE SAME ONE WHO HURT YOUR SISTER, DAN--
--AND I'M NOT GOING TO REST UNTIL THIS SO-CALLED GHOST RIDER IS BROUGHT IN.
X-RAY
DO YOU BELIEVE THAT SOME OF THESE PAPERS ARE ACTUALLY CALLING HIM A HERO? IF YOU WANT MY OPINION HE'S A KILLER, BOY. A COLD BLOODED KILLER.
DON'T YOU WORRY ABOUT BARB. EVER SINCE HE SHOWED UP AT THE HOSPITAL LAST NIGHT I'VE PUT MEN ON EVERY FLOOR.
BUT THE PAPERS SAY THAT HE HELPED TWO KIDS-- BROUGHT THEM HERE.
NONSENSE! HE WAS JUST TRYING TO COVER HIS BUTT. ALL HE WANTED TO DO WAS THROW US OFF HIS SCENT AND--
ER--EXCUSE ME, CAPTAIN DOLAN, I WANT TO GO SEE HOW BARB'S DOING.
OF COURSE, SON, GO AHEAD.

BARB?
I NEED YOUR HELP AGAIN. I'M SO CONFUSED.
WHEN I RIDE THAT MOTORCYCLE IT FEELS LIKE I'M TRANSFORMED INTO SOME SORT OF A MONSTER.
I CAN'T BELIEVE THE THINGS THAT I-- IT--DOES. IT'S SO BRUTAL.
THIS IS ALL SO CRAZY. I DON'T WANT IT TO HAPPEN ANYMORE, BUT I CAN'T BRING MYSELF TO GET RID OF THAT BIKE.
I--UH, IT--DID SAVE TWO KIDS' LIVES TODAY. IF I AM THIS POWERFUL GHOST RIDER--
--WHY CAN'T I SAVE YOU?

AT THAT MOMENT...
BRING NO MORE REPORTS OF FAILURE, CHAPMAN!
THOSE CANNISTERS BELONG IN MY HANDS. DO WHATEVER IS NECESSARY TO GET THEM BACK.
MY ENTIRE OPERATION... MY CITY... WILL BE JEOPARDIZED IF THEY FALL INTO THE WRONG HANDS--
--GET THEM NOW!

AND ELSEWHERE...
OUR CLIENTS PAY FOR RESULTS.
FIND THE CHILDREN, THIS GHOST RIDER, OR WHOEVER WILL LEAD YOU TO THE CANNISTERS--
--THEN LOCATE THE CANNISTERS--
--AND KILL ALL THE WITNESSES!
DAILY BUGLE
ALLEGED "CRIMINAL" GHOST RIDER SAVES CHILD!
TO BE CONTINUED...

addition to the issues covered in this volume, Marvel launched many other "firsts" in the early 1990s: ongoing and limited series, ackup serials, reprint series and one-shots, graphic novels, adaptations and more.

JANUARY 1990

ARVEL: 1989 — THE YEAR IN REVIEW began yearly magazine-sized parody series.

INISHER/WOLVERINE: AFRICAN SAGA was a print one-shot.

TH MAN #10 changed the series' title from th Man: The Ultimate Ninja.

OBOCOP #1 began an ongoing series based the movie character.

ARVEL COMICS PRESENTS #46 began a ort serial starring Devil-Slayer.

FEBRUARY 1990

AMOR THE SUB-MARINER #1 began an ngoing series.

TEELTOWN ROCKERS #1 began a limited eries.

VENGERS SPOTLIGHT #31 began a short ackup serial starring USAgent.

LASTIC FORKS #1 began an Epic limited eries.

AGA OF THE ORIGINAL HUMAN TORCH #1 egan a limited series.

ENSATIONAL SHE-HULK: CEREMONY #1 egan a limited series.

LIVE BARKER'S NIGHTBREED #1 began Epic ongoing series based on the movie haracters.

IHUMANS SPECIAL was a one-shot.

IARVEL COMICS PRESENTS #48 began short serial starring Spider-Man and olverine.

TREET POET RAY #1 began a limited series, e sequel to a Blackthorne Publishing series.

TALKERS #1 began an Epic ongoing series.

-MEN CLASSIC #46 changed the series' title om Classic X-Men.

MARCH 1990

AMP CANDY #1 began a short ongoing series ased on the animated TV character.

LSEWHERE PRINCE #1 began an Epic limited eries.

-MEN: SPOTLIGHT ON…STARJAMMERS #1 egan a limited series.

IARVEL SUPER-HEROES #1 began a quarterly ngoing anthology series, which featured a erial starring Speedball.

OMORROW KNIGHTS #1 began an Epic mited series.

ERO #1 began a limited series.

IARVEL COMICS PRESENTS #50 began a hort serial starring Comet Man.

APRIL 1990

LACK KNIGHT #1 began a limited series.

MARVEL AGE PREVIEW #1 began a sporadic short yearly promotional series.

GUARDIANS OF THE GALAXY #1 began an ongoing series.

MAY 1990

CAPTAIN AMERICA #372 began a backup serial starring Battlestar.

MARVEL COMICS PRESENTS #53 began a short serial starring Stingray.

WOLVERINE BATTLES THE INCREDIBLE HULK was a reprint one-shot.

AVENGERS #319 began a backup serial starring the Avengers Crew.

MARVEL COMICS PRESENTS #54 began serials starring Werewolf By Night and Hulk & Wolverine.

PUNISHER ARMORY #1 began a sporadic ongoing reference series.

JUNE 1990

STEVEN BRUST'S JHEREG: THE GRAPHIC NOVEL was a magazine-sized Epic novel adaptation.

TALES FROM THE HEART OF AFRICA: THE TEMPORARY NATIVES was an Epic one-shot.

BRUTE FORCE #1 began a limited series.

PUNISHER: NO ESCAPE began a sporadic ongoing series of Punisher one-shots.

NEW MUTANTS SUMMER SPECIAL was a one-shot.

SPIDER-MAN #1 began an ongoing series.

SPIDER-MAN VS. WOLVERINE was a reprint one-shot.

IMPOSSIBLE MAN SUMMER VACATION SPECTACULAR #1 began a short yearly series.

KNIGHTS OF PENDRAGON #1 began an ongoing series; the first Marvel series produced in the United Kingdom but sold simultaneously in the U.K. and U.S.A.

MARVEL FANFARE #52 began a short serial starring the Black Knight.

MARVEL COMICS PRESENTS #57 began a short serial starring the Sub-Mariner.

ROBOCOP 2 MOVIE ADAPTATION #1 began a limited series reprinting Marvel's movie adaptation.

JULY 1990

THANOS QUEST #1 began a limited series.

X-FACTOR: PRISONER OF LOVE was a one-shot.

DARKMAN #1 began a limited series reprinting Marvel's movie adaptation.

WILD CARDS #1 began an Epic limited series based on the novel characters.

AUGUST 1990

ESPERS TPB was an Epic reprint collecting the Eclipse Comics series.

MARVEL COMICS PRESENTS #60 began serials starring Poison and Scarlet Witch.

FRED HEMBECK SELLS THE MARVEL UNIVERSE was a reprint one-shot.

MIGHTY MOUSE #1 began an ongoing series based on the animated TV character.

SEVEN BLOCK was an Epic one-shot.

CLOAK AND DAGGER #14 changed the series' title from The Mutant Misadventures of Cloak and Dagger.

SEPTEMBER 1990

CADILLACS AND DINOSAURS #1 began an Epic limited series reprinting the Kitchen Sink Xenozoic Tales comics.

NOMAD #1 began a limited series.

OCTOBER 1990

CAPTAIN AMERICA #380 began a short backup serial starring USAgent.

MARVEL COMICS PRESENTS #64 began serials starring the Fantastic Four and Ghost Rider & Wolverine.

FAFHRD AND THE GRAY MOUSER #1 began an Epic limited series novel adaptation.

THE LAST AMERICAN #1 began an Epic limited series.

ZORRO #1 began an ongoing series starring the novel and movie character.

HOLLYWOOD SUPERSTARS #1 began an Epic limited series.

OFFICIAL HANDBOOK OF THE MARVEL UNIVERSE: MASTER EDITION #1 began an ongoing reference series.

NOVEMBER 1990

SON OF YUPPIES FROM HELL was a humor one-shot.

ALIEN LEGION: ON THE EDGE #1 began an Epic limited series.

ATOMIC AGE #1 began an Epic limited series.

HARVEY KURTZMAN'S STRANGE ADVENTURES was a magazine-sized hardcover Epic humor one-shot.

BARBIE #1 began an ongoing series based on the toy line.

BARBIE FASHION #1 began an ongoing series based on the toy line.

MARVEL COMICS PRESENTS #68 began a serial starring Shanna the She-Devil.

MARVEL POSTER BOOK began a sporadic ongoing series of magazine-sized poster books.

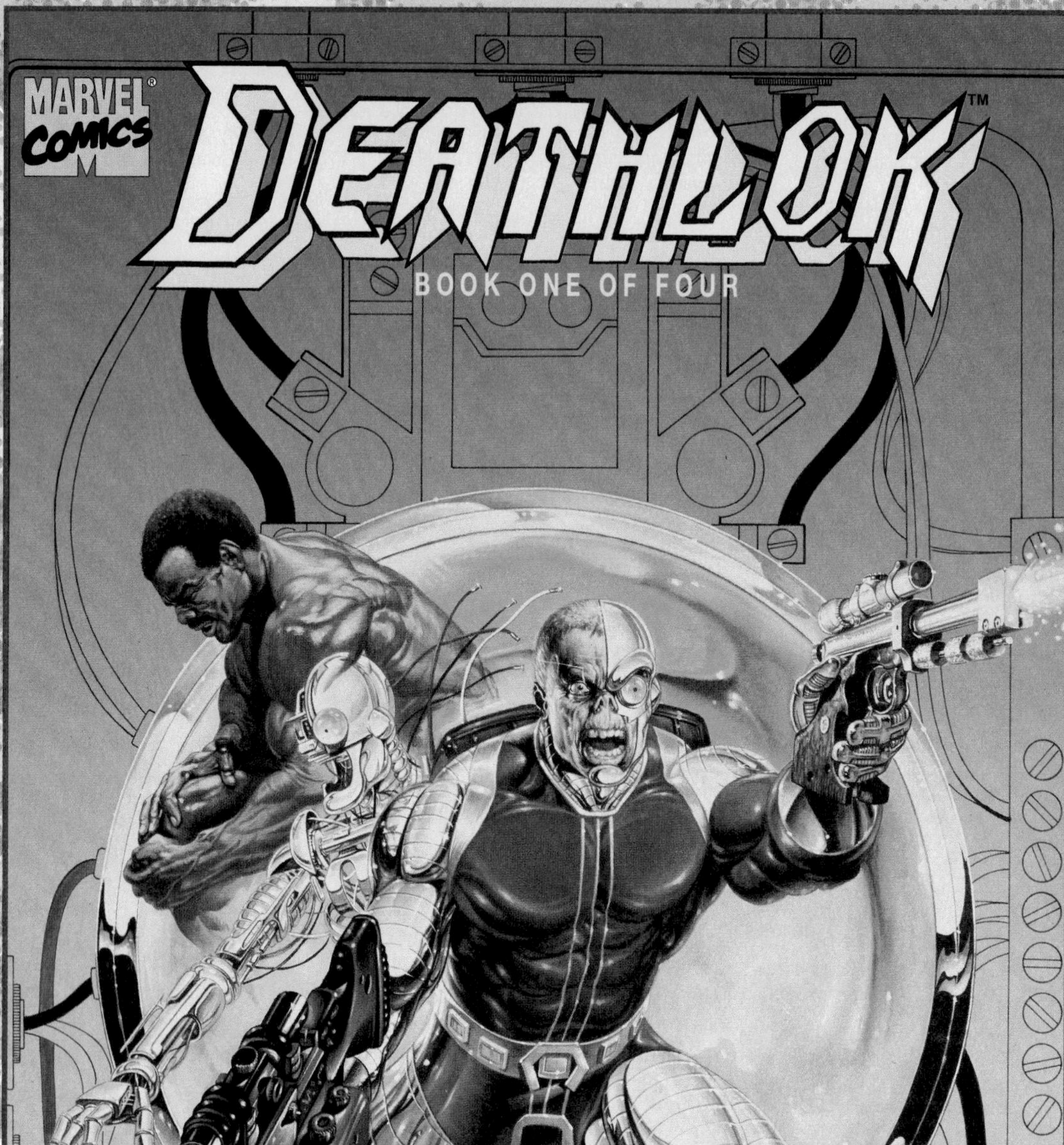
MARVEL COMICS
DEATHLOK™
BOOK ONE OF FOUR
JUSKO 89

DEATHLOK #1, published in May 1990, began a limited series that revamped the 1970s character, introducing pacifist Michael Collins as a new version of the cyborg soldier. It was soon followed by an ongoing series.

DEATHLOK™

BOOK ONE

THE BRAINS OF THE OUTFIT

Dwayne McDuffie
Gregory Wright
WRITERS

Jackson Guice
PENCILER

Scott Williams
INKER

Gregory Wright
with
aul Mounts & Brad Vancat
COLORISTS

Richard Starkings
LETTERER

COVER ILLUSTRATION

Tom Brevoort
ASSISTANT EDITOR

Bob Budiansky
EDITOR

Tom DeFalco
EDITOR IN CHIEF

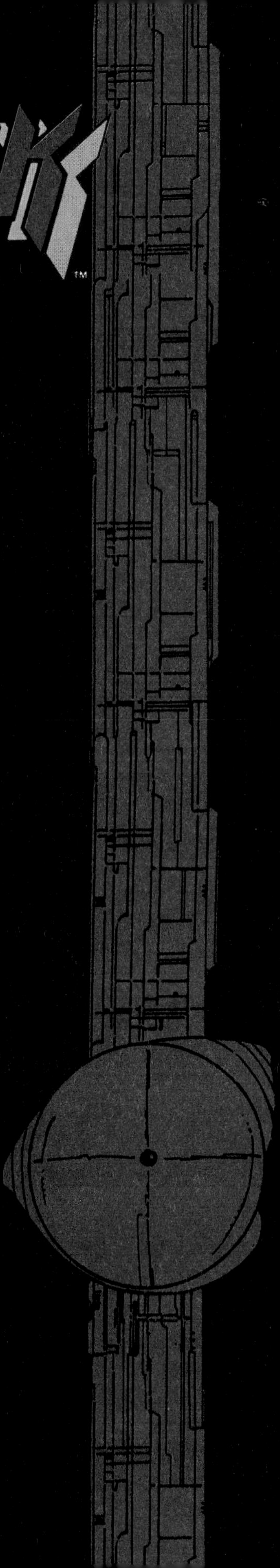

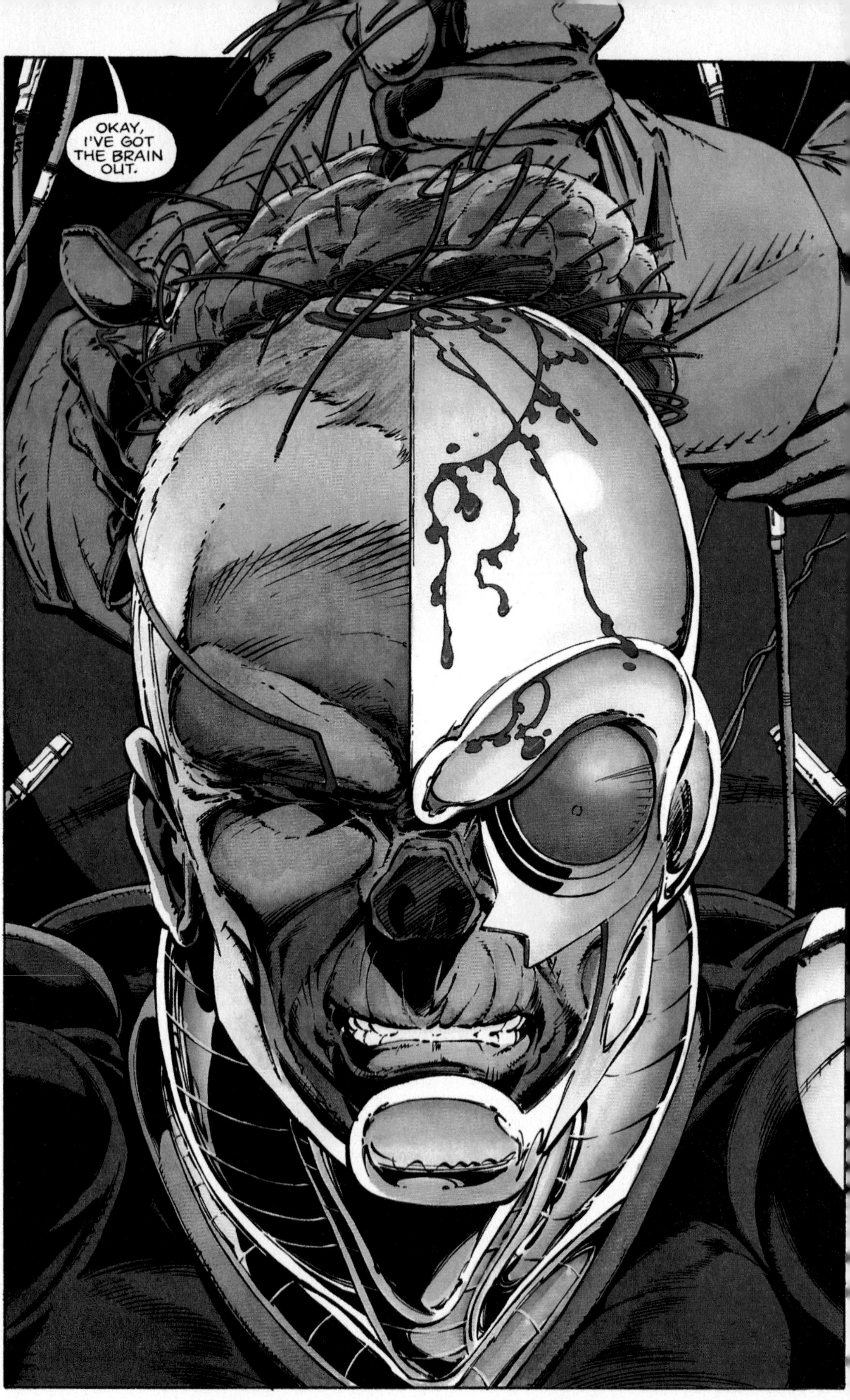
OKAY, I'VE GOT THE BRAIN OUT.

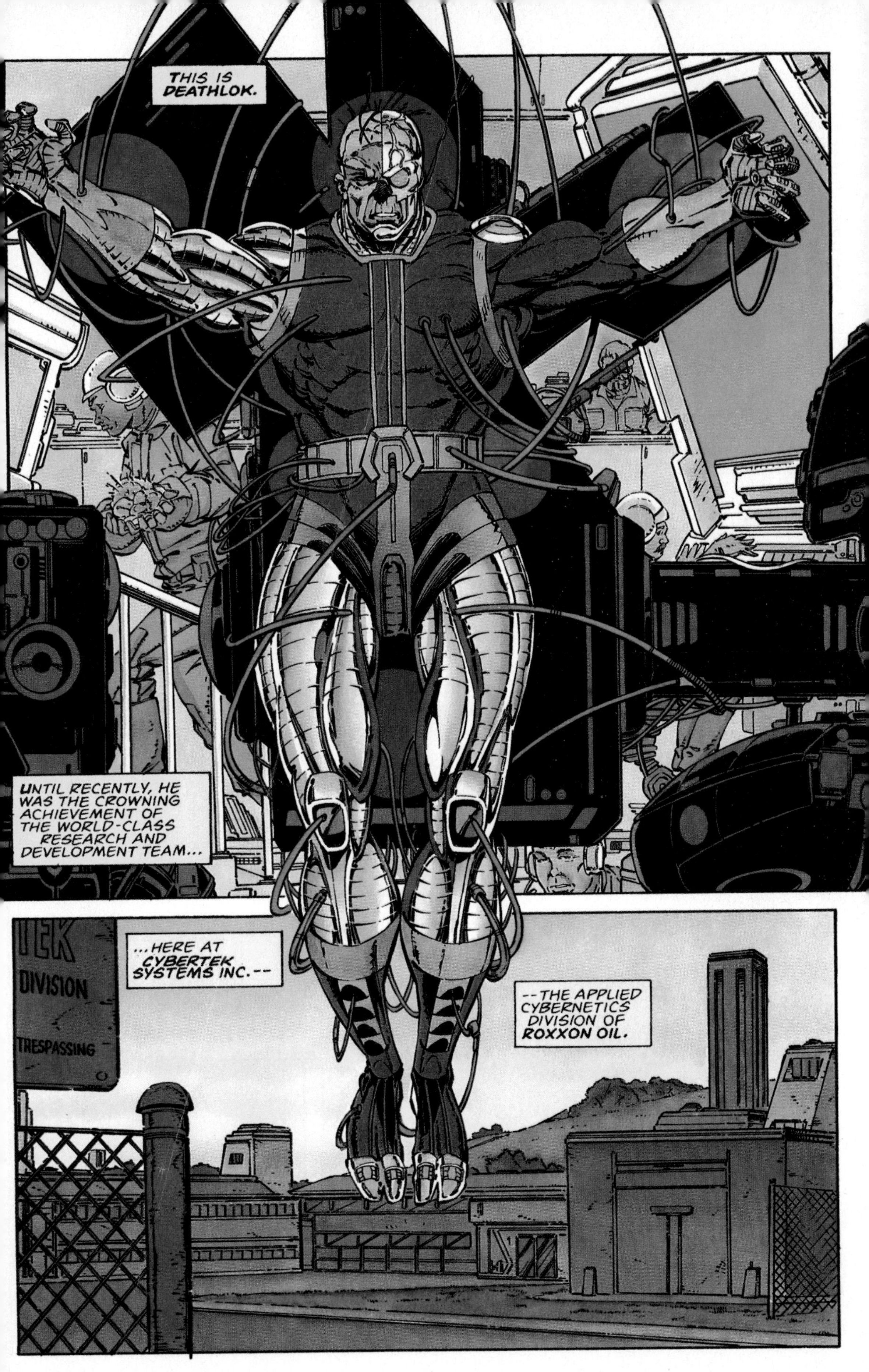

THIS IS DEATHLOK.
UNTIL RECENTLY, HE WAS THE CROWNING ACHIEVEMENT OF THE WORLD-CLASS RESEARCH AND DEVELOPMENT TEAM...
...HERE AT CYBERTEK SYSTEMS INC.--
EK
DIVISION
TRESPASSING
--THE APPLIED CYBERNETICS DIVISION OF ROXXON OIL.

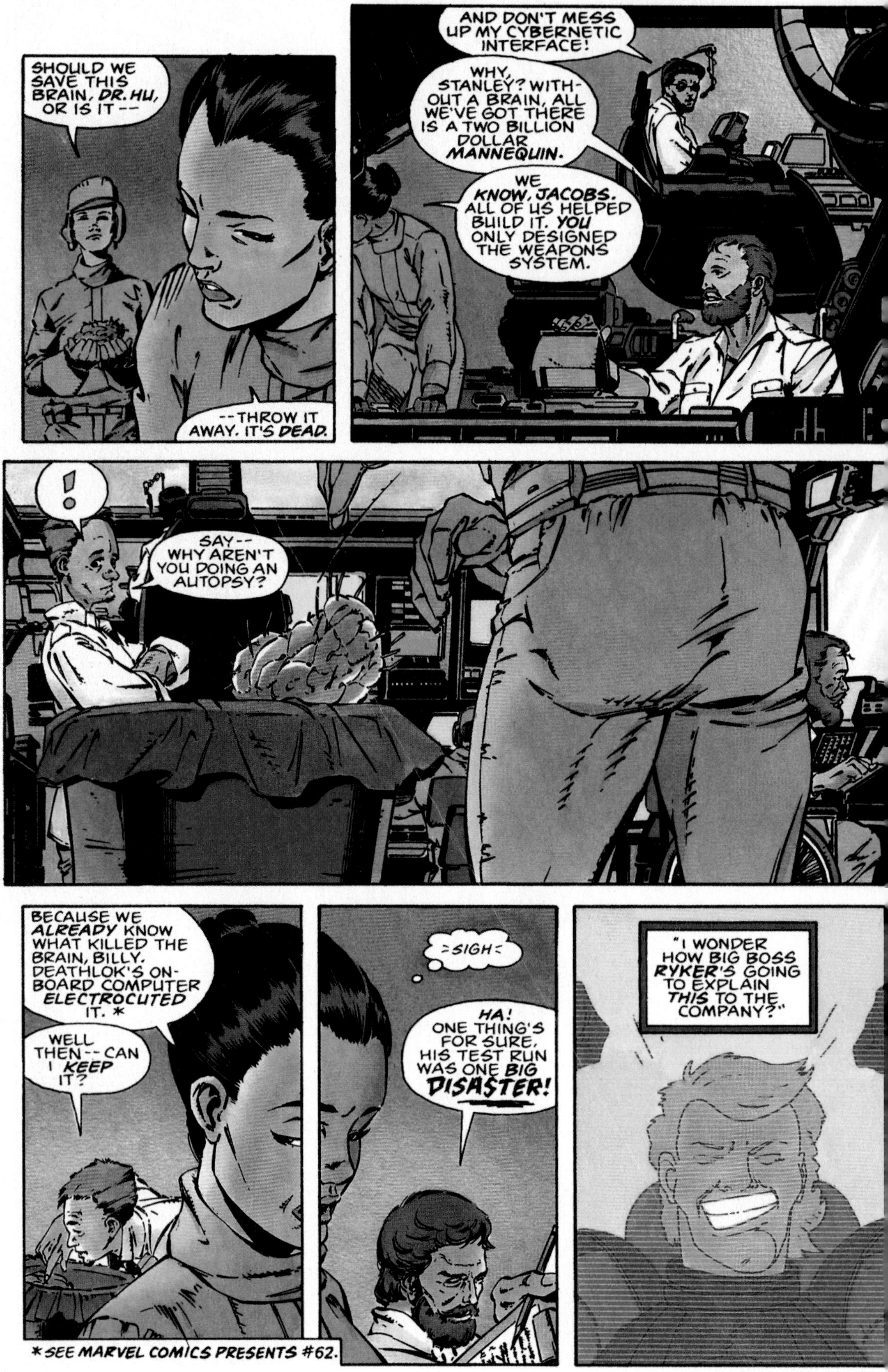
SHOULD WE SAVE THIS BRAIN, DR. HU, OR IS IT --
--THROW IT AWAY. IT'S DEAD.
AND DON'T MESS UP MY CYBERNETIC INTERFACE!
WHY, STANLEY? WITH-OUT A BRAIN, ALL WE'VE GOT THERE IS A TWO BILLION DOLLAR MANNEQUIN.
WE KNOW, JACOBS. ALL OF US HELPED BUILD IT. YOU ONLY DESIGNED THE WEAPONS SYSTEM.
!
SAY-- WHY AREN'T YOU DOING AN AUTOPSY?
BECAUSE WE ALREADY KNOW WHAT KILLED THE BRAIN, BILLY. DEATHLOK'S ON-BOARD COMPUTER ELECTROCUTED IT. *
WELL THEN--CAN I KEEP IT?
=SIGH=
HA! ONE THING'S FOR SURE. HIS TEST RUN WAS ONE BIG DISASTER!
"I WONDER HOW BIG BOSS RYKER'S GOING TO EXPLAIN THIS TO THE COMPANY?"
* SEE MARVEL COMICS PRESENTS #62.

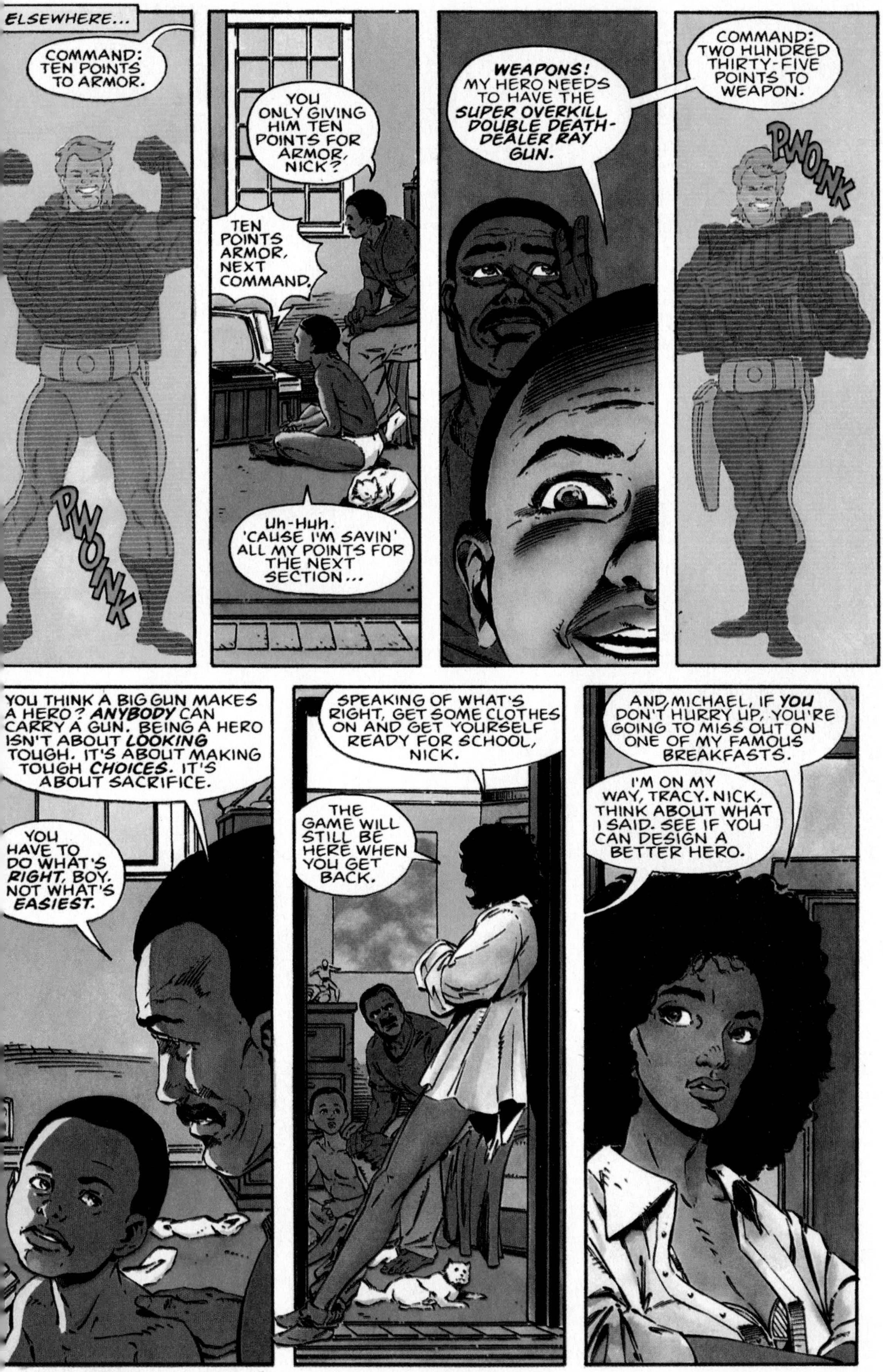
ELSEWHERE...
COMMAND: TEN POINTS TO ARMOR.
PWONK
YOU ONLY GIVING HIM TEN POINTS FOR ARMOR, NICK?
TEN POINTS ARMOR, NEXT COMMAND.
Uh-Huh. 'CAUSE I'M SAVIN' ALL MY POINTS FOR THE NEXT SECTION...
WEAPONS! MY HERO NEEDS TO HAVE THE SUPER OVERKILL DOUBLE DEATH-DEALER RAY GUN.
COMMAND: TWO HUNDRED THIRTY-FIVE POINTS TO WEAPON.
PWONK
YOU THINK A BIG GUN MAKES A HERO? ANYBODY CAN CARRY A GUN. BEING A HERO ISN'T ABOUT LOOKING TOUGH. IT'S ABOUT MAKING TOUGH CHOICES. IT'S ABOUT SACRIFICE.
YOU HAVE TO DO WHAT'S RIGHT, BOY. NOT WHAT'S EASIEST.
SPEAKING OF WHAT'S RIGHT, GET SOME CLOTHES ON AND GET YOURSELF READY FOR SCHOOL, NICK.
THE GAME WILL STILL BE HERE WHEN YOU GET BACK.
AND, MICHAEL, IF YOU DON'T HURRY UP, YOU'RE GOING TO MISS OUT ON ONE OF MY FAMOUS BREAKFASTS.
I'M ON MY WAY, TRACY. NICK, THINK ABOUT WHAT I SAID. SEE IF YOU CAN DESIGN A BETTER HERO.

YOU KNOW, TRACY, I'M AFRAID I'M NOT SPENDING ENOUGH TIME WITH NICK.
I SPEND ALL DAY WRITING SOFT-WARE FOR HIGH-TECH ARTIFICIAL LIMBS --
--AND SOME-WHERE NICK HAS PICKED UP THE IDEA THAT A HERO IS ANY MUSCLEHEAD WITH A BIG GUN.
YOU DON'T HAVE TO WORRY ABOUT NICK'S VALUES. HE KNOWS THE DIFFERENCE BETWEEN REAL LIFE AND A GAME.
AND BESIDES, YOU HELP DEFINE HIS VALUES IN THE BEST POSSIBLE WAY --
-- BY EXAMPLE.

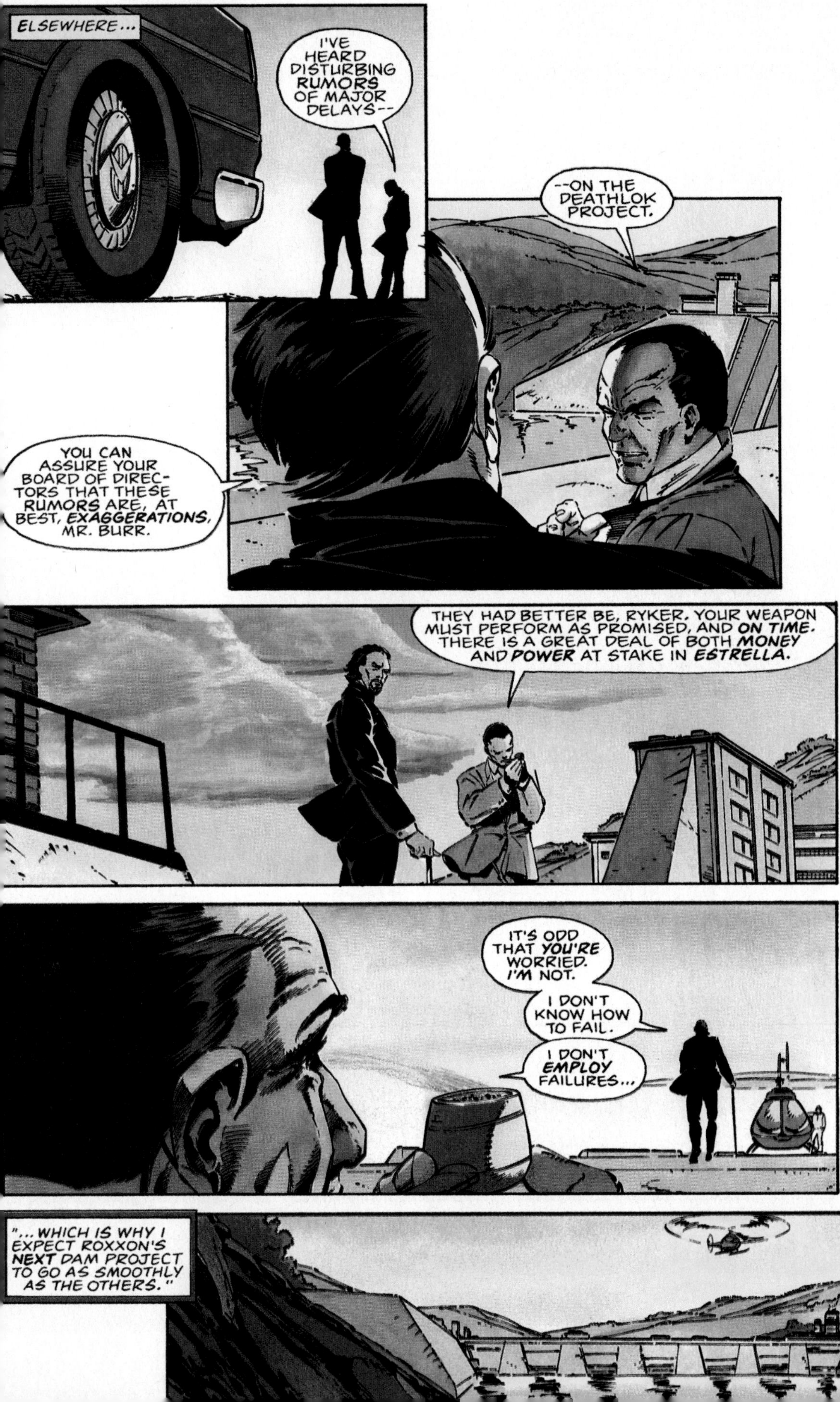
ELSEWHERE...
I'VE HEARD DISTURBING RUMORS OF MAJOR DELAYS--
--ON THE DEATHLOK PROJECT.
YOU CAN ASSURE YOUR BOARD OF DIRECTORS THAT THESE RUMORS ARE, AT BEST, EXAGGERATIONS, MR. BURR.
THEY HAD BETTER BE, RYKER. YOUR WEAPON MUST PERFORM AS PROMISED, AND ON TIME. THERE IS A GREAT DEAL OF BOTH MONEY AND POWER AT STAKE IN ESTRELLA.
IT'S ODD THAT YOU'RE WORRIED. I'M NOT.
I DON'T KNOW HOW TO FAIL.
I DON'T EMPLOY FAILURES...
"...WHICH IS WHY I EXPECT ROXXON'S NEXT DAM PROJECT TO GO AS SMOOTHLY AS THE OTHERS."

LATER THAT MORNING...
THE CYBERNETICS LAB AT CYBERTEK.
THIS IS HOW IT'S GOING TO BE.
YOU WILL LOCATE AND NEUTRALIZE THE FAULT IN THE CYBORG AND HAVE IT READY FOR A BRAIN TRANSPLANT TOMORROW.
C'MON, MR. RYKER, WE'LL NEVER BE READY THAT FAST.
OF COURSE WE WILL, JACOBS. THAT IS, IF DR. HU CAN HAVE IT PREPPED FOR SURGERY IN TIME.
I'LL MANAGE.
I STILL CAN'T BELIEVE WE FOUND SOMEONE STUPID ENOUGH TO VOLUNTEER THE FIRST TIME.
I DON'T THINK IT'LL BE A PROBLEM, STANLEY. NOT IF ONE ASKS IN THE PROPER MANNER...
SEE THAT THE WORK IS COMPLETED...
...OR I MAY BE FORCED TO ASK ONE OF YOU.

WHILE IN ANOTHER SECTION OF THE BUILDING...
HAS MR. COLLINS COME IN YET?
NO, BUT WHEN HE DOES, HE'S NOT GOING TO BE HAPPY.
I'M HERE. WHY AIN'T I HAPPY?
DON'T WORRY, MICHAEL. I'M NOT HAPPY EITHER.
MORNIN', JIM. WHAT'S THE PROBLEM HERE?
BILLY HANSEN WENT CRAZY.
"WENT?"
YEAH. HE WANTS EXTENSIVE REVISIONS ON THAT BIG OPERATING SYSTEM WE WORKED ON. AND HE WANTS THEM TODAY.
NO PROBLEM. TELL EVERYBODY TO TAKE IT EASY. I'LL GO UP AND TALK TO HARLAN.
I'M SURE HE'LL GIVE US MORE TIME.

AND UPSTAIRS...
HI, LAURIE, COULD YOU TELL HARLAN WE'RE HERE TO SEE HIM?
MR. RYKER IS TIED UP IN WEAPONS TESTING WITH BEN JACOBS. HE DOESN'T WISH TO BE DIS-TURBED.
C'MON, JIM. LET'S LOOK INTO THIS *OURSELVES.*
NOW WHY ARE THEY LIGHTING A FIRE UNDER OUR BUTTS ALL OF A SUDDEN?
THIS REALLY ISN'T WOR THE FUS MICHAEL
TAP TAP TAP
I'M SURE THEY'LL EXPLAIN IT ALL TOMORROW.
CYBERTEK SYSTEMS
MAIN MENU
User: Michael Collins, Director: Computer Software Systems Unit
TASK?
Access: "Operating System/Ryker File"
ACCESS DENIED. IMPROPER PASSWORD.
INSUFFICIENT CLEARANCE.

"INSUFFICIENT CLEARANCE"?
HA! THAT WON'T STOP ME.

OPEN: OP SYSTEM BACKDOOR.

PASSWORD?
"Hi, honey. I'm Home!"

ENTRY GRANTED. ALL FILES AVAILABLE.
Access: "Project: Deathlok/Ryker File"
LASER DISK VIDEO FOOTAGE AVAILABLE.

WHAT'S "DEATHLOK"? YOU KNOW ANYTHING ABOUT THIS? I'M ACCESSING THE VIDEO.
YOU'RE NOT GOING TO LIKE IT.
I'M NOT GOING TO LIKE WHAT?
TAP TAP

I DON'T BELIEVE IT! THEY TRICKED ME INTO WORKING ON A WEAPONS PROJECT.
DWORMAN, YOU KNEW ABOUT THIS.
EVERYBODY WHO COULD HANDLE IT KNEW.
HOW COULD YOU WORK ON THIS? DIDN'T YOU REALIZE--
ORGANIC SYSTEM
CAUSED BY
--THERE'S A HUMAN BRAIN IN THERE?
EVERYBODY WHO COULD HANDLE IT KNEW. I'LL TALK TO YOU LATER.

THAT EVENING...
AW, LOOK OUT!
BABY WHAT'S WRONG?
IT'S JUST THAT... HOW WOULD YOU FEEL IF I HAD TO GIVE UP MY JOB... ON MORAL GROUNDS?
I DIDN'T MARRY A JOB, MICHAEL. YOU KNOW THAT. I MARRIED A MAN.
SIT DOWN AND WORK THIS THROUGH. WHATEVER IT IS. I'LL FINISH THE DISHES.
THANKS, TRACE-- BUT NO WIFE OF MINE IS DOING ANY DISHES. THAT'S WHAT WE HAD THE KID FOR.
NICK!

MORNING...
...WEAPONS TESTING FACILITY, CYBERTEK...
THIS PROJECT WE'VE BEEN WORKING ON, IT ISN'T JUST ARTIFICIAL LIMBS. IT'S SOME KIND OF SOLDIER ROBOT! I FOUND VIDEO IN YOUR COMPUTER FILE, HARLAN. YOU COULDN'T HAVE KNOWN ANYTHING ABOUT THIS. COULD YOU?
OF COURSE NOT, MICHAEL. WE'LL GO TO MY OFFICE, AND YOU CAN SHOW ME WHAT YOU'VE FOUND.
I DON'T KNOW HOW YOU GUYS IN THE WEAPONS DIVISION LIVE WITH YOURSELVES.

FACE IT, RYKER, DEATHLOK'S JUST A BUSTED TOY. MY CYBERTANK HAS ALWAYS BEEN THE SUPERIOR WEAPON.
SHEER FIREPOWER ISN'T EVERYTHING, JACOBS.
ONCE DEATHLOK IS BACK ON LINE, I'M CONFIDENT HE'LL PROVE HIMSELF EQUALLY FORMIDABLE. BUT UNTIL THEN--
RYKER! WE'VE GOT TO TALK, NOW!
RYKER'S OFFICE, MOMENTS LATER...
LET'S GATHER UP ALL OF THE EVIDENCE AND GO TO THE NEWSPAPERS. WE'VE GOT TO DO SOMETHING ABOUT THIS.
MY SENTIMENTS EXACTLY.
PWEWT
UHNN!
LAURIE? GET DOCTORS HU AND KIMBLE TO THE LAB AND GET A MED TEAM TO ME IMMEDIATELY.
THEN GET TRACY COLLINS ON THE PHONE.

HELLO? OH HI, HARLAN. NICE TO HEAR FROM YOU.
I'M AFRAID I HAVE SOME... TERRIBLE NEWS FOR YOU, TRACY--
--IT'S ABOUT MICHAEL...
DAYS LATER. THE FEDERATIVE REPUBLIC OF ESTRELLA.
ALTHOUGH POISED ON THE BRINK OF INDUSTRIALIZATION, IT IS STILL A COUNTRY THAT IS MOSTLY COVERED BY LUSH RAIN FOREST.
FFFFFFFSS
OVER A THIRD OF ESTRELLA'S LAND DRAINS INTO THE AMAZON RIVER, WHICH WATERS THE RAIN FOREST.
SSHOOOO
DRY LAND TO BUILD ON IS HARD TO COME BY IN THESE PARTS.
WHUMP
BUT THE SUCCESS-FUL ENTREPRENEUR MAKES HIS OWN OPPORTUNITIES.

HISSSSSSS
<LUCKY FOR US IT WAS A DUD. A MISSILE SO LARGE COULD HAVE DESTROYED THE ENTIRE RESISTANCE.> *
*TRANSLATED FROM THE PORTUGUESE.
IT'S NOT A DUD.
ZZRAK
KERAATCH
HEAVY INDUSTRY HAS ARRIVED IN ESTRELLA.

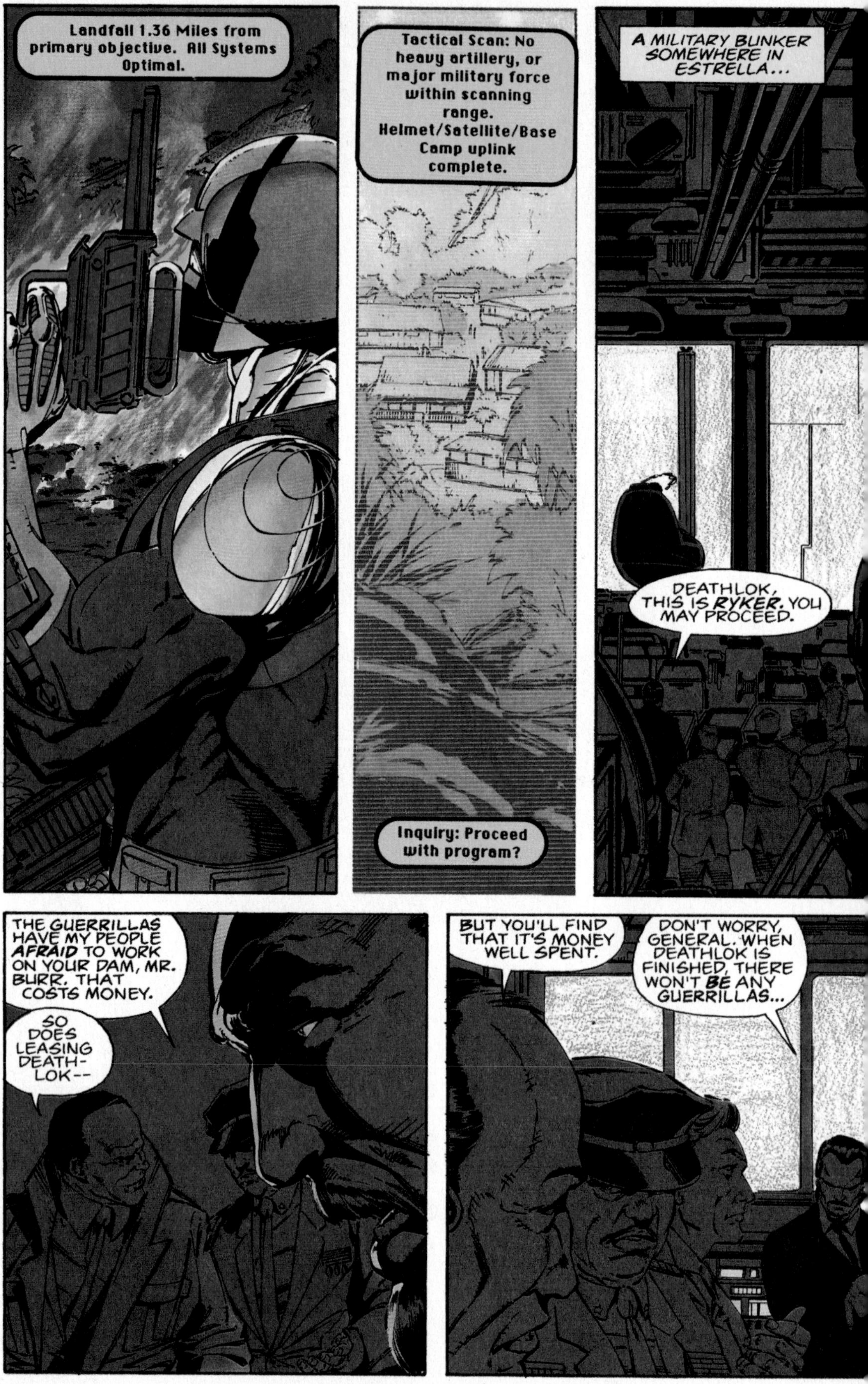
Landfall 1.36 Miles from primary objective. All Systems Optimal.
Tactical Scan: No heavy artillery, or major military force within scanning range. Helmet/Satellite/Base Camp uplink complete.
Inquiry: Proceed with program?
A MILITARY BUNKER SOMEWHERE IN ESTRELLA...
DEATHLOK, THIS IS RYKER. YOU MAY PROCEED.
THE GUERRILLAS HAVE MY PEOPLE AFRAID TO WORK ON YOUR DAM, MR. BURR. THAT COSTS MONEY.
SO DOES LEASING DEATH-LOK--
BUT YOU'LL FIND THAT IT'S MONEY WELL SPENT.
DON'T WORRY, GENERAL. WHEN DEATHLOK IS FINISHED, THERE WON'T BE ANY GUERRILLAS...

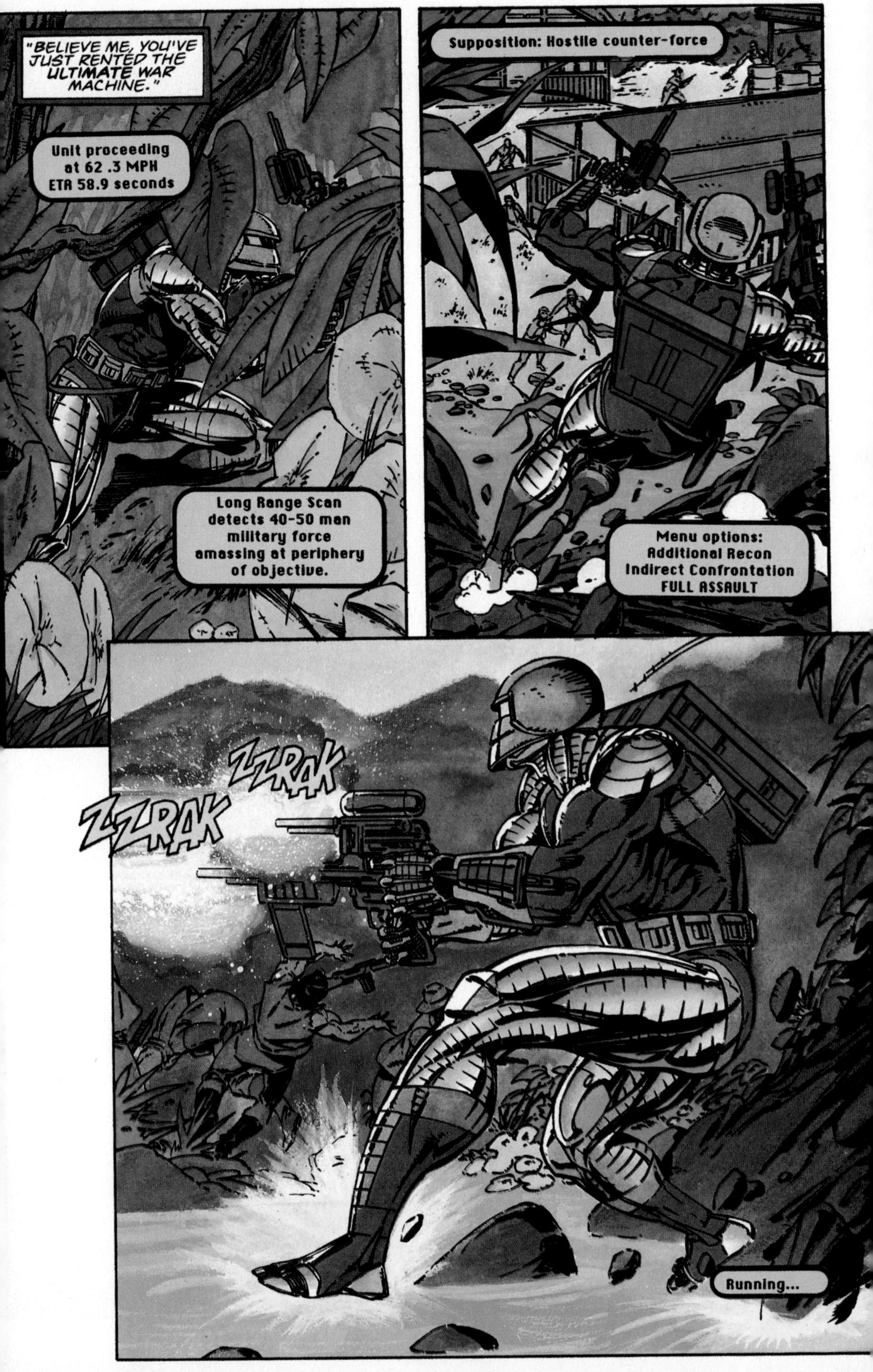
"BELIEVE ME, YOU'VE JUST RENTED THE ULTIMATE WAR MACHINE."
Unit proceeding at 62 .3 MPH ETA 58.9 seconds
Long Range Scan detects 40-50 man military force amassing at periphery of objective.
Supposition: Hostile counter-force
Menu options: Additional Recon Indirect Confrontation FULL ASSAULT
ZZRAK
ZZRAK
Running...

AAARUAGH!
ZZRAK
ZZRAK
AIEEE!
ZZRAK
ZZRAK
SKLUTCH
ZZRAK
ZZRAK

Tactical Scan:
3 Lifeforms. Indications of armament.
Assumption: Hostile.
Menu Options:
Indirect Confrontation
Additional Recon
FULL ASSAULT
UHHN!
HARLAN SHOT ME!
K'RATACH
ERROR
ERROR
ERROR
ERROR
ERROR
<MARY, MOTHER OF MERCY!>
MY GOD! WHAT'S GOIN' ON? WHERE AM I?
Programming fault.
ZZRAK
THIS IS MICHAEL COLLINS. WHO'S TALKING? I CAN'T SEE YOU!

WAITAMINUTE. I CAN SEE.
ZZRAK
IT'S ME! I'M SHOOTING PEOPLE!
I'M RESPONSIBLE FOR THIS.
I'VE GOT TO STOP IT, BUT I CAN'T!
Programming fault located. Source: organic software.
ZZ
ZZRAK
NO. IT CAN'T BE TRUE...
ZZRAK
Self-Repair routines running.
...SOMEHOW, I'M INSIDE OF DEATHLOK!
ZZRAK

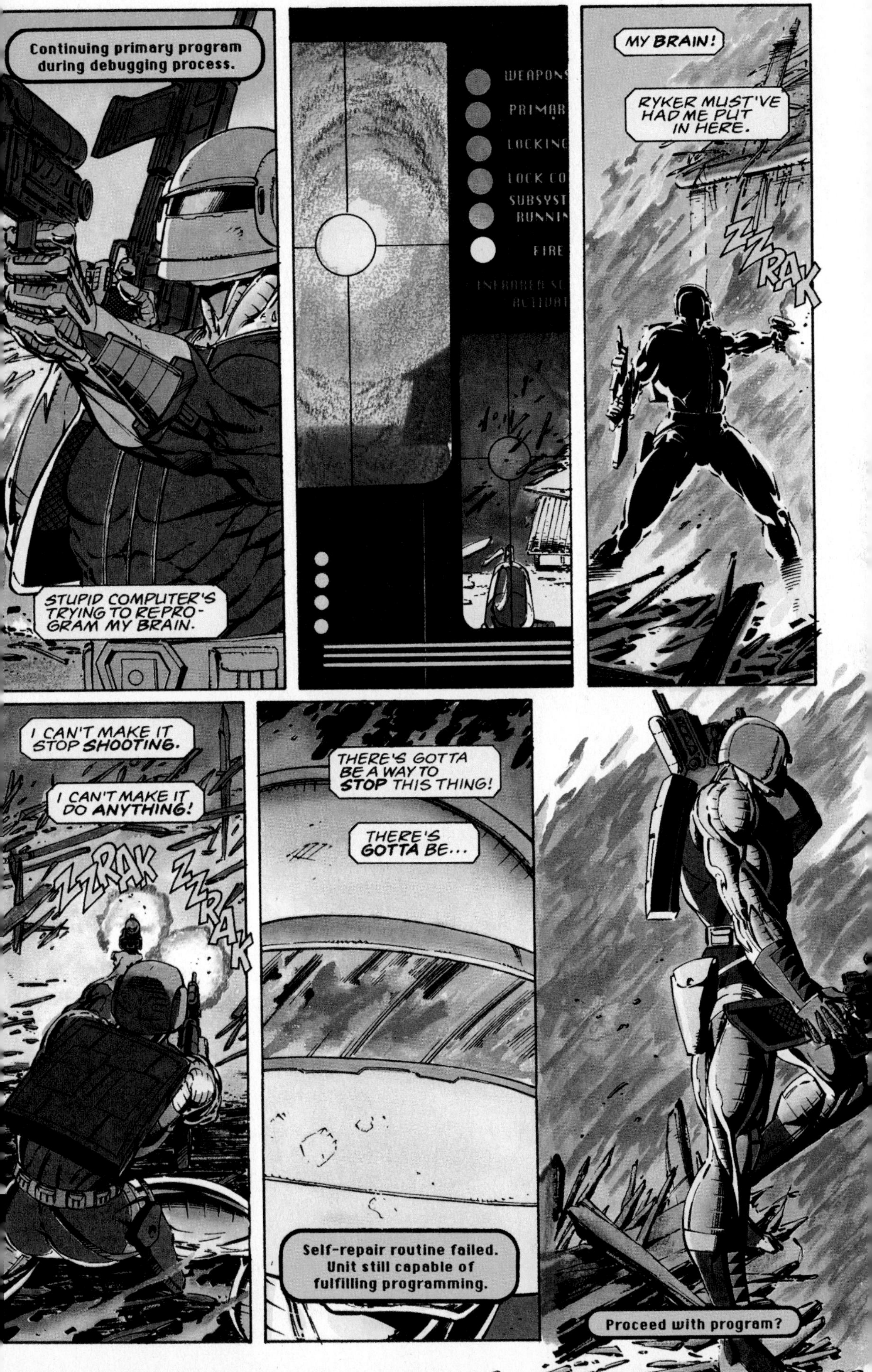
Continuing primary program during debugging process.
STUPID COMPUTER'S TRYING TO REPROGRAM MY BRAIN.
WEAPONS
PRIMAR
LOCKING
LOCK CO
SUBSYST
RUNNIN
FIRE
MY BRAIN!
RYKER MUST'VE HAD ME PUT IN HERE.
ZZRAK
I CAN'T MAKE IT STOP SHOOTING.
I CAN'T MAKE IT DO ANYTHING!
ZZRAK
ZZRAK
THERE'S GOTTA BE A WAY TO STOP THIS THING!
THERE'S GOTTA BE...
Self-repair routine failed. Unit still capable of fulfilling programming.
Proceed with program?

Uh Oh. LOOKS LIKE WE'VE GOT A LITTLE GLITCH. MAYBE WE SHOULD BRING HIM IN.
BRING HIM IN..?!
RYKER...
TOLD YA IT WOULD HAPPEN AGAIN.
IT'S NOT OVER.
DEATHLOK, THIS IS RYKER. PROCEED.
Running.
ZZRAK
RYKER, NO! DON'T MAKE ME DO THIS YOU SON OF A B
Tactical scan: Unarmed lifeform 20 meters, 0.85 degrees.

Lifeform now armed and hostile.
Menu Options:
Additional Recon
Indirect Confrontation
FULL ASSAULT
NO! YOU CAN'T!
BRAKKA BRAKKA BRAKKA BRAKKA
Countermanding order received.
PWEE
PWEE
PWEE
Programming altered.
Subroutine selection cancelled.
Program completed. Returning to basecamp for debriefing and repairs.
I STOPPED IT! I WONDER IF I CAN MAKE IT DO ANYTHING ELSE?
THAT CONCLUDES OUR BUSINESS, GENERAL. YOU CAN PUT YOUR MEN BACK TO WORK IMMEDIATELY.
"COUNTERMANDING ORDER"? WHERE DID THAT COME FROM?
HE SHOULDN'T HAVE LET THAT LITTLE GIRL LIVE.

DAYS LATER...
COMPUTER WHERE ARE WE?
Cybertek, Main Lab, Paterson, New--
I KNOW WHERE CYBERTEK IS. WHY CAN'T WE MOVE?
Unit is in storage position. Motor functions have been shut down externally..
TERRIFIC.
I WANT TO KNOW RIGHT NOW WHERE THIS "COUNTERMANDING ORDER" CAME FROM. IS THIS COMPUTER REPROGRAMMING ITSELF?
NO WAY. COMPUTERS ONLY DO WHAT PEOPLE TELL 'EM.
COMPUTER OPEN ACCESS TO MAIN OPERATING SYSTEM.
Access granted.
ALL RIGHT THEN, WHO TOLD HIM?
MAYBE THE BRAIN IS OVERRIDING THE COMPUTER. LIKE LAST TIME.

WELL, I'LL BE--
ARE YOU IN THERE, COLLINS?
YOU KNOW, IF HE IS, THE NEW OPERATING SYSTEM WOULD PREVENT THE COMPUTER FROM TORCHIN' THE BRAIN IN SELF-DEFENSE.
BUT THE BRAIN IS ONLY SUPPOSED TO BE FOR STORAGE.
AT LEAST THAT WAS THE PLAN.
SO YOU'RE TELLING ME THAT COLLINS' BRAIN IS CONTROLLING MY WAR MACHINE?
ER-- SOMETHING LIKE THAT.
WELL, WHAT SHALL WE DO, BILLY? WE NEED A BRAIN IN THE CYBORG, BUT NOT ONE RUNNING THE SHOW.
AND WE DON'T HAVE TIME TO APPROPRIATE ANOTHER "VOLUNTEER."
SAY. WE COULD BIT-MAP MICHAEL'S MEMORY--
--AND DUMP IT FROM THE BRAIN!

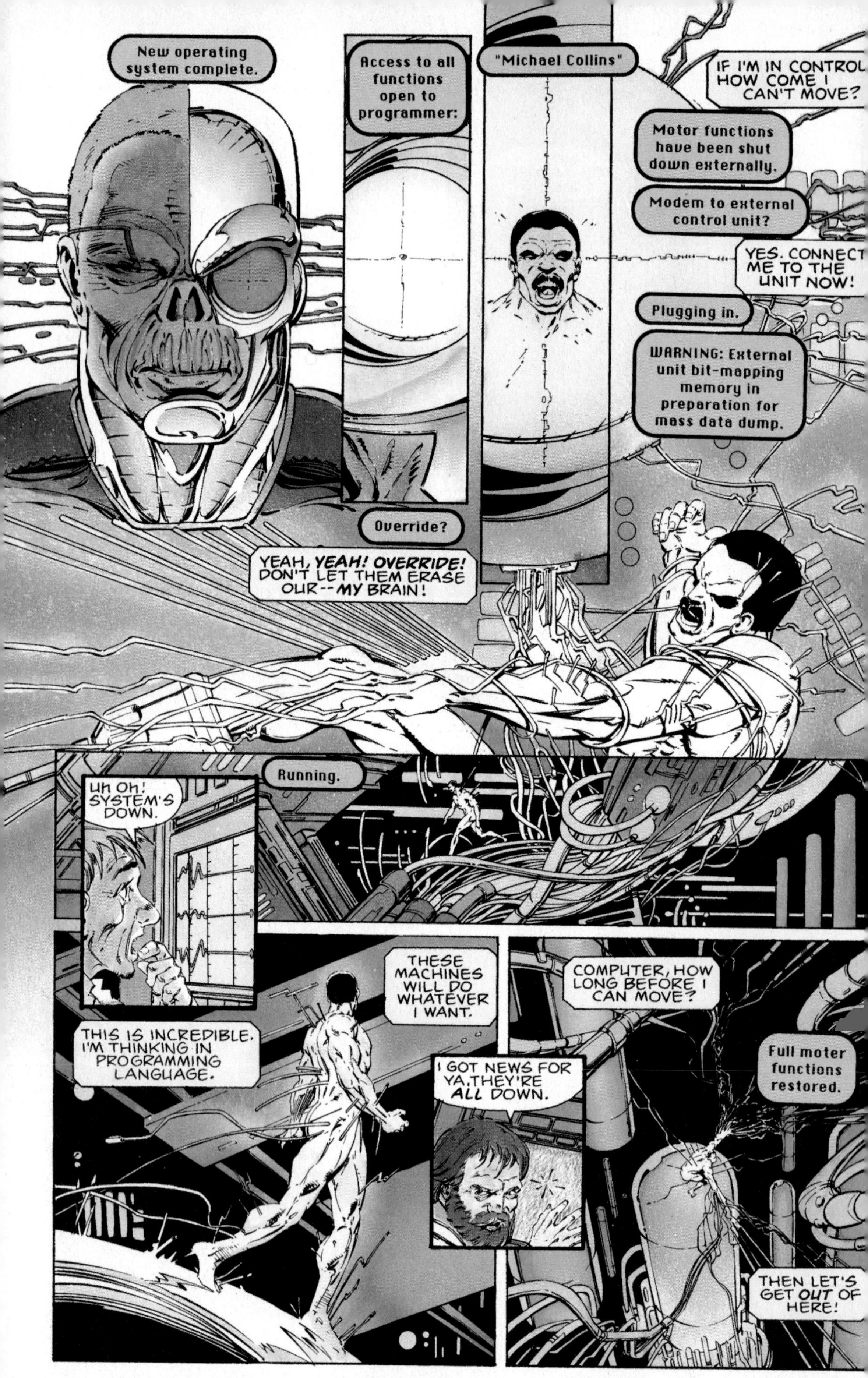
New operating system complete.
Access to all functions open to programmer:
"Michael Collins"
IF I'M IN CONTROL HOW COME I CAN'T MOVE?
Motor functions have been shut down externally.
Modem to external control unit?
YES. CONNECT ME TO THE UNIT NOW!
Plugging in.
WARNING: External unit bit-mapping memory in preparation for mass data dump.
Override?
YEAH, YEAH! OVERRIDE! DON'T LET THEM ERASE OUR-- MY BRAIN!
Running.
Uh Oh! SYSTEM'S DOWN.
THIS IS INCREDIBLE. I'M THINKING IN PROGRAMMING LANGUAGE.
THESE MACHINES WILL DO WHATEVER I WANT.
I GOT NEWS FOR YA.THEY'RE ALL DOWN.
COMPUTER, HOW LONG BEFORE I CAN MOVE?
Full moter functions restored.
THEN LET'S GET OUT OF HERE!

SHIZT
SHIZT
ARRRAUGH!
ZDAT
ZDAT
ZDAT
NO! IT'S BROKEN FREE!
Helmet seal complete. All systems functioning
CLUMP
CALL SECURITY. SEAL ALL EXITS!
FINE BY ME.
SKRUNCH

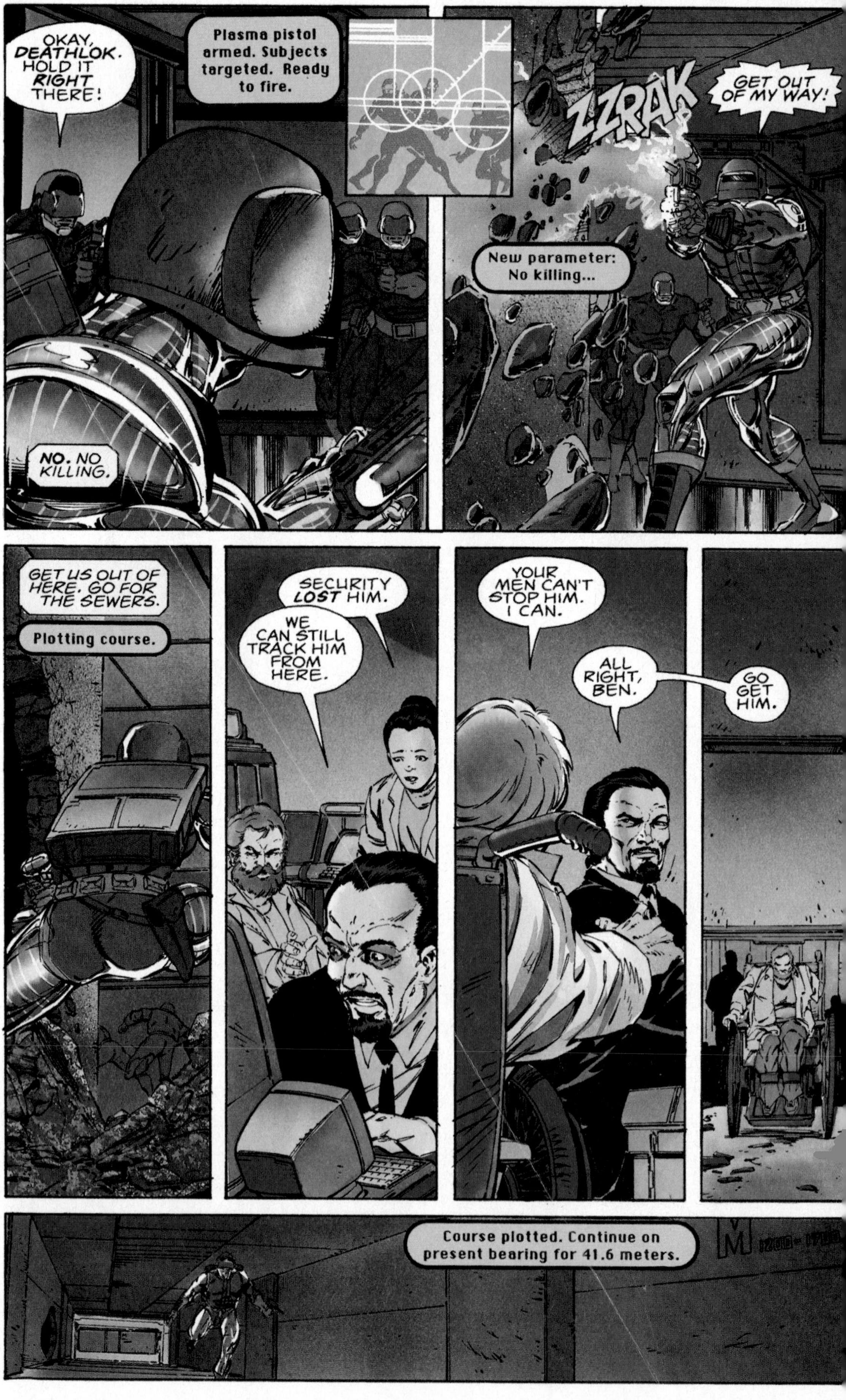

OKAY, DEATHLOK. HOLD IT RIGHT THERE!
Plasma pistol armed. Subjects targeted. Ready to fire.
NO. NO KILLING.
ZZRAK
GET OUT OF MY WAY!
New parameter: No killing...
GET US OUT OF HERE. GO FOR THE SEWERS.
Plotting course.
SECURITY LOST HIM.
WE CAN STILL TRACK HIM FROM HERE.
YOUR MEN CAN'T STOP HIM. I CAN.
ALL RIGHT, BEN.
GO GET HIM.
Course plotted. Continue on present bearing for 41.6 meters.

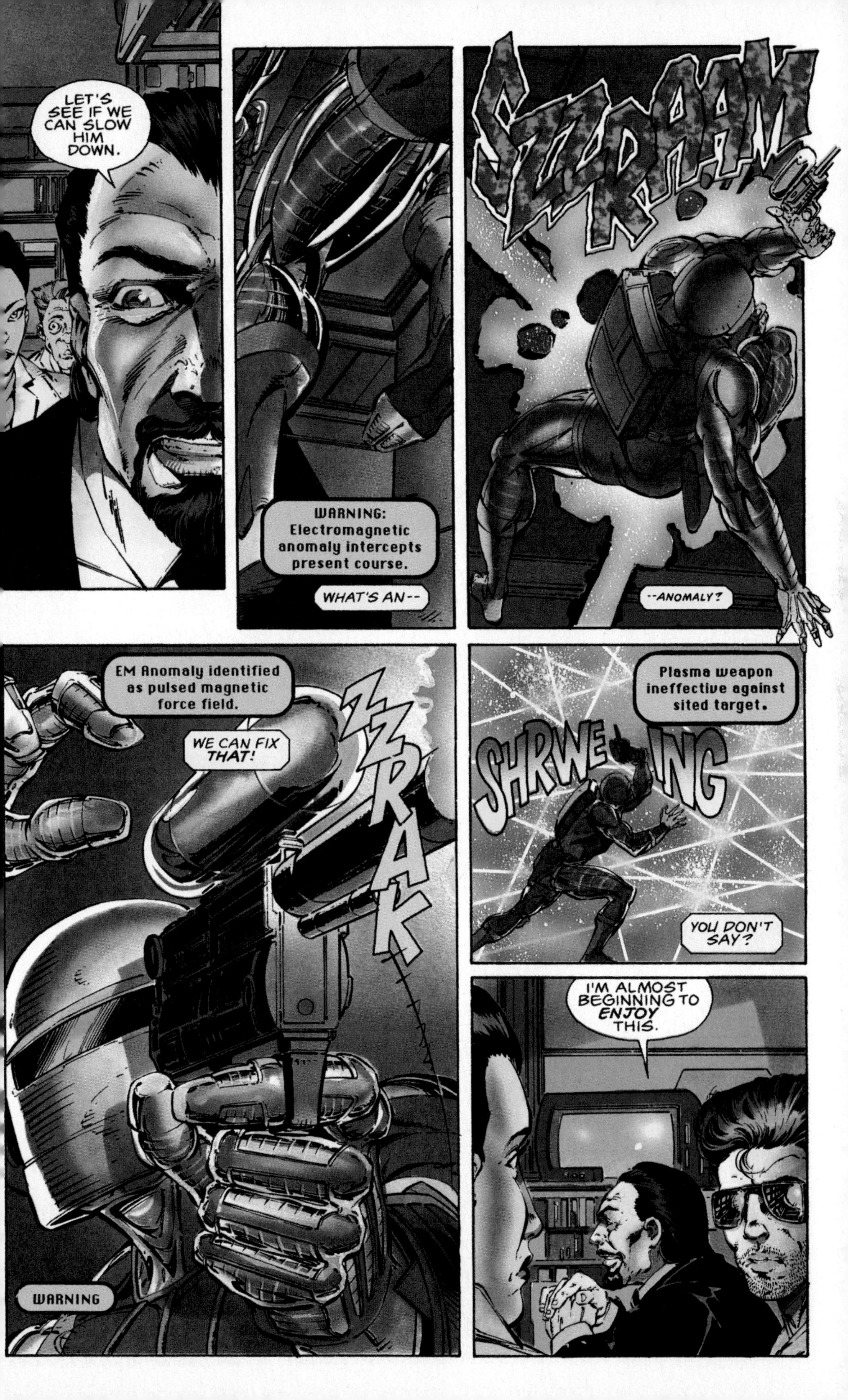
LET'S SEE IF WE CAN SLOW HIM DOWN.
WARNING: Electromagnetic anomaly intercepts present course.
WHAT'S AN--
--ANOMALY?
EM Anomaly identified as pulsed magnetic force field.
WE CAN FIX THAT!
ZZRAK
WARNING
Plasma weapon ineffective against sited target.
SHRWE ING
YOU DON'T SAY?
I'M ALMOST BEGINNING TO ENJOY THIS.

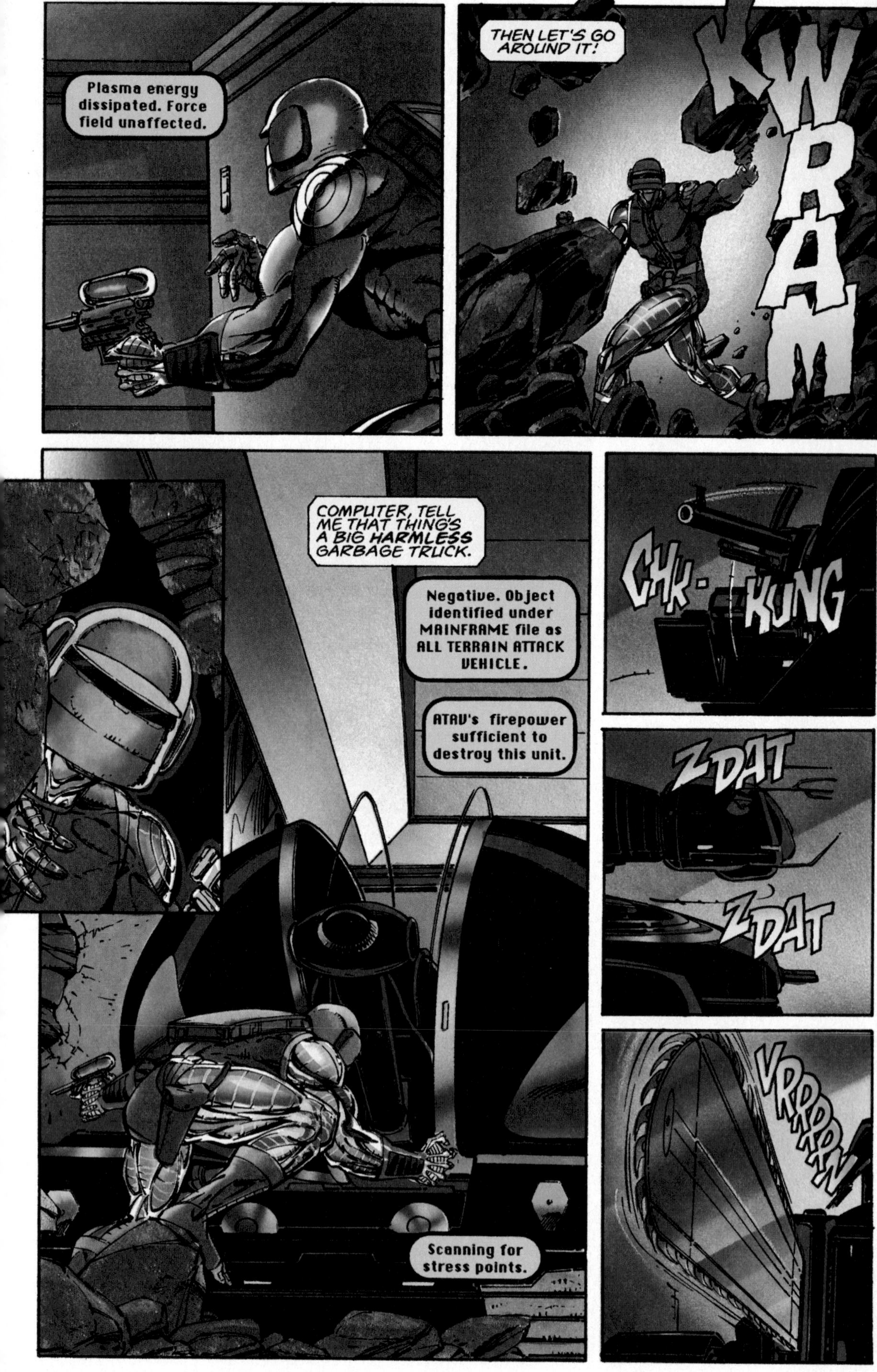
Plasma energy dissipated. Force field unaffected.
THEN LET'S GO AROUND IT!
KWRAM
COMPUTER, TELL ME THAT THING'S A BIG HARMLESS GARBAGE TRUCK.
Negative. Object identified under MAINFRAME file as ALL TERRAIN ATTACK VEHICLE.
ATAV's firepower sufficient to destroy this unit.
Scanning for stress points.
CHK-KUNG
ZDAT
ZDAT
VRRRRRN

Sensors identify ATAU pilot as Ben Jacobs.
"No killing" parameter still in effect.
JACOBS?! HOW'D HE GET DOWN HERE BE-FORE ME?
Unit being tracked and telemonitored through helmet transponder.
WE CAN'T HAVE THAT NOW, CAN WE?
WHAT'S GOING ON?
ZZRAK
Targeting to neutralize weapons systems.
Internal systems re-evaluation: Removal of helmet has increased vulnerability as follows: Negative function; transponder, air filter, rebreather, optical filter, uplink. Exposed organics now vulnerable to impact.
DO YOU MIND? I'M TRYING TO WORK.
SORRY, BOSS, WE LOST THE SIGNAL.
THEN WE'D BETTER CHECK THIS OUT OURSELVES.

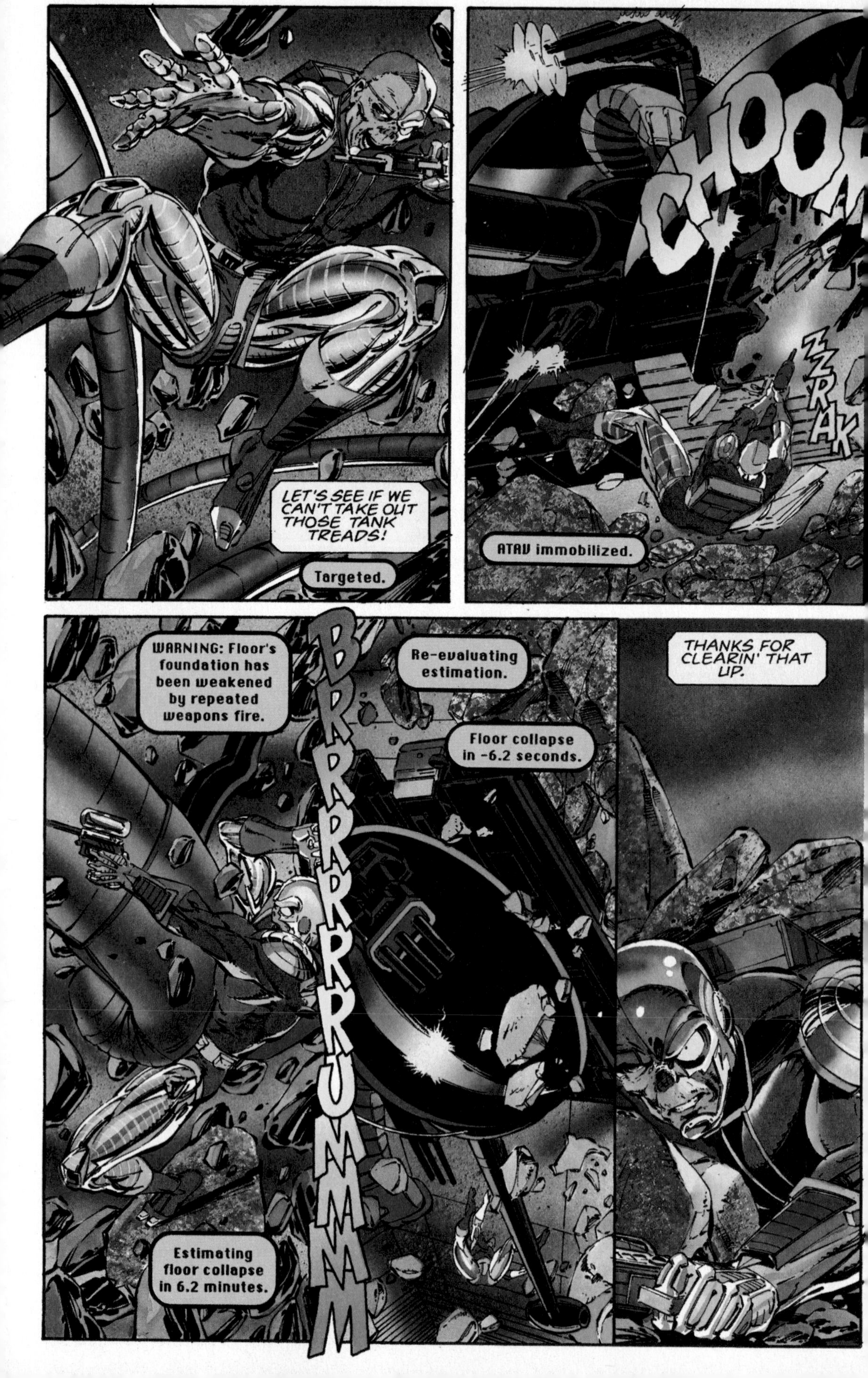
LET'S SEE IF WE CAN'T TAKE OUT THOSE TANK TREADS!
Targeted.
CHOOM
ZZRAK
ATAV immobilized.
WARNING: Floor's foundation has been weakened by repeated weapons fire.
Estimating floor collapse in 6.2 minutes.
BRDRDRDRDRRUMMMMM
Re-evaluating estimation.
Floor collapse in ~6.2 seconds.
THANKS FOR CLEARIN' THAT UP.

PUM PUM PUM
PWOOM
Unit undamaged. All systems functional.
ATAV severely damaged.
ZZRAK
YEAH. THAT SUCKER'S DEAD IN THE WATER.
ZZRAK
ZZRAK
ZZRAK
LET'S JUST MAKE SURE.
AND SPEAKING OF DEAD...
NO! STAY BACK! PLEASE!
SAY GOODNIGHT, BEN!
G'NIGHT BEN?

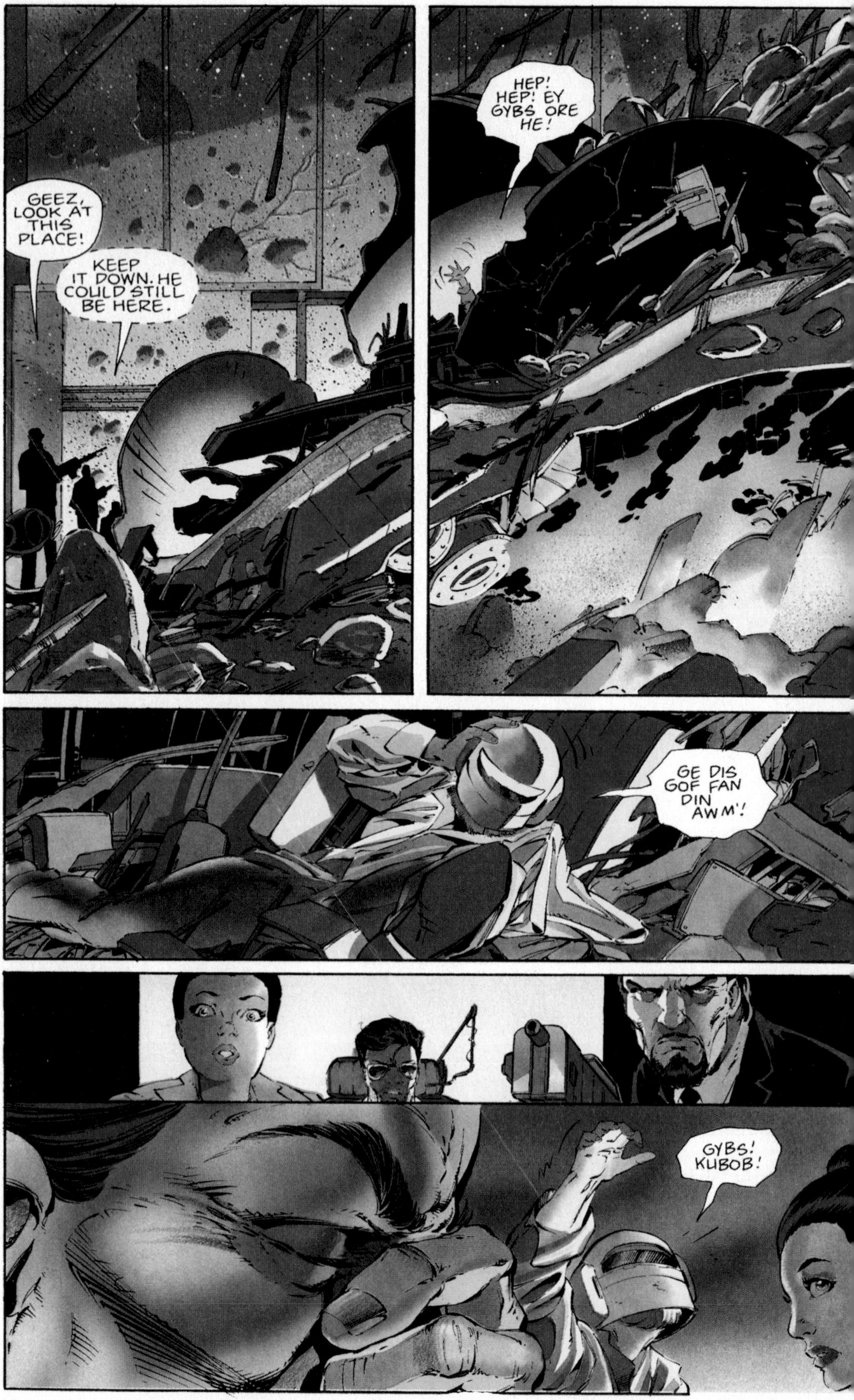
GEEZ, LOOK AT THIS PLACE!
KEEP IT DOWN. HE COULD STILL BE HERE.
HEP! HEP! EY GYBS ORE HE!
GE DIS GOF FAN DIN AWM'!
GYBS! KUBOB!

Entering municipal sewer system. No evidence of pursuit within sensor range.
SO WE LOST 'EM. NOW WHAT?
Collating options.
WHO ASKED YOU?
You did.
>SIGH<
GOTTA GO SEE TRACY.
SHE'LL KNOW WHAT TO DO.

SHE'LL UNDERSTAND.
NICK, YOU'VE BEEN PLAYING THAT GAME FOR A LONG TIME. DON'T YOU THINK IT'S TIME YOU CRACKED A SCHOOL BOOK?
IN A MINUTE. I CAN'T QUIT PLAYING TILL I BEAT THIS THING.
YOU CAN PLAY THE GAME AFTER YOU FINISH YOUR HOME-WORK...
WELL...

...JUST DON'T PLAY ALL NIGHT AGAIN.
I'LL GET THE DOOR.
BECAUSE I'M YOUR HUSBAND.
IT'S ME... MICHAEL.

NO! YOU'RE SOME KIND OF MONSTER!
WAIT! PLEASE...
SLAM
MOM..?
NICK?! IS THAT MY BOY?
P-PLEASE! JUST GO AWAY! HE'S NOT YOUR BOY!
SURE HE IS...
...MAKE HIM WASH THE DISHES. THAT'S WHAT WE HAD HIM FOR.
M-MICHAEL?

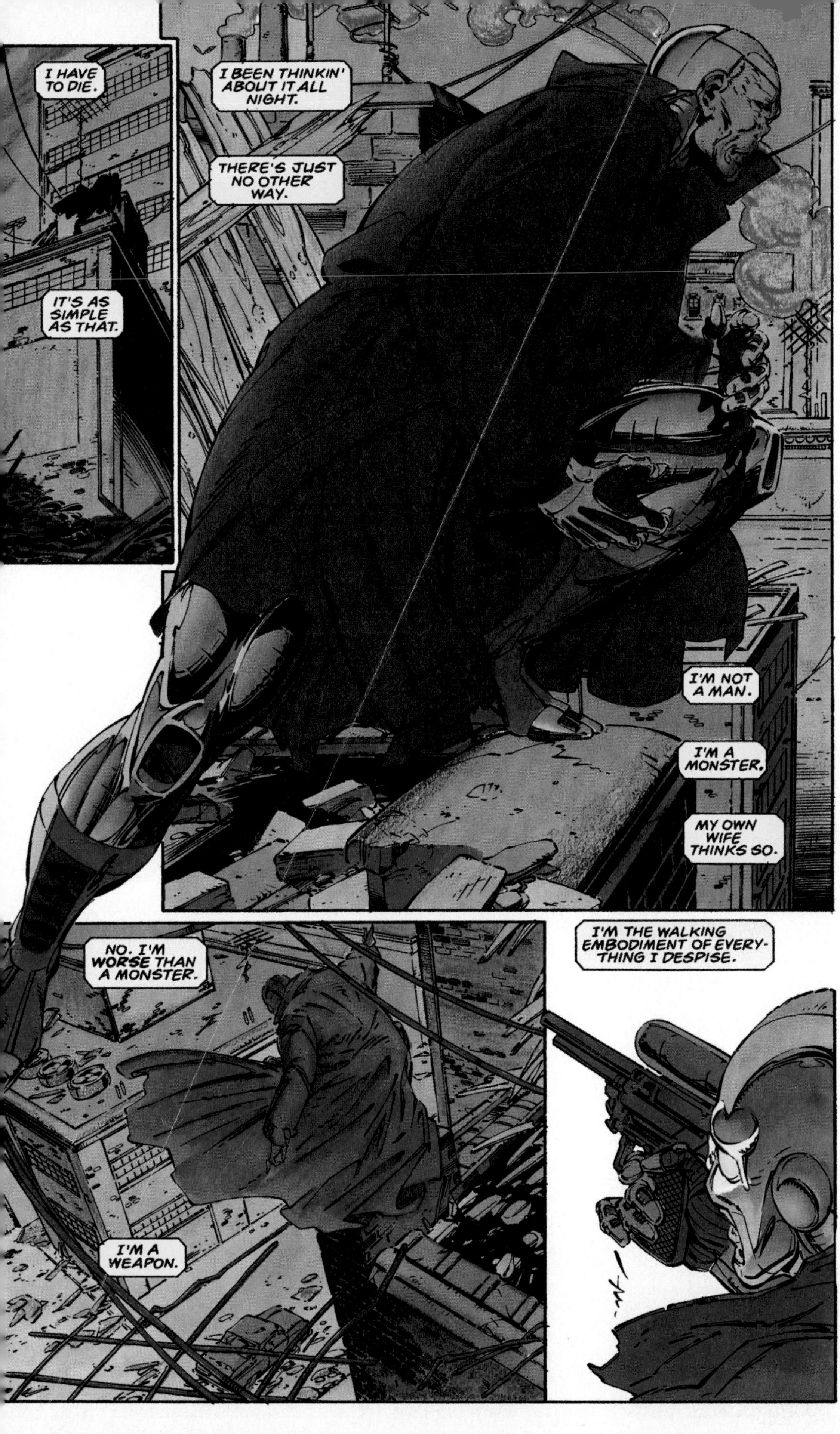
I HAVE TO DIE.
I BEEN THINKIN' ABOUT IT ALL NIGHT.
THERE'S JUST NO OTHER WAY.
IT'S AS SIMPLE AS THAT.
I'M NOT A MAN.
I'M A MONSTER.
MY OWN WIFE THINKS SO.
NO. I'M WORSE THAN A MONSTER.
I'M A WEAPON.
I'M THE WALKING EMBODIMENT OF EVERY-THING I DESPISE.

I HAVE TO DIE.
IT'S NOT THAT SIMPLE.
THEY'D JUST FIND THE BODY--
--AND IT WOULD ALL START OVER AGAIN.
I GOTTA DESTROY THE MACHINE.
SHIK
NO.
I CAN'T JUST KILL THE MAN.
Preparing for cybernetic systems overload.
ZDAT
ZDAT
ZDAT
All surge protection systems defeated.
External powerlines carrying sufficient current to permanently fuse Deathlok systems and destroy organic software.

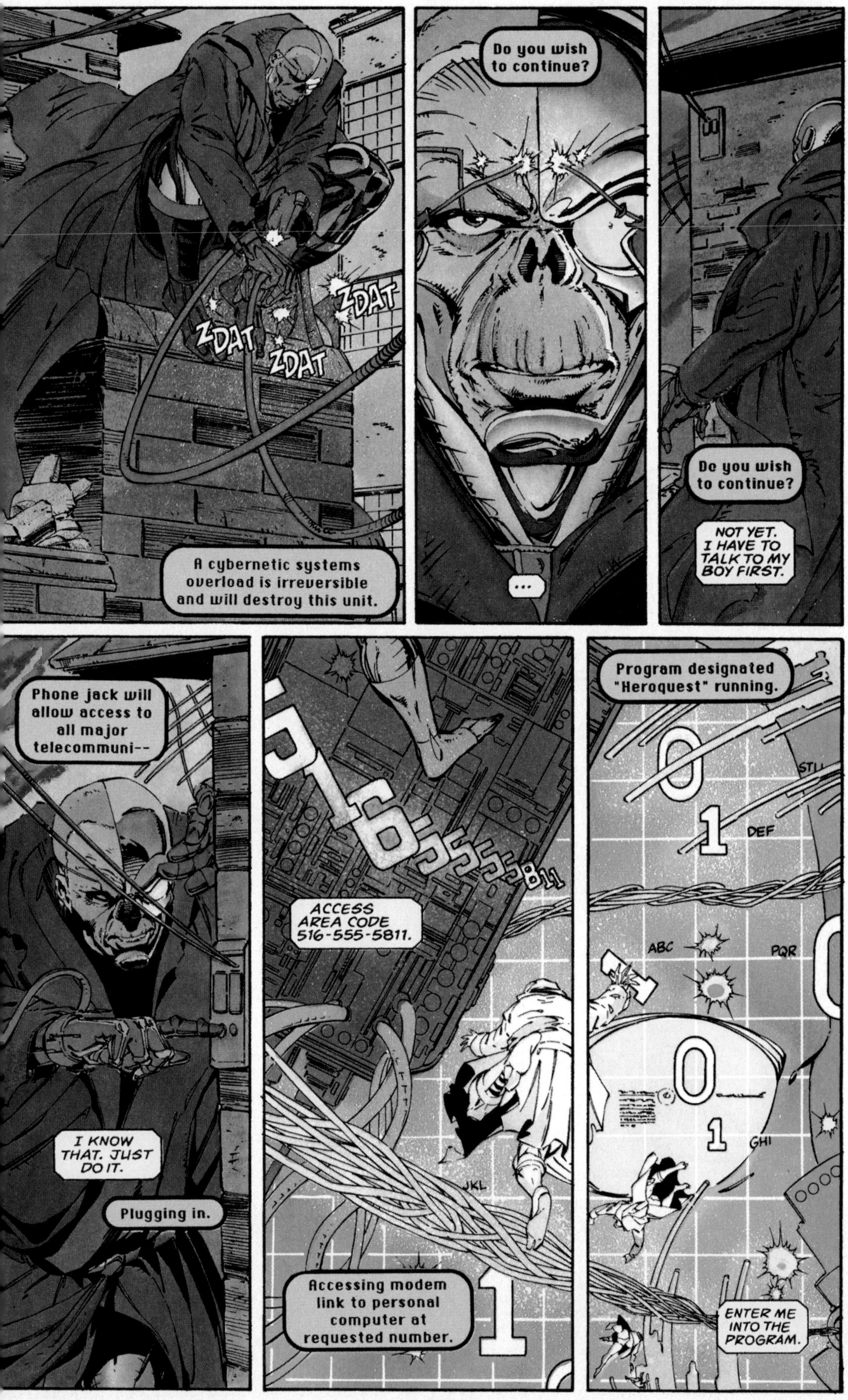
ZDAT
ZDAT
ZDAT
A cybernetic systems overload is irreversible and will destroy this unit.
Do you wish to continue?
...
Do you wish to continue?
NOT YET. I HAVE TO TALK TO MY BOY FIRST.
Phone jack will allow access to all major telecommuni--
I KNOW THAT. JUST DO IT.
Plugging in.
5165555811
ACCESS AREA CODE 516-555-5811.
Accessing modem link to personal computer at requested number.
Program designated "Heroquest" running.
ENTER ME INTO THE PROGRAM.

HEROQUEST VERSION 4.2. CONTINUE LAST GAME OR START A NEW ONE?
COMMAND: CONTINUE LAST GAME.
TWO EVIL KNIGHTS FROM THE GORGE OF MAGALONG APPROACH. ATTACK OR FLEE?
COMMAND: ATTACK WITH AX.
TAP
TAP
YOU HAVE WOUNDED THE EVIL KNIGHTS, BUT HAVE LOST YOUR MOUNT AND AX. DO YOU TAKE PRISONERS?
COMMAND: NO PRISONERS, JUST KILL 'EM WITH SWORD

WOINK
HOLD UP A MINUTE, uh, KNIGHT.
HEY, KID! WHAT DO YOU THINK YOU'RE DOING?
WE'RE NOT KILLING ANYBODY WITH ANYTHING--!
Th-THIS SN'T HOW THE AME WORKS! Wh-WHERE DID OU COME FROM?!
I'M YOUR--! uh, YOUR FATHER INCLUDED ME IN THE PROGRAM... IN CASE YOU FORGOT THE PURPOSE OF HEROQUEST.
A HERO WOULD FIND A BETTER WAY THAN THE WAY YOU'RE PLAYING THIS GAME.
BUT IT'S TOO HARD THAT WAY.
YOU HAVE TO DO WHAT'S RIGHT, BOY. NOT WHAT'S EASIEST.
THAT'S WHAT... DAD USED TO SAY.

... BUT HE'S NOT HERE ANY MORE.
WHEREVER HE IS, THAT DOESN'T MAKE IT ANY LESS TRUE.
YOU WANT TO WIN AT THIS GAME, YOU'VE GOTTA LEARN HOW TO BE A HERO.
I... I WILL.
TEK
DELETE
PAUSE
INPUT
SAVE

Phone link disconnected.
Continue with cybernetics systems overload?
...
Continue with cybernetics systems overload?
I DON'T THINK SO.
" YOU WANT TO WIN AT THIS GAME...
"...YOU'VE GOTTA LEARN HOW TO BE A HERO."

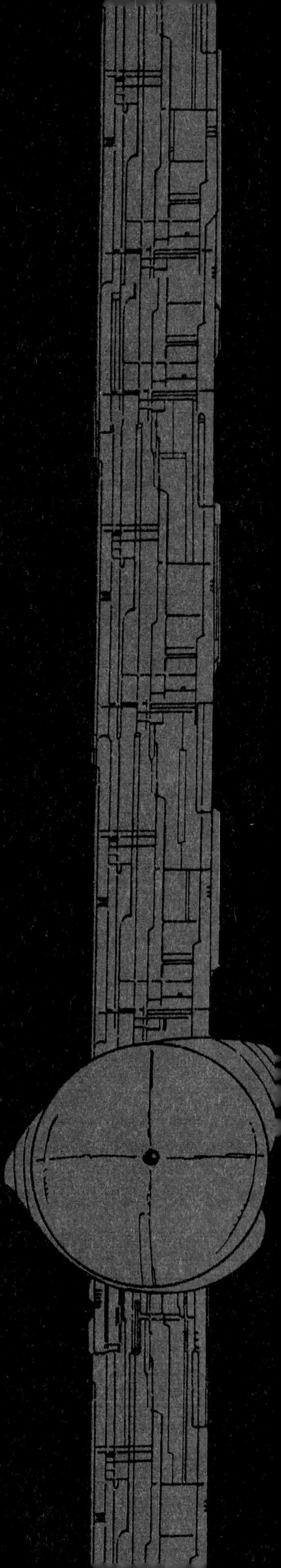

NEXT:
JESUS SAVES

THE MAN...IN THE MACHINE

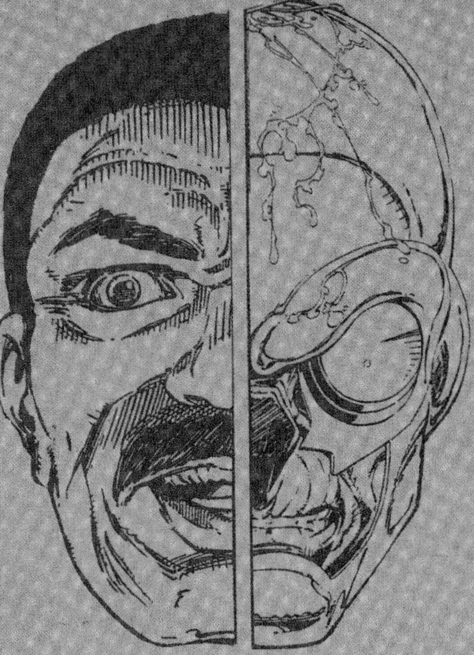

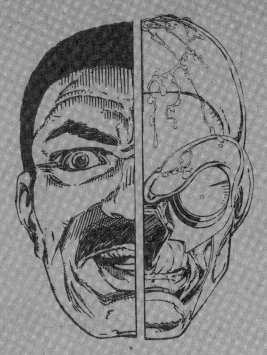

Research scientist **Michael Collins** discovers that the project in advanced cybernetics which he heads for the mammoth **Roxxon Corporation** is in actuality an attempt to create the ultimate **death-machine for hire**--an unliving, programmable **cyborg** of immense power. Collins seeks to bring the nightmarish project to a halt, but is rewarded for his high moral stance by being **murdered**...and then brought back, locked inside the death-machine, becoming the very thing he loathes and fears most--**DEATHLOK!**

$3.95 U.S.
$4.95 Can.
ISBN# 0-87135-668-6

[redacted]

Deathlok #1 inside-cover art by Jackson Guice

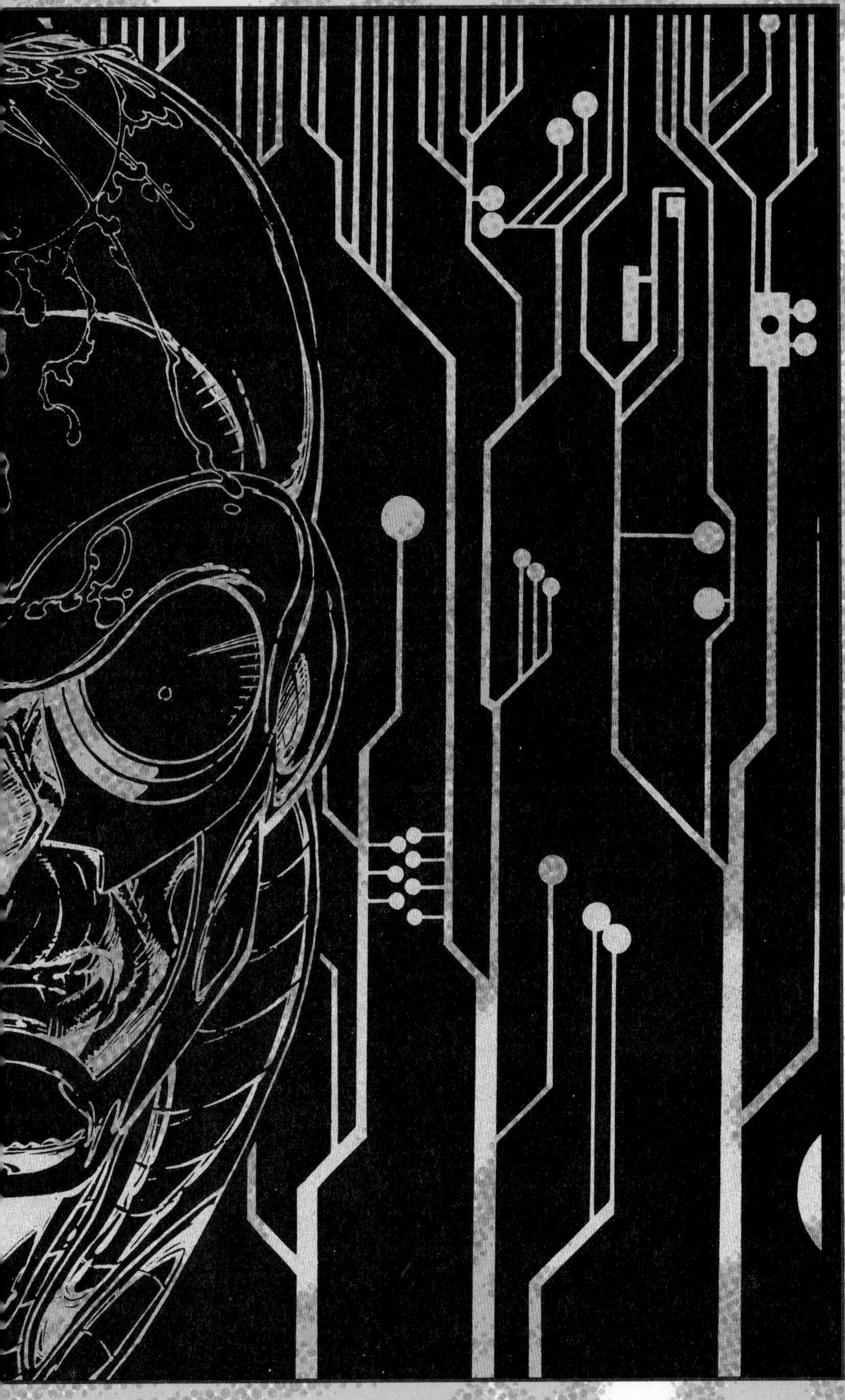

MARVEL COMICS
HEROES FOR THE 90'S--!
THE NEW WARRIORS
$1.00 US
$1.25 CAN
1
JULY
UK 60p
APPROVED BY THE COMICS CODE AUTHORITY
NAMORITA
FIRESTAR
KID NOVA
MARVEL BOY
SPEEDBALL
AND INTRODUCING--
NIGHT THRASHER
FANTASTIC 1st ISSUE!

NEW WARRIORS #1, published in May 1990, began an ongoing series starring the teenage superteam that debuted during the recent "Acts of Vengeance" event.

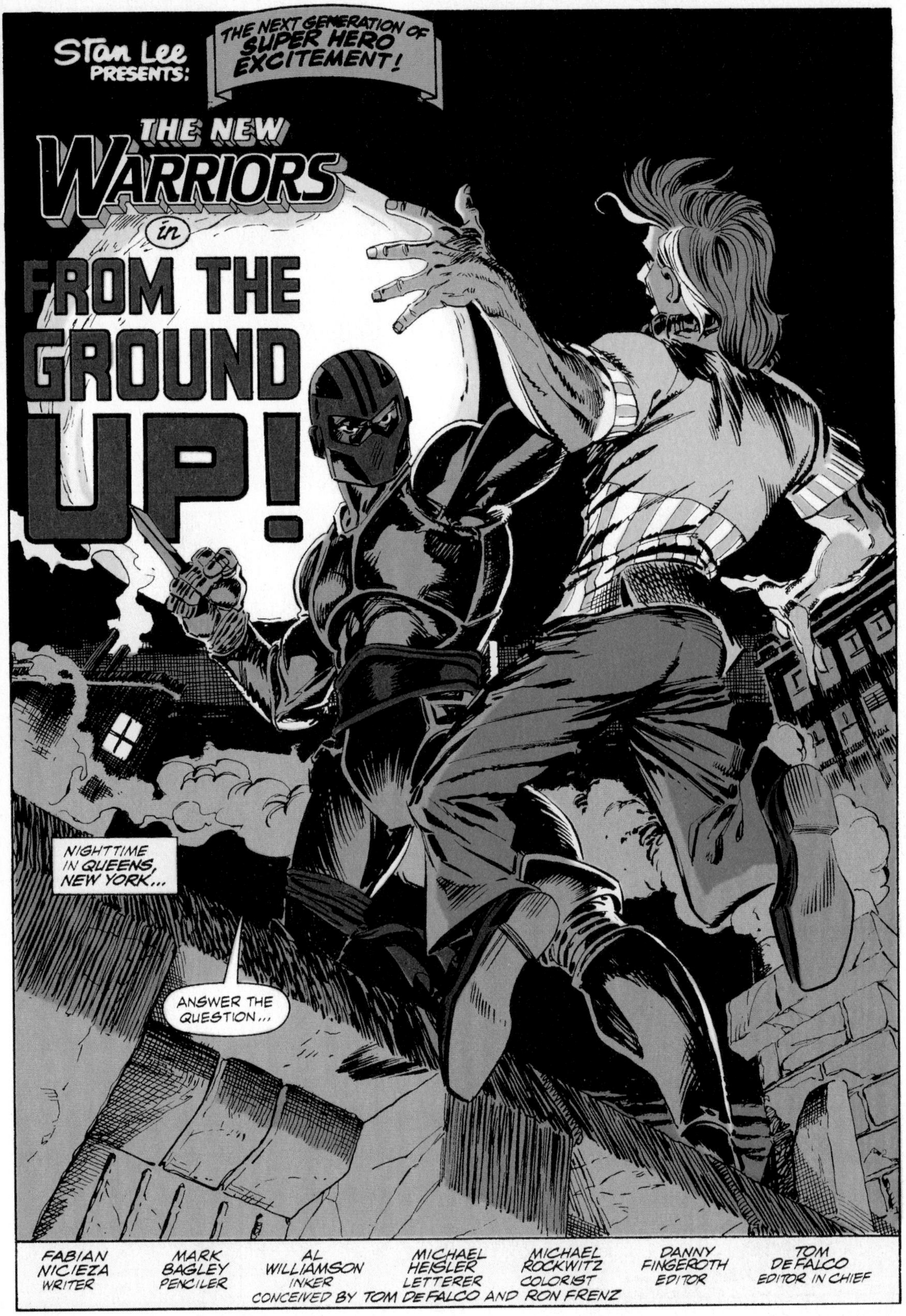

Stan Lee PRESENTS:
THE NEXT GENERATION OF SUPER HERO EXCITEMENT!
THE NEW WARRIORS in
FROM THE GROUND UP!
NIGHTTIME IN QUEENS, NEW YORK...
ANSWER THE QUESTION...
FABIAN NICIEZA WRITER
MARK BAGLEY PENCILER
AL WILLIAMSON INKER
MICHAEL HEISLER LETTERER
MICHAEL ROCKWITZ COLORIST
DANNY FINGEROTH EDITOR
TOM DEFALCO EDITOR IN CHIEF
CONCEIVED BY TOM DEFALCO AND RON FRENZ

...ARE YOU OR AREN'T YOU RICHARD RIDER?
YEAH--
NFFGH
--YEAH!
THANKS.
YAAAAAAAA
OH MAN OH MAN OH MAN
OHMANOHMANOHMAN
EEEK
?
OH, MAN! OH, MAN!!
I CAN FLY AGAIN!!
YOU KNEW I USED T'BE NOVA?
BUT HOW'D'JOU KNOW I STILL HAD MY POWERS IN ME?
I DIDN'T.

YOU WHAT?
YOU COULDA KILLED ME!!
MAYBE.
BUT I DIDN'T...
...I ONLY GAVE YOU BACK THE ONE THING YOU WANTED MORE THAN ANYTHING ELSE IN THE WORLD.
NOW I WANT SOMETHING FROM YOU...
MORNING IN MANHATTAN.
EVEN FOR THE MOST JADED OF NEW YORKERS, THE SIGHTS WHICH ARE USUALLY SEEN IN FRONT OF AVENGERS MANSION CAN BOGGLE THE MIND.
AVENGERS MANSION
HOT DOG
MAYBE THIS ONE ONLY REGISTERS HALFWAY ON THE "BOGGLE SCALE."
FUNKY TIGHTS. WHO'RE YOU?
YOU CAN CALL ME MARVEL BOY!
ANYTHIN' YOU SAY. YOU AN AVENGER OR SOMETHIN'?
NOT YET, FRIEND, BUT GIVE ME HALF AN HOUR!
BETTER NOT LET MYSELF GET TOO COCKY...
SECURITY SYSTEMS?!
ALL RIGHT!!
SHIK
SHIK
ONCE THE AVENGERS SEE MY TELEKINETIC POWERS IN ACTION, THEY'LL BEG ME TO JOIN THEM!
SHIK
SHIK

OKAY. LET ME GO.
BREEP:- RETINAL SCAN IDENTIFICATION ACKNOWLEDGED:- SUBJECT: VANCE ASTRO:- GROUP AFFILIATION: GUARDIANS OF THE GALAXY:- CROSS REFERENCE FILE #112A-D:-
DISENGAGE SECURITY CODE THREE.
A LITTLE TOO YOUNG TO BE A THOUSAND YEARS OLD, AREN'T YOU, SON?
CAPTAIN AMERICA?!
AND I'M TO TAKE IT YOU'RE VANCE ASTRO?
ASTROVIK. I GUESS I'M THE GUY THE MAN YOU KNOW IS GOING TO GROW UP TO BE... UHM...
...YOU FOLLOW ALL OF THAT?
HAH--YES, SON, I DO.
BEN GRIMM FILLED US IN ON YOUR CURRENT STATUS SOME TIME AGO. WE LIKE TO KEEP OUR FILES AS COMPLETE AS POSSIBLE.
HEY, THE THING TOLD YOU ABOUT ME? BEN'S MY FRIEND.
THEN THAT MAKES YOU MY FRIEND, TOO, VANCE.
WHAT CAN I DO FOR YOU?
I'M HERE TO JOIN THE AVENGERS!
I SEE...
...WELL, YOU'RE A LITTLE TOO YOUNG STILL, AND WE DON'T HAVE THE TRAINING FACILITIES NEEDED TO TEACH YOU...
WHY DON'T YOU TRY AGAIN IN A FEW YEARS, VANCE?
YES, SIR...
OKAY?
SURE...
WHAT AN IDIOT I WAS!
WALKING IN THERE LIKE I OWNED THE PLACE!
NOW WHAT?
I CAN'T BE AN AVENGER UNLESS I GET THE EXPERIENCE AND I WON'T GET THE EXPERIENCE UN-LESS I BECOME AN AVENGER.
I'LL JUST BLAME IT ALL ON JOSEPH HELLER...
MARVEL BOY!
WHO--?
THE NAME'S NIGHT THRASHER. THIS IS NOVA. YOU WANT TO JOIN A GROUP, DO YOU?

AFTERNOON IN QUEENS.
A QUIET NEIGHBORHOOD HAS BEEN TURNED UPSIDE-DOWN BY A MODERN-DAY NIGHTMARE: GROUNDSOIL CONTAMINATION.
THREE CHILDREN HAVE DEVELOPED CANCER OVER THE PAST YEAR, ANOTHER FIVE, LEUKEMIA. THE SCHOOL PLAYGROUND HAS BEEN CLOSED DOWN AND THE EXPERTS HAVE FINALLY BEEN CALLED IN.
G-T
GENETECH
THE NEW YORK DEPARTMENT OF ENVIRONMENTAL PROTECTION HAS HIRED GENETECH, A NEW COMPANY WHOSE SPECIALTY IS SUPERHUMAN GENETIC RESEARCH.
AND A CLASS FROM EMPIRE STATE UNIVERSITY'S DEPARTMENT OF ENVIRONMENTAL SCIENCE HAS COME FOR A FIELD ASSIGNMENT.
IS ALL OF THIS COMMOTION NECESSARY, MS. TRUESDALE?
I MEAN, DOESN'T IT HAVE A NEGATIVE EFFECT ON THE COMMUNITY?
GOOD QUESTION, NITA, LET'S GO STRAIGHT TO THE SOURCE FOR THE ANSWER...
...SET IT UP IN SECTOR C...
NO PROB, WALT.
MR. ROSEN, ONE OF MY STUDENTS WANTS TO KNOW HOW ALL OF THIS AFFECTS THE SURROUNDING COMMUNITY.
WELL, LINDA, THERE ARE NO EASY ANSWERS...
HOW ABOUT GIVING US SOME HARD ONES, THEN?
AHEM. AND YOU ARE--?
NITA PRENTISS. NAMORITA PRENTISS.
THE SUB-MARINER'S COUSIN?
FASCINATING.
WELL, MISS PRENTISS, AT THIS PARTICULAR SITE, WE'RE STILL TRYING TO COME UP WITH THE QUESTIONS!
THE ANSWERS ALWAYS SEEM TO TAKE CARE OF THEMSELVES...

MIDTOWN MANHATTAN.
YOU LIVE HERE? BY YOURSELF?
NO, MARVEL BOY, I HAVE TWO LEGAL GUARDIANS.
YOU RICH OR SOMETHIN'?
OR SOMETHING.
DO YOUR GUARDIANS KNOW ABOUT ALL OF THIS EQUIPMENT?
DO THEY KNOW ABOUT YOUR CRIMEFIGHTING?
THEY ENCOURAGE IT.
THEY HAVE TAUGHT ME ALL I KNOW AND GIVEN ME ALL I NEED TO WAGE MY WAR.
NOW WHY DON'T YOU TELL US EXACTLY WHAT YOU KNOW...
...STARTING WITH: HOW DID YOU FIND OUT ABOUT MY IDENTITY?
THE SAME WAY HE FINDS OUT ABOUT ANYTHING, BOY-- THROUGH HARD WORK.
YES, CHORD. WITHOUT ORGANIZATION, IN-FORMATION AND DE-TERMINATION, LIFE BECOMES A SERIES OF UNCERTAIN STEPS TOWARDS AN UNKNOWN GOAL.
WONDERFUL. DID ROSEY GRIER OVER HERE TAKE CONFUCIUS TO GET FORTUNE COOKIES OR DOES SHE ALWAYS TALK LIKE THAT?
RELAX YOUR LIPS, SON. RESPECT TAI'S WISDOM.
EXCUSE ME, MA'AM, EXACTLY WHAT GOAL IS NIGHT THRASHER WALKING TOWARDS?
MY PARENTS WERE MURDERED WHEN I WAS A BOY.
I'M GOING TO MAKE ALL CRIMINALS PAY FOR WHAT THEY DO.
BUT I NEED HELP TO DO IT. THAT'S WHERE YOU GUYS--
--AND HOPEFULLY ONE OTHER--COME IN. CHORD--?
ACCESSING.
THIS IS THE BEST SYSTEM I'VE EVER SEEN!

DOES THIS HAVE MORE CAPACITY THAN A CRAY?
NOT QUITE. BUT IT'S GOT MORE GIGABYTES THAN A MACINTOSH!
HEY, DWAYNE, I LIKE THIS KID BETTER THAN THE ONE WITH THE BUCKET ON HIS HEAD.
I'M IN.
MASSACHUSETTS ACADEMY
THAT'S THE RITZY PLACE NEAR BOSTON!
I COULDN'T GET ACCEPTED THERE. I COULDN'T AFFORD THE TUITION ANYWAY...
TWO-FOUR-FOUR-MARY-MARY-VICTOR.
YOU SURE ABOUT THIS? WE TRIP ANY ALARMS...
HELLFIRE CLUB?!
"ACCESS ONLY?"
WHOA HERE-- THIS IS NASTY TERRITORY!
HOW DID YOU GET THEIR BACK-DOOR?
FIRESTAR
JONES, ANGELICA
MONEY TALKS.
AND START THINKING IN TERMS OF "WE"--
THAT'S HOW YOU FOUND OUT ABOUT ME!
YOU HACKED INTO THE FANTASTIC FOUR'S SYSTEMS!
I CAN'T GET INTO THE FF'S SYSTEMS-- THEY'RE TOO ADVANCED.
THEN HOW? AFTER I RETURNED TO EARTH, I WENT TO REED RICHARDS--
--HOPING HE COULD RESTORE MY POWERS--
EXACTLY. HE DID A COMPLETE ANALYSIS OF YOU AND FOUND OUT THAT YOUR POWERS HAD BEEN BURIED SO DEEP WITHIN YOU--
--THAT ONLY A 35% CHANCE OF THEIR RESURGENCE EXISTED. THEN HE PROVIDED SHIELD WITH THE DATA--
AND WHEN SHIELD COLLAPSED, YOU TAPPED INTO THEIR SYSTEMS AND GOT PROFESSOR RICHARDS' REPORT, RIGHT?
HOW LONG HAVE YOU BEEN AT THIS? DID YOU FIND OUT ABOUT ME THE SAME WAY?
DID YOU SEE THAT HOT DOG VENDOR OUTSIDE OF AVENGERS MANSION?

HE GETS FIVE HUNDRED A MONTH TO TELL ME WHO GOES IN AND OUT. TODAY, HE CALLED ME ABOUT YOU.
SMOOTH. AND THIS FIRESTAR PERSON?
THE FINAL PIECE OF THE PUZZLE.
WEST MORRIS, NEW JERSEY...
PUMPKIN-- I KNOW YOU'RE HAPPY I'M HOME-- BUT IF YOU GET ANY HAIR ON MY SWEATER--
BRIIING
BRII
OFF THE BED--
HELLO?
ANGELICA JONES?
WE KNOW WHO YOU ARE. WE KNOW WHAT YOU CAN DO.
SO WILL THE WORLD IF YOU DON'T COME TO THE PENTHOUSE OF THE AMBROSE BUILDING ON 57TH AND LEXINGTON.
THIRTY MINUTES.
H-HELLO? WHO--WHO IS THIS?
CLIK
NO.
NO!
NO!
MEANWHILE, IN SPRINGDALE, NEW YORK...
I DON'T WANT TO GO
I DON'T WANT TO GO
I DON'T WANT TO GO
I DON'T WANT TO GO
351
Amtrak
OH, CALM DOWN AND GET ON THE TRAIN!
MOM, I DON'T WANT TO GO TO ANOTHER ART GALLERY OPENING! I MEAN, JUST SHOOT ME IN THE HEAD NOW, YOU KNOW?
DON'T BE SO MELODRAMATIC, ROBBIE.
BESIDES, WHEN WE'RE IN NEW YORK, MAYBE WE'LL LOOK FOR THAT NEW TV YOU'VE BEEN WHINING ABOUT.

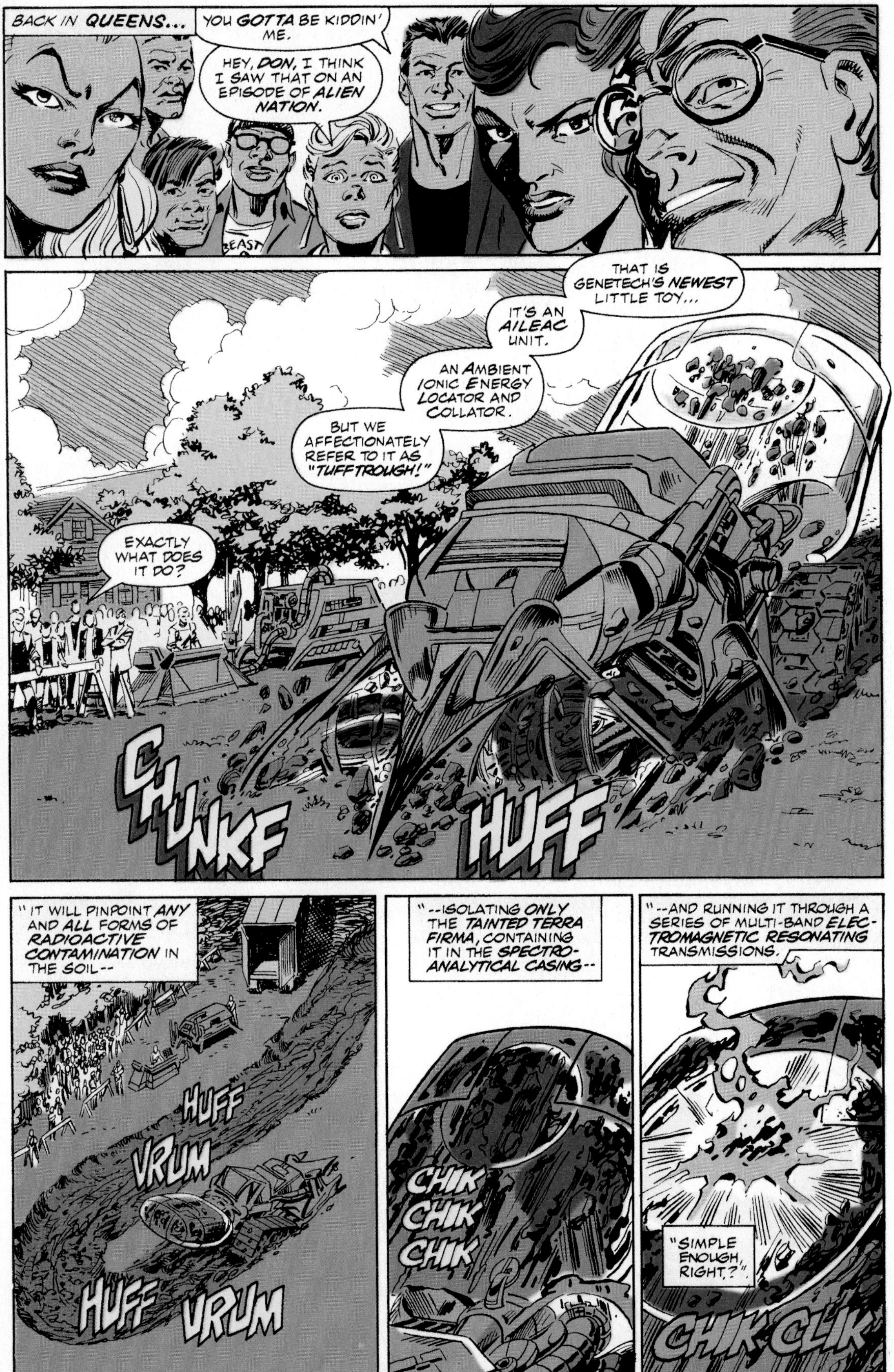
BACK IN QUEENS...
YOU GOTTA BE KIDDIN' ME.
HEY, DON, I THINK I SAW THAT ON AN EPISODE OF ALIEN NATION.
BEAST
THAT IS GENETECH'S NEWEST LITTLE TOY...
IT'S AN AILEAC UNIT.
AN AMBIENT IONIC ENERGY LOCATOR AND COLLATOR.
BUT WE AFFECTIONATELY REFER TO IT AS "TUFFTROUGH!"
EXACTLY WHAT DOES IT DO?
CHUNKF
HUFF
"IT WILL PINPOINT ANY AND ALL FORMS OF RADIOACTIVE CONTAMINATION IN THE SOIL--
HUFF
VRUM
HUFF
VRUM
"--ISOLATING ONLY THE TAINTED TERRA FIRMA, CONTAINING IT IN THE SPECTRO-ANALYTICAL CASING--
CHIK
CHIK
CHIK
"--AND RUNNING IT THROUGH A SERIES OF MULTI-BAND ELECTROMAGNETIC RESONATING TRANSMISSIONS.
"SIMPLE ENOUGH, RIGHT?"
CHIK CLIK

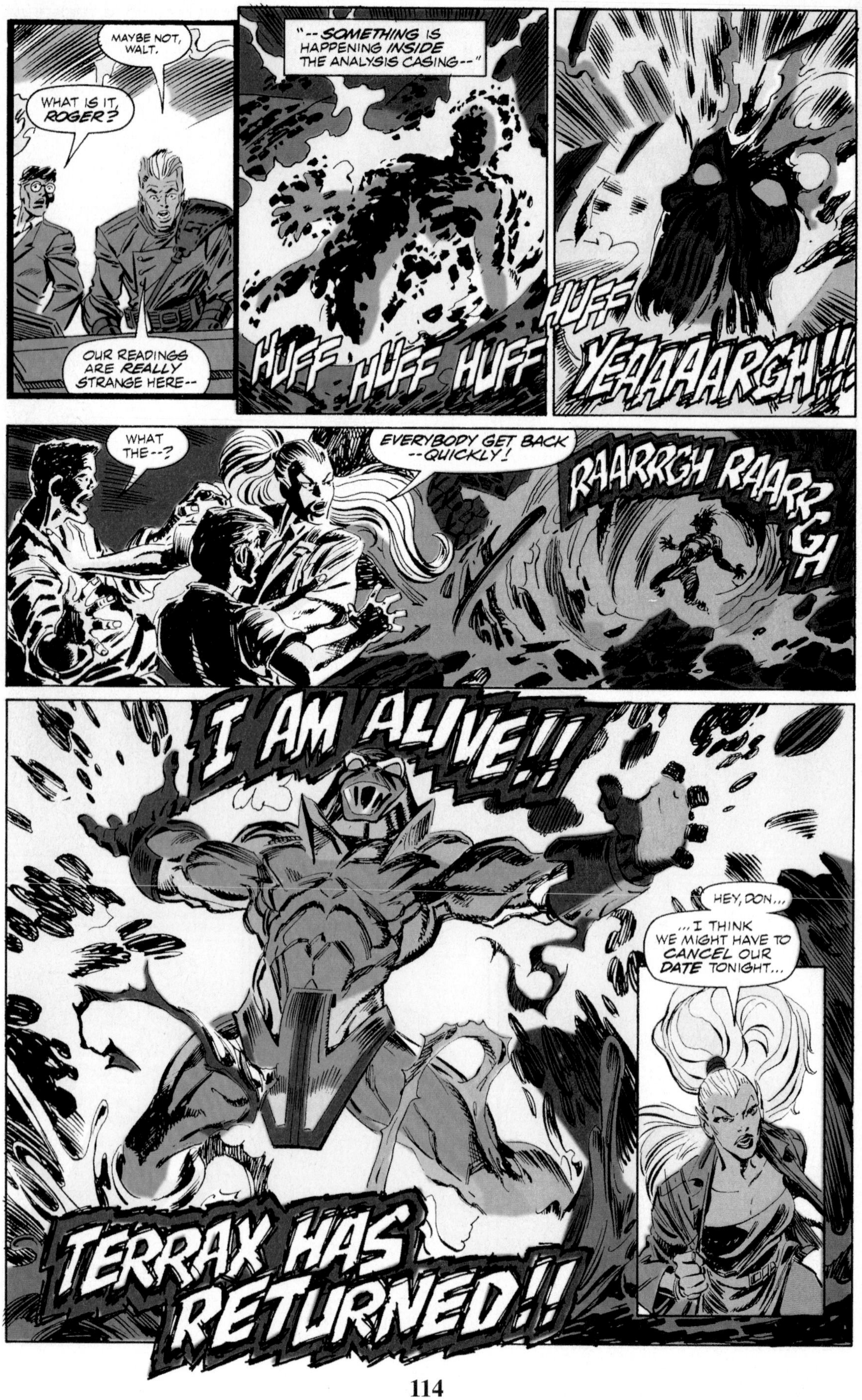

MAYBE NOT, WALT.
WHAT IS IT, ROGER?
OUR READINGS ARE REALLY STRANGE HERE--
"--SOMETHING IS HAPPENING INSIDE THE ANALYSIS CASING--"
HUFF HUFF HUFF HUFF
YEAAAARGH!!
WHAT THE--?
EVERYBODY GET BACK --QUICKLY!
RAARRGH RAARRRGH
I AM ALIVE!!
HEY, DON...
...I THINK WE MIGHT HAVE TO CANCEL OUR DATE TONIGHT...
TERRAX HAS RETURNED!!

MEANWHILE, BACK AT THE AMBROSE BUILDING...
YOU SURE THIS FIRESTAR IS GOING TO APPRECIATE YOUR TACTICS, THRASHER?
HE DON'T CARE, MARVEL BOY.
IF YOU AIN'T NOTICED YET, NIGHT THRASHER HAS A REAL INTERESTING WAY OF MAKING NEW FRIENDS...!
I'M NOT TRYING TO MAKE NEW FRIENDS, NOVA, I'M TRYING TO--
I KNOW, I KNOW, "WAGE A WAR ON CRIME," BLAH, BLAH, BLAH!
I'M NOT SO SURE I WANNA BE ON YOUR TEAM. BUT I'M GONNA WATCH YOU LIKE A HAWK TILL I FIGURE YOU OUT, BUDDY!
LISTEN-- DO YOU HEAR...
WHO ARE YOU?!
SHLOKRAK
HOW DID YOU FIND OUT ABOUT ME?!
THAT'S FIRESTAR?
CALM DOWN.
IT WAS HIS IDEA!
WE WANT YOU TO JOIN OUR GROUP.
IT SEEMED LIKE THE QUICKEST WAY TO GET YOU HERE.
YOU COULD HAVE TRIED ASKING!

RUMMMBLE!!
WAS THAT YOU?
N-NO!
THE CHANCES OF AN EARTH-TREMOR IN THIS AREA... NEARLY IMPOSSIBLE!
COME ON!
JUST LIKE I THOUGHT.
THE POLICE BAND HAS POSTED A PRIORITY-CODE 666.
WHAT'S THAT?
IT'S A SUPER-HUMAN ACTIVITY ALERT. THERE'S TROUBLE THAT THEY CAN'T HANDLE.
THE BULLETIN SAYS IT'S HAPPENING IN QUEENS.
IT'LL TAKE TOO LONG TO GET THE CHOPPER GOING...
YOU HAVE A HELICOPTER?
MARVEL BOY CAN'T FLY FAST OR FAR ENOUGH ON HIS OWN.
NOVA, YOU CARRY HIM.
FIRESTAR, WE APOLOGIZE FOR OUR METHODS, BUT WE NEED YOUR HELP--!
OUR METHODS?
CAN YOU CARRY ME ALL THE WAY TO QUEENS?
GEE, I'M NOT REALLY SURE...
I GUESS WE'LL FIND OUT...
...SOMEWHERE OVER THE EAST RIVER!

QUEENS.
WHO ARE YOU, EARTH-PIG, TO CONFRONT ME ALONE?
ARE YOU A SUICIDAL FLESHLING?
IS PROTECTING THIS MUDBALL PLANET SO IMPORTANT TO YOU?
I'M BEGINNING TO WONDER MYSELF!
WHY DON'T YOU TRY AND CATCH ME, TERRY-BABY--? THEN WE'LL TRADE GRIPES ABOUT MOTHER EARTH TOGETHER!
BRAM
I THINK I REMEMBER THIS GEEK--HE FOUGHT THE FANTASTIC FOUR!
THE WAY HE CONTROLS THE LAND MAKES ME FEEL LIKE A FISH OUT OF WATER!
I WANNA GET HIM AWAY FROM THE CROWDS--
--BUT NOW WE'RE HEADING TOWARDS TOO MANY HOUSES...!
GONNA HAVE TO GET THIS OVER WITH--
POOM

--NOW!
NOW--I CRUSH YOU, FLITTING INSECT!
THROOM
KUMPOM!
OUCH OUCH OUCH
WHERE'S MY COUSIN WHEN I NEED HIM?
OR THE AVENGERS?
OR WOLFPACK, EVEN...
MY VICTORY OVER YOU WILL NOT BE COMPLETE, EARTH-PUP, UNTIL I AM COMPLETE!
UPON PLUNGING MY FIST INTO THIS MAELSTROM OF METAL--
--I WILL TRIGGER MY COSMIC POWERS AND--
--RECREATE MY AXE OF VENGEANCE!
ALL THE BETTER WITH WHICH TO SEVER OUR RELATIONSHIP!

BACK AWAY FROM HER!
WHO--?
--ARE THESE BRAVE NEW WARRIORS WHO HAVE BURST ONTO THE SCENE?
WAY COOL!
CHANNEL 7
GUYS LIKE THAT'LL GET THE BABES EVERY TIME!
THOUGH THESE SUPER-POWERED YOUTHS HAVE YET TO BE IDENTIFIED, BILL, THEIR COURAGE CANNOT BE DOUBTED!
HEEEY, MOM, CAN I GO TO QUEENS AND FIGHT A PSYCHO SUPER-VILLAIN WITH A BUNCH OF PUBESCENT SUPER HEROES?
HMMM. THINK I'VE GOT IT NARROWED DOWN TO THREE CHOICES...
OF COURSE, HONEY...
NOW THIS ONE IS CABLE-READY, YOU SAY?
WELL, SHE DID SAY YES, SO TECHNICALLY, I'M NOT DITCHIN' HER...
BESIDES, WHAT'S SHE GONNA DO-- GROUND ME?
DOUBTFUL, CONSIDERING WHO SHE'S DEALIN' WITH HERE!
MEN'S WEAR
HEY!
THANKS, MISTER--
SHOULD BE JUST ENOUGH TO TRIGGER THE OLD...
...KINETIC FIELD AND TURN ME INTO--
SPEEDBALL, THE MASKED MARVEL!!
YEEEHAAA!

MEANWHILE--
BACK, GNAT!
FIRESTAR-- TAKE OUT THE AXE!
GT
SHIVAK
AAGH!
GET THIS CURSED HEAT OFF OF ME!
I WON'T BE BURNED TO DEATH AGAIN!*
* SEE FANTASTIC FOUR #260 --DILIGENT DANNY.
AGAIN?
DON'T TAKE YOUR OLD GRUDGES OUT ON US!
POM
SKASHUNCH

EVERYONE--HIT HIM NOW WHILE HE'S BLINDED!
BLINDED?
HAH HA HAHA
NESCIENT, INSIGNIFICANT MOTE!
I WAS ABLE TO SEE IN THE DARKEST REACHES OF SPACE!
HOW CAN MERE SMOKE HARM ME?
ALLOW ME TO SHOW YOU THE WONDERS OF THE UNIVERSE I HAVE SAMPLED--!
THIS IS A METEOR!
URK
THANKS FOR THE ASSIST.
SURE, BUT WHAT DO WE DO ABOUT TERRAX?
WAIT, LISTEN TO ME--IF MY THEORIES ARE CORRECT, THIS CREATURE CAN BE STOPPED! LISTEN TO ME!
I DON'T SEE AS HOW WE HAVE MUCH CHOICE, MISTER.
SET ME DOWN, MARVEL BOY. HELP THE OTHERS.
HE KEEPS DEFLECTING MY BURSTS WITH DEBRIS!
AWAY FROM ME, I SAID! DON'T YOU EVER STOP?!
THAT'S THE PROBLEM WITH US, TERRY...

...OUR REACH ALWAYS EXCEEDS OUR GRASP!
WHAT?
OR IN THIS CASE, MAYBE NOT.
HOGHJ
YEEAAAAAAA
LOOK OUT, BABE!
THROOM
WHY DID TERRAX SCREAM LIKE THAT?
AND WHY DID THAT PUNK RISK SUICIDE BY CALLING ME "BABE"?
RARRRGH!
FWOOSH
OUR GOOD BUDDY'S STARTING TO LOSE IT, FOLKS.
FWOOSH
HEY-- DON'CHOO MEAN--
KRUMM
POKKA
POKKA
POKKA
POKKA
POKKA
--OUR GOOD MUDDY!

IT'S THAT NEW KID-- SPEEDBALL--!
AND THAT "BUBBLE-FIELD" OF HIS SEEMS TO BE CHIPPING INTO TERRAX!
THOSE BUBBLES MUST HAVE SUBSTANCE TO THEM. I WONDER IF...
HEY SPUDS, THIS IS COOL! THE TOUGHEST GUY I EVER FOUGHT BEFORE NOW WAS THE STICKER!
IF I CAN CONTAIN THAT KINETIC FIELD--
--THIS IS GOING TO REALLY HURT--
--KEEP THE PRESSURE UP-- ALLOW THE FIELD TO B-BUILD INSIDE MY T-TEKE BUBBLE--
--THEN IF I'M RIGHT ABOUT SPEEDBALL'S FIELD, THE K-KINETIC MOTION OF THE-- MOLECULES-- SHOULD REACH A-- MAXIMUM POINT--
MUGGFHRHJUFF
THWAFOOM
NOW!!
NNGHRHGH!
EEEYAARGH!!!
CHIGGA
CHIGGA
CHIGGA
CHIGGA
CHIGGA
CHIGGA
CHIGGA
CHIGGA
CHIGGA

MRUGHWARRGHYYEARY!!!II
I WILL KILL YOU ALL!
ANYONE GET THE NUMBER OF THE DERMATOLOGIST THAT HIT ME?
DID IT WORK?
SURE. HE'S MADDER THAN EVER NOW.
HE KEEPS USING THE GROUNDSOIL TO REPLENISH HIMSELF!
NOVA! NAMORITA! YOU HAVE TO--
WE KNOW WHAT WE HAVE TO DO!
LAST THING I WANNA DO IS HEAR YOU ORDERIN' ME.
HE'S A GOOD FRIEND I TAKE IT?
ACTUALLY, WE JUST MET LAST NIGHT.
YOU, THOUGH, I COULD BECOME GOOD FRIENDS WITH.
YOU LIVE IN QUEENS?
YEAH! HOW'D'JOU KNOW?
NEVER MIND.
FLY AS HIGH AS YOU CAN!
WHAT DIFFERENCE COULD THAT--
AGGA-AGGA-AHHHRR
BLUE BLAZES! HE'S FALLING APART!
AAAAAA
DID YOU JUST SAY "BLUE BLAZES?"
SORRY, OLD HABIT
TUM TROOM!

SUFFERING SHAD... WE JUST KILLED HIM!
HE KNEW.
THAT SON OF A-- HE KNEW!!
THRASHER! YOU LET US KILL HIM!!
NO, I DIDN'T.
I DID. SORT OF.
THE FIRST TIME YOU YOUNGSTERS LIFTED TERRAX OFF THE GROUND, OUR SENSORS REGISTERED ENORMOUS STRESS TO HIS SYSTEM.
TERRAX WAS A DIS-EMBODIED SENTIENT ENERGY FORM WHICH REQUIRED CONSTANT GROUNDSOIL REPLENISHMENT.
ONCE REMOVED FROM THE GROUND, THE AMBIENT ENERGY WAS UNABLE TO KEEP THE AMALGAMATED FORM SUBSTANTIAL.
SO IT WASN'T REALLY ALIVE AT ALL?
YOU COULD THINK OF IT THAT WAY.
BUT DOESN'T TERRAX'S DISSOLUTION STILL KEEP THIS AREA CONTAMINAT-ED?
I WOULDN'T WORRY ABOUT THAT, MARVEL BOY.
"SUFFERIN' SHAD?"
SORRY, OLD HABIT
WE CAN TAKE CARE OF THINGS FROM HERE, KIDS.
CAP! AND THAT'S QUASAR AND SHE-HULK!
HELLO, CAPTAIN. I'M WALTER ROSEN.
"KIDS?"
YOU SEEM TO HAVE HELPED WITH THE SITUATION HERE, KIDS, BUT THE AVENGERS SHOULD TAKE OVER NOW.

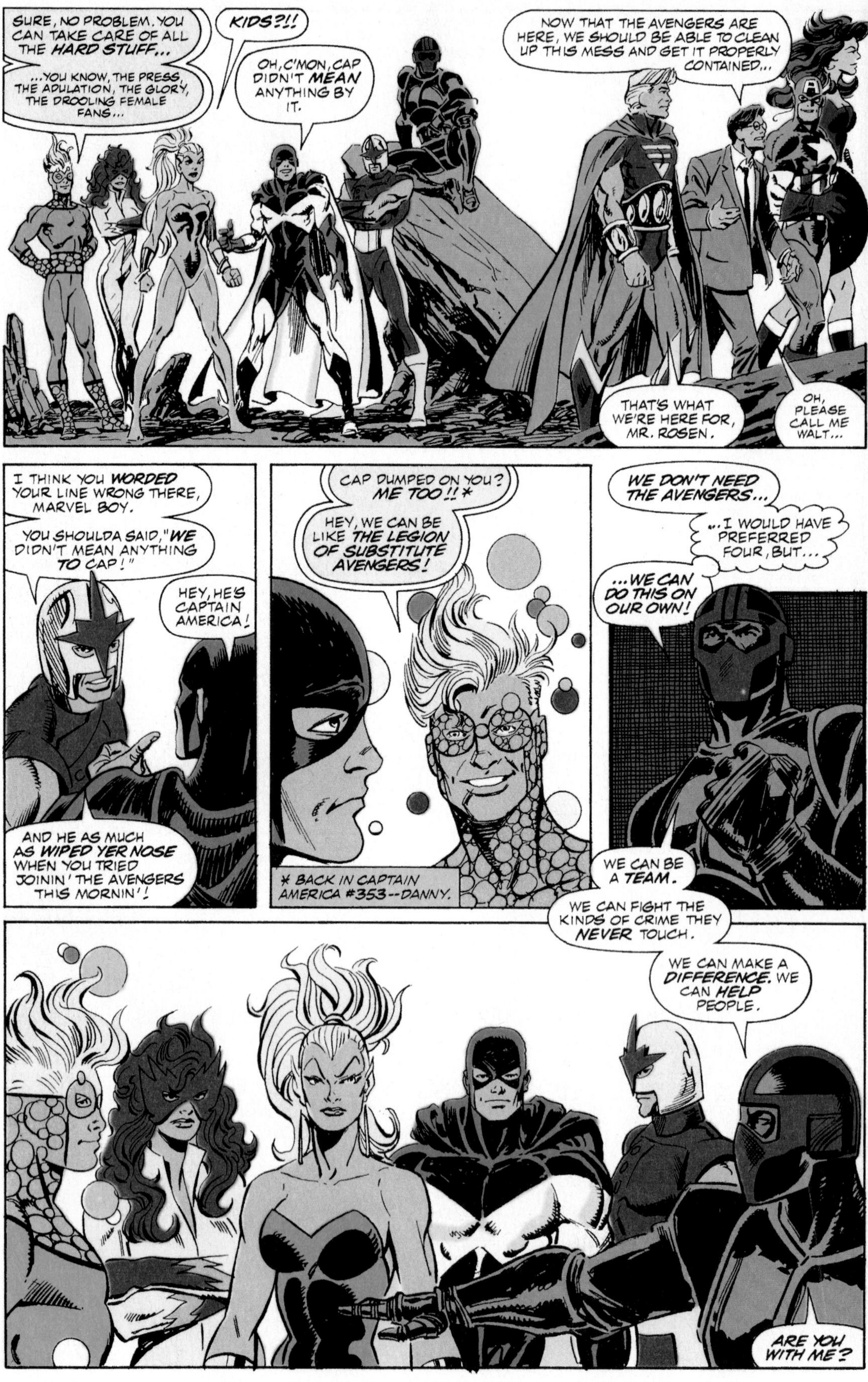
SURE, NO PROBLEM. YOU CAN TAKE CARE OF ALL THE HARD STUFF...
...YOU KNOW, THE PRESS, THE ADULATION, THE GLORY, THE DROOLING FEMALE FANS...
KIDS?!!
OH, C'MON, CAP DIDN'T MEAN ANYTHING BY IT.
NOW THAT THE AVENGERS ARE HERE, WE SHOULD BE ABLE TO CLEAN UP THIS MESS AND GET IT PROPERLY CONTAINED...
THAT'S WHAT WE'RE HERE FOR, MR. ROSEN.
OH, PLEASE CALL ME WALT...
I THINK YOU WORDED YOUR LINE WRONG THERE, MARVEL BOY.
YOU SHOULDA SAID, "WE DIDN'T MEAN ANYTHING TO CAP!"
HEY, HE'S CAPTAIN AMERICA!
AND HE AS MUCH AS WIPED YER NOSE WHEN YOU TRIED JOININ' THE AVENGERS THIS MORNIN'!
CAP DUMPED ON YOU? ME TOO!! *
HEY, WE CAN BE LIKE THE LEGION OF SUBSTITUTE AVENGERS!
* BACK IN CAPTAIN AMERICA #353--DANNY.
WE DON'T NEED THE AVENGERS...
...I WOULD HAVE PREFERRED FOUR, BUT...
...WE CAN DO THIS ON OUR OWN!
WE CAN BE A TEAM.
WE CAN FIGHT THE KINDS OF CRIME THEY NEVER TOUCH.
WE CAN MAKE A DIFFERENCE. WE CAN HELP PEOPLE.
ARE YOU WITH ME?

FIRESTAR--?
I DON'T KNOW ABOUT THIS...
NOVA--?
THAT'S THE SPIRIT GUYS!
IS IT JUST ME...
...OR IS THIS AN INCREDIBLY DRAMATIC AND EMOTIONAL TURNING POINT IN OUR LIVES?
I REALLY DON'T KNOW ABOUT THIS...
BUCK UP, RED, IT'LL BE COPACETIC!
WHAT DO WE CALL OURSELVES?
HOW ABOUT THE "IMBECILES?"
COS' I MUST BE ONE TO BE DOING THIS!
I HEARD A REPORTER CALL US SOMETHING KINDA COOL...
...HOW ABOUT...
THE NEW WARRIORS
THAT'S IT. END OF DISCUSSION.
AND THE BEGINNING OF A LEGEND...

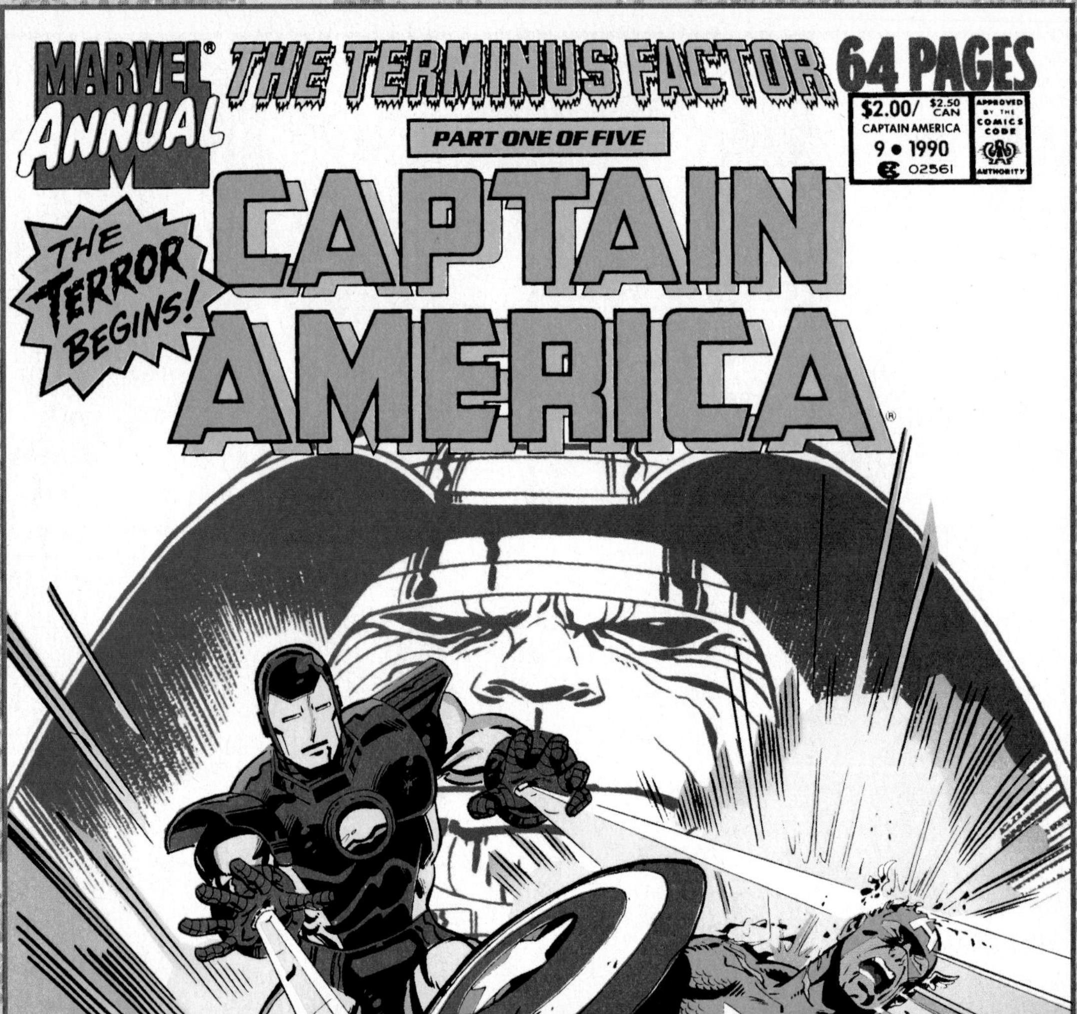
MARVEL® ANNUAL
THE TERMINUS FACTOR
64 PAGES
$2.00/ $2.50 CAN
CAPTAIN AMERICA
9 • 1990
02561
APPROVED BY THE COMICS CODE AUTHORITY
PART ONE OF FIVE
CAPTAIN AMERICA®
THE TERROR BEGINS!

CAPTAIN AMERICA ANNUAL #9, published in July 1990, included a story starring Nomad, former sidekick of the 1950s Captain America. This story set the stage for Nomad's limited series, which was soon followed by an ongoing series.

NOMAD
WALKING THE LINE
TOO HOT A DAY IN SAVANNAH, GEORGIA FOR A FUNERAL.
TOO HOT TO SEE YOUR OWN FAILURES BEIN' LAID TO REST. BUT I CAN'T IGNORE THE TRUTH.
I'M THINKIN' REAL FLOWERY STUFF HERE. NOT MY STYLE. I'M A FIGHTER BY NATURE. PREFERABLY ON THE RIGHT SIDE OF THE LAW, THOUGH WHATEVER IT TAKES IS FINE BY ME.
HER NAME WAS PATTY JOPLIN. SHE WAS A RUNAWAY, A DRUG ADDICT, AND MY INFORMANT.
I THOUGHT HER DRUG DEALER -- HER PIMP -- UMBERTO SAFILIOS HAD DONE IT. WAS SURE OF IT. WAS WRONG.
MAYBE IT WAS HIM THOUGH. OR MAYBE IT COULDA BEEN SOME D.E.A. AGENTS COVERIN' THEIR OWN BUTTS.
SEE, PATTY HAD FOUND OUT ABOUT THINGS SHE SHOULDN'T HAVE. KNOWLEDGE KILLED HER.

FABIAN NICIEZA WRITER · DON HUDSON PENCILER · TOM MORGAN INKER · PAT BROSSEAU LETTERER · ED LAZELLARI COLORIST

SO NOW I'M HERE 'CAUSE I WANT TO FIND OUT MORE ABOUT HER. MORE ABOUT HOW SHE LIVED AND WHY SHE DIED.
ME, I'M NOT SCARED OF A LITTLE KNOWLEDGE.
HER PARENTS ARE MILLER AND PATRICIA JOPLIN. OLD SOUTHERN MONEY. WHY WOULD SHE WANT TO RUN AWAY FROM SUCH A LIFE?
...IN EARTH AS IT IS IN HEAVEN... ASHES TO ASHES...
R.I.P.
WAIT--THAT GUY GIVIN' HIS CONDOLENCES--
--WHERE ARE THE #$%@*! BINOCULARS--
SAFILIOS?!
WHAT'S HE DOIN' HERE? HOW CAN HE WALTZ IN AND OUT PRETTY AS YOU PLEASE?
HE'S SHAKIN' THE FATHER'S HAND, KISSIN' THE MOTHER'S CHEEK... AND HE WAS PATTY'S PIMP!
IF HE DIDN'T PULL THE TRIGGER HIMSELF, HE AT LEAST HAD A PART IN HER DEATH--IN RUININ' HER LIFE WITH DRUGS AND SEX...
WHAT'S GOIN' ON HERE?

ONLY WAY TO FIND OUT IS TO FOLLOW SAFILIOS TO THE SAVANNAH AIRPORT.
FOLLOW HIS STRETCH LIMO WITH THE TV ANTENNA ON THE TRUNK AND THE FULLY-LOADED BAR IN THE BACK.
A REGULAR TRIUMPH FOR THE AMERICAN DREAM, RIGHT?
WATCH THE SCUM PARADE AROUND LIKE HE DESERVES WHAT HE'S GOT IN THIS WORLD.
AND ALL OF HIS LITTLE BOYS WHO STICK TO HIM LIKE SWEAT ON AN ARM-PIT--HOW FAR WILL SAFILIOS GO FOR THEM?
I TOL' JOU TO HAVE THE JET READY WHEN--
SHUT UP, SAFILIOS!
I CAN BREAK THIS CREEP'S HAND REAL EASY. I CAN ALSO BREAK THE GLASS IN HIS HAND.
NOW YOU WOULDN'T WANT ME TO HURT YOUR BOY, WOULD YOU?
NO, EES OKAY--HE HAS A MEDICAL PLAN.
NOW LET'S TALK ABOUT US, EH?
JOU COME ALL DE WAY TO GEORGIA TO SEE ME?
I LOVE JOU, NOMAD--I DO--JOU ARE MY FAVORITE HERO. EES TRUE.
WHY DID YOU COME TO PATTY'S FUNERAL, YOU PIG?!
TELL ME!
NNNRGHH

I COME 'CAUSE I WAS EENVITED. HOW COME JOU COME?
I--I CAME BECAUSE SOMEONE WHO KNEW THE TRUTH HAD TO.
EH-HEH
HA-HAH
AH-HAH-HAH-HA-HAH
MISTAKE.
KCHISH
AAGH--!
NFFF--RRNN--
BLEED QUIETLY, MARTINSON.
SUCH A TUFF GUY, EH, NOMAD?!
JOU THEENK YOU KNOW THE TRUTH?
GO TO HER FATHER! GO SEE HER FATHER! LEARN WHAT TRUTH EES!
FIND OUT HOW MUCH JOU DON' KNOW ABOUT!
TOO CLOSE TO LOSIN' IT THERE. THAT WOULDN'T'VE HELPED ME...OR PATTY...

GO SEE HER FATHER, SAFILIOS SAID. AND HIS VOICE...
...I NEVER HEARD HIS VOICE LIKE THAT BEFORE-- SO CLOSE TO LOSIN' IT... BUT HE HELD BACK--
--'COS IT WOULDN'T'VE HELPED HIM... OR PATTY?
I'M THINKIN' TOO MUCH. IT TAKES ME TWO HOURS TO GET TO THE JOPLIN ESTATE. THE RADIO DON'T WORK AND THEN I START THINKIN' TOO MUCH.
I DON'T LIKE THINKIN' TOO MUCH. I'M A SIMPLE GUY BY NATURE. I HAVE A FIST, FIND ME A FACE, THE TWO MEET. EASY.
EXCUSE ME, SIR-- THIS IS A PRIVATE PARTY.
Y'ALL LOOKIN' FOR A COSTUME BALL, YOU HAVE THE WRONG PLACE.
I HAVE MY INVITATION RIGHT HERE.
TRAK
I GUESS YOU COULD SAY NATURE CALLS.
KHAK

SO MUCH FOR THE SUBTLE APPROACH.
HOW DOES CAP ALWAYS MANAGE TO DO THIS WITH-OUT BUSTIN' HALF A DOZEN HEADS IN?
IT'S THE HEAT THAT DOES IT TO ME. MAKES ME ANGRIER.
HEY, YOU--
I'M WEARIN' A KEVLAR JACKET, AN' IT'S SIX HUNDRED DEGREES OUT! REGULAR EINSTEIN, I AM.
AS IF I HAVE TO WORRY ABOUT ANY OF THESE RENT-A-COPS NAILIN' ME WITH A GUNSHOT!
SO WHILE SPEEDY GONZALEZ IS TRYIN' TO FIGURE OUT WHAT HAPPENED TO HIS PALS...
CHAK
OKAY, SO NOW I THINK PEOPLE HAVE NO-TICED ME.
AN' THEY'LL CALL THE COPS, AN' THAT'LL BE ANOTHER STATE I HAVE AN OUTSTANDING WARRANT IN.

GEEZ-- HOW DOES CAP DO IT? MAYBE I SHOULD JOIN THE AVENGERS OR SOMETHIN', THAT WAY I'LL BE ALLOWED TO BUST SKULLS AT WILL.
I'M NOT HERE TO HURT ANYONE, MA'AM.
I-- I KNEW PATTY-- I'M JUST TRYING TO GET SOME ANSWERS. I'M LOOKING FOR YOUR HUSBAND.
I UNDERSTAND.
HE IS INSIDE THE STUDY RIGHT NOW.
FESTIVITIES ARE NOT HIS PREFERENCE.
ESPECIALLY WHEN THE FESTIVITIES ARE PART OF YOUR ONLY DAUGHTER'S FUNERAL.
ME AND MY MEN'LL GET HIM NOW, MRS. JOPLIN!
JUST GET SOME MEDICAL ATTENTION-- AND ONCE YOU'VE STOPPED BLEEDING, HENNISON-- GET A GUN ...A LARGE GUN... JUST IN CASE.
HOUSE IS HUGE. I GREW UP IN PLACES THAT WERE SMALLER THAN THE CLOSETS IN HERE.
PLACE SMELLS OLD. SMELLS RICH. I HATE THAT SMELL.
IN THE STUDY, SHE SAID. THERE.
WHY DO I KNOW I AIN'T GONNA LIKE WHAT I FIND?

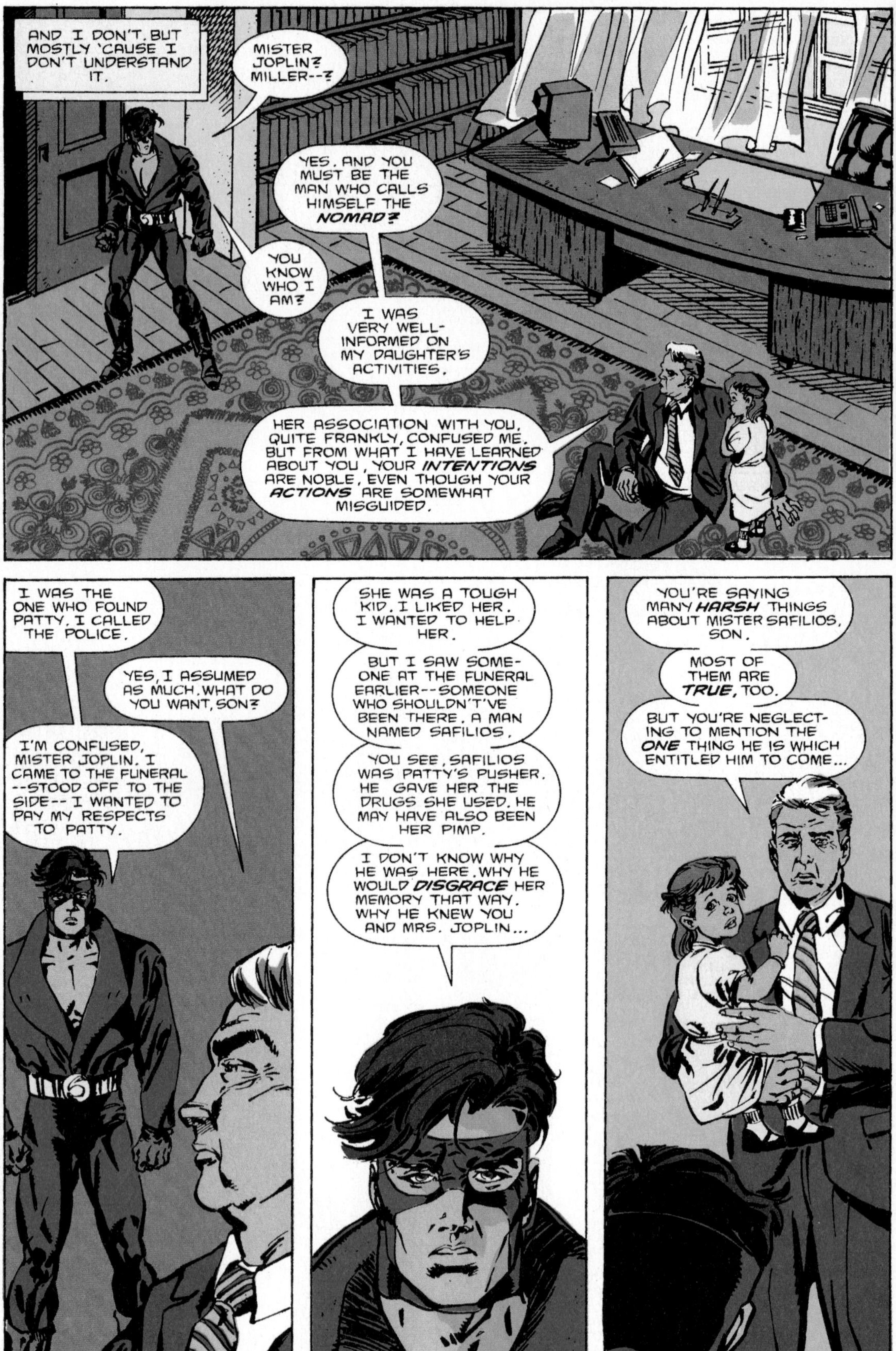
AND I DON'T. BUT MOSTLY 'CAUSE I DON'T UNDERSTAND IT.
MISTER JOPLIN? MILLER--?
YES. AND YOU MUST BE THE MAN WHO CALLS HIMSELF THE NOMAD?
YOU KNOW WHO I AM?
I WAS VERY WELL-INFORMED ON MY DAUGHTER'S ACTIVITIES.
HER ASSOCIATION WITH YOU, QUITE FRANKLY, CONFUSED ME. BUT FROM WHAT I HAVE LEARNED ABOUT YOU, YOUR INTENTIONS ARE NOBLE, EVEN THOUGH YOUR ACTIONS ARE SOMEWHAT MISGUIDED.
I WAS THE ONE WHO FOUND PATTY. I CALLED THE POLICE.
YES, I ASSUMED AS MUCH. WHAT DO YOU WANT, SON?
I'M CONFUSED, MISTER JOPLIN. I CAME TO THE FUNERAL --STOOD OFF TO THE SIDE-- I WANTED TO PAY MY RESPECTS TO PATTY.
SHE WAS A TOUGH KID. I LIKED HER. I WANTED TO HELP HER.
BUT I SAW SOMEONE AT THE FUNERAL EARLIER--SOMEONE WHO SHOULDN'T'VE BEEN THERE. A MAN NAMED SAFILIOS.
YOU SEE, SAFILIOS WAS PATTY'S PUSHER. HE GAVE HER THE DRUGS SHE USED. HE MAY HAVE ALSO BEEN HER PIMP.
I DON'T KNOW WHY HE WAS HERE. WHY HE WOULD DISGRACE HER MEMORY THAT WAY. WHY HE KNEW YOU AND MRS. JOPLIN...
YOU'RE SAYING MANY HARSH THINGS ABOUT MISTER SAFILIOS, SON.
MOST OF THEM ARE TRUE, TOO.
BUT YOU'RE NEGLECTING TO MENTION THE ONE THING HE IS WHICH ENTITLED HIM TO COME...

...UMBERTO SAFILIOS IS ALSO THE FATHER OF MY GRANDCHILD.
!
YOU SEEM SURPRISED. I THOUGHT YOU KNEW.
IF HE'S THE CHILD'S FATHER-- THEN YOU KNEW WHERE PATTY WAS ALL ALONG-- SHE WASN'T A RUNAWAY--
OH, BUT SHE WAS. THEN TWO YEARS AGO, WHEN SHE WAS SEVENTEEN, PATTY SHOWED UP WITH THIS CHILD UNDER HER ARM.
SHE DIDN'T WANT SAFILIOS TO HAVE THEIR CHILD, BUT SHE COULDN'T STAY EITHER. SHE HAD TOLD SAFILIOS OF CERTAIN-- IMPROPRIETIES-- IN MY BUSINESS DEALINGS.
AS LONG AS HE HAD THAT KNOWLEDGE, I WOULD BE BEHOLDEN TO HIM. AS LONG AS I HAD HIS CHILD, HE WOULD BE BEHOLDEN TO ME. STALEMATE. LIFE GOES ON.
AND THAT'S ACCEPTABLE TO YOU?
THAT'S LIFE, SON...
...HE SAID, "WHAT ARE YOU GOING TO DO BUT PLAY THE HANDS YOU'RE DEALT?" I DON'T KNOW.
I DON'T HAVE AN ANSWER, BUT IT GIVES ME SOMETHING TO THINK ABOUT ON THE LONG DRIVE BACK TO MIAMI.

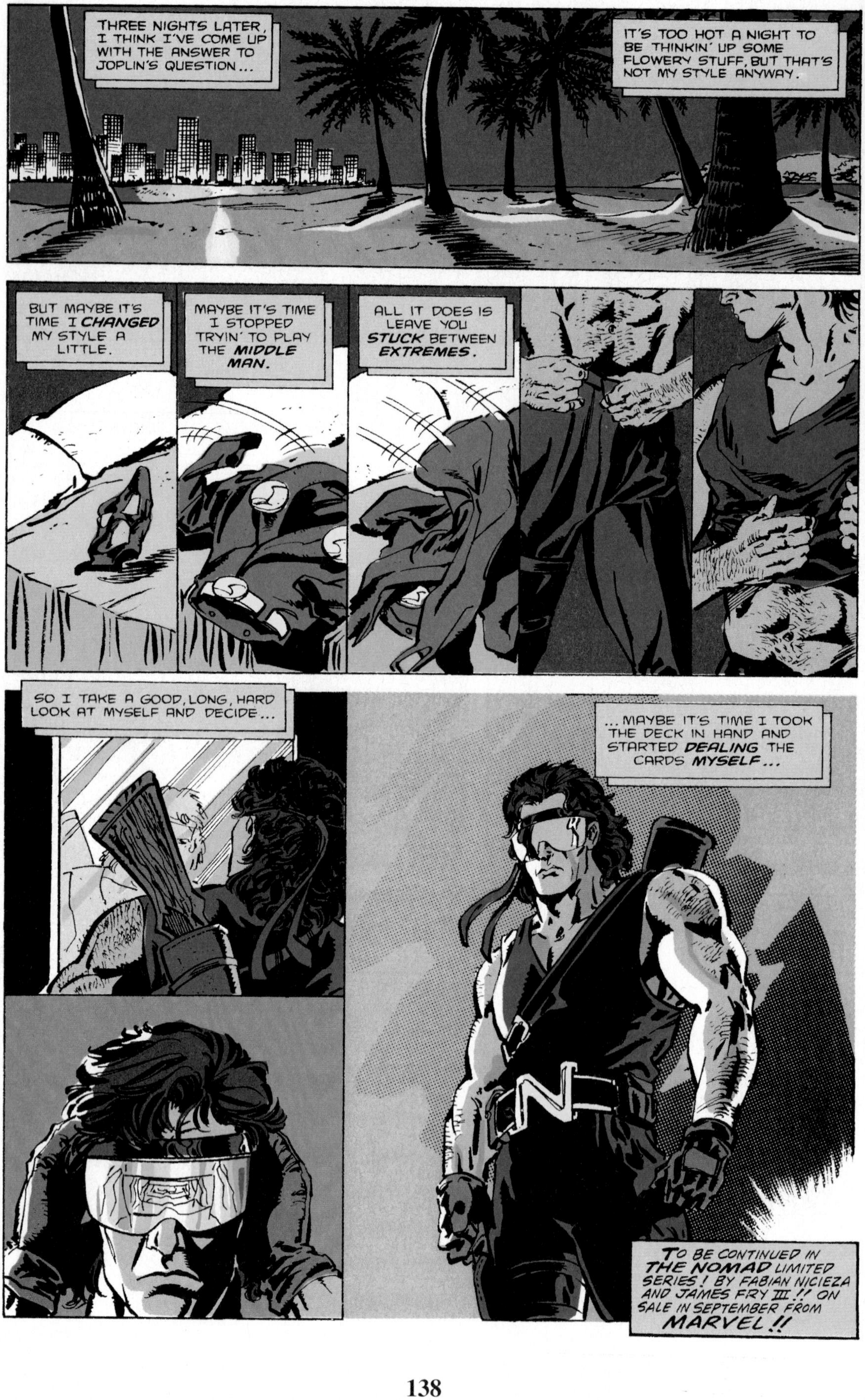
THREE NIGHTS LATER, I THINK I'VE COME UP WITH THE ANSWER TO JOPLIN'S QUESTION...
IT'S TOO HOT A NIGHT TO BE THINKIN' UP SOME FLOWERY STUFF, BUT THAT'S NOT MY STYLE ANYWAY.
BUT MAYBE IT'S TIME I **CHANGED** MY STYLE A LITTLE.
MAYBE IT'S TIME I STOPPED TRYIN' TO PLAY THE **MIDDLE MAN.**
ALL IT DOES IS LEAVE YOU **STUCK** BETWEEN **EXTREMES.**
SO I TAKE A GOOD, LONG, HARD LOOK AT MYSELF AND DECIDE...
...MAYBE IT'S TIME I TOOK THE DECK IN HAND AND STARTED **DEALING** THE CARDS **MYSELF**...
TO BE CONTINUED IN THE NOMAD LIMITED SERIES! BY FABIAN NICIEZA AND JAMES FRY III!! ON SALE IN SEPTEMBER FROM MARVEL!!

MARVEL COMICS
FOOLKILLER
©1990 MARVEL ENT. GROUP, INC.
$1.75 US
$2.25 CAN
1
OCT
UK 60p
APPROVED BY THE COMICS CODE AUTHORITY
PART 1 OF TEN
SO MANY FOOLS, SO LITTLE TIME!

FOOLKILLER #1, published in August 1990, began a limited series featuring former Foolkiller Greg Salinger, and introducing his successor Kurt Gerhardt.

MAD...AS IN ANGRY
STEVE GERBER, J.J. BIRCH & TONY DEZUNIGA
PHIL FELIX, LETTERS. CRAIG ANDERSON, EDITOR.
GREG WRIGHT, COLORS. TOM DEFALCO, ED. IN CHIEF.
LIVE A POEM--
--OR DIE A FOOL!

I SAID THE WORDS. I LAUGHED THE LAUGH.
I WALKED THE TALK AND TALKED THE WALK.
SHE WAS ALREADY DEAD--ROTTING, DECAYING, PUTRID.
I FIRED ANYWAY.
INSTEAD OF THE PURIFYING WHITE LIGHT, THE FIRE THAT BURNS AWAY FOOLS...
...THE GUN SHOT MUCUS.
A REEKING, LEAPING RIVER OF DISEASE. AND IN ITS CURRENTS SWAM BITS OF FLESH.
CHARRED, DEAD FLESH.
HUMAN.
PIECES OF... MY VICTIMS.
SO MUCH SICKNESS, SO MUCH DEATH. I WAS WADING IN A SEA OF PAIN.
MY STOMACH WAS CHURNING.
SO WAS THE MUCUS.
I HAD TO GET OUT.

NATURALLY, THE DOORS WERE LOCKED.
HOW CAN ONE ESCAPE THE VERY CONTENT OF ONE'S OWN LIFE?
AND THAT, OF COURSE, IS WHAT THE DILAPIDATED HOUSE REPRESENTED.
MY FORMER LIFE. MY OLD CONCEPTS OF THE WORLD AND MYSELF.
CRUMBLING DOWN AROUND ME.
THE MUCUS, WHICH HAD RISEN IN A GREAT WAVE, WAS MY ILLNESS--THE GUMMY EMOTIONAL JUICE IN WHICH MY INSANITY WAS SUSPENDED.
ALONG WITH MY CRIMES.
AND MY GUILT.
THEN, THE WAVE FELL UPON ME, ENGULFING ME IN ITS CLINGING FILTH.
OOZING INTO MY MOUTH. SLITHERING UP MY NOSTRILS WITH EACH DESPERATE BREATH.
I SCREAMED.
I CLAWED AT THE DEADLY VEIL AND AT MY OWN SKIN.
I WANTED TO PEEL THEM BOTH FROM ME.
THEN, EVERYTHING CHANGED.

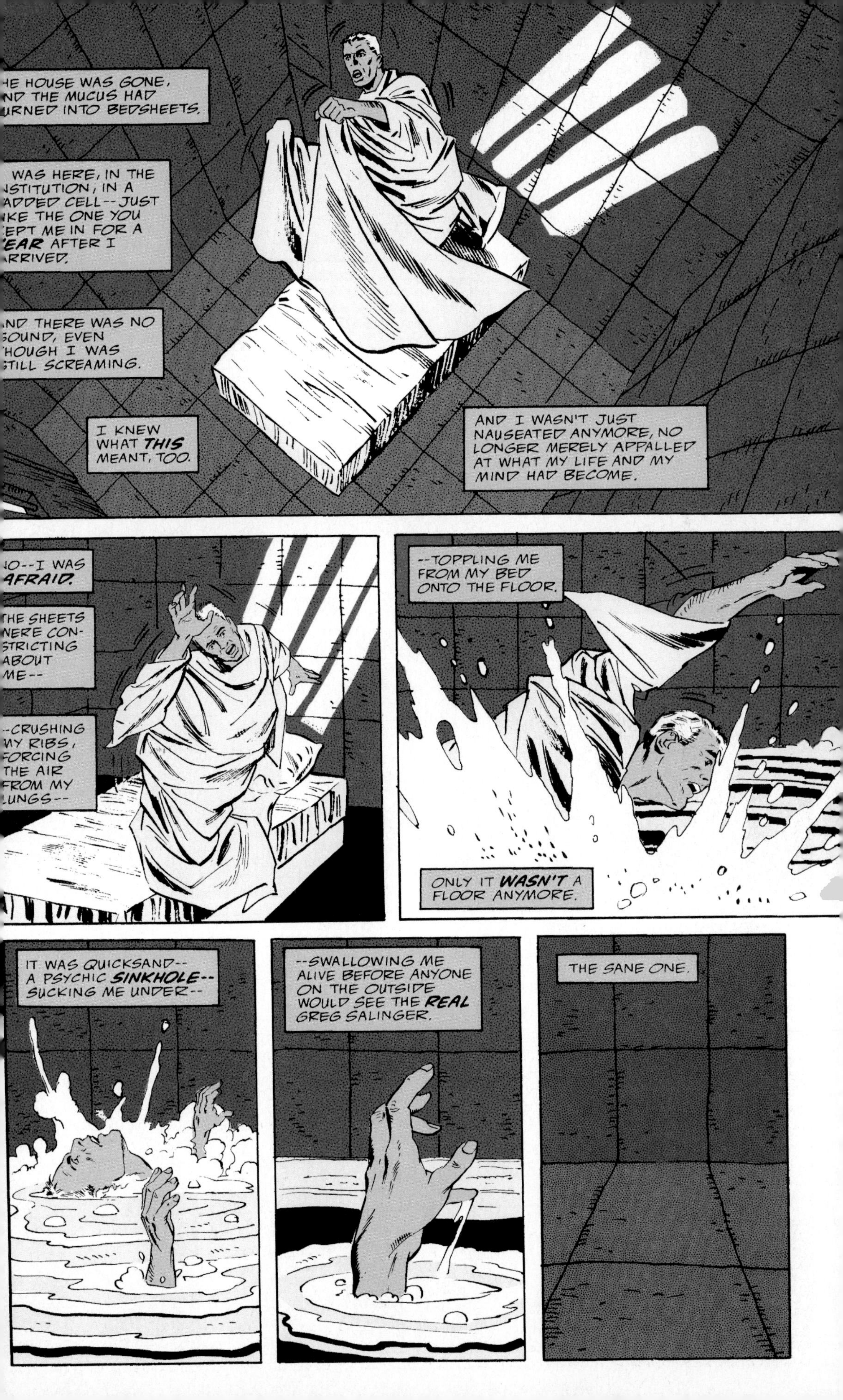
HE HOUSE WAS GONE, ND THE MUCUS HAD URNED INTO BEDSHEETS.
WAS HERE, IN THE NSTITUTION, IN A ADDED CELL--JUST IKE THE ONE YOU EPT ME IN FOR A EAR AFTER I RRIVED.
ND THERE WAS NO SOUND, EVEN HOUGH I WAS TILL SCREAMING.
I KNEW WHAT THIS MEANT, TOO.
AND I WASN'T JUST NAUSEATED ANYMORE, NO LONGER MERELY APPALLED AT WHAT MY LIFE AND MY MIND HAD BECOME.
O--I WAS AFRAID.
HE SHEETS WERE CON-STRICTING ABOUT ME--
--CRUSHING MY RIBS, FORCING THE AIR FROM MY UNGS--
--TOPPLING ME FROM MY BED ONTO THE FLOOR.
ONLY IT WASN'T A FLOOR ANYMORE.
IT WAS QUICKSAND--A PSYCHIC SINKHOLE--SUCKING ME UNDER--
--SWALLOWING ME ALIVE BEFORE ANYONE ON THE OUTSIDE WOULD SEE THE REAL GREG SALINGER.
THE SANE ONE.

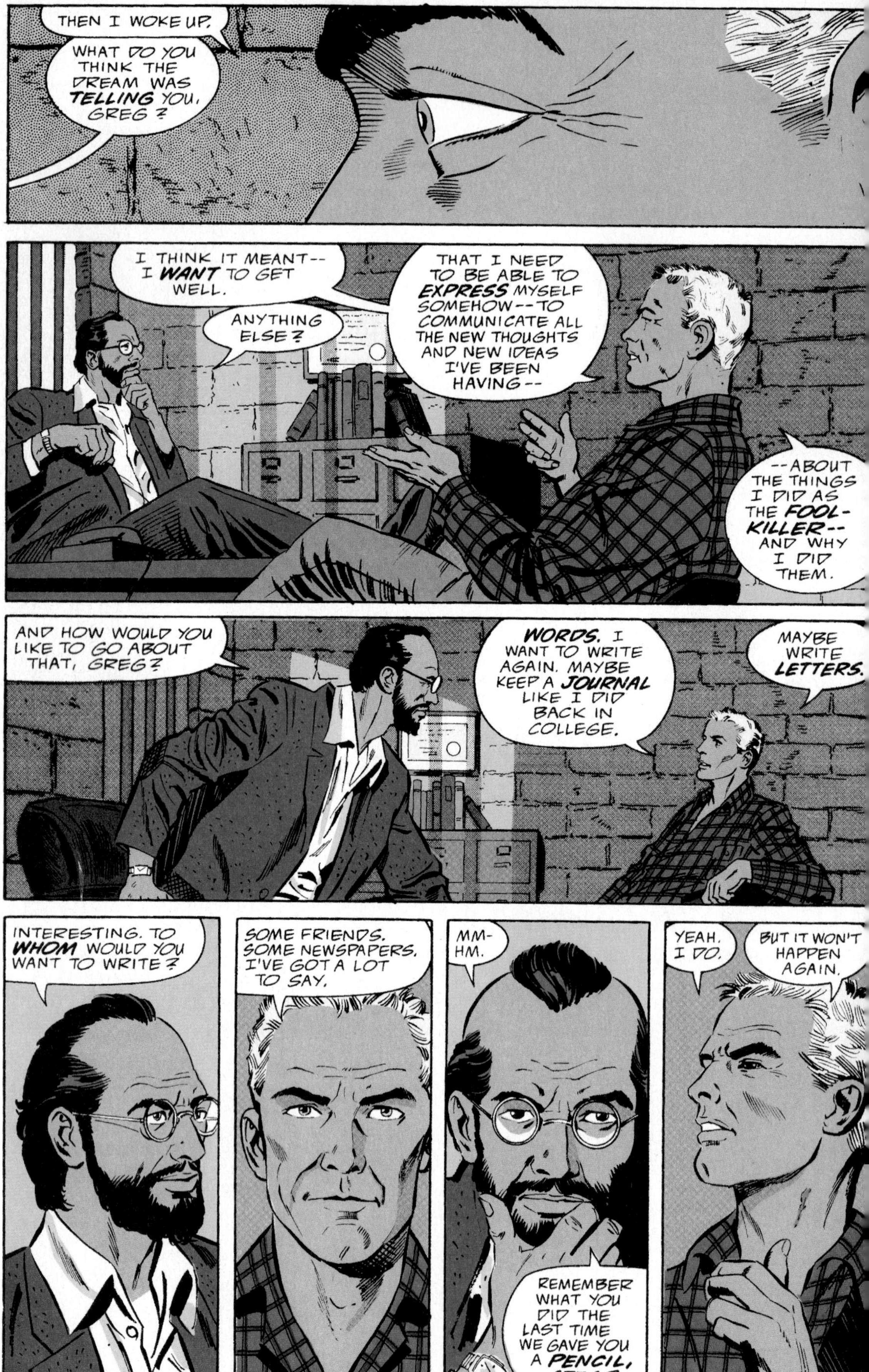

THEN I WOKE UP.
WHAT DO YOU THINK THE DREAM WAS TELLING YOU, GREG?
I THINK IT MEANT-- I WANT TO GET WELL.
ANYTHING ELSE?
THAT I NEED TO BE ABLE TO EXPRESS MYSELF SOMEHOW--TO COMMUNICATE ALL THE NEW THOUGHTS AND NEW IDEAS I'VE BEEN HAVING--
--ABOUT THE THINGS I DID AS THE FOOL-KILLER-- AND WHY I DID THEM.
AND HOW WOULD YOU LIKE TO GO ABOUT THAT, GREG?
WORDS. I WANT TO WRITE AGAIN. MAYBE KEEP A JOURNAL LIKE I DID BACK IN COLLEGE.
MAYBE WRITE LETTERS.
INTERESTING. TO WHOM WOULD YOU WANT TO WRITE?
SOME FRIENDS. SOME NEWSPAPERS. I'VE GOT A LOT TO SAY.
MM-HM.
REMEMBER WHAT YOU DID THE LAST TIME WE GAVE YOU A PENCIL, GREG?
YEAH, I DO.
BUT IT WON'T HAPPEN AGAIN.

THE BRONX, NEW YORK.
I TRIED TO WARN HIM --DAMN IT, ELEANOR, I DID!
HE WOULDN'T LISTEN-- HE LAUGHED AT ME-- CALLED ME A "WORRY WART"...!
I DIDN'T WORRY ENOUGH. I SHOULD HAVE INSISTED--
YOU DID WHAT WAS POSSIBLE. WILLY COULD BE A VERY STUBBORN MAN.
A STUBBORN, BLIND FOOL, YOU MEAN. IT WAS HIS LEAST ENDEARING TRAIT.
NO MATTER WHAT, HE HAD TO BE RIGHT. NO ONE COULD PERSUADE HIM OF ANYTHING.
CAN I PERSUADE YOU NOT TO GO INTO WORK THIS AFTERNOON?
YOU'RE IN NO SHAPE TO PROCESS LOAN APPLICATIONS.
I'VE GOT NO CHOICE. WYNDHAM MADE IT CLEAR HE EXPECTS ME IN.
ON THE DAY OF YOUR FATHER'S FUNERAL? THAT'S OBSCENE.
YEAH. I'LL GRAB THE BUS. I WANT YOU TO TAKE A TAXI HOME.
AND DON'T TELL ME IT'S TOO EXPENSIVE.

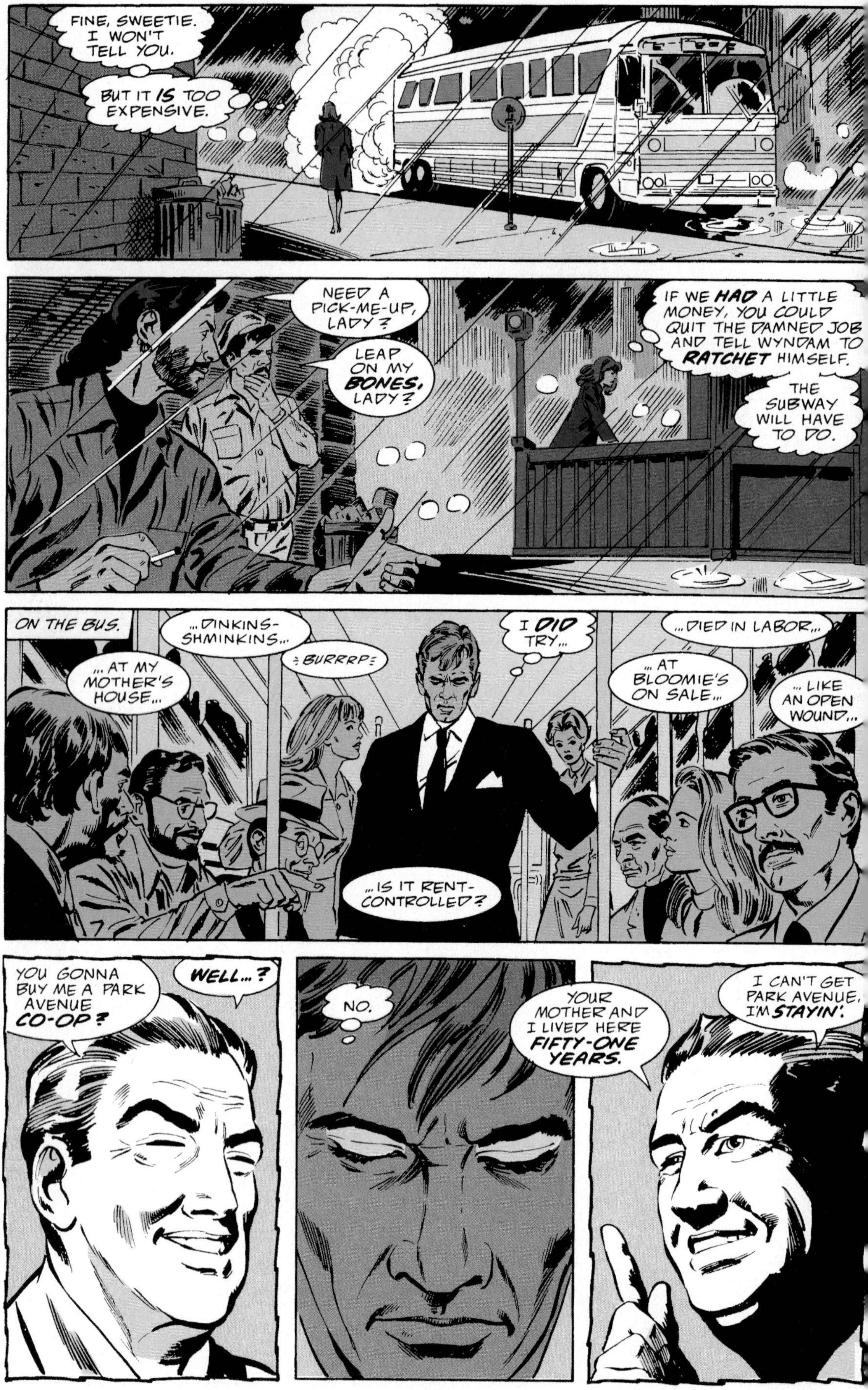
FINE, SWEETIE. I WON'T TELL YOU.
BUT IT IS TOO EXPENSIVE.
NEED A PICK-ME-UP, LADY?
LEAP ON MY BONES, LADY?
IF WE HAD A LITTLE MONEY, YOU COULD QUIT THE DAMNED JOB AND TELL WYNDAM TO RATCHET HIMSELF.
THE SUBWAY WILL HAVE TO DO.
ON THE BUS.
...DINKINS-SHMINKINS...
...AT MY MOTHER'S HOUSE...
BURRRP
I DID TRY...
...DIED IN LABOR...
...AT BLOOMIE'S ON SALE...
...LIKE AN OPEN WOUND...
...IS IT RENT-CONTROLLED?
YOU GONNA BUY ME A PARK AVENUE CO-OP?
WELL...?
NO.
YOUR MOTHER AND I LIVED HERE FIFTY-ONE YEARS.
I CAN'T GET PARK AVENUE, I'M STAYIN'.

WHO IN THEIR RIGHT MIND'S GONNA ROB ME?
EVERYBODY IN THE NEIGHBORHOOD KNOWS I GOT NOTHIN'! A ROBBER WOULD LOSE MONEY ON ME IF HE FIGURED IN HIS TIME!
ENTER
DRUGS
THE NEIGHBORHOOD IS CHANGING, DAD. THE GANGS ARE MOVING IN.
THEY DON'T STOP TO ASK WHETHER IT'S WORTH THEIR WHILE TO MUG YOU.
BELIEVE ME, YOU'RE TAKING YOUR LIFE IN YOUR HANDS WALKING THESE STREETS.
...BUT AVOID THE CORNED BEEF...
...UNDER THE WEATHER...
...MY CHOLESTEROL...
WERE YOU LAUGHING WHEN THEY DRAGGED YOU INTO THE ALLEY?
PINE BLUFF?
DON'T POINT!
...NOT YOUR BUSINESS!
"I DOUBT IT, DAD.
"HOW 'BOUT WHEN THEY BOOSTED YOUR WALLET...
"...AND FOUND OUT YOU ONLY HAD SIX BUCKS ON YOU?
"YEAH. MAYBE THEN.
"BUT NOT FOR LONG-- EH, DAD?
"NOT FOR LONG."

WANT TO HEAR A GOOD ONE, DAD?
THEY ENJOYED BASHING IN YOUR SKULL SO MUCH, THEY LEFT YOU THE SIX DOLLARS.
THAT'S HOW MUCH THINKING WAS GOING ON, DAD.
SILVER EAG
BUS STOP
YOU WERE WORTH MORE TO THEM AS ENTERTAINMENT.
BUT WHAT THE HECK-- YOU GOT THINGS YOUR WAY. GOT TO LAUGH IN MY FACE.
UNTIL THOSE LAST FEW SECONDS, YOU COULD BELIEVE YOU'D BEEN RIGHT ABOUT EVERYTHING, EVERY DAY OF YOUR LIFE.
AND ALL IT COST YOU WAS LEAVING YOUR BRAINS ON A GRIMY PATCH OF PAVE-MENT.
GERHARDT! I NEED TO SEE YOU ABOUT THE WALKER APPLI-CATION!
KURT GERHARDT LOAN OFFICER
JUST... GIVE ME A MOMENT, MR. WYNDHAM.

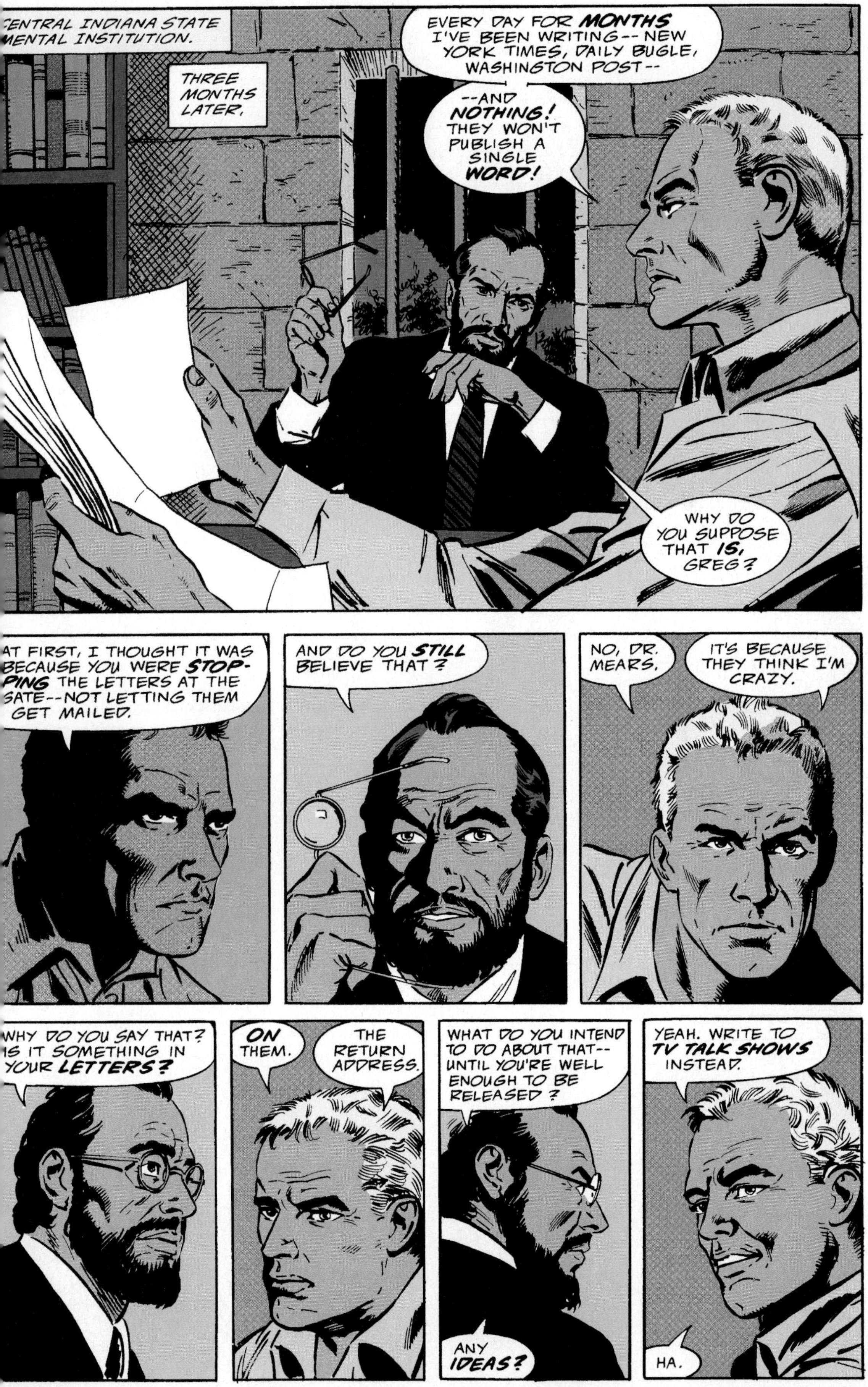
CENTRAL INDIANA STATE MENTAL INSTITUTION.
THREE MONTHS LATER.
EVERY DAY FOR MONTHS I'VE BEEN WRITING-- NEW YORK TIMES, DAILY BUGLE, WASHINGTON POST--
--AND NOTHING! THEY WON'T PUBLISH A SINGLE WORD!
WHY DO YOU SUPPOSE THAT IS, GREG?
AT FIRST, I THOUGHT IT WAS BECAUSE YOU WERE STOPPING THE LETTERS AT THE GATE--NOT LETTING THEM GET MAILED.
AND DO YOU STILL BELIEVE THAT?
NO, DR. MEARS.
IT'S BECAUSE THEY THINK I'M CRAZY.
WHY DO YOU SAY THAT? IS IT SOMETHING IN YOUR LETTERS?
ON THEM.
THE RETURN ADDRESS.
WHAT DO YOU INTEND TO DO ABOUT THAT-- UNTIL YOU'RE WELL ENOUGH TO BE RELEASED?
ANY IDEAS?
YEAH. WRITE TO TV TALK SHOWS INSTEAD.
HA.

RIVERDALE, NEW YORK.
...BECAUSE SILVER EAGLE WAS DE-CLARED INSOLVENT, THAT'S WHY.
MANAGEMENT WON'T SUFFER. THERE'S FEDERAL BAIL-OUT MONEY.
BUT TO KEEP THEIR SALARIES INFLATED, THEY'VE GOT TO "TRIM THE FAT."
ARE YOU SURE THAT'S THE ONLY REASON THEY LET YOU GO?
KURT, YOU'VE BEEN HORRIBLY DEPRESSED SINCE YOUR FATHER DIED.
I MEAN, THAT'S TO BE EXPECTED, OF COURSE, BUT--
--AND THIS ISN'T MEANT AS CRITICISM--
--BUT IS IT POSSIBLE YOU LET YOUR MOOD AFFECT YOUR WORK?
ELEANOR, LET ME ASK YOU SOMETHING.
DO YOU REALLY FIND IT SO DIFFICULT TO BELIEVE IN EXECUTIVE INCOMPETENCE-- AND PROBABLY CORRUPTION--
--THAT YOU FIND IT MORE COMFORTING TO BLAME THEIR MISTAKES ON YOUR HUSBAND?
DO YOU?!
KURT, I--
WHAT? SAY IT!
I'M SORRY.
TRULY I AM.
I HOPE YOU MEAN THAT.
IF YOU DON'T, I'VE GOT NOTHING LEFT.
WHAT DID I DO WRONG, ELEANOR?
WHY IS MY LIFE SUDDENLY FALLING TO PIECES...?

INDIANA.
THOSE ARE ALL THE SAME MEMO -- BUT EACH ONE'S ADDRESSED TO A DIFFERENT PERSON--!
HOW DO YOU DO THAT ?!
IT'S CALLED MERGE PRINTING. YOU TYPE SPECIAL CODES INTO THE DOCUMENT FILE--
--AND WHEN YOU PRINT OUT, THE WORD PROCESSOR READS IN AN ADDRESS LIST THAT CORRESPONDS TO THE CODES.
WOW.
S IT HARD? OULD I LEARN O USE THAT MACHINE?
VELL, YOU'D NEED R. MEARS'S PERMISSION, F COURSE--
--BUT I'M SURE I COULD TEACH YOU THE PROGRAM EASILY ENOUGH.
AS A MATTER OF FACT, I THINK IT WOULD BE AN EXCELLENT IDEA FOR GREG TO LEARN THE COMPUTER.
I'M PLEASED TO SEE YOU SHOW SUCH CURIOSITY.
IT INDICATES YOU'RE MAKING REAL PROG-RESS.
REALLY?
EW YORK.
FIVE YEARS WITH SILVER EAGLE. THEY MUST HAVE LIKED YOUR WORK.
WAS IN NE FOR A ROMOTION HEN, UH...
...YOU KNOW.
I'M AFRAID WE HAVE NO OPENINGS JUST NOW...
I SEE...
...BUT I'D LIKE TO KEEP YOUR RESUME AND APPLICATION ON FILE, JUST IN CASE.
OF COURSE. THANK YOU.

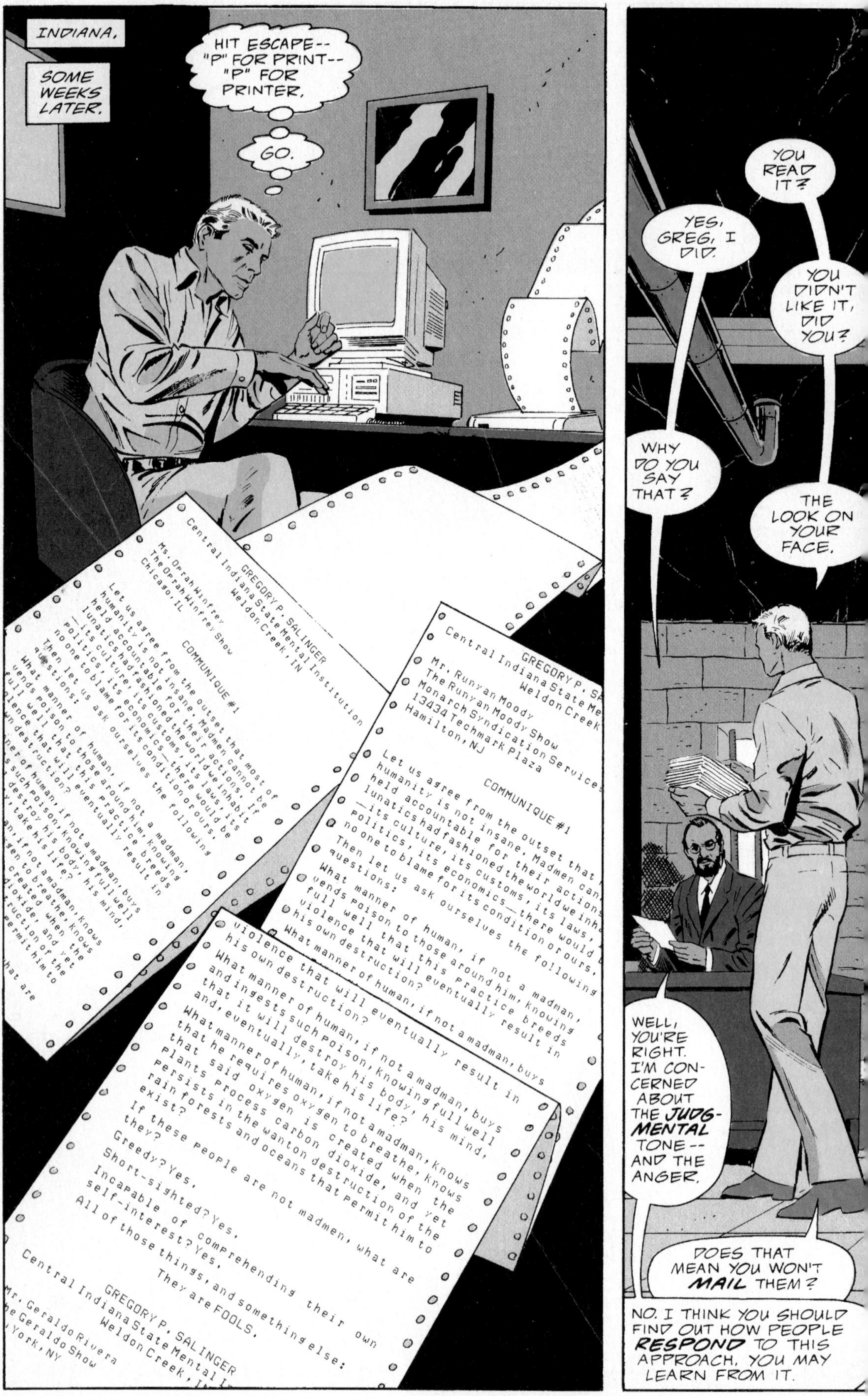
INDIANA.
SOME WEEKS LATER.
HIT ESCAPE-- "P" FOR PRINT-- "P" FOR PRINTER.
GO.
GREGORY P. SALINGER
Central Indiana State Mental Institution
Weldon Creek, IN
Ms. Oprah Winfrey
The Oprah Winfrey Show
Chicago, IL
COMMUNIQUE #1
Let us agree from the outset that most of humanity is not insane. Madmen cannot be held accountable for their actions. If lunatics had fashioned the world we inhabit —its culture, its customs, its laws, its politics, its economics—there would be no one to blame for its condition or ours.
Then let us ask ourselves the following questions:
What manner of human, if not a madman, vends poison to those around him, knowing full well that this practice breeds
Mr. Runyan Moody
The Runyan Moody Show
Monarch Syndication Services
13434 Techmark Plaza
Hamilton, NJ
COMMUNIQUE #1
Then let us ask ourselves the following questions:
What manner of human, if not a madman, vends poison to those around him, knowing full well that this practice breeds violence that will eventually result in his own destruction?
What manner of human, if not a madman, buys
violence that will eventually result in his own destruction?
What manner of human, if not a madman, buys and ingests such poison, knowing full well that it will destroy his body, his mind, and, eventually, take his life?
What manner of human, if not a madman, knows that he requires oxygen to breathe, knows that said oxygen is created when the plants process carbon dioxide, and yet persists in the wanton destruction of the rain forests and oceans that permit him to exist?
If these people are not madmen, what are they?
Greedy? Yes.
Short-sighted? Yes.
Incapable of comprehending their own self-interest? Yes.
All of those things, and something else:
They are FOOLS.
GREGORY P. SALINGER
Central Indiana State Mental I
Weldon Creek, I
Mr. Geraldo Rivera
he Geraldo Show
York, NY
YOU READ IT?
YES, GREG, I DID.
YOU DIDN'T LIKE IT, DID YOU?
WHY DO YOU SAY THAT?
THE LOOK ON YOUR FACE.
WELL, YOU'RE RIGHT. I'M CONCERNED ABOUT THE JUDGMENTAL TONE-- AND THE ANGER.
DOES THAT MEAN YOU WON'T MAIL THEM?
NO. I THINK YOU SHOULD FIND OUT HOW PEOPLE RESPOND TO THIS APPROACH. YOU MAY LEARN FROM IT.

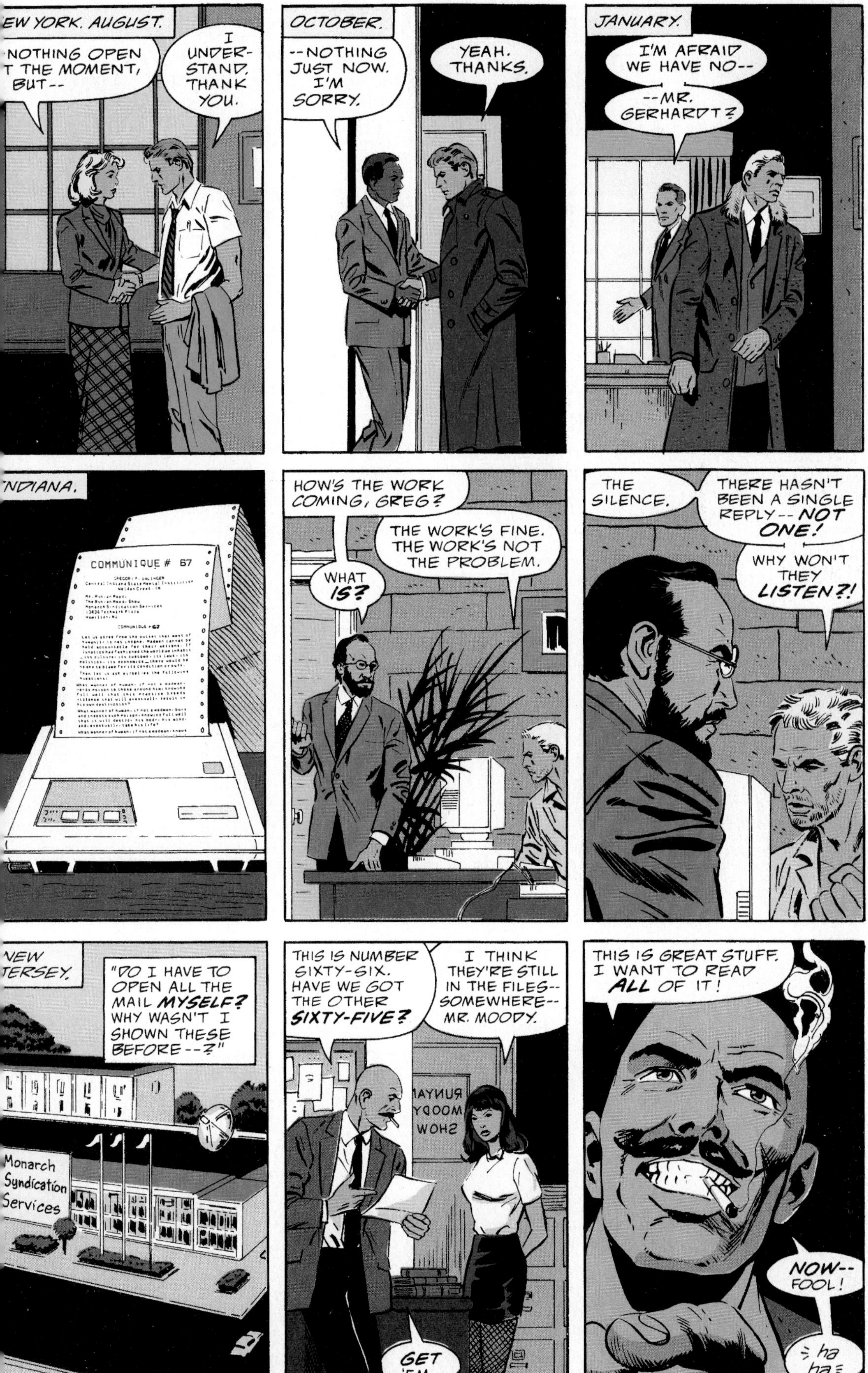

EW YORK. AUGUST.
NOTHING OPEN T THE MOMENT, BUT--
I UNDER-STAND. THANK YOU.
OCTOBER.
--NOTHING JUST NOW. I'M SORRY.
YEAH. THANKS.
JANUARY.
I'M AFRAID WE HAVE NO--
--MR. GERHARDT?
NDIANA.
COMMUNIQUE # 67
HOW'S THE WORK COMING, GREG?
THE WORK'S FINE. THE WORK'S NOT THE PROBLEM.
WHAT IS?
THE SILENCE.
THERE HASN'T BEEN A SINGLE REPLY-- NOT ONE!
WHY WON'T THEY LISTEN?!
NEW JERSEY.
"DO I HAVE TO OPEN ALL THE MAIL MYSELF? WHY WASN'T I SHOWN THESE BEFORE--?"
Monarch Syndication Services
THIS IS NUMBER SIXTY-SIX. HAVE WE GOT THE OTHER SIXTY-FIVE?
I THINK THEY'RE STILL IN THE FILES-- SOMEWHERE-- MR. MOODY.
RUNYAN MOODY SHOW
GET 'EM.
THIS IS GREAT STUFF. I WANT TO READ ALL OF IT!
NOW-- FOOL!
ha ha

RIVERDALE.
THE EVICTION NOTICE CAME TODAY, KURT.
OUR SAVINGS ARE GONE. WE'VE SOLD ALL THE BOOKS AND HALF THE FURNITURE.
YOU'VE BEEN OUT OF WORK SEVEN MONTHS AND IMPOSSIBLE TO TALK TO FOR THREE MONTHS LONGER THAN THAT.
I CAN'T TAKE IT ANYMORE, KURT.
WHEN DO YOU WANT ME TO MOVE OUT?
AS SOON AS POSSIBLE. I'VE... ALREADY CALLED A LAWYER.
SHOULDN'T HAVE BOTHERED. I'LL SETTLE FOR THE COMPUTER AND MY CLOTHES.
YOU CAN HAVE THE REST.
WHAT LITTLE IS LEFT...
JERSEY. ONE WEEK LATER.
THAT'S RIGHT--AN INTERVIEW.
WE'RE IN 145 MARKETS. YOU'LL BE ABLE TO SPEAK YOUR MIND VIRTUALLY COAST-TO-COAST.
MR. MOODY, I--UH--DON'T KNOW WHAT TO SAY--I WASN'T EXPECTING--
YES, OF COURSE, I WANT TO-- IT'S JUST--
OH! GOOD! YOU DO UNDERSTAND THAT! IT'S M-E-A-R-S. DR. MEARS.
NEW YORK CITY.
ARE YOU KIDDING? YOU BET YOU'RE HIRED! WHEN CAN YOU START?
IS MONDAY OKAY?
I'M JUST MOVING INTO MY NEW PLACE.
BURGER CLOWN
MONDAY IT IS! FOUR P.M. SHARP--FOR THE DINNER AND SNACK SHIFT.
THANK YOU, BOBBY--VERY MUCH.

NDIANA. MONDAY.
T'S MOODY HIM-SELF, DR. WIGGINS. WHAT SHALL I TELL HIM?
THAT I'VE GIVEN THE MATTER CAREFUL CONSIDERATION AND REGRETFULLY MUST CONCLUDE--
GOD. FOR ONCE IN YOUR LIFE, GIVE A DIRECT ANSWER!
HE MEANS "NO."
MR. MOODY, I'M AFRAID OUR CHIEF-OF-STAFF FEELS IT WOULD BE IN-APPROPRIATE--AND UP-SETTING TO OTHER PATIENTS--TO ALLOW A TELEVISION CREW--
THAT'S CORRECT. IT MEANS "NO." I'M VERY SOR-- WHAT?
I SAID, TELL HIM IT MIGHT MAKE A MORE INTERESTING SHOW, ANYWAY, IF WE SET UP OUTSIDE AND PUT ON SOME GUESTS--
--TO DISCUSS WHETHER MENTAL PATIENTS CAN BE DENIED FIRST AMENDMENT RIGHTS BY GRANOLA-SUCKING, DICTATORIAL THERAPISTS.
YEAH. SURE. I'LL HANG ON.
TELL HIM...
...I'LL CALL HIM BACK.
EW YORK. FOUR P.M.
INDA KLEIN, HIS IS KURT ERHARDT.
KURT, HIS IS INDA.
BURGER CLOWN
PLEASED TO MEET YOU, LINDA.
LIKE-WISE.
SUIT UP IN BACK, KURT--
--AND THEN I'LL HAVE LINDA SHOW YOU THE BASICS--
--PORTION CONTROL, THE MENU, CASH REGISTERS--ALL THAT STUFF.

11:30 P.M.
YOU LOOK BUSHED, KURT. WHY DON'T YOU TAKE A BREAK?
CAN YOU HANDLE THE COUNTER ALONE?
OH, YEAH, IT'LL BE SLOW TILL MIDNIGHT, WHEN THE MOVIES LET OUT.
IF YOU SAY SO. THANKS, LINDA...!
BURGER CLOWN
SHE'S RIGHT--I AM TIRED, MORE THAN I REALIZED.
BUT IT FEELS A LOT BETTER THAN THE ACHE AND FRUSTRATION OF POUNDING THE PAVEMENT.
I CAN'T EVEN GET ANGRY ABOUT MY "COMEDOWN" ANYMORE. SO WHAT IF MY BOSS IS JUST OVER HALF MY AGE?
BOBBY AND LINDA ARE BOTH GOOD KIDS--AND HARD WORKERS. I'D HIRE EITHER ONE OF THEM IF I STILL--
YO! KURT!
JUST WANTED TO LET YOU KNOW--YOU DID TERRIFIC FOR YOUR FIRST DAY.
MOST O' THE TRAINEES TAKE FOREVER JUST TO LEARN THE REGISTERS...!
THANKS, BOBBY.
I KNEW THE BANKING EXPERIENCE WOULD COME IN HANDY FOR SOME--
BLAM!
OH, HELL...!

STAY IN YOUR SEATS AN' KEEP QUIET--AN' NOBODY'LL HAVETA GET HURT!
MAYBE.
BOTH HANDS ON TOP O' THE COUNTER, BABE!
THAT'S RIGHT-- NOW OPEN THE REGISTER AN' GIMME THE CASH!
BOBBY...?
DO IT.
DON'T RESIST.
SIX BUCKS.
KILL FOR SIX BUCKS.
SPEED IT UP, SWEETIE--
--I AIN'T GOT ALL NIGHT.
I'M TRYING-- I SWEAR! IT WON'T OPEN!
DIE FOR SIX BUCKS.

DON'T JERK ME AROUND, BABE. YOU THINK I WON'T CUT YA, YOU'RE DEAD WRONG!
I'M NOT! TRY IT YOURSELF--YOU'LL SEE--!
SIX BUCKS.
KURT-- DON'T--!
SIX BUCKS!
WHA'--?
I'LL RIP OUT YOUR HEART FOR SIX BUCKS!
I'LL TEAR YOUR FACE OFF-- FOR SIX BUCKS!
I'LL BREAK YOUR--
THOK!
--BREAK--
--YOUR--
--FOR SIX--
MAN, AM I SICK O' THIS GUY.
CHUK!
SIX
CHUD!
BUCKS
CHOT!
SISH
KLUD!
B--

ROOSEVELT HOSPITAL EMERGENCY ROOM.
11:50 P.M.
"STAB WOUNDS... BULLET WOUNDS... BURNS, MUTILATIONS, PUNCTURES... LOOK AT THEM.
"CLUTCHING THEMSELVES. MOANING. WEEPING. SITTING IN PUDDLES OF THEIR OWN BLOOD."
LOOK AT ME-- ONE MORE PIECE OF WOUNDED MEAT AMONG A HERD...!
WHAT?
I'M SORRY, KURT. I DIDN'T HEAR--
WHAT'S HAPPENED TO PEOPLE--WHAT'S HAPPENED TO CIVILIZATION--
--THAT THIS KIND OF CRUELTY COULD BECOME COMMONPLACE?
WHAT KIND OF VICIOUS, SUB-HUMAN BRUTES COMMIT THESE ATROCITIES?
WHY AREN'T THEY HERE?
HOW COME THEY NEVER DIE?

KURT'S APARTMENT.
WEDNESDAY.
WE'RE ALL HOSTAGES, YOU KNOW THAT? HOSTAGES OF RANDOM, SENSELESS BRUTALITY--
JUST SIP THE CHICKEN SOUP, WILL YOU? DON'T THINK ABOUT THAT.
MAKES YOU WONDER, THOUGH--WHAT IF THE TABLES GOT TURNED?
WHAT IF SOMEBODY MADE THEM THE HOSTAGES?
MADE WHO--?
THE PARASITES--
--THE ANIMALS!
WHAT IF THERE WERE RANDOM EXECUTIONS INSTEAD OF RANDOM CRIMES, LINDA?
HOW MANY OF THEM DO YOU THINK WOULD HAVE TO DIE--
--BEFORE THEY FIGURED OUT THEY WEREN'T WANTED...?
KURT, THAT'S SICK. HOW CAN WE CALL OURSELVES CIVILIZED IF--
OLD ARGUMENT... DOESN'T WASH ANYMORE.
WE'RE NOT CIVILIZED--DON'T YOU SEE THAT? IT'S--A LIE--!
THIS IS ANOTHER AGE--OF BARBARISM!
BOBBY WANTS YOU TO TAKE THE REST OF THE WEEK OFF--GET YOUR STRENGTH BACK.
YOU'LL DO THAT, WON'T YOU?
YEAH. WILL YOU STOP BY AGAIN IN A DAY OR TWO?
I'LL... TRY.

FRIDAY NIGHT.
CENTRAL INDIANA STATE MENTAL INSTITUTION
EVERYBODY GETS BUTTERFLIES BEFORE A SHOW--YOU'RE GONNA BE BRILLIANT, GREG.
JUST SAY WHAT YOU WROTE IN YOUR LETTERS.
MSS
THE PEOPLE WANT TO HEAR YOU, GREG.
THEY'RE YOUR FRIENDS. I'M YOUR FRIEND. THERE'S NO REASON TO BE NERVOUS.
YOU CAN STILL BACK OUT OF THIS IF YOU WANT, GREG.
DO YOU?
NO.
ATTABOY! JUST REMEMBER--IT'S GONNA BE A CONVERSATION, NOT A PERFORMANCE.
JUST IGNORE THE LIGHTS, IGNORE THE CAMERAS, AND TALK TO ME.
SAME WITH THE PEOPLE WHO CALL IN. PHONE CALL'S A PHONE CALL.
I CAN DO THAT... I'M SURE I CAN...!
NEW YORK.
NINE P.M.
TONIGHT--LIVE FROM INDIANA--IS THIS THE COLLAPSE OF WESTERN CIVILIZATION?
ARE LIBERALS AND CRIMINALS DESTROYING OUR WAY OF LIFE?
RUNYAN MOODY ASKS--
--THE FOOL-KILLER!
RUNYAN MOODY SHOW
CONTINUED.

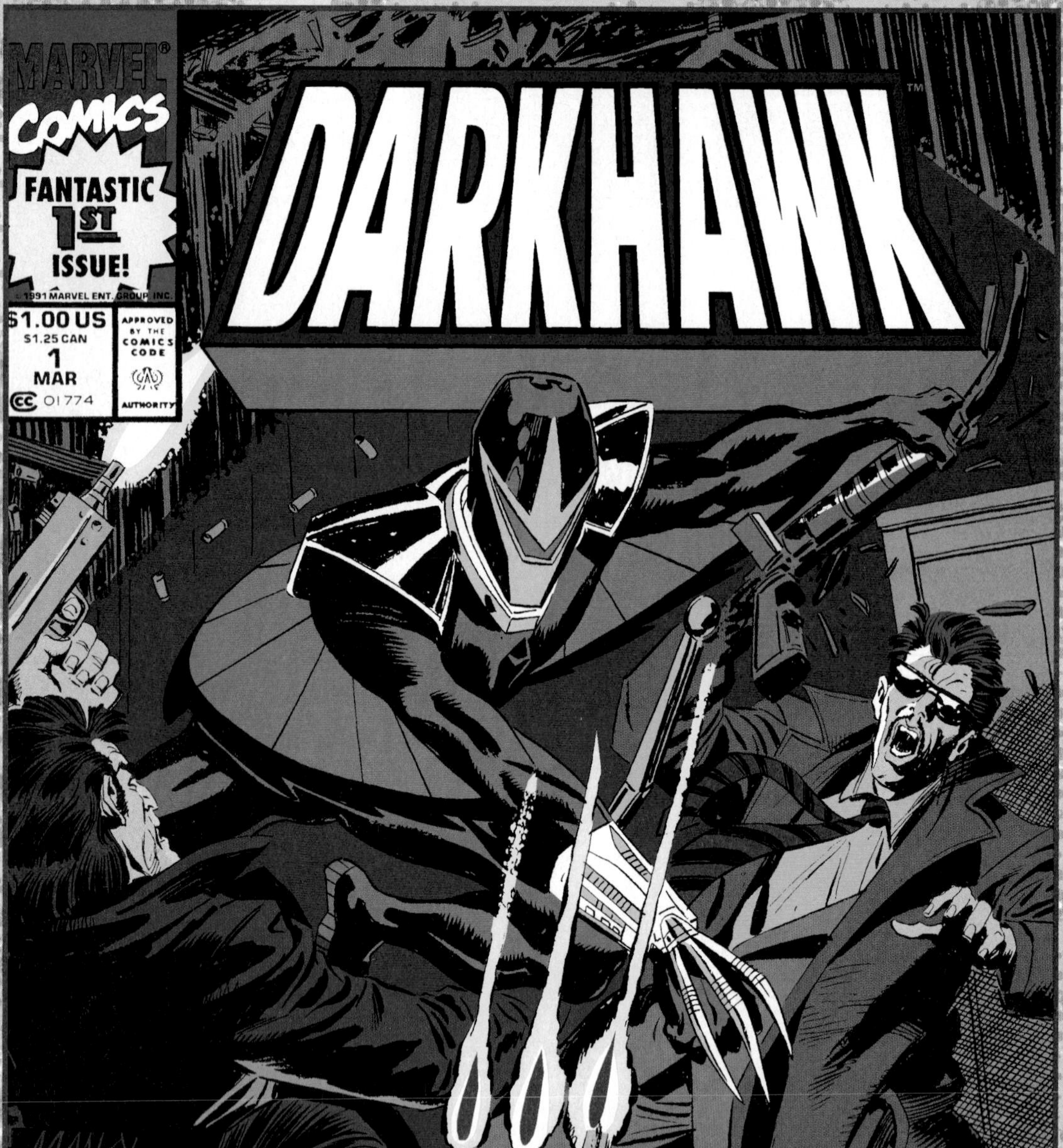
MARVEL COMICS
FANTASTIC 1ST ISSUE!
DARKHAWK
©1991 MARVEL ENT. GROUP, INC.
$1.00 US
$1.25 CAN
1
MAR
01774
APPROVED BY THE COMICS CODE AUTHORITY
MANLEY
DAWN OF THE DARKHAWK!

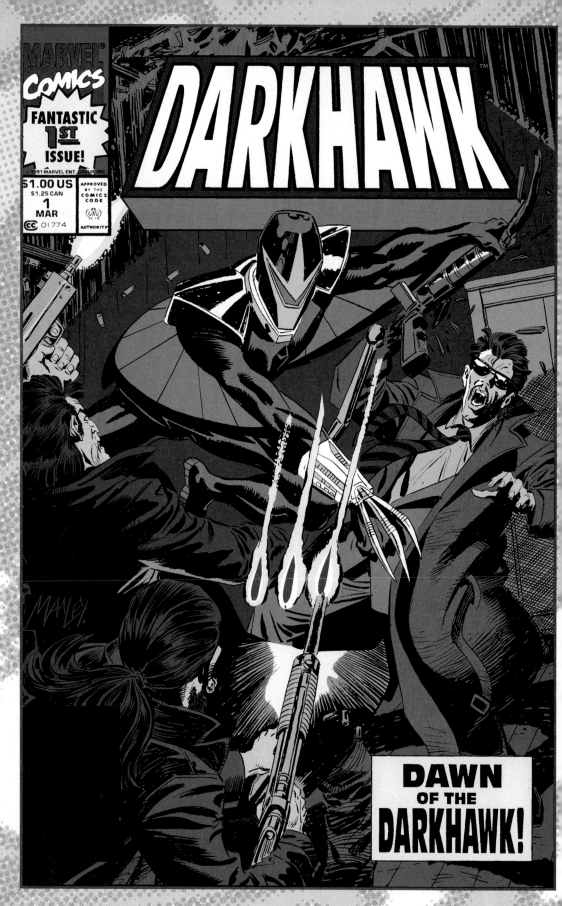

DARKHAWK #1, published in January 1991, introduced the mysterious armored hero in an ongoing series.

STAN LEE PROUDLY PRESENTS THE PREMIERE ADVENTURE OF THE GREATEST HERO OF THE NINETIES...
DAWN OF THE DARKHAWK
MANLEY
DARKHAWK CREATED BY TOM DEFALCO AND MIKE MANLEY.
DANNY FINGEROTH WRITER
MIKE MANLEY ARTIST
JOE ROSEN LETTERER
JOE ROSAS COLORIST
HOWARD MACKIE EDITOR
TOM DEFALCO EDITOR IN CHIEF

THEY SAY YOU CAN JUDGE A MAN BY HIS ENEMIES.
THIS IS THE HOBGOBLIN. HE DOESN'T KNOW IT YET...
...BUT HE'S SOON GOING TO BECOME THE SWORN ENEMY OF A HERO WHO DOESN'T EVEN EXIST YET.
DID YOU FIND IT--?!

DON'T DIS-APPOINT ME, BAZIN--
VROOOOSH
--TELL ME THAT YOU'VE FOUND IT!
BE PATIENT, MY FRIEND, AND CALL ME PHILIPPE.
MY AGENTS ARE FOLLOWING UP A LEAD--
--AND, AS SURELY AS THEY FOUND THIS EXQUISITE PIECE OF 4th CENTURY EGYPTIAN--
SKZZZT!
FIND THE OBJECT WE'VE AGREED ON--
--OR RISK PUTTING ME IN A REAL-LY BAD MOOD...
...PHILIPPE.
I'LL ADD THE COST OF THE VASE TO YOUR BILL.
I'LL PAY ANY PRICE IF YOU GET ME WHAT I WANT.
YOU HAVE NO IDEA WHAT PRICE YOU WILL PAY, FOOL.

QUEENS, NEW YORK...
WONDERLAND AMUSEMENT PARK. IT USED TO BE THE PLACE TO GO FOR CHEAP THRILLS.
TIMES CHANGE. IT CLOSED THREE YEARS AGO.
IT'S SLATED TO BE DEMOLISHED IN A FEW DAYS.
WONDERLAND
SHOOTING GALLERY
TONIGHT, THERE'S SOME DECIDEDLY UNAMUSING ACTION GOING ON THERE.
COME ON, OLD MAN. YOU MUST'VE SEEN IT SOMEWHERE.
BOYS--WHY WOULD SAINT JOHNNY LIE?
ONCE THE PARK'S GONE--I'M JUST ANOTHER HOMELESS STATISTIC--
--WHAT'VE I GOT TO GAIN BY LYING?
THE CLUES ALL LEAD HERE. AND YOU HAUNT THIS PLACE.
NOW, DON'T MAKE US BREAK--
STOP.
YOU SURE, MR. BAZIN?
QUITE SURE.
HERE, MR.--SAINT--JOHNNY...
...MAYBE THIS WILL SOFTEN YOUR HOLIER-THAN-THOU STANCE.
SPLASH
WHEN YOU FINISH DRINKING THAT UP--
--CALL THE NUMBER ON THE BAND.
PERHAPS YOUR MEMORY WILL HAVE IMPROVED BY THEN.

MORNING. NEW YORK COUNTY COURTHOUSE.
OH, GREAT...
...I STOP FOR A QUICK LUNCH...
...GET LOST IN MY NOTES...
...AND I'M TEN MINUTES LATE FOR COURT. SOME ASSISTANT D.A. I TURNED OUT TO BE...
GRACE POWELL...?
HMMM... YES...?
CAFETERIA
THIS IS FOR YOU.
LEAVE WELL ENOUGH ALONE--AND PROSPER.
OTHERWISE--SUFFER THE CONSEQUENCES.
UNLESS THAT'S A SIGNED CONFESSION--
--TELL YOUR BOSS TO KEEP HIS MONEY--AND HIS THREATS--
--TO HIMSELF.
GOT THAT, MESSENGER BOY?
I REALLY DON'T KNOW SPECIFICALLY WHO THE ENVELOPE IS FROM--
--BUT YOUR MESSAGE WILL BE CONVEYED.
THIS...THIS ISN'T WHAT THEY TOLD ME IT'D BE LIKE IN LAW SCHOOL.
DOESN'T MATTER. I'VE GOT A HALF DOZEN CASES TO PROSECUTE TODAY...
...AS SOON AS I CAN STAND UP.
IT TAKES A FEW MINUTES, BUT STAND SHE DOES...

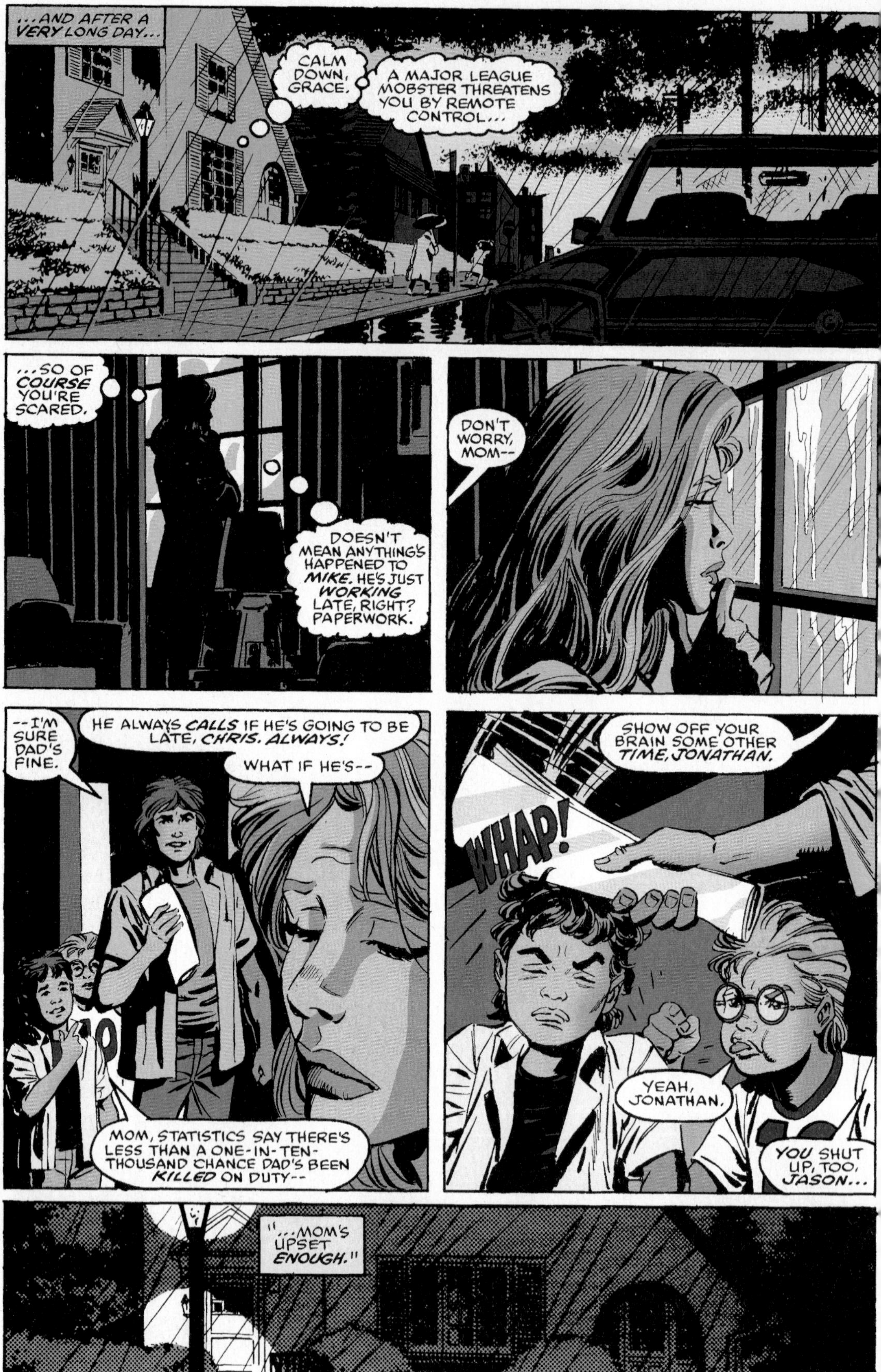
...AND AFTER A VERY LONG DAY...
CALM DOWN, GRACE.
A MAJOR LEAGUE MOBSTER THREATENS YOU BY REMOTE CONTROL...
...SO OF COURSE YOU'RE SCARED.
DOESN'T MEAN ANYTHING'S HAPPENED TO MIKE. HE'S JUST WORKING LATE, RIGHT? PAPERWORK.
DON'T WORRY, MOM--
--I'M SURE DAD'S FINE.
HE ALWAYS CALLS IF HE'S GOING TO BE LATE, CHRIS. ALWAYS!
WHAT IF HE'S--
MOM, STATISTICS SAY THERE'S LESS THAN A ONE-IN-TEN-THOUSAND CHANCE DAD'S BEEN KILLED ON DUTY--
SHOW OFF YOUR BRAIN SOME OTHER TIME, JONATHAN.
WHAP!
YEAH, JONATHAN.
YOU SHUT UP, TOO, JASON...
"...MOM'S UPSET ENOUGH."

HONEY--
--YOU CAN'T LEAVE THE BACK DOOR UNLOCKED. NOT THESE DAYS.
MIKE!
DAD!
I WAS SO WORRIED--AND YOU ALMOST GAVE ME A HEART ATTACK SNEAKING IN!
"SNEAKING"? I JUST DIDN'T WANT TO MUDDY UP THE WALL-TO-WALL.
WE WERE WORRIED, DAD --I THOUGHT MAYBE BAZIN...
NOT TODAY. HAD MY HANDS FULL WITH SOME DEALERS ON GRAND STREET. THANK GOD FOR KEVLAR VESTS.
MIKE, I...
...I WAS THREATENED BY ONE OF BAZIN'S GOONS TODAY.
HONEY--MAYBE IT'S TIME FOR US BOTH TO GIVE UP--GET OUT OF THIS SEWER OF A CITY BEFORE IT'S TOO LATE.
IF ONLY OUR SIDE HAD--
--AN EDGE.
THAT'S WHAT YOU ALWAYS SAY, DAD. BUT I NEVER HEARD YOU SO DEMORALIZED BEFORE.
WISH THERE WAS SOMETHING I COULD DO.
DON'T WISH YOUR LIFE AWAY LIKE I DID, CHRIS.
I WISHED I COULD BE SOME KIND OF HERO--AND ALL I AM IS A TARGET FOR LOWLIFES.
YOU ARE A HERO, DAD.
SURE, JASON. TELL ME THAT ONCE YOU MISS A MEAL.

SOON...
WELL, COME ON... LET'S AT LEAST PRETEND TO MAKE SOME CAREFREE FAMILY SMALL TALK.
HEY, DAD... I'VE GOT A QUESTION.
GO AHEAD, JASON.
YOU PROMISED TO TAKE ME AND JON OVER TO WONDERLAND BEFORE THEY TEAR IT DOWN. HOW 'BOUT TONIGHT?
WE'LL DO IT THIS WEEKEND, JASON-- IF I DON'T HAVE TO WORK OVERTIME.
WAY COOL, DAD!
BUT, SUNDAY AFTERNOON...
HEY, GUYS-- CHILL OUT. I'M TRYING TO STUDY.
CHRIS-- JUST 'CAUSE MOM AND DAD HAVE TO WORK TODAY DOESN'T MEAN YOU CAN'T TAKE US TO WONDERLAND!
I TOLD YOU, JON-- I PROMISED MOM WE WOULDN'T LEAVE THE HOUSE.
BING BONG
OUTSIDE-- THOSE SHADOWS--!
OH, NO KIDNAPPERS --NOT TODAY.
COME OUT AND PLAY, CHRIS!
GENE! REBECCA! I TOLD YOU I HAD TO WATCH THE TWINS--!
GET REAL, CHRIS. THEY'RE ELEVEN! YOU STAYED ALONE AT THEIR AGE.
COME ON. A QUICK SODA AT JASOL'S.
WELL...
GUYS! IF MOM CALLS, I'M IN THE BATHROOM.
BUT--
I'LL BE BACK IN FIFTEEN MINUTES--WITH MILK SHAKES!
GET GOING!

THEY'RE GONE!
MY BABIES ARE GONE!
I TRUSTED YOU, CHRIS--
--AND NOW THEY'RE GONE!
KIDNAPPED BY BAZIN, FOR ALL WE KNOW!
I BLEW IT, MOM, I ADMIT IT--!
CALL THE POLICE--
--BUT, MEANWHILE, I BET I KNOW WHERE THEY WENT!
AND...
MISTER--DID YOU SEE MY BROTHERS? TWINS.
SURE DID, SON. JUST DON'T HIT ME.
HUH?
THEY WENT TO THE HAWK'S PLACE--THE FUNHOUSE.
THANKS, OLD MAN. I'LL BUY YOU A CASE OF THAT ROTGUT--
--AFTER I FIND 'EM.
THE MAN CALLED SAINT JOHNNY LOOKS DEEP INTO HIS BOTTLE...
...AND WONDERS WHY HE WOULD GIVE THIS YOUNG MAN INFORMATION HE WOULDN'T SELL DAYS BEFORE FOR A THOUSAND DOLLARS.

YEAH! I HEAR THEIR VOICES...
FUN HOUSE
TICKETS
...COMING FROM UP HERE...!
THERE THEY...
...ARE!
YOW!
YAAAH! DON'T HURT US!
SERVES YOU RIGHT FOR GETTING ME IN TROUBLE!
YOU SAID FIFTEEN MINUTES, YOU DIDN'T COME BACK AFTER AN HOUR!
OH, SO TWO WRONGS MAKE A--
SHHH--! SOMEBODY'S COMING-- MAYBE A SECURITY GUARD...?
HUH? A BUNCH OF GUYS--
--AND DAD?!

GO AHEAD, POWELL. TAKE IT-- WITH MR. BAZIN'S COMPLIMENTS.
IT'S ALL THERE--
--FIFTY THOUSAND, IN TWENTIES LIKE WE AGREED.
YOU'LL GET YOUR MONEY'S WORTH.
YEAH, YER A MAN OF HONOR, AIN'TCHA, POWELL?
YOU--
WHOK!
--LOUSY--
BEHIND ME--
--GOTTA MOVE--!
BYOW!
KWOK!
I TOLD THE BOSS YA CAN'T TRUST A CROOKED COP.
I'M GONNA WHACK 'IM AND--
NO! STOP!
HEY! LOOKIE HERE--
--SOME PAIN-IN-THE-NECK INNOCENT BYSTANDERS TO BLOW AW--

NOOOOOOOO!
BYOW!
JASON! JONATHAN! RUN!!
THEY AIN'T GOIN' NOWHERE--
RUN!
FWASH!
BYOW!
BYOW!
BYOW!
MOVE, GUYS-- MOVE!
KREK
SHRUMMMMMM!
THE FLOOR--
HAAAAALP!
NOOOOOO--!

OOMPH GOTCHA, JON!
TOMATOES
OWW!
YOU OKAY, JASON?
M-MY ARM HURTS... BUT... I THINK I'M OKAY.
THOSE BOARDS MUST'VE BEEN ROTTING FOR YEARS. BUT MAYBE IT'LL BE A LUCKY BREAK FOR US.
Y-YEAH. MAYBE THERE'S A WAY OUT THROUGH THE BASEMENT.
LET'S SEE.
MAN-- LOOK AT THIS STUFF. GIVES ME THE CREEPS.
THEY'RE JUST OLD FUNHOUSE PROPS OR SOMETHING. WE'VE GOT BIGGER PROBLEMS.
YA SURE DO, KID.
GET IN THIS CLOSET.
BUT--
NOW.
KLIK
OKAY. I LOCKED 'EM IN, SO AT LEAST...
...I'LL DIE FIRST.
NO! CAN'T THINK LIKE THAT.
KRASH!
YOW!
I'LL THROW EVERYTHING I CAN GET MY HANDS ON.
WE'RE DOWN HERE WITH YOU NOW, PUNK. ONE BULLET'S ALL IT'LL TAKE.
AIM AT UNF THIS, SMART GUY!
METAL SHELVING-- OUGHT TO BLOCK THEIR WAY FOR A MINUTE--!
NOW, MAYBE THERE'S SOMETHING BACK HERE--

--I CAN USE AS A WEAPON--SOME KIND OF "EDGE".
HAH--THAT'S WHAT DAD WAS ALWAYS TALKING ABOUT...
...BEFORE HE GAVE UP.
WHAT I WOULDN'T GIVE FOR THE POWER TO TRASH THOSE MISERABLE--
HUH?

I...I FEEL LIKE I'M SURGING WITH POWER!
ONLY...I'M NOT ME! EXCEPT I AM.
SO I MUST BE DREAMING...!
UNGH THIS SHELF MUST WEIGH A TON!
THOSE KILLERS--! THEY WANT TO MURDER ME--MY DAD--MY BROTHERS--
SHWOOOOOM!
THAT BLAST-- COMING OUT OF MY CHEST--?!
NOW I KNOW IT'S A DREAM.
AND IF THAT'S THE CASE--
--I MAY AS WELL GO FOR BROKE!
HERE, GUYS--
--HAVE A BIG METAL OBJECT!
KRAAASH!
WHOEVER YOU ARE--
BYOW
--YOU'RE DEAD!
BYOW
WHOSE VOICE WAS COMING OUT OF ME?!
AND HOW'M I DODGING THESE BULLETS--!!

YOU HAVE INVADED THE LAIR OF THE, UH, EDGE-MAN. THE THREE YOUTHS ARE IN MY CHARGE.
BEGONE--OR PAY THE PRICE!
DID I SAY THAT?
WHOEVER YOU ARE--YOU'RE ONLY ONE GUY--
--GET 'IM!
OWW! KNIFE CUT ME--BAD!
I DON'T THINK THIS IS A DREAM--!
TRY THIS ON FOR SIZE, WEIRDO!
GGGK
...N--NOOOO...
DANGER HIGH VOLTAGE
KWOK!
KWAM!
MAN! IT'S LIKE THEY DON'T WEIGH ANYTHING!

LOOKS LIKE THAT KNOCKED THE FIGHT OUT OF--
NO!
WHOEVER-- WHATEVER-- YOU ARE--
KRAAZZLE!
--I'M SAYING YOU CAN'T STAND UP TO THIS JUICE!
FRAZATT!
WHOA--! I BET HE'S RIGHT! I FELT THAT!
BODY SEEMS FAST ENOUGH TO EVADE HIM, BUT I'VE GOT TO TAKE THE OFFENSIVE--
--SEE IF I CAN FIRE ONE OF THOSE BLASTS AGAIN. CONCENTRATE... CONCENTRATE--
VRAKOOOM!
YEAH!
BUT MY AIM'S NO GOOD--DON'T WANNA BRING THE PLACE DOWN ON ME--AND MY FAMILY!
SKRAAKLE!
I CAN'T BE-LIEVE IT--BUT YOU HAVE THE POWER, DON'T YOU--?! THE POWER HOBGOBLIN AND MY BOSS ARE AFTER--!
WELL, THEY CAN GET IT FROM YOU AFTER THE AUTOPSY.
I'M DONE! HE'S GONNA KILL ME--!

FEAR'S FREEZING ME! CAN'T LET IT-- CAN'T!
DREAM OR NO DREAM, CHRIS--
HIGH VOLTAGE
--MOVE!
AAAAAAA
AAAAAA
SKZZZZZ
HE...HE'S DEAD...
...NEVER SAW A DEAD GUY BEFORE...
THE FINAL SURGE SHORTED OUT THE ENTIRE BASEMENT, RENDERING THE CABLE HARMLESS...

...AND, A FEW MINUTES LATER...
THESE TWO'RE STILL OUT. JUST AS WELL.
NOW WHAT DO I DO WITH THEM? CALL THE POLICE...?
BAMM! BAMM! BAMM!
HEY! WHAT'S GOING ON OUT THERE?!
LET US OUT!
THE TWINS! GOT TO--
WHOA--!
MY ARM...!
MY WHOLE BODY--!
THEY'LL SEE ME--WHAT'LL I TELL THEM--?!

WHAT'LL I TELL *ME*?!
OH, MAN! I'M SOME KIND'A *FREAK!* ***FOREVER!***
IT *CAN'T* BE. THERE'S GOT TO BE *SOME* WAY I CAN CHANGE--
HUH?
WHEW! GET OUTTA MY *LIFE!*
HANG ON, GUYS!
I'LL LET YOU OUT IN A SEC!
GOT TO FIND--
CHRIS--!
--DAD...
I SAW WHAT WAS GOING ON...
TELL ME IT WASN'T WHAT IT *LOOKED* LIKE.
TELL ME. PLEASE.
I...I *CAN'T*, CHRIS.
TAKE CARE OF YOUR MOM AND THE KIDS FOR ME.

DAD!
EXIT
GONE.
OT DOGS
CHRIS SEARCHES THE AREA, BUT TO NO AVAIL...
...AND, SOON...
OKAY, GUYS, YOU'RE FREE NOW. EVERY-THING'S O--
YOU STINK, CHRIS! WE COULD OF DIED IN THERE! I HATE YOU!
HOW...HOW'S YOUR ARM, JASON?
HURTS. I THINK DAD'LL HAVE TO TAKE ME TO THE DOCTOR.
UH... RIGHT.
THE AMULET...!
I'LL CATCH UP IN A SECOND, JAS.
"AN EDGE AGAINST CRIME."
OKAY, DAD. MAYBE YOU COULDN'T LIVE UP TO YOUR OWN IDEALS.
THAT DOESN'T MEAN I CAN'T.
IF IT DOESN'T KILL ME FIRST.

IT IS NEARLY A FULL DAY BEFORE CHRIS IS ABLE TO LEAVE HIS FAMILY AND RETURN TO WONDERLAND...
...BUT BY THAT TIME...
YEAH, THE FUNHOUSE WENT DOWN WITH THREE WOMPS OF THE OL' WRECKIN' BALL.
YOU'D THINK WITH THAT STIFF THEY FOUND IN THERE, THEY'D'VE HELD OFF DEMOLITION.
BUT, HEY--WE WERE TOLD TO DO IT ASAP.
UH... THANKS, GUYS.
NOW I'LL NEVER KNOW ANY MORE ABOUT THE AMULET.
POWER'S GOT TO BE USED--NOT ABUSED...
...BY A DARKHAWK.
HUH--WHAT'D YOU SAY--
--OLD MAN...?
GONE.
TWO DAYS LATER...
AAAGGGH!

MOM! JASON HIT ME!
JON STARTED IT, MOM!
HE SAID DAD WAS A CROOK!
WELL, HE IS-- WE SAW HIM--!
BOTH OF YOU-- BE QUIET! IT'S NOT AS SIMPLE AS IT--
RRNGG! RRNGGG!
HELLO.
YES.
YES, I UNDERSTAND.
WHO WAS IT, MOM? WAS IT DAD?
NO. IT WAS... NOBODY...
MOM--!
A MAN SAID: "LAY OFF BAZIN-- OR YOU'LL HAVE ONE LESS KID TO FEED." OH, CHRIS--!
EASY, MOM...
THIS IS ALL WRONG. MY FAMILY'S FALLING APART...
...WHILE BAZIN TOYS WITH PEOPLE'S LIVES LIKE THEY WERE NOTHING.
IF ONLY I HAD THE POWER TO--!
GUESS I CAN'T AVOID IT ANYMORE. I DO HAVE THE POWER. THE QUESTION IS...

"...DO I HAVE THE NERVE...?"
SCARED. WHAT IF I GET STUCK AS THAT CREATURE?
I'VE GOT A LEAD, HOBGOBLIN. CITY BUREAUCRACY GOT IT BURIED UNDER A HUNDRED TONS OF RUBBLE BEFORE I COULD STOP THEM, BUT--
SO I'LL DIG. IF THIS IS THE OBJECT OF POWER THAT I'M HUNTING FOR...
I THINK IT IS. A BEING OF GREAT POWER WAS THERE. KILLED ONE OF MY MEN.
WHAT DID THIS "BEING" LOOK LIKE?
MY MEN SAID HE LOOKED TERRIFYING.
"GOOD. I LIKE 'TERRIFYING'."
I DID IT. THERE'S NO TURNING BACK.
I ♥ BROOKLYN
LOOK OUT, BAZIN. THIS IS THE AGE OF--
--WHAT NAME DID THAT OLD WINO SAY. OH, YEAH--
DARKHAWK!
YEAH. DARKHAWK.
"READY OR NOT, WORLD--HERE I COME!"
YOUR HUNT BEGINS ACROSS THE RIVER, AT THE OLD WONDERLAND PARK IN QUEENS.
I'M LEAVING NOW--
--AND I'LL KILL ANYONE WHO GETS IN MY WAY!
NEXT MONTH: MORE SECRETS OF THE AMULET REVEALED AS DARKHAWK AND SPIDER-MAN BATTLE HOBGOBLIN!

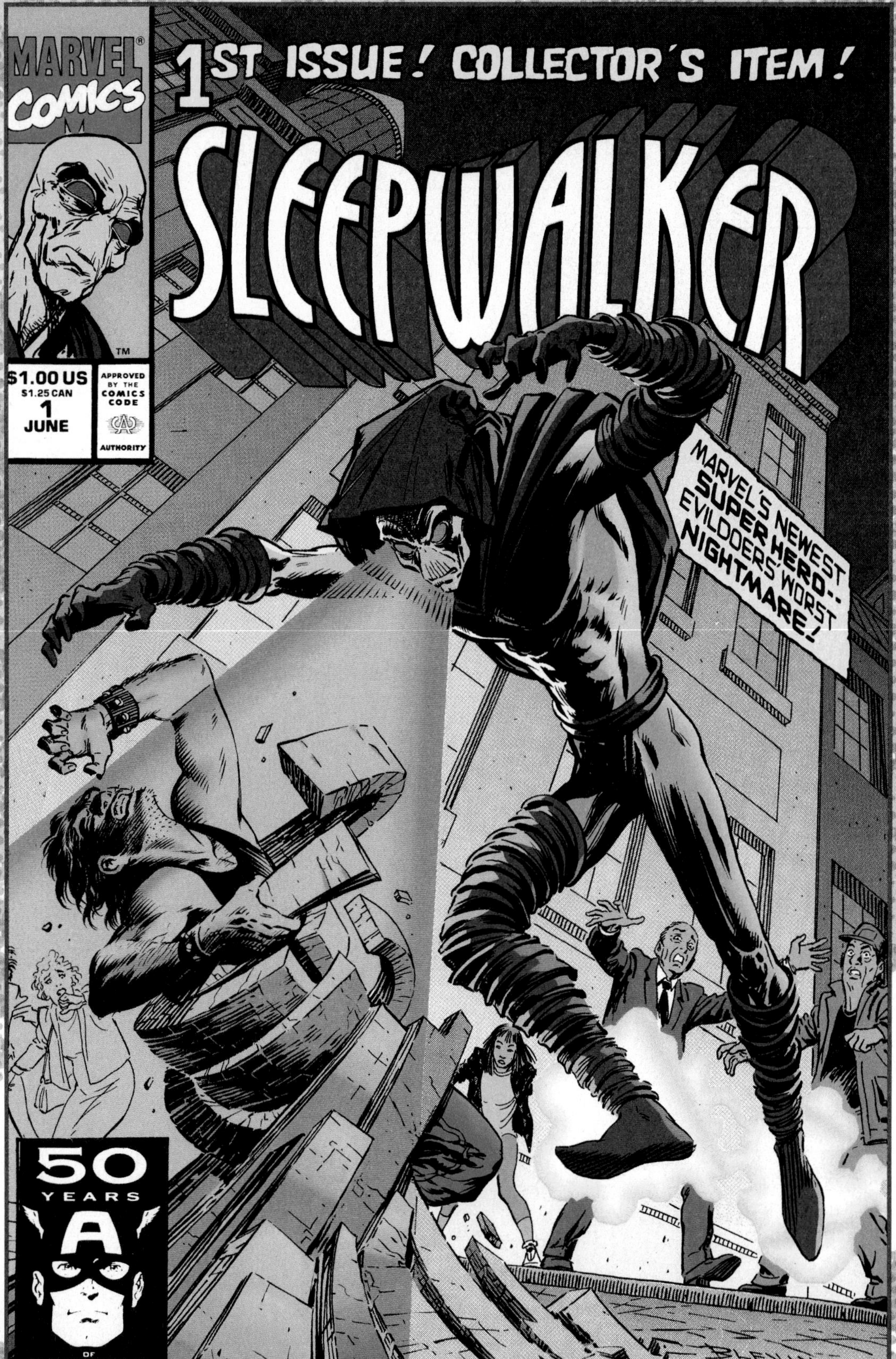
MARVEL®
COMICS
1ST ISSUE! COLLECTOR'S ITEM!
SLEEPWALKER
TM
$1.00 US
$1.25 CAN
1
JUNE
APPROVED BY THE COMICS CODE AUTHORITY
MARVEL'S NEWEST SUPER HERO--
EVILDOERS' WORST NIGHTMARE!
50 YEARS
A
OF CAPTAIN AMERICA
1941 – 1991
BLEVINS

SLEEPWALKER #1, published in April 1991, introduced the eerie other-dimensional hero in an ongoing series.

A PICKUP BASKETBALL GAME IN A CITY SCHOOLYARD...
...FOR MANY IT OFFERS A CHANCE TO COMPETE, TO EXERCISE, TO SOCIALIZE...
... FOR A SELECT FEW, A CHANCE TO EXCEL...
HEY!
THWAK
BOINK
DUNK IT!
BLOCK 'IM!
BUT SOMETIMES, EVEN FOR A PLAYER AS GIFTED AS RICK SHERIDAN...
...A MOMENT OF SEEMING TRIUMPH...

...CAN SUDDENLY TURN TO ONE OF UTTER TERROR!
SLEEPWALKER CREATED BY BOB BUDIANSKY
TO SLEEP PERCHANCE TO SCREAM!
BOB BUDIANSKY, WRITER & COLORIST BRET BLEVINS, ARTIST
TOM ORZECHOWSKI, LETTERER DON DALEY, EDITOR TOM DeFALCO, EDITOR IN CHIEF

Uh, H-HEY, G-G--
--G-GUH--
SSSS
--GUYS!
GUII--
--IIIEEEKS!!

MAN, I'VE BEEN IN A LOT OF GAMES BEFORE, BUT I'VE NEVER BEEN DEFENSED LIKE THAT!
WHAT A DREAM!
RRR..!
NO, RAMBO--
...ROWR
--IT'S TOO EARLY. THAT WASN'T THE ALARM GOING OFF--
CLIK
LOVE CRAZY
MY FAVORITE WIFE
MURDER, HE SAYS
--THAT WAS ME. AND I DON'T HAVETA GET UP UNTIL--
CLIK
CLIK
6:30
--OOH, THAT HURTS.
Y'KNOW, SOMETIMES I THINK I TRAINED YOU TOO WELL FOR YOUR OWN GOOD... AND MINE.
BUT YOU'RE STILL A PRETTY GOOD DOG FOR A DOG.
...SOME EYEWITNESSES CLAIMED THEY SAW SPIDER-MAN...
...BUT SOURCES IN THE POLICE DEPARTMENT SAY THE CRIMINAL KNOWN AS 8-BALL WAS BEHIND THE THEFT.
CLIK
YOU'D WAKE UP, TOO, BOY, IF YOU HAD THE DREAM I HAD.
IT WAS SO... SO REAL!
CLIK

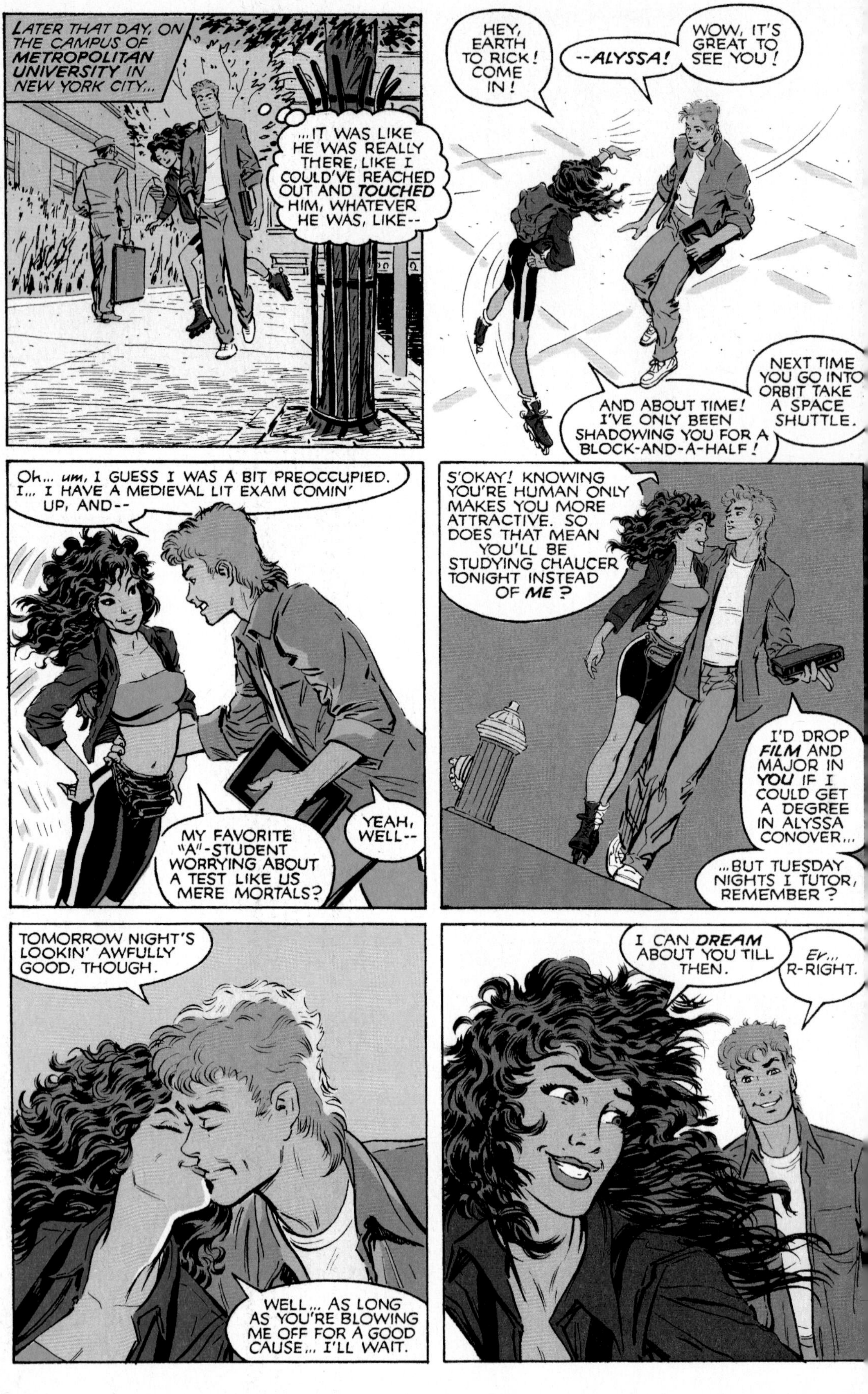
LATER THAT DAY, ON THE CAMPUS OF METROPOLITAN UNIVERSITY IN NEW YORK CITY...
...IT WAS LIKE HE WAS REALLY THERE, LIKE I COULD'VE REACHED OUT AND TOUCHED HIM, WHATEVER HE WAS, LIKE--
HEY, EARTH TO RICK! COME IN!
--ALYSSA!
WOW, IT'S GREAT TO SEE YOU!
AND ABOUT TIME! I'VE ONLY BEEN SHADOWING YOU FOR A BLOCK-AND-A-HALF!
NEXT TIME YOU GO INTO ORBIT TAKE A SPACE SHUTTLE.
Oh... um, I GUESS I WAS A BIT PREOCCUPIED. I... I HAVE A MEDIEVAL LIT EXAM COMIN' UP, AND--
MY FAVORITE "A"-STUDENT WORRYING ABOUT A TEST LIKE US MERE MORTALS?
YEAH, WELL--
S'OKAY! KNOWING YOU'RE HUMAN ONLY MAKES YOU MORE ATTRACTIVE. SO DOES THAT MEAN YOU'LL BE STUDYING CHAUCER TONIGHT INSTEAD OF ME?
I'D DROP FILM AND MAJOR IN YOU IF I COULD GET A DEGREE IN ALYSSA CONOVER...
...BUT TUESDAY NIGHTS I TUTOR, REMEMBER?
TOMORROW NIGHT'S LOOKIN' AWFULLY GOOD, THOUGH.
WELL... AS LONG AS YOU'RE BLOWING ME OFF FOR A GOOD CAUSE... I'LL WAIT.
I CAN DREAM ABOUT YOU TILL THEN.
Er... R-RIGHT.

LATER THAT NIGHT...
NOT SO FAST, RAMBO--YOU TOOK A NAP TODAY. I DIDN'T.
I TOLD YOU BUMS TO STAY AWAY FROM HERE!
WHAT'S THE PROBLEM, MR. E.?
THEY ARE! THEY HANG OUT HERE ALL DAY AND DRINK AND PEDDLE DRUGS! ACH!
LOOK AT THE MESS THEY MAKE!
THE EPSTEINS OWN THIS BUILDING. I THINK YOU'D BE WISE TO LISTEN TO THEM, AND LEAVE.
WHAT YOU GONNA DO ABOUT IT IF WE DON'T, BOY SCOUT?
IT'S NOT ME YOU HAVE TO WORRY ABOUT--
--IT'S HIM.
GRR?
C'MON, SAL. LET'S FIND SOMEPLACE WHERE WE DON'T GOTTA LISTEN TO NO COMEDIANS!
NEXT TIME I'LL POINT MORE THAN MY FINGER AT THAT JERK!
DON'T JUST STAND AROUND, RICK. YOU'RE NOT GETTIN' YOUR ROOM FOR FREE FOR NOTHIN', Y'KNOW. YOU'RE THE JANITOR--
--CLEAN UP!
SLAM
YOU'RE WELCOME.

MINUTES LATER...
YAWN
STAY OUT OF MY WAY, RAMBO. I WOULDN'T WANT YOU...
...TO GET SQUASHED!
WHUMP
?
ZZZZZ
1:45
Ahhh...
SUN, SURF, SAND! IT DOESN'T GET ANY BETTER THAN THIS!
I STAND CORRECTED--
--ALYSSA!
WHAT ARE YOU DOING HERE?!
ANYTHING YOU WANT ME TO DO, RICK.
RIGHT ANSWER!

Huh--?!
ALYSSA, WATCH OUT BEHIND YOU!
OH NO, I'M NOT GONNA LET YOU USE THAT THING ON ME AGAIN!
ALYSSA, RUN!
CAN'T YOU HEAR ME-- RUN!!
HEY-- WHAT'S HAPPENING TO THE GROUND?!
WHAT'S HAPPENING TO YOU?!

NO!
NOOO!!
IT'S THAT MEDALLION!
YOU'RE NOT THROWING ME DOWN A PIT AND GETTING RID OF ME THAT EASILY, BUG-FACE!
EVERY TIME YOU SHOW UP, YOU START MESSIN' WITH IT AND THINGS GET CRAZY!
NOT THIS TIME!
HE-- HE'S GONE!
I MADE HIM DISAPPEAR!
AWRRIGHT!

BRREEEEP
8:00
Ahh... I NEEDED THAT.
HAVEN'T SLEPT SO WELL IN DAYS.
BRR... COLD OUTSIDE.
Hmm... I DON'T REMEMBER LEAVING THE WINDOW OPEN LAST NIGHT. STRANGE.
HEY, RAMBO. I'M AWAKE. DON'T BOTHER TO--
CLIK
...tick tock tick tock...
AW, WHAT THE HECK...
CLIK
...AND TO TELL US ABOUT THAT ATTEMPTED ROBBERY...
...tick tock people...
... HE'S JUST A CREATURE OF HABIT.
CLIK
...HERE'S YVONNE McMURRAY REPORTING FROM BROOKLYN.
...time's slipping away...
ANYWAY, WHO CARES? I FEEL SO GOOD THIS MORNING.
SLAMM
THANK YOU, BRIAN.
MUST BE BECAUSE OF THAT DREAM. I DON'T KNOW WHO THAT CREATURE WAS...
CONTRARY TO EARLIER REPORTS...
CLIK
people of the world...

≥YAWN≤ ...BUT AFTER WHAT I DID TO HIM...
I'M IN BROOKLYN AT THE SCENE OF THE ATTEMPTED BURGLARY.
...from sea to shining s...
CLIK
...I DON'T THINK HE'LL BE PAYING ME ANY MORE VISITS WHILE I'M SLEEPING--
HEY, I KNOW THAT BUILDING. IT'S JUST A FEW BLOCKS AWAY.
MR. FRANK BAYLOR IS THE NIGHT WATCHMAN HERE.
COULD YOU TELL US WHAT YOU SAW?
ABOUT QUARTER TO FIVE THIS MORNIN' A COUPLA GUYS BROKE INTO THE WARE-HOUSE.
ONE OF 'EM HELD A GUN TO MY HEAD, THREATENED TO BLOW IT OFF--
--UNTIL THIS--THIS THING SHOWED UP AND SCARED 'EM ALL AWAY!
I- IT LOOKED KINDA HUMAN, BUT IT WASN'T!
IT WAS SOME KINDA BUG-EYED MONSTER!
POLICE ARTISTS DREW THIS SKETCH BASED ON EYEWITNESSES' TESTIMONY.
CALL: 555-3689
THAT... THAT'S HIM!

CONEY ISLAND AMUSEMENT PARK, THAT NIGHT...
CYCLONE
WOW!
C'MON, LET'S GO FOR ANOTHER SPIN ON THE CYCLONE, RICK!
WONDER WHEEL
RICK?
Oh, SORRY, ALYSSA. I WAS... DISTRACTED.
DEAD IS MORE LIKE IT.
DIDN'T YOU NOTICE WE WERE ON A 100-MILES-AN-HOUR ROLLER COASTER AND I WAS SCREAMING SO LOUD THAT MY MOTHER BACK IN MICHIGAN COULD HEAR ME?
I'M STILL WEIRDED OUT BY THAT NEWS REPORT THIS MORNING. THAT CREATURE LOOKED JUST LIKE THE ONE IN MY DREAM.
I'VE NEVER HAD A PREMONITION LIKE THAT BEFORE.
AND THEN I WOKE UP... AND THE WINDOW WAS OPEN!
MAYBE MR. CREATURE DROPPED IN FOR A VISIT WHILE HE WAS IN THE NEIGHBORHOOD.
I HADN'T THOUGHT OF THAT...
RICK, I'M KIDDING! LIGHTEN UP!
LOOK, IF YOU WANT TO WORRY ABOUT SOME REAL CREATURES...
...LET'S DO THE HAUNTED HOUSE! THERE'S BUNCHES OF 'EM IN THERE!
MAYBE I SHOULD TAKE YOU HOME, ALY. I'M TIRED AND--
AND I'M TIRED OF YOU BEING TIRED!
C'MON!
TRUST ME, THIS'LL BE FUN!

OOHOOOO
RIP
REAL SCARY.
GIVE IT A CHANCE. THE BETTER STUFF COMES LATER.
RIGHT.
HEY, THAT ONE'S PRETTY RADICAL, RICK.
RICK?
ZZZZZ
!
R-RICK, WAKE UP--
--WAKE UP!

HUH?!
IT WAS... IT WAS SO REAL!
IN FACT, IT LOOKED JUST LIKE THE CREATURE YOU DESCRIBED.
THE SPOOK I JUST SAW...
WHAT DID?
... WHILE YOU WERE ASLEEP.
SOON, ON A STREET IN BROOKLYN'S PARK SLOPE SECTION...
SORRY I HAVEN'T BEEN TOO MUCH FUN TONIGHT, ALYSSA.
ANYONE CAN HAVE AN OFF NIGHT--
--EVEN YOU.
BUT NOW YOU OWE ME.
FAIR ENOUGH.
I'LL BE COMING AROUND TO COLLECT REAL SOON.
BUT TRY TO GET SOME SLEEP IN THE MEAN-TIME, OKAY?
SLEEP...
...HOW CAN I EVER SLEEP AGAIN?

IN THE DAYS THAT FOLLOW, RICK CAN'T SLEEP FOR FEAR OF RELEASING THE MONSTER, AND THE CONSEQUENCES ARE DEVASTATING...
I'M OPEN!
NICE PASS, RICKO!
NEXT TIME PASS IT TO A TEAMMATE INSTEAD!
Um, TONIGHT'S ENGLISH LESSON IS ABOUT PROPOSITIONS... PROHIBITIONS...
...er, PREPOSITIONS.
¿QUÉ?
YOU WERE SUPPOSED TO STOP A LEAK, NOT START A FLOOD, RICK.
THE POOR BOY IS TIRED, MORRIS.
YOU SHOULD GET MORE REST, DEAR.
... AND AS YOUR PROFESSOR, I MUST SAY I'M SURPRISED AT THE SHARP, SUDDEN DROP IN YOUR GRADES.
GOTTA STAY AWAKE... CAN'T LET THAT CREATURE COME BACK WHILE I'M SLEEPING... GOTTA FIND A WAY TO STOP IT...
MR. JAVA

RICK'S NEIGHBORHOOD, FOUR NIGHTS LATER...
LEE'S FOODS
24 HOURS • 7 DAYS A WEEK
I'M WORRIED ABOUT YOU, RICK.
YOU LOOK AWFUL.
IT... IT'S THESE *TESTS,* ALYSSA. HAVEN'T BEEN ABLE TO GET MUCH SLEEP LATELY.
STEWED Prunes
OAT BRAN INSTANT COFFEE
SALTINES
HERE IT IS--
--*COFFEE.*
YOU'VE BEEN DRINKING TOO MUCH OF THAT LATELY.
HELPS KEEP ME AWAKE...
...SO I CAN...
...STUDY.
BUT YOU NEVER HAD TO STUDY SO MUCH BEFORE.
ONLY A FEW MORE DAYS TILL MY TESTS ARE OV--
YOU HEARD ME--HAND OVER THE CASH!
HUH--?!
HEY, NATE, LOOK WHO'S HERE--
--IT'S THE *BOY SCOUT!*
WHATSAMATTER, NO PUPPY TO PROTECT YOU THIS TIME?!
THAK
UNG!!
RICK!

STAY DOWN THERE AND YOU WON'T GET HURT! UNDERSTAND?!
GRAB THE GIRL TILL WE GET TO THE CAR!
DONE!
UHH... MY HEAD! GOTTA STAY CONSCIOUS...
...CAN'T LET... THEM TAKE ...ALYSSA...
...CAN'T LET...
...THE CREATURE...
...COME...
...OUT...
BUT THE BLOW TO HIS HEAD PROVES TOO MUCH FOR RICK TO WITHSTAND, AND SO...
...AS HE SLIPS INTO UNCONSCIOUSNESS...

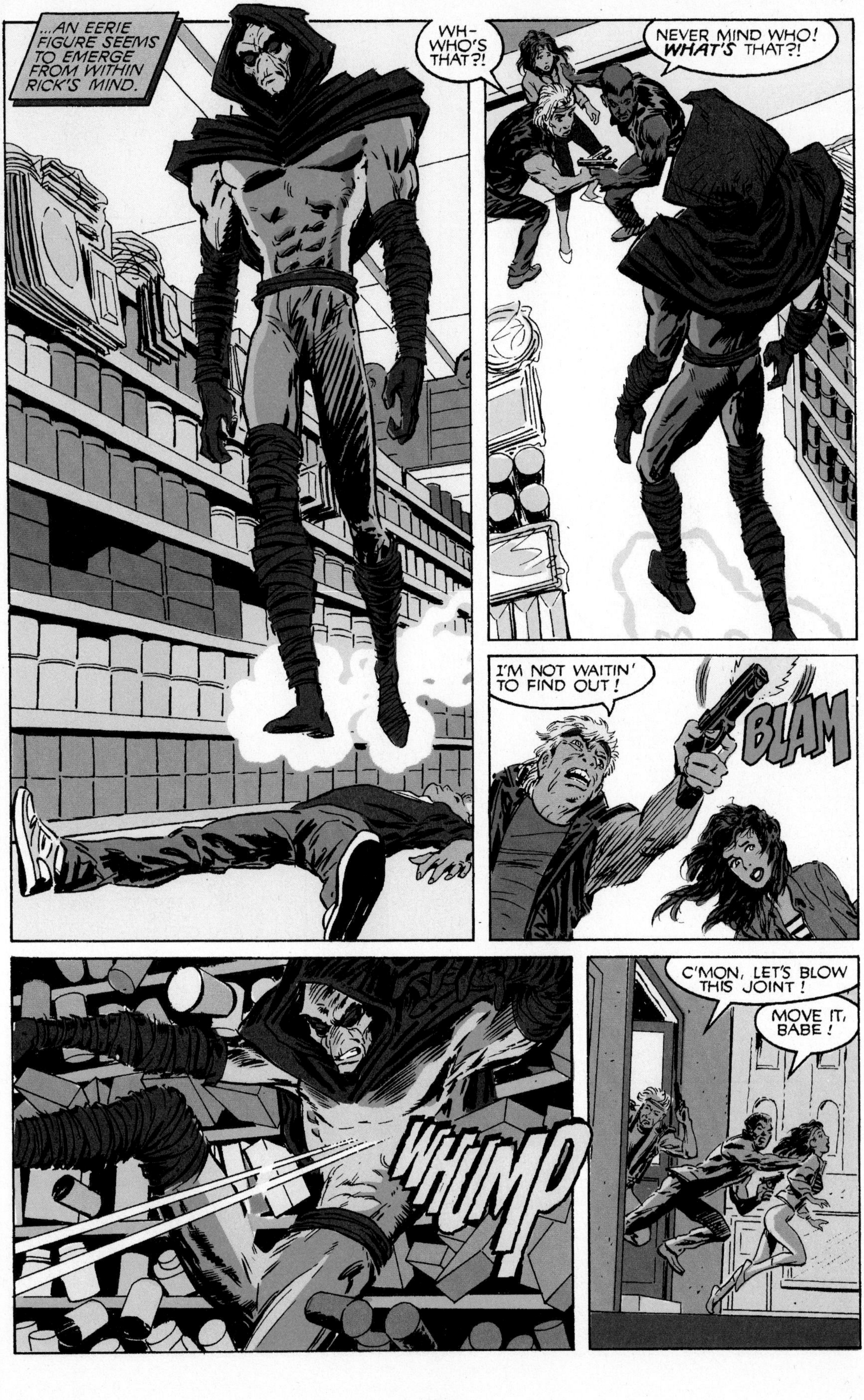
...AN EERIE FIGURE SEEMS TO EMERGE FROM WITHIN RICK'S MIND.
WH- WHO'S THAT?!
NEVER MIND WHO! WHAT'S THAT?!
I'M NOT WAITIN' TO FIND OUT!
BLAM
WHUMP
C'MON, LET'S BLOW THIS JOINT!
MOVE IT, BABE!

MISTER, ARE YOU--
--WHAT THE?!
C-CAN... CAN I HELP YOU... UP?!
BUT THE MYSTERIOUS BEING DOESN'T WAIT FOR AN ANSWER--
--HE ACTS!
SCREE
HEY, WHERE'D THAT COME FROM?!
WONK
IT'S THAT FREAK! HE'S SHOOTIN' SOME WEIRD BEAM AT IT, CAUSIN' IT TO BEND!
STEP ON THE GAS!
I AM!

HE FLIPPED US!
BOING
YIIEEE!!
OOF!
HEY--!
BONK
THIS MAILBOX-- IT'S ALIVE!
SLAM
U.S. MAIL
YOU MORON! HANDSOME JUST STUCK IT TO YOU WITH THAT BEAM O' HIS!
HE'S THE ONE WHO'S ALIVE--
--BUT NOT FOR LONG!
WOMP

KILL HIM! HE'S SOME KINDA MONSTER!
KILL HIM!
I SAW WHAT YOU DID TO THAT BOY!
GET OUT OF OUR NEIGHBORHOOD!
THAT'S IT! RIP HIS UGLY FACE OFF!
BONK
AGHH!
WHAT'S HE DOIN'?!
THE PAVEMENT--
--IT'S SWALLOWIN' US UP!!
NICE TRICK, MELON-HEAD!
LET'S SEE YA DO THAT AGAIN WITH YOUR BRAINS SPLATTERED ALL OVER THE STREET!
Huh--?!

N-NO, PLEASE...
...P-PLEASE DON'T FRY MY FACE OFF!
NOOOO!!
AR-ARE YOU OKAY?
HOW'D I GET UP HERE?!
ARE YOU OKAY?

NO PARKING
WH-WHO ARE YOU?
I AM A SLEEP-WALKER.
MISTER--!
WHA--?!
HUH--?!
RICK, RICK--WHAT HAPPENED TO YOU?!
DON'T WORRY ABOUT ME--WHAT HAPPENED TO YOU?!
THAT CREATURE FROM THE HAUNTED HOUSE--HE POPPED OUT OF NOWHERE AND CAUGHT THE TWO ROBBERS.
AND THEN HE DISAPPEARED--RIGHT BEFORE YOU WALKED OUT OF THE STORE!
OH, NO...
RICK--ARE YOU ALL RIGHT?
IT-IT'S TRUE! WHEN I'M NOT CONSCIOUS... THAT MONSTER COMES OUT!
HOW'M I EVER GONNA SLEEP AGAIN?
RICK--?!
RICK, YOU'VE GOT TO TELL ME--ARE YOU ALL RIGHT!?!
I...I DON'T KNOW, ALYSSA. I JUST DON'T KNOW...
NEXT
THE MYSTERY OF SLEEPWALKER DEEPENS! RICK LOSES MORE SLEEP! AND MARVEL'S MOST SPHERICAL SUPER-VILLAIN DEBUTS--
The ENIGMATIC 8-BALL!

DECEMBER 1990

ARVEL COMICS #1 HC was a hardcover print of Marvel's very first comic book.

ASTER OF KUNG FU: BLEEDING BLACK was one-shot.

EKTRA LIVES AGAIN was an oversized Epic aphic novel.

ARVEL COMICS PRESENTS #69 began a ort serial starring Daredevil.

ARTS AND MINDS was a magazine-sized ic graphic novel.

E NEW ADVENTURES OF CHOLLY AND YTRAP: TILL DEATH DO US PART #1 began Epic limited series.

JANUARY 1991

L SUPERPRO SUPER BOWL SPECIAL was a e-shot.

D MCKEEVER'S METROPOL #1 began an ic ongoing series.

ARVEL ILLUSTRATED: THE SWIMSUIT ISSUE as a magazine-sized parody one-shot.

ARVEL COMICS PRESENTS #72 began a rial featuring the origin of Wolverine.

IE DESTROYER was a one-shot based on the vel characters.

FEBRUARY 1991

EUTENANT BLUEBERRY #1: THE IRON HORSE gan a magazine-sized Epic graphic novel ries reprinting translated French comics.

GHTCAT was a one-shot.

OXIC AVENGER #1 began an ongoing series sed on the movie character.

ARVEL TALES #248 began a sporadic serial arring Petey, the young Peter Parker.

OCTOR STRANGE/GHOST RIDER SPECIAL as a reprint one-shot.

ARVEL FANFARE #56 began a short serial arring Shanna the She-Devil.

MARCH 1991

LACK PANTHER: PANTHER'S PREY #1 began limited series.

WEET XVI #1 began an ongoing series.

EADLY FOES OF SPIDER-MAN #1 began a nited series.

EATHLOK SPECIAL #1 began a limited reprint eries.

HE ORIGINAL ADVENTURES OF CHOLLY & YTRAP was a magazine-sized Epic reprint ne-shot.

ARVEL QUARTERLY REPORT: 1ST QUARTER 991 began a thrice-yearly ongoing series corporate stock report foldouts done in seudo-comic style.

APRIL 1991

ARVEL COMICS PRESENTS #77 began a nort serial starring Nick Fury and Dracula.

CAR WARRIORS #1 began an Epic limited series.

DAMAGE CONTROL #1 began a limited series.

SAMURAI CAT #1 began an Epic limited humor series based on the novel characters.

THOR #433 featured Eric Masterson adopting the Thor identity and taking over the series' lead role.

MAY 1991

CAPTAIN AMERICA #387 began a short backup serial starring the Red Skull.

ALPHA FLIGHT SPECIAL #1 began a limited reprint series.

ORIGINAL GHOST RIDER RIDES AGAIN #1 began a limited reprint series.

PUNISHER: P.O.V. #1 began a limited series.

DOUBLE DRAGON #1 began a limited series based on the video game characters.

INFINITY GAUNTLET #1 began a limited series.

MARVEL SUPER-HEROES #6 began a short serial starring the X-Men.

NEW MUTANTS ANNUAL #7 began a short backup serial starring Freedom Force.

THE OLYMPIANS #1 began a sporadic Epic limited series.

DEATHLOK #1 began an ongoing series.

JUNE 1991

MARVEL COMICS PRESENTS #82 began a serial starring Firestar.

AMAZING SPIDER-MAN ANNUAL #25 began a short backup serial starring the Outlaws.

PUNISHER SUMMER SPECIAL #1 began a yearly ongoing series.

NFL SUPERPRO SPECIAL EDITION was a reprint one-shot.

JULY 1991

TERMINATOR 2: JUDGMENT DAY was a comic-sized one-shot reprint of Marvel's movie adaptation.

WONDER MAN #1 began an ongoing series.

TERMINATOR 2: JUDGMENT DAY #1 began a limited series reprinting Marvel's movie adaptation.

THE TRANSMUTATION OF IKE GARUDA #1 began a sporadic Epic limited series.

AVENGERS: DEATH TRAP, THE VAULT was a magazine-sized one-shot, the first not to bear the "Marvel Graphic Novel" branding.

MARVEL COMICS PRESENTS #85 began a serial starring the Beast.

THE ADVENTURES OF CAPTAIN AMERICA #1 began a limited series.

ALIEN LEGION: TENANTS OF HELL #1 began an Epic limited series.

MARVEL MILESTONE EDITION: X-MEN #1 began a sporadic series featuring facsimile reprints of various important Marvel comics.

AUGUST 1991

NFL SUPERPRO #1 began an ongoing series.

X-MEN #1 began an ongoing series.

CAPTAIN PLANET AND THE PLANETEERS #1 began an ongoing series based on the animated TV characters.

SEPTEMBER 1991

CAPTAIN AMERICA #394 began a short backup serial starring B.A.D. Girls, Inc.

CAPTAIN CONFEDERACY #1 began an Epic limited series, the sequel to a Steeldragon Press series.

ETERNALS: THE HEROD FACTOR was a one-shot.

LEGION OF NIGHT #1 began a limited series.

PIRATES OF DARK WATER #1 began a limited series based on the animated TV characters.

EPIC LITE was an Epic humor one-shot.

SPIDER-MAN SAGA #1 began a limited reference series.

TOMB OF DRACULA #1 began an Epic limited series.

SLEEZE BROTHERS: SOME LIKE IT FRESH was an Epic one-shot.

CLIVE BARKER'S BOOK OF THE DAMNED: A HELLRAISER COMPANION #1 began an Epic limited series based on the movie characters.

OCTOBER 1991

MARVEL COMICS PRESENTS #90 began a serial starring Cable and Ghost Rider.

WEAVEWORLD #1 began an Epic limited series novel adaptation.

BILL & TED'S EXCELLENT COMIC BOOK #1 began an ongoing series based on the movie characters.

THE DESTROYER #1 began a limited series based on the novel characters.

HELLRAISER/NIGHTBREED: JIHAD #1 began an Epic limited series based on the characters from both movies.

MARSHAL BLUEBERRY: THE LOST DUTCHMAN'S MINE was a magazine-sized Epic graphic novel reprinting translated French comics.

NOVEMBER 1991

AN AMERICAN TAIL: FIEVEL GOES WEST #1 began a limited series reprinting Marvel's movie adaptation.

MARVEL COMICS PRESENTS #93 began a short serial starring Nova (Frankie Raye).

HOOK was a comic-sized one-shot reprint of Marvel's movie adaptation.

MARVEL HOLIDAY SPECIAL #1 began a yearly ongoing series.

X-FORCE #1, published in June 1991, began an ongoing series starring the hard-hitting mutant strike force formerly known as the New Mutants.

X-FORCE
APPROVED BY THE COMICS CODE AUTHORITY
LIEFELD.

X-FORCE
MARVEL COMICS
CABLE
X-FORCE
MARVEL COMICS
SHATTERSTAR
X-FORCE
MARVEL COMICS
DEADPOOL
X-FORCE
MARVEL COMICS
SUNSPOT & GIDEON
MARVEL COMICS
X-FORCE

X-Force #1 was bagged with one of several different trading cards.
Art by Rob Liefeld.

NTARCTICA. JUNE 4. SEVEN SILENT GURES STAND MOTIONLESS, ROODING, ALONE WITH THEIR HOUGHTS...
... AND THE WEIGHT OF THE ROAD THEY HAVE CHOSEN TO FOLLOW...
...ONCE THEY WERE CHILDREN, DELIGHTING IN A DREAM...
. NOW, THEY RE SOLDIERS, IGHTING FOR HE FREEDOM OF THEIR KIND.
SENSOR SCAN CHECKS OUT?
YUP. WE'RE RIGHT ABOVE THEM.
AND THE ELECTRO-MAGNETIC SCRAMBLER HAS MUSSED UP THEIR DEFENSE SYSTEMS, RIGHT?
DO YOU EVEN NEED TO ASK, KIDDO?
LET'S DO IT, THEN.
REMEMBER, THEY'RE PACKING A LOT OF FIREPOWER.
AS ARE WE. WE HAVE WAITED LONG ENOUGH FOR THIS OPPORTUNITY.
I KNOW.
TODAY, THE TERRORIST ACTIONS OF THE MUTANT LIBERATION FRONT...
...COME TO AN END!
A FORCE TO BE RECKONED WITH

SOME WOULD CALL THEM HEROES, SOME WOULD CALL THEM REBELS. THEY FIGHT FOR A FADING DREAM IN A WORLD OF NIGHTMARES --
CANNONBALL
DOMINO
WARPATH
FERAL
THE NEXT GENERATION OF MUTANTS ACTION BROUGHT TO YOU BY:
ROB LIEFELD - EVERYTHING BUT...
FABIAN NICIEZA - WORDS
CHRIS ELIOPOULOS - LETTERS
BRAD VANCATA - COLOR ART
BOB HARRAS - BAGGY EYES
TOM DeFALCO - BAGGY BOSS

STAN LEE PRESENTS
X-FORCE
Children of the atom, born as mutants with fantastic powers and abilities--bound together as soldiers fighting a dirty war for the survival of their species.
CABLE
SHATTERSTAR
BOOM BOOM
[redacted]

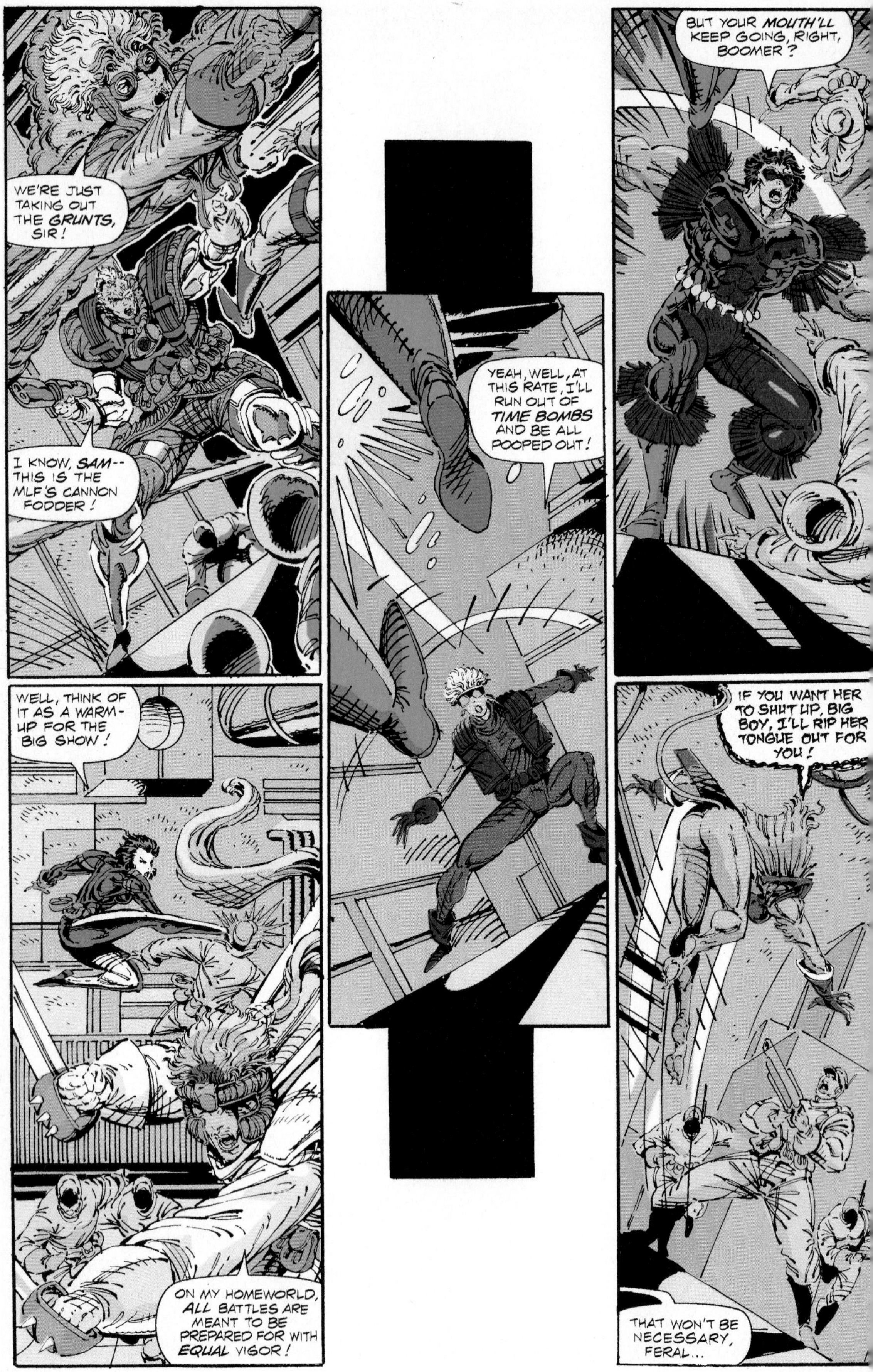

WE'RE JUST TAKING OUT THE GRUNTS, SIR!
I KNOW, SAM-- THIS IS THE MLF'S CANNON FODDER!
WELL, THINK OF IT AS A WARM-UP FOR THE BIG SHOW!
ON MY HOMEWORLD, ALL BATTLES ARE MEANT TO BE PREPARED FOR WITH EQUAL VIGOR!
YEAH, WELL, AT THIS RATE, I'LL RUN OUT OF TIME BOMBS AND BE ALL POOPED OUT!
BUT YOUR MOUTH'LL KEEP GOING, RIGHT, BOOMER?
IF YOU WANT HER TO SHUT UP, BIG BOY, I'LL RIP HER TONGUE OUT FOR YOU!
THAT WON'T BE NECESSARY, FERAL...

THOOM
... BUT WE'LL KEEP YOUR OFFER IN MIND, THANK YOU.
CABLE-- ACTIVITY AT MARK 32!
FOREARM, KAMIKAZE, WILDSIDE, AND REAPER!
I TOLD YOU TO LEARN OUR METHOD OF TELLING TIME--
--ONE O'CLOCK TO TWELVE-- DON'T USE THAT MARK GARBAGE FOR POSITIONING AGAIN!
UNDERSTOOD. CAN I ATTACK NOW?
YEAH, HAVE A PARTY.
OOOH-- SIC 'EM, TIGER!
WHOEVER IS FOOL ENOUGH TO LEAD THE ATTACK IS MINE!

COME TO PLAY, BUFFOON...
...COME TO DIE!
SHIN
KLIN
THE KILLING GAME IS BEST LEFT TO THOSE WILLING TO KILL, SHATTERSTAR!
YOU DOUBT MY HONOR AS A WARRIOR?
THAT IS YOUR SECOND MISTAKE, REAPER...

SHAKK
...YOUR FIRST WAS IN CHOOSING TO DO BATTLE WITH ME!
NNFF-- YOU WON'T KILL ME -- WOOGH-- IT'S NOT YOUR WAY--
MY WAY AND THE WAY OF MY MATES MAY BE TWO COMPLETELY DIFFERENT THINGS, REAPER...

...LUCKY FOR YOU...
CHAK
... I AM WILLING TO TEMPER MY ACTIONS ON THIS WORLD TO SUIT THOSE OF MY NEW COMRADES IN ARMS!
FOR THE TIME BEING, AT LEAST.
YOU GET STRONGER EVERY TIME WE MEET, FOREARM...
...KIND OF REMINDS ME OF SOMEONE ON MY TEAM...
...THE BOY KEEPS GETTING STRONGER AND STRONGER...
BUT NOT STRONG ENOUGH TO HELP YOU, EH, CABLE?

KAPOW!
I WOULDN'T SAY THAT...
NICE SHOT, WARPATH.
THANK YOU.
NONE OF THIS MATTERS--WE CAN TAKE AS MANY OF THEIR PIECES AS THEY OFFER, BUT WE HAVE TO NAIL THE KING...

...WE HAVE TO NAIL STRYFE!
INDEED YOU DO, CABLE... INDEED YOU DO...
THUMBELINA, CONTACT ZERO-- BEGIN TELEPORTATION OF THE REMAINING MLF MEMBERS TO A SAFER LOCATION.
WHAT OF THE FOUR IN DIRECT COMBAT NOW?
THEY ARE LOST TO US FOR NOW.
BETTER TO LOSE SOME FINGERS IN ORDER TO SAVE THE WHOLE HAND, NO?

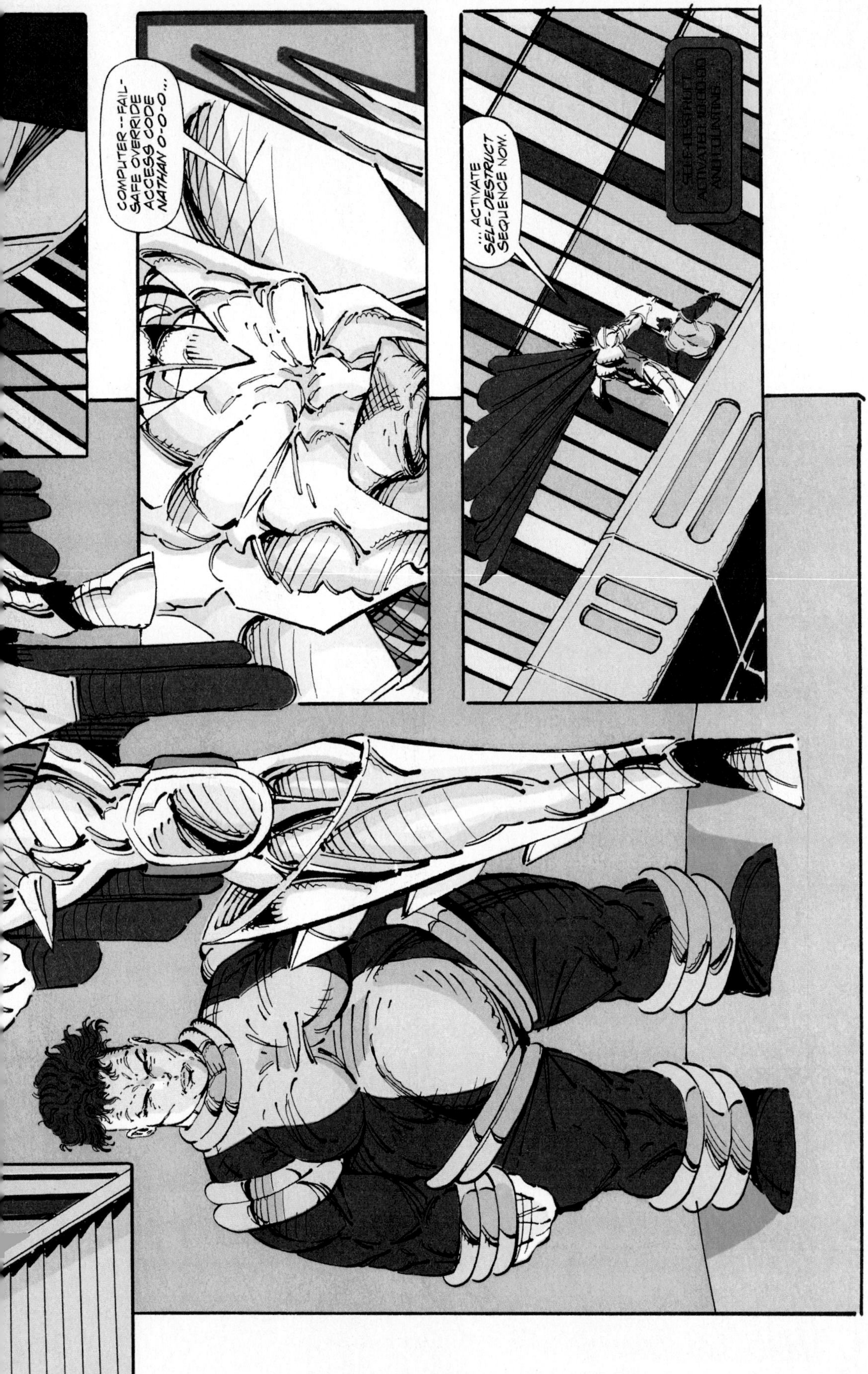

COMPUTER -- FAIL-SAFE OVERRIDE ACCESS CODE NATHAN 0-0-0-0...
... ACTIVATE SELF-DESTRUCT SEQUENCE NOW.
SELF-DESTRUCT ACTIVATED 10:00:00 AND COUNTING

954 AND COUNTING
YO-- WILDSIDE!
YOU SCRATCH MY BACK... I'LL SCRATCH YOURS!!
OOH. PROMISES, PROMISES. MUST BE MY ANIMAL MAGNETISM...
KITTY-CAT'S PURRRRFECTLY PREPARED TO FIGHT, HUH?
OKEY-DOKEY...

LET'S MAKE YOU HACK UP A FURBALL-- WHUDDYASAY, WHUDDYASAY?!
I SAY YOU TALK TOO MUCH...
HACK
WHAT'S THE MATTER... CAT GOT YOUR TONGUE?
OH YEAH, SHE DOES...
SNAP!
I'LL COME AROUND TO HEAR WHAT YOU HAVE TO SAY REAL SOON... SAY IN A FEW MONTHS WHEN YOUR JAW HEALS...

9:42:33 AND COUNTING
FERAL -- DID YOU KILL HIM?
NOOOO -- BUT IF YOU GIVE ME A MINUTE...
DOWN, TIGER -- SHEATHE THE CLAWS -- YOU CAN KILL IN SELF-DEFENSE, NOT FOR SPORT!
I WALK AWAY TODAY AND THAT'S ONE MORE PERSON WHO COULD NAIL ME TOMORROW!
RRRUMMMMBBBLE
WHAT NOW? THE PLACE IS FALLING APART -- FALL BACK, TEAM!

FSHMMMM
ZHURRO-- GUD TUHC U--
ZERO PORTED WILDSIDE AWAY! WHAT'S THEIR GAME?
THEY RETREAT LIKE WHIPPED PUPS!
THERE HAS TO BE MORE TO IT THAN THAT!
SQUAD--TWELVE O'CLOCK--UP ON THE LANDING--
STRYFE!

YOU'RE DEAD. END OF STORY.
POONTH POONTH POONTH
I THINK NOT, NATHAN-- OR WHATEVER IT IS YOU'RE CALLING YOURSELF THIS TIME...
...I THINK NOT.
FSHMMM
FSHAK
HE GOT AWAY!
STAB HIS EYES!
HE GOT AWAY AGAIN!!

SHOOMP
GOOD ADVICE, FOREARM TRIED SNEAKIN' UP ON YOU. THIS PLACE IS COMING APART FASTER THAN OUR BATTLE PLAN.
MULTIPLE CHARGES THROUGHOUT THE COMPLEX...
...STRYFE MUST HAVE ACTIVATED A SELF-DESTRUCT SYSTEM...
WHAT THE--
OKAY, WAKE UP! PAY ATTENTION, YOU OLD FOOL!
SCOUT CRAFT-ONE--LOCK ON TO OUR COORDINATES--
--BODYSLIDE BY SIX--
SHYYNN
THE WHOLE JOINT'S ROCKIN', BOSS!

SHY YNN
SCOUT--MAINTAIN AUTO-FUNCTION--TAKE OFF, DOUBLE-TIME!
FRRSHWO
KRAKA TA THOOM
THIS IS WHAT WE WERE PLANNIN' FOR?
SEEMED KINDA SIMPLE FOR SIX WEEKS O' TRAININ'.
ALL THAT COUNTS IS THAT HE GOT AWAY AGAIN...
MANHATTAN. JUNE 5. 8:34 A.M.

SCOUT -- OVERRIDE AUTO -- IMPLEMENT MANUAL --
YOU JUST KNOW HOW I LOOOOVE TO HIT THE GAS MYSELF...
SVVYEESH
IT GOES DOWN IN THE WIN COLUMN -- THAT'S WHAT COUNTS.
AIN'T THERE A LITTLE MORE TO IT THAN WINNIN' AND LOSIN'?
WHAT ABOUT THE KINDA FASHION STATEMENT WE MAKE?
THAT SHOULD COUNT FER SOMETHIN', RIGHT BIG MUCK-A-MUCK?

THE MAJESTIC PENTHOUSE APARTMENT OF A VERY MYSTERIOUS MAN NAMED GIDEON.
SWEEP PATTERN RIGHT, 'BERTO-- I HAVE THE LEFT!
I HAVE PERFORMED THESE KINDS OF EXERCISES SINCE I WAS BUT A CHILD, MY FRIEND.
I CAN DO THEM IN MY SLEEP!
SHKLUNG
WELL, KIDDO, MUCH AS I DISAGREE WITH MANY OF THE PHILO-SOPHIES OF YOUR FORMER MENTOR, CHARLES XAVIER--
I KNOW, I KNOW-- THE ONE YOU DO AGREE WITH IS THAT ONLY THROUGH CONSTANT PRACTICE CAN WE HONE OUR MUTANT ABILITIES TO THEIR RAZOR'S EDGE.
THAT'S ANOTHER ONE I CAN GO THROUGH IN MY SLEEP!
NEVERTHELESS, MR. SMART ALECK-- IT PAYS TO BE PREPARED -- IN BUSINESS AND IN PLEASURE. IT COULD MEAN THE DIFFERENCE BETWEEN LIFE AND DEATH!
AND I HAVE BEEN, GIDEON-- HAVEN'T I?
ROBERTO...IN THE LAST SIX MONTHS I HAVE SEEN YOU GRASP THE INTRICACIES OF BUSINESS AS IF BORN TO THE ROLE..

OUR LATE FATHER WOULD BE PROUD OF YOU ... AS AM I.
YOU HAVE COME A LONG WAY IN A SHORT TIME.
I WOULD CERTAINLY SAY SO. IN FACT, IT'S TIME TO ADVANCE YOU TO THE NEXT STEP...
... YOU HAVE LEARNED TO UNDERSTAND POWER...
... NOW YOU HAVE TO LEARN HOW TO USE IT!
THE JANKOS STOCK BUYOUT?
THREE O'CLOCK. WORLD TRADE CENTER.
BRING SEVERAL TOURNIQUETS.
NO LONGER AM I THE NEW MUTANT-- THE NOVICE STUDENT.
THEY'RE GOING TO NEED SOME WHEN WE BLEED THEM TO DEATH!
THE PUPIL LEARNS EVERY DAY...

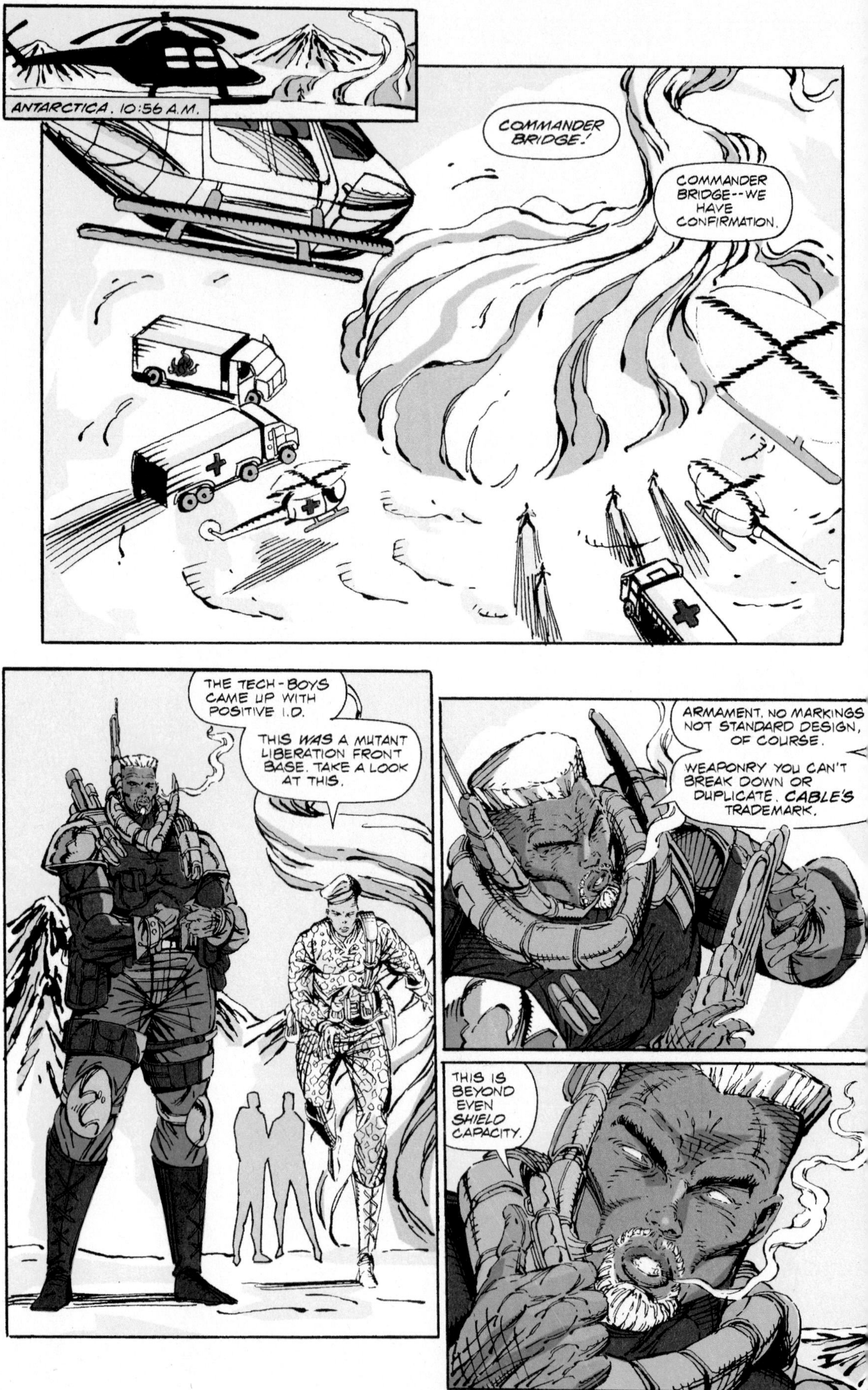

ANTARCTICA. 10:56 A.M.
COMMANDER BRIDGE!
COMMANDER BRIDGE--WE HAVE CONFIRMATION.
THE TECH-BOYS CAME UP WITH POSITIVE I.D.
THIS *WAS* A MUTANT LIBERATION FRONT BASE. TAKE A LOOK AT THIS.
ARMAMENT. NO MARKINGS NOT STANDARD DESIGN, OF COURSE.
WEAPONRY YOU CAN'T BREAK DOWN OR DUPLICATE. *CABLE'S* TRADEMARK.
THIS IS BEYOND EVEN *SHIELD* CAPACITY.

CONTACT FURY. TELL HIM THE SIT-OP IS UNDER CONTROL.
YES, COMMANDER ANYTHING ELSE?
YES. CALL ME GEORGE. I DON'T LIKE TITLES OR LABELS.
HERO. VILLAIN. HUMAN. MUTANT. NONE OF IT MATTERS SQUAT TO ME.
ONLY RIGHT AND WRONG.
AND IN THIS PARTICULAR CASE, IT'S STARTING TO BECOME CRYSTAL CLEAR.
CABLE AND HIS LITTLE ARMY OF TOY SOLDIERS HAVE TO BE BROUGHT DOWN!
THE ADIRONDACK MOUNTAINS IN UPSTATE NEW YORK. 2:26 P.M.

PLACE IS REALLY STARTIN' T'COME 'ROUND, SIR.
AH HAD READ PROFESSOR XAVIER'S FILES ON LARRY TRASK'S OLD SENTINEL BASE...
...I DIDN'T THINK IT WAS STILL AROUND.
IT'S GOT EVERYTHIN WE NEED. COMPUTER SET-UP'S GREAT.
REC-ROOM AND THE FACILITIES'RE OKAY, TOO.
BOOM BOOM HOOKED UP THE TV SATELLITE SO WE CAN GET TWO HUNDRED CHANNELS!
AND SHE STILL CAN'T FIND NOTHIN' T'WATCH.
BOOMER'S ALREADY CALLIN' IT LE CHALET SCHWARZKOPF.
THE READY ROOM'S PERFECT FOR MISSION PREP.
LIVIN' QUARTERS ARE KINDA CRAMPED. FRANKLY, WE WERE ALL KINDA HOPIN' T'HAVE OUR OWN ROOMS.
UHM... ARE YOU LISTENIN' TO ME?
YUP.
NEED A HAND WITH THE DIAGNOSTIC CHECK?
NOPE.
CAN I ASK YOU A QUESTION?
YUP.
WE HAD THE MLF IN THE PALM OF OUR HANDS YESTERDAY.
WHY'D WE LET 'EM GET AWAY?

WE SEVERELY CRIPPLED BOTH THEIR OPERATIONS AND THEIR MANPOWER.
TO HAVE TRIED TO GO BEYOND THAT WOULD HAVE JEOPARDIZED OUR UNIT MORE THAN I WOULD HAVE PREFERED.
AH WASN'T SURE THAT YOU CARED ABOUT US ONE WAY OR THE OTHER.
I DO.
BUT YOU HELD US BACK. ARE YOU AFRAID OF STRYFE KILLING ONE OF US THE WAY HE KILLED YOUR SON?
AH... THAT... A SLIGHT MISCONCEPTION... BORN OF YOUR OLD FRIEND RICTOR'S NAIVETTÉ...
THE YOUNG MAN IN QUESTION WAS NAMED TYLER.
HE WAS LIKE A SON TO ME, NOT MY FLESH AND BLOOD.
A PART OF MY SOUL MAYBE... BUT NOT MY BODY.
WE WORKED TOGETHER, MUCH LIKE I DO WITH X-FORCE NOW.
AFTER A YEAR OR SO WE DRIFTED APART...

HE HOOKED UP WITH STRYFE AND THE MLF.
THEN WHAT HAPPENED?
HE DIED DURING A TERRORIST OPERATION.
IT WAS A POSITION HE WAS PLACED IN BY STRYFE.
I HAVE SEVERAL REASONS FOR WANTING TO SEE THAT ARMORED MAGGOT DEAD.
TYLER'S DEATH IS ONLY ONE OF THEM.
YOU NEVER TOLD ME ANY OF THIS. WHY?
YOU NEVER ASKED.
EVERY DAY I LEARN SOME-THIN' ABOUT YOU THAT EITHER MAKES ME WANNA BUST YOU ONE OR RESPECT YOU EVEN MORE.
WAIT--DON'T TELL ME--RE-ENACTING YOUR FAVORITE SCENES FROM "LOVE CONNECTION," RIGHT?
DON'T YOU KNOW IT.
SAM--THE OTHERS ARE WAITING FOR YOU UPSTAIRS.
DOMINO. A PLEASURE AS ALWAYS.
SHOOT--I'M LATE FOR OUR WORKOUT!

ATER,
OLKS...
MOOD WAS THICK ENOUGH TO CUT WITH A BUZZSAW--
--WHAT WERE YOU TWO BEEF-BAGS TALKING ABOUT?
SAM WAS ASKING ABOUT TYLER.
I TAKE IT THE CURIOSITY WAS PROVOKED?
WELL, THEY WERE ALL JUST WONDERING WHAT THE GRUDGE MATCH AGAINST STRYFE WAS ALL ABOUT.
HOW MUCH MORE DID YOU DECIDE TO DISCLOSE TO THEM?
OH, I TOLD THEM ABOUT THAT BEAUTY MARK IN THE SHAPE OF A MAGNUM ON YOUR--
HEY!
WHAT DO YOU THINK YOU'RE DOING?!!
SIMPLIFYING MY GRUNT WORK.
DON'T WORRY--I WOULDN'T HAVE DONE IT IF ANYONE ELSE WAS AROUND.
WELL, IF YOU'RE GOING TO HOLD BACK ON TELLING THESE KIDS EVERYTHING THERE IS TO KNOW ABOUT YOU--
--YOU'D BETTER BE PREPARED TO SING LIKE A CANARY IF THEY CATCH YOU PULLING STUNTS LIKE THAT!

WHEN IT'S TIME FOR THEM TO LEARN, THEY'LL LEARN.
FINE -- JUST DON'T EXPECT THEM TO JUMP THROUGH HOOPS WITHOUT BARKING ONCE IN A WHILE.
THEIR BARK IS NOTHING COMPARED TO MY BITE.
FROM NOW ON JUST BE A LITTLE MORE DISCREET--OKAY--?!
MANHATTAN. THE WORLD TRADE CENTER. 2:59 P.M.
THE JANKOS MEETING. GIDEON AND DACOSTA.
STEP RIGHT THIS WAY, SIRS.
CAN I GET YOU ANYTHING?
THE NAME OF THE PERFUME YOU'RE WEARING--
--IF I COULD OWN ITS MANUFACTURES, I COULD OWN MEN'S MINDS AS READILY AS YOU MOST SURELY DO.
NOT NOW...
:SIGH: VERY WELL THEN, AN ESPRESSO, IF YOU PLEASE.
CERTAINLY SIR.
IT'S CALLED THE ALLURE.
THEN IT IS APTLY NAMED...

GIDEON, MR. DACOSTA, IF YOU COULD PLEASE HAVE A SEAT, WE CAN BEGIN.
IS SHE--?
AND THEN SOME.
PRETTY ENOUGH TO PITY.
I AM ARIANNA JANKOS.
THIS MEETING WAS CALLED IN ORDER TO BUY OUT WHAT REMAINS OF MY COMPANY HOLDINGS AGAINST MY BETTER WISHES.
ALLOW ME TO INTRODUCE TO YOU A GENTLEMAN WHO IS GOING TO PREVENT THAT FROM HAPPENING.
HIS NAME IS TOM CASSIDY.
HE'S HERE TO MAKE ALL OF YOU A COUNTER-OFFER YOU SIMPLY CAN'T REFUSE!
AFTERNOON, LADIES AND GENTS...

THAT'S BLACK TOM! HE'S BANSHEE'S COUSIN!
NOT HERE. NOT NOW.
DROGA! HIS HISTORY IS REPLETE WITH TERRORIST ACTS!
WE WAIT. WE BIDE OUR TIME. WE SEE WHAT HIS GAME IS.
LEARN HOW TO WIN THE HAND WITH THE CARDS YOU'RE DEALT.
THE LOVELY LADY, ARIANNA HAS REQUESTED THE PLEASURE OF MY COMPANY TO ASSURE THAT SHE DOES NOT LOSE HERS.
IN ORDER TO DO THA WE'LL NEED TO EXTOR SCADS OF MONEY FROM YOUR RESPECTI CORPORATIONS.
INDEED... SCADS...
SO FOR THE NEXT FEW HOURS... DAYS... WEEKS, EVEN--
--YOU WILL ALL BE MY UNWILLING GUESTS!
TO BE LESS COY ABOUT THE DEAL--CALL YOURSELVES MY HOSTAGES!

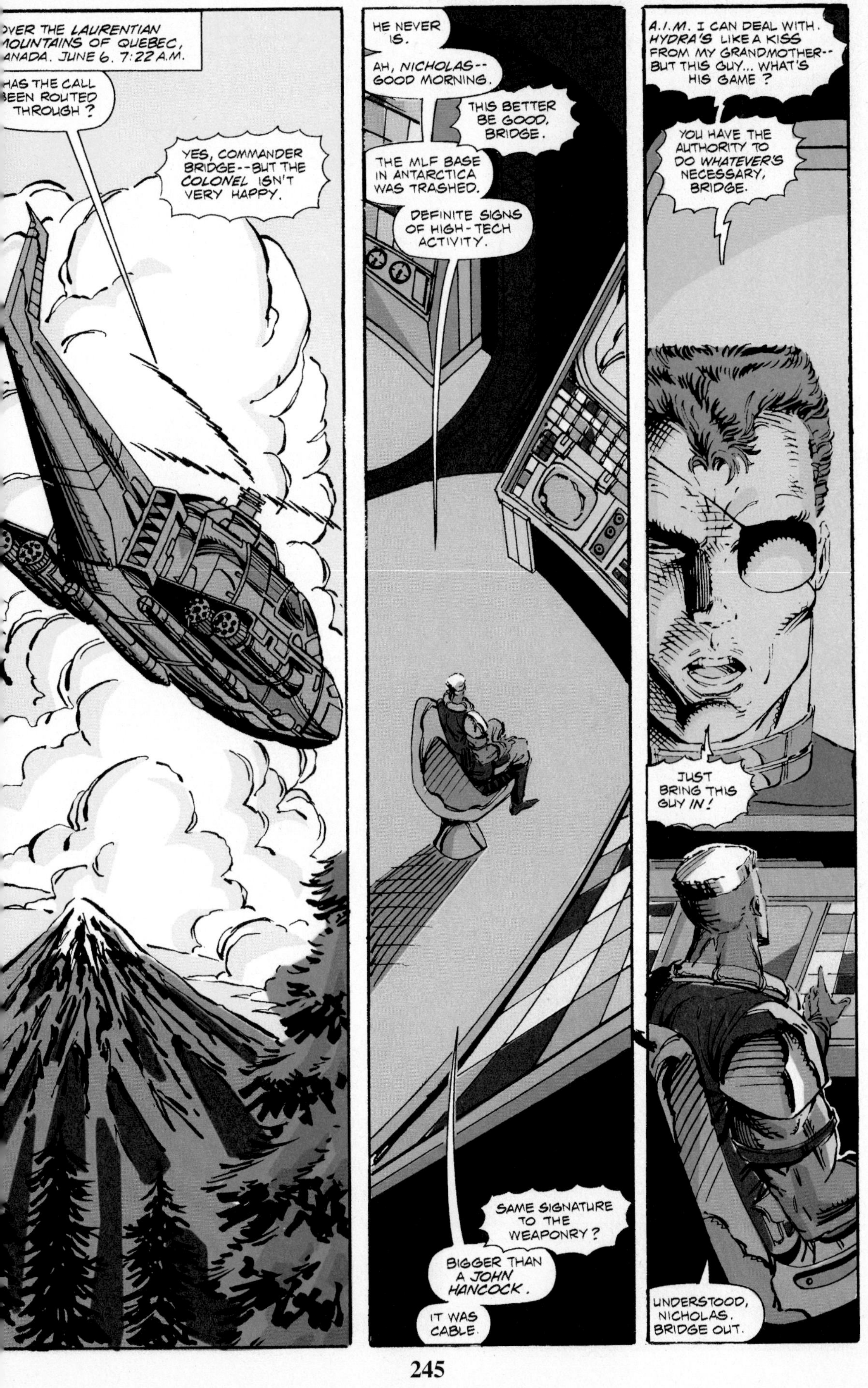
OVER THE LAURENTIAN MOUNTAINS OF QUEBEC, CANADA. JUNE 6. 7:22 A.M.
HAS THE CALL BEEN ROUTED THROUGH?
YES, COMMANDER BRIDGE--BUT THE COLONEL ISN'T VERY HAPPY.
HE NEVER IS.
AH, NICHOLAS--GOOD MORNING.
THIS BETTER BE GOOD, BRIDGE.
THE MLF BASE IN ANTARCTICA WAS TRASHED.
DEFINITE SIGNS OF HIGH-TECH ACTIVITY.
SAME SIGNATURE TO THE WEAPONRY?
BIGGER THAN A JOHN HANCOCK.
IT WAS CABLE.
A.I.M. I CAN DEAL WITH. HYDRA'S LIKE A KISS FROM MY GRANDMOTHER--BUT THIS GUY... WHAT'S HIS GAME?
YOU HAVE THE AUTHORITY TO DO WHATEVER'S NECESSARY, BRIDGE.
JUST BRING THIS GUY IN!
UNDERSTOOD, NICHOLAS. BRIDGE OUT.

IT HAD TO COME DOWN TO THIS, DIDN'T IT ?
I SHOULDN'T BE SURPRISED.
OUT OF ALL OF US. YOU WERE ALWAYS AN ENIGMA...
...THE SILENT EXPLOSION WE CALLED YOU...
PATCH ME THROUGH ON A SECURITY ACCESS LINE TO GENERAL CLARKE IN CANADIAN MILITARY.
I WANT DEPARTMENT K BROUGHT IN ON THIS.
BRIDGE TO COMM-CENTER.
COMM-CENTER HERE.
IT'S TIME TO CALL IN WEAPON X!
OF COURSE--
TO BE CONTINUED!

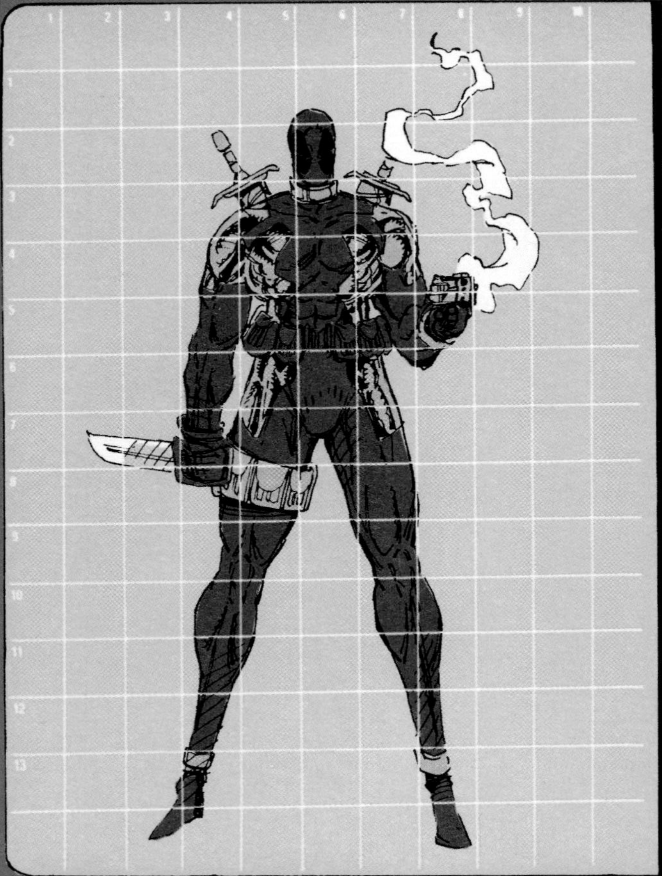

Listing 245.7

DEADPOOL

The man you have to love to hate and hate to love. As hard as it may be to believe, Deadpool gives even mercenaries a bad name. I've only tangled with him once, when Tolliver hired him to come after me, but that was enough.

For all his incessant blabbing, Deadpool is still an incredibly capable opponent, having mastered several fighting techniques from savate to chewing someone's ear off!

He's also shown himself to be proficient in multiple weapons-use, ranging from bolos to a bo staff. Known weapons preferences include: long sword, throwing stars, garrote wires, small-range cluster bombs and of course, his mouth.

Though my personal experience with Deadpool is limited, former associates of mine from the Wild Pack have had extensive dealings with him. Unfortunately, save for Domino, I haven't maintained contact with any of them (the past is best left buried, I always say).

According to some reports, Deadpool's desire for wealth and material gain has been so strong, that he has actually been known to switch allegiances to the other side in the middle of a fight if the price was right!

This information could be put to good use should the situation arise where one of my soldiers' lives was threatened by this imbecilic, but deadly, assassin.

On a personal note, for purely selfish reasons, I'd love another crack at this guy. He deserves to enjoy the feel of my fist in his big mouth once or twice. Or three times . . .

CABLE GUIDE

A LOOK INTO THE FILES OF X-FORCE'S MYSTERIOUS LEADER.

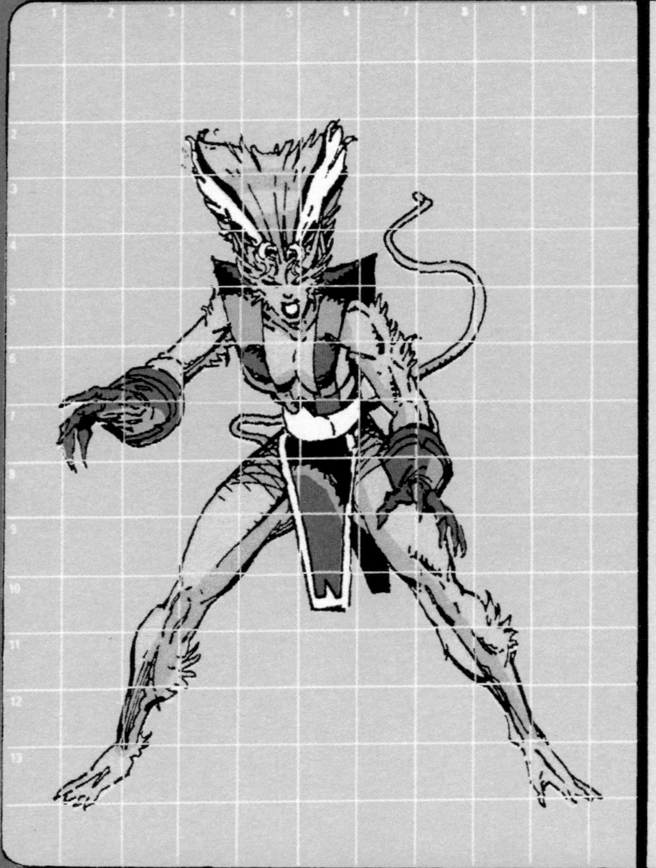

Listing 240.4

FERAL

A dangerous, enigmatic young woman, whose short tenure with our unit has fostered more questions regarding her past, present and future than answers. Feral, who's chosen not to reveal whether she has any other name, is a mutant with feline features and attributes.

Her reflexes and acrobatic abilities are remarkable: her sensory perceptions are enhanced to animal levels--her superior sight and sense of smell alone make her an ideal interdiction operative.

It is not her fighting skills I can call into question, because they are excellent. Nor is it her determination or perseverance over adversity, which are forged in steel. My real doubts, and they're doubts which are increasing almost every day, is Feral's personality.

She is, at times, a ferocious, almost bestial fighter, and at others a coy, deferential, manipulative vamp. More and more, I realize that she has the psychological attributes of a house cat--domesticated, but capable of malicious intent, fickle, contradictory behavior and hair-trigger violent tendencies.

Feral will sit on your lap, purring for attention one second, and just as easily kill a passing bird and drop it at your feet for approval the next. She has shown an inclination (say it--a preference) for killing. Normally, I would laud that attribute in one of my soldiers, but in Feral, I see a potential for trouble.

What if she can't control herself--or worse, we can't control her? What will I have to do then? I think I'd rather not find out...

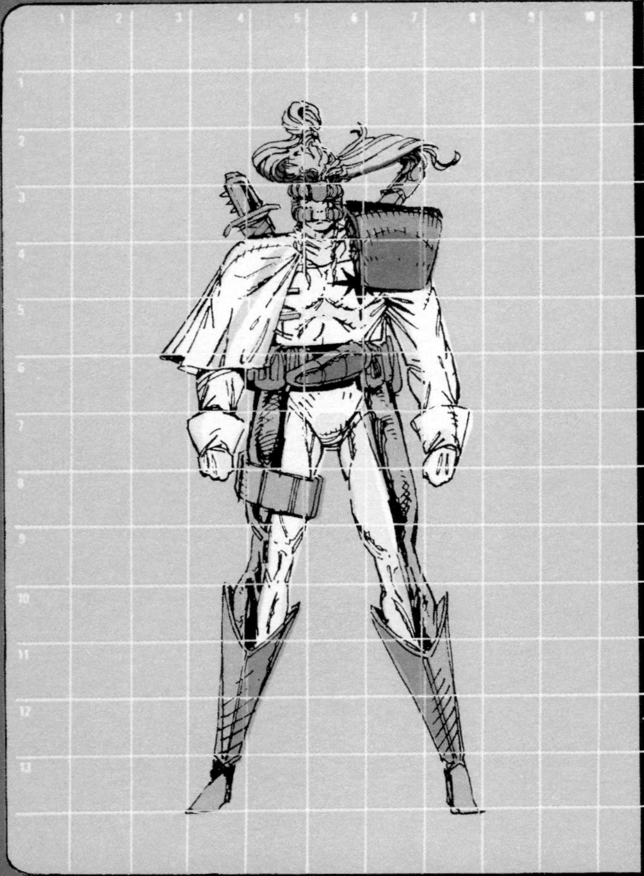

Listing 240.3

SHATTERSTAR

This mysterious warrior from another dimension appeared in our former bunker base seeking the help of the X-Men in combating the tyrannical rulers of his homeworld.

He found something better instead. He found us.

His interdimensional transportaion equipment was destroyed in the ensuing battle against the forces of his homeworld and Shatterstar has been exiled on Earth (I know, I know, it sounds ridiculous to me, too).

In return for his services in our fighting unit, I have promised him that we will aid his cause. I just never told him when.

For now, I need Shatterstar more than his homeworld needs us. He is a perfectly honed fighting machine, versed in several forms of interpersonal combat techniques as well as text book military strategy. Of my entire unit, he is most willing to accomplish his assignment no matter the personal or physical cost.

This could be a result of his enhanced biorestorative metabolism, which allows him to heal himself far faster than a normal human. Shatterstar claims to be genetically bred to be an ultimate arena warrior on his homeworld's video network slaughter games. Lending credence to his claim is the fact that his speed, strength and stamina are all of superhuman proportion.

If Shatterstar better learns to communicate with his fellow soldiers both in the field and off, he will become a more valuable addition to the cause. Until then, he is a wild card who, when used to his maximum potential, can exceed his liabilities.

I'll just have to keep a close eye on him . . .

CABLE GUIDE

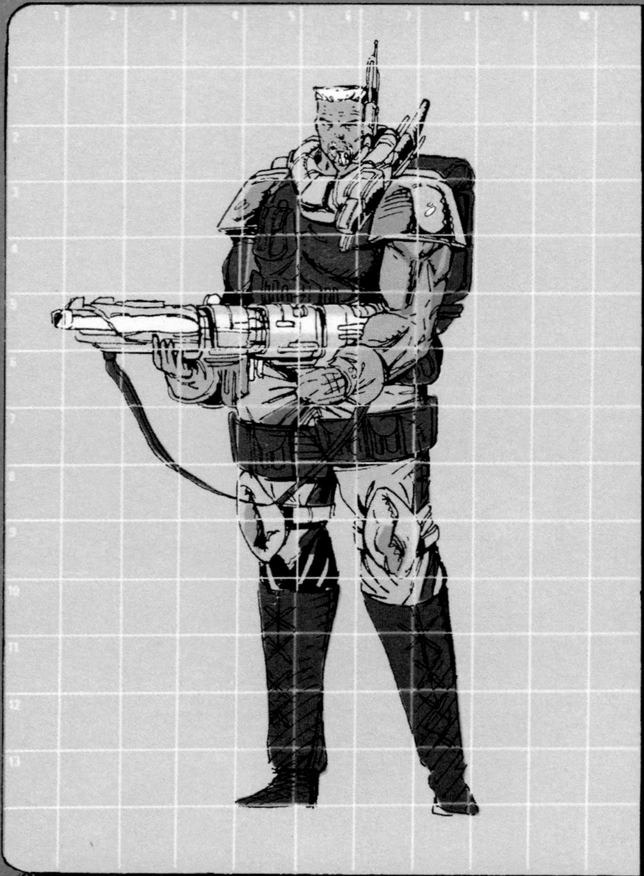

Listing 242.5

BRIDGE, G.W.

There were times and then there were times (didn't I say somewhere else that the past is best left buried? Maybe I lied. Or maybe I changed my mind). There was a time when a young man named Bridge was a part of an elite mercenary outfit called the Wild Pack.

Well, he's not so young anymore, but he's still a part of something elite-like and mercenary-like . . . it's called the elite establishment. Bridge is a commander in SHIELD.

Word has it that he's so good at what he does, that he no longer has to report in to anybody and can set his own agenda. Unfortunately, his agenda often contradicts with my own.

We were part of something pretty fun back then. I called him Sammy Davis Sr. (it involves a long story about the Wild Pack being compared to the 1950's Rat Pack, which included Sammy Davis Jr. and Sammy was a small guy and Bridge is about thirty-two feet tall . . . just forget about it). He called me Ol' Blue Eye (a Cyclopean reference to Frank Sinatra. . . I'm explaining myself to a computer diary . . .). There were six of us and we raised cane over the world. We had a party. We got drunk a lot. We made some money.

I called it my geographical initiation phase. I had to learn as much about the world order—economically and socialogically—in as short a time as possible, so what better way than working to destabilize most of the political systems in the country for cold, hard cash?

Things are still cold and hard, but it's not cash anymore. It's life.

You do what you have to do, G.W. . . . but if your agenda comes crashing butt-screaming, spittle-slapping right into mine . . . I'll do what I always have . . . I'll survive . . .

. . . no matter what the cost.

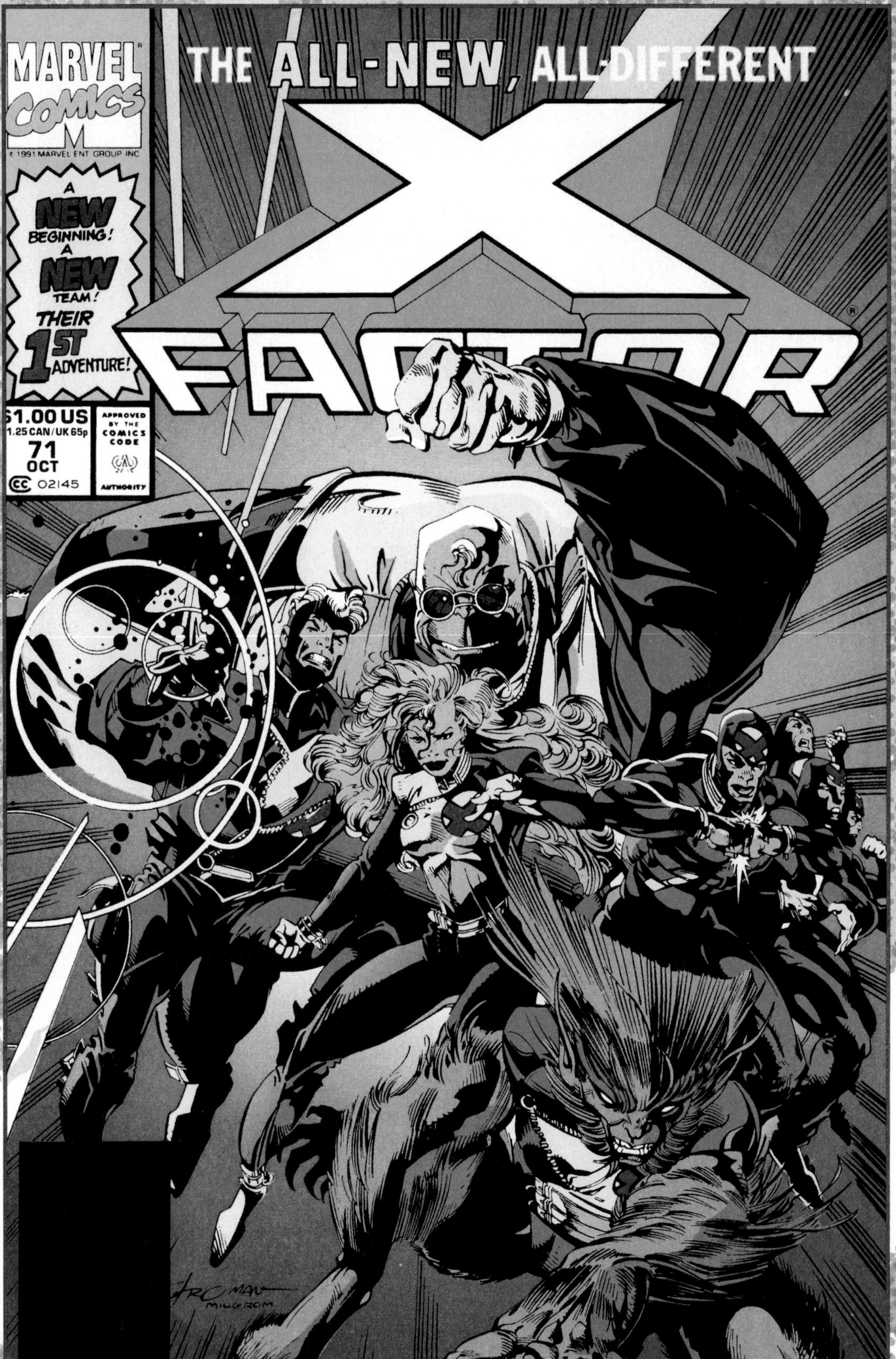
MARVEL COMICS
© 1991 MARVEL ENT GROUP INC
THE ALL-NEW, ALL-DIFFERENT
X-FACTOR
A NEW BEGINNING! A NEW TEAM! THEIR 1ST ADVENTURE!
$1.00 US
$1.25 CAN/UK 65p
71
OCT
02145
APPROVED BY THE COMICS CODE AUTHORITY

X-FACTOR #71, published in August 1991, switched the series' focus from the original team members to an all-new team, with a completely different lineup, which used the same name.

STAN LEE PRESENTS...
CUTTING THE MUSTARD
EXCUSE ME...
YA GOT ANY GREY POUPON?
A NEW DIRECTION, MEASURED TO X-ACTING STANDARDS BY
PETER DAVID WRITER
LARRY STROMAN PENCILER
AL MILGROM INKER
MICHAEL HEISLER LETTERER
GLYNIS OLIVER COLORIST
BOB HARRAS EDITOR
TOM DeFALCO EDITOR IN CHIEF

OF COURSE WE DO... GUIDO, IS IT?
GUIDO IT IS.
OF COURSE WE DO, GUIDO-IT-IS. AFTER ALL, HERE AT X-FACTOR, WE HAVE IT ALL.
ARMORY, VEHICLES, AND OF COURSE...
GREY POUPON.
SO TELL ME, MZ... DANE, IS IT?
DANE IT IS. LORNA.
YOU ONE'A THOSE TYPES WHAT BABBLES WHEN THEY'RE NERVOUS, DANE-IT-IS-LORNA?
IS IT THAT OBVIOUS?
WELL... OKAY, LOOK... THE GUY THEY'RE APPROACHING TO HEAD UP THIS WHOLE OPERATION...
SPLATT
-UHH!- STUPID MAYO JAR.
WE HAVE A HISTORY, Y'KNOW?

IF ALEX COMES HERE, IT'LL BE THE FIRST TIME IN AGES WHERE THERE'S NOTHING TO KEEP US APART.
YOU WANT I SHOULD HOSE YOU TWO DOWN? THAT IT?
CHOMP
THAT'S NOT THE PROBLEM.
ALTHOUGH YOU MIGHT HAVE TO.
THEN AGAIN, MAYBE YOU WON'T. OHHHH...
YOU SEE... SO MUCH HAS HAPPENED TO US...
WE'VE BEEN SO MUCKED UP, IN MIND AND BODY, SO MANY TIMES...
HOW DO I KNOW THAT THERE'S ANY RELATIONSHIP TO GO BACK TO, Y'KNOW?

UFFFFF!
POK
STUPID FREAKING MAYO JAR.
HERE. GIMME A HAND WITH THIS.
SURE.
LOOK, DANE-IT-IS-LORNA... IF THE GUY'S DUMB ENOUGH TO LET YA GO...
...JUST CLEARS THE WAY FOR US.
US?
YOU AND ME US?
GUIDO, WE REALLY DON'T KNOW EACH OTHER.
A 90'S GUY LIKE ME SAYS WHAT HE FEELS.
I'M WHATCHA CALL "SENSITIVE." 'COURSE, SOME BLORK GOT A PROBLEM WITH THAT...
CAN YOU OPEN THIS STUPID THING?
...THEN I'LL DEFENESTRATE HIM.
HUH?
VRRT VRRT
WHAT'S WITH THIS STUPID MAYO JAR? IT...
OH FOR CRYING OUT LOUD, LET ME TAKE IT.
WHAT'S A "BLORK?"

I CAN'T REALLY GO INTA IT WITH LADIES PRESENT.
WELL, THE HECK WITH IT. I HAVE BETTER THINGS TO DO.
LIKE WHAT?
Miracle Whip
BONK
THIS IS CRAZY. EVEN MY MAGNETIC POWERS CAN'T PRY THE LID OFF.
LIKE FINDING SOMEPLACE TO LIVE, JAMIE.
MAYBE YOU WERE FORTUNATE ENOUGH TO HAVE SOME FRIENDS TOURING EUROPE WHO WANT YOU TO HOUSE-SIT THEIR CONDO, BUT SOME OF US DON'T GET THINGS HANDED TO THEM.
IS IT MY FAULT I'VE GOT RICH FRIENDS?
YES.
ALEX... I HOPE YOU TAKE THE JOB.
AND I'M PETRIFIED THAT YOU WILL.

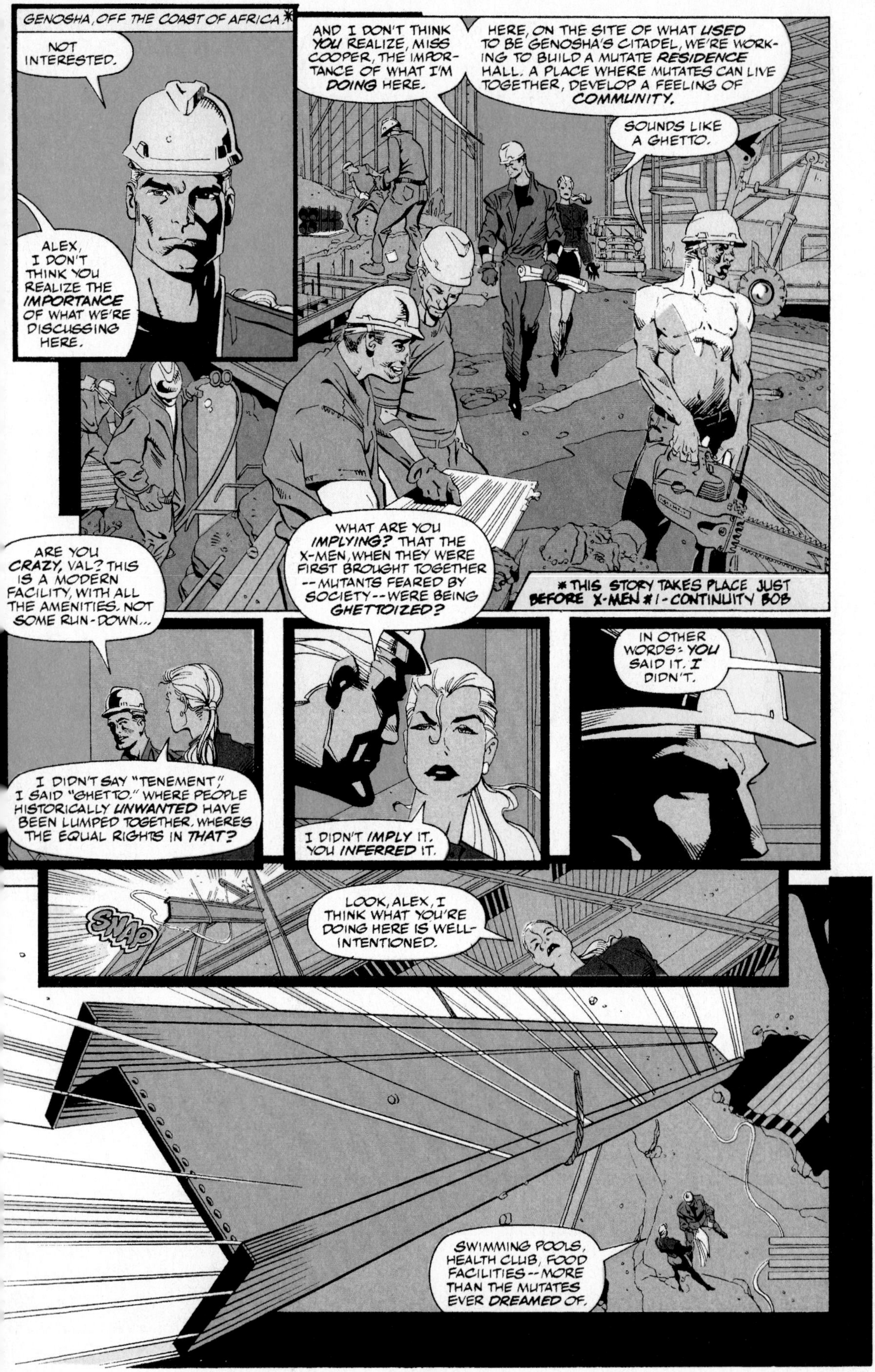
GENOSHA, OFF THE COAST OF AFRICA.*
NOT INTERESTED.
ALEX, I DON'T THINK YOU REALIZE THE IMPORTANCE OF WHAT WE'RE DISCUSSING HERE.
AND I DON'T THINK YOU REALIZE, MISS COOPER, THE IMPORTANCE OF WHAT I'M DOING HERE.
HERE, ON THE SITE OF WHAT USED TO BE GENOSHA'S CITADEL, WE'RE WORKING TO BUILD A MUTATE RESIDENCE HALL. A PLACE WHERE MUTATES CAN LIVE TOGETHER, DEVELOP A FEELING OF COMMUNITY.
SOUNDS LIKE A GHETTO.
ARE YOU CRAZY, VAL? THIS IS A MODERN FACILITY, WITH ALL THE AMENITIES. NOT SOME RUN-DOWN...
WHAT ARE YOU IMPLYING? THAT THE X-MEN, WHEN THEY WERE FIRST BROUGHT TOGETHER --MUTANTS FEARED BY SOCIETY--WERE BEING GHETTOIZED?
*THIS STORY TAKES PLACE JUST BEFORE X-MEN #1-CONTINUITY BOB
I DIDN'T SAY "TENEMENT," I SAID "GHETTO." WHERE PEOPLE HISTORICALLY UNWANTED HAVE BEEN LUMPED TOGETHER. WHERE'S THE EQUAL RIGHTS IN THAT?
I DIDN'T IMPLY IT. YOU INFERRED IT.
IN OTHER WORDS: YOU SAID IT. I DIDN'T.
SNAP
LOOK, ALEX, I THINK WHAT YOU'RE DOING HERE IS WELL-INTENTIONED.
SWIMMING POOLS, HEALTH CLUB, FOOD FACILITIES--MORE THAN THE MUTATES EVER DREAMED OF.

BUT THE U.S. GOVERNMENT IS LOOKING AT THE BIG PICTURE, AND YOU SHOULD--
LOOK OUT!!
I'VE GOT YE, ALEX! HOLD ON!
WHUMP
OOOF!
RAHNE, ARE YOU NUTS?! WHERE'D YOU COME FR--
VAL! MOVE!
CRIPES!

HAVE YOU LOST YOUR MIND?! WHAT, YOU THINK JUST BECAUSE YOU'RE A GOVERNMENT LIAISON, YOU'RE INVULNERABLE?!
WHY DIDN'T YOU MOVE?!
BECAUSE I WANTED TO SEE IF, WHEN YOU ACT FROM INSTINCT INSTEAD OF THINKING, YOU COULD MAKE THE RIGHT CHOICE.

WASHINGTON, D.C. ...
WELL DONE, LOCKJAW. YOU HAVE INDEED TRANSPORTED US TO THE NATION'S CAPITAL.
IT'S PERFECTLY EVIDENT. THE AIR FAIRLY REEKS OF SANCTIMONIOUS-NESS.
ROXXON
SHUT DOWN ROXXON!
ROXXON'S RAPING THE ENVIRONMENT!
I AM LOOKING FOR THE HEAD-QUARTERS OF X-FACTOR.
NEVER HEARD OF THEM.
RUN! EVERYBODY BACK! THERE'S BEEN A BOMB THREAT! IT'S GOING OFF IN TWO MINUTES!
"NEVER HEARD OF THEM." NOW THAT SOUNDS PROMISING.

GET OUT OF HERE! HURRY!
I'M LOOKING FOR X-FACTOR.
WHO CARES? DIDN'T YOU HEAR ME?! RUN!
YOU WANT RUNNING?
I WILL SHOW YOU RUNNING.
HUMANS. INSANITY.
THE THINGS
I MUST DO
JUST TO GET
SIMPLE DIRECTIONS.
HERE IS YOUR BOMB.
YOU LUNATIC! IT'S ABOUT TO BLOW...
...UP?
NOW THAT I HAVE YOUR ATTENTION...
I AM SEEKING X-FACTOR. I UNDERSTAND THEY'RE ON EMBASSY ROW.
THAT'S, UH... A MILE WEST, THAT WAY.
EXCELLENT. WE'LL BE THERE IN A FLASH.

GENOSHA...
RAHNE, I APPRECIATE YOUR EFFORTS...BUT YOU DIDN'T HAVE TO "RESCUE" ME.
I KNOW, ALEX. IT'S JUST... I SAW YOU IN DANGER, AND I COULDNA CONTROL MUHSELF.
YOU CONTROLLED YOURSELF JUST FINE WHEN IT CAME TO ME, THOUGH, DIDN'T YOU, MISS SINCLAIR?
SKUFPH
YEAH, AND THAT WAS PRETTY BLASTED STUPID ON YOUR PART, MISS COOPER.
WHAT WERE YOU TRYING TO PROVE, JUST STANDING THERE LIKE THAT? INSTEAD OF THE SHOWER YOU JUST NEEDED, YOU WOULD'VE NEEDED AN UNDERTAKER.
WHEN YOU SAW THE GIRDER FALLING, YOU ACTED ON INSTINCT.
THAT'S WHEN YOU'RE AT YOUR BEST, ALEX. WHEN YOU THINK TOO MUCH, YOU GET SCREWED UP...
AND I BELIEVE YOU'RE THINKING TOO MUCH NOW ABOUT JOINING X-FACTOR, AND SCREWING UP WHAT IS YOUR FIRST, BEST DESTINY. YOU'RE DENYING YOUR INSTINCT.
DENYING WHAT? THE CHANCE TO LEAD SOME GOVERNMENT-FORMED INTERVENTION GROUP? THE CHANCE TO HAVE MORE LIVES DEPENDING ON ME?
THE CHANCE TO DO SOME GOOD. TO DE-GHETTOIZE MUTANTS INSTEAD OF BUILDING NEW ONES.
KNOK KNOK
LOOK, VALERIE, MY MIND'S MADE...
...UP?

HELLO, ALEX.
MAY WE COME IN?
UH... SURE.
SCOTT? PROFESSOR?
Oh, Professor!!!
ALEX... LET'S TALK.
SO, RAHNE, DARLING... CAN I OFFER YOU ANY-THING? A DRINK? SANDWICH?
KIBBLES AND BITS?

IT'S AN EXCELLENT OPPORTUNITY, ALEX. WITH THE BREAKUP OF FREEDOM FORCE, THE GOVERNMENT IS IN THE POSITION OF HAVING THEIR FIRST PUBLICIZED ASSOCIATION WITH MUTANTS BLOWING UP IN THEIR FACES.
MUTANTS HAVE BEEN VERY HIGH-PROFILE OF LATE, THANKS TO THE GENOSHAN INCURSION. A POSITIVE FACE ON MUTANT/ GOVERNMENT RELATIONS BENEFITS ALL.
THEY WANT WINDOW DRESSING. NICE, POLITE CUDDLY MUTANTS TO TAKE HEAT IN DIFFICULT SITUATIONS. "GOVERNMENT MUTIES." I'D BE A SMILING FRONT MAN, AN UNCLE A-TOM-IC.
NOT INTERESTED.
ALEX, IT WOULDN'T BE THAT WAY. LOOK... THE PRESIDENT IS VERY MUCH BEHIND THIS PROJECT, AND CONSIDERING HIS VOTER APPROVAL RATE, THAT'S POWERFUL SUPPORT.
IS THIS WHAT THE GREAT DREAM HAS COME TO, PROFESSOR? PLAYING POLITICS?
THE STAKES ARE FAR HIGHER THAN THAT, ALEX. WE KNOW WHAT A FUTURE OF UNCHECKED MUTANT SUSPICION COULD HOLD. HOW WOULD YOU FEEL IF MISERABLE FATES BEFELL YOUR BRETHREN... A FATE YOU MIGHT HAVE STAVED OFF, HAD YOU NOT BEEN SO SELF-ABSORBED.
GREAT. IF I PASS THIS UP, THEN MUTANTKIND GOES DOWN THE CHUTE AND IT'S MY FAULT? IF IT'S SO IMPORTANT, THEN YOU DO IT.
I CAN'T BE EVERYWHERE. WE NEED SOMEONE HEADING THIS WE CAN TRUST. YOU'D BE A GOVERNMENT STRIKE GROUP, JUST LIKE DELTA FORCE. YOU'D COME AND GO AS NEEDED, DRAW A HEALTHY PAYCHECK... AND, OF COURSE, BE WITH LORNA...
LORNA...?

LORNA?
PIETRO?! MY LORD... YOU LOOK LIKE DEATH WARMED OVER!
EVER... THE FLATTERER...
UHHHH...
GUIDO!! GET OVER HERE! WE GOT COMPANY!
SO HE JUST FAINTED DEAD AWAY, HUH?
THAT'S RIGHT. PUT HIM THERE ON THE COUCH.
YEAH, WELL, IT WAS THAT OR STICK HIM ON THE MANTEL.
I DON'T UNDERSTAND. LAST I HEARD, QUICK-SILVER WAS ON THE WEST COAST WITH THAT BRANCH OF THE AVENGERS. WHAT'S HE DOING HERE?
NOT TOO WELL, FROM THE LOOK OF HIM. I THINK HE'S COMIN' AROUND, THOUGH.

THANK YOU ALL FOR YOUR CONCERN. I AM FEELING SOMEWHAT...
MADROX, ISN'T IT? YES... MADROX. WHAT ARE YOU DOING?
I WAS ASKING LOCKJAW WHAT WAS WRONG WITH YOU. BUT HE WASN'T ANSWERING. I KNOW IT'S HARD FOR HIM TO SPEAK, BUT...
SPEAK...?
HEH, HEH HEHHHH HEH...
WHAT'S SO BLASTED FUNNY?
YOU'VE... HA HAHH HA... YOU'VE BEEN TALKING TO BEN GRIMM, HAVEN'T YOU?
I'VE PLAYED CARDS WITH HIM, YEAH. HE TOLD ME THAT LOCKJAW WAS A DEFORMED INHUMAN, NOT A DOG.
HERE, SPEEDY GONZALES. OPEN THIS WHILE YOU EXPLAIN.
GLADLY. MADROX... ANSWER ME THIS. IF LOCKJAW IS A DEFORMED INHUMAN, THEN WHY HAVE THE INHUMANS ALWAYS TALKED TO HIM LIKE A DOG? WOULDN'T THAT BE SOMEWHAT PATRONIZING?
WELL... I GUESS. BUT THEN WHY--?
BECAUSE HE'S A DOG. IT WAS A JOKE, MADROX. GORGON AND KARNAK UTILIZED LOCKJAW'S ANTENNA AS A HIGH-POWERED TRANSMITTER, AS A PRANK ON THEIR OLD FRIEND, GRIMM.
AND GRIMM, THINKING HE'D FOUND A SOUL MATE, APPARENTLY SWALLOWED IT. YOU MEAN HE STILL HASN'T CAUGHT ON? FOR HEAVEN'S SAKE, DON'T BE THE ONE TO TELL HIM.
DON'T BE SO SMUG, FLEET FOOT. I BET YOU'D'VE BEEN FOOLED IF SOMEONE HAD PULLED THE SAME STUNT ON YOU.
ME? OF... COURSE NOT. I'D NEVER BE SO ...UHM... GULLIBLE.
PIETRO... WHAT ARE YOU DOING HERE? DON'T TAKE THIS WRONG, BUT... YOU LOOK OLDER THAN BEFORE. MORE TIRED.
YOU'RE CORRECT, LORNA, AND MY IMPULSIVE EXTINGUISHING OF A BOMB THREAT ONLY AGGRAVATED MY SITUATION...
THAT SITUATION BEING THAT MY POWER...

...IS KILLING ME.
I'M PLEASED YOU DECIDED TO COME ALONG, RAHNE.
ACH, OF COURSE AH DID, ALEX. WE'RE A TEAM, YOU AND ME.
SPEAKING OF TEAMS (SHE SAID BY WAY OF CLEVER SEGUE)...
HERE'S PHOTOS OF YOURS.
GUIDO... FORMER BODYGUARD FOR AN OFF-WORLD ROCKER NAMED LILA CHENEY. BUILT LIKE A TANK.
JAMIE MADROX, THE MULTIPLE MAN. CREATES REPLICAS OF HIMSELF. HE'S HIS OWN BEST FRIEND. ANY QUESTIONS?
LORNA DANE, A.K.A. POLARIS... RECENTLY REACQUIRED HER MASTERY OF MAGNET-ISM. YOU'VE... MET.
AN OBSERVATION: YOU, VAL COOPER, SEEM TO BE ENJOYING THIS TREMENDOUSLY.
OH, I AM. I HAVE A BROTHER WHO'S AN FBI AGENT, AND I AM SO TIRED OF HIM TELLING ME ABOUT THESE EXCIT-ING CASES HE GETS...
LIKE, FOR INSTANCE, THIS GIRL THEY FOUND. SHE WAS DEAD... WRAPPED IN PLASTIC...
BUT THAT STUFF WILL BE TAME COMPARED TO WHAT X-FACTOR GETS INVOLVED WITH.

SOMEONE HAS DONE SOMETHING TO ME. I DON'T KNOW HOW, BUT THEY'VE TURNED MY POWER AGAINST ME.
WHAT DO YOU MEAN?
IT STARTED LAST WEEK. EVERY TIME I USE MY VELOCITY, MY METABOLISM SPEEDS UP, ACCELERATING MY AGING. I'VE LEARNED THAT SOME EVIL INDIVIDUAL IS BEHIND IT, AND HE'S BASED SOMEWHERE HERE IN THE WASHINGTON AREA.
PARK
HOW DO YOU KNOW?
BECAUSE OF THIS POSTCARD I GOT IN THE MAIL. HERE, MADROX... READ IT.
"DEAR MR. SILVER: HA HA. I HAVE TURNED YOUR POWER AGAINST YOU. YOU'LL NEVER FIND ME. SINCERELY: AN EVIL INDIVIDUAL." AND IT'S GOT A D.C. POSTMARK.
THAT'S TERRIBLE! WHAT WOULD MAKE SOME-ONE DO SOMETHING LIKE THIS?
YOU ASK ME, I BLAME SOCIETY.

BUT YOU WERE WITH THE W.C.A. WHY NOT BRING THEM IN ON THIS?
I HAD RESOLVED TO PART COMPANY WITH THEM. THEY DO NOT APPRECIATE MY TALENTS.
THE COMPUTERS INDICATED THAT X-FACTOR WAS FORMING IN THE D.C. AREA AND...
ACTUALLY, IT ALREADY HAS FORMED.
ALEX!
AWWWW...
HMMMPH.
QUICKSILVER? WHAT ARE YOU DOING HERE?
AN EVIL INDIVIDUAL HAS TURNED MY POWERS AGAINST ME.
WHY?
YOU ASK ME, I BLAME SOCIETY.
THAT SEEMS TO BE THE CONSENSUS. BY THE WAY, I CAN'T GET THIS MAYO JAR OPEN. I DON'T THINK ANYONE CAN.

OH REALLY? GET A LOAD OF... THIS!
PLASMA BLASTS FOR A MAYO JAR?! ISN'T THAT A BIT OF OVER...
FWAAM
KILL?
PUFF
AW, FOR CRYIN' OUT LOUD!
OH, YOU PEOPLE. HONESTLY. GIVE IT HERE.
BONK
YOU JUST RAP IT A COUPLE TIMES...
THERE. OPEN. NOW...
SKRUK SKRUK
TELL US ABOUT THIS EVIL INDIVIDUAL...

HEEH HEH HEH HEH...OH, I GOT 'EM GOOD.
THIS LITTLE UNBREAKABLE JAR I WHIPPED UP ON MUIR ISLAND... COMPLETE WITH UNREMOVABLE LID EXCEPT WHEN MY LITTLE REMOTE CONTROL DEVICE ALLOWS IT TO BE OPENED...
QUICKSILVER THINKS INHUMANS CAN PULL PRACTICAL JOKES? HE HASN'T SEEN JOKES UNTIL HE'S CROSSED SWORDS WITH JAMIE MADROX.
KNOCK KNOCK
NOW WHO COULD THAT BE AT THIS TIME OF NIGHT? ASIDE FROM X-FACTOR, NO ONE KNOWS I'M STAYING AT THIS CONDO.
IT'S PROBABLY JUST A SALESMAN. STILL...
YES? CAN I HELP Y--
CHUK
BOOM BOOM BOOM

ARRRHHHHH!!!
CRASH

TO BE CONTINUED...

MARVEL COMICS
WARLOCK
and the INFINITY WATCH
THE GATHERING OF THE WATCH
$1.75 US
$2.15 CAN
2
MAR
01897
APPROVED BY THE COMICS CODE AUTHORITY
© 1992 MARVEL ENT. GROUP INC.

While issue #1 featured Adam Warlock alone, WARLOCK AND THE INFINITY WATCH #2, published in January 1992, introduced Adam's handpicked cosmic team in an ongoing series.

JIM
STARLIN
WRITER
ANGEL
MEDINA
PENCILS
TERRY
AUSTIN
INKS
JACK
MORELLI
LETTERS
IAN
LAUGHLIN
COLORS
CRAIG
ANDERSON
EDITOR
TOM
DeFALCO
CHIEFTAN

WARLOCK AND THE
INFINITY WATCH
THE SHIP LAYS DEAD IN THE ETHER. HER EVERY FUNCTION HAS BEEN SYSTEMATICALLY TERMINATED.
HER ATTACKERS WERE DEFINITELY NOT GOING FOR THE QUICK KILL.
GATHERING THE
WATCH!

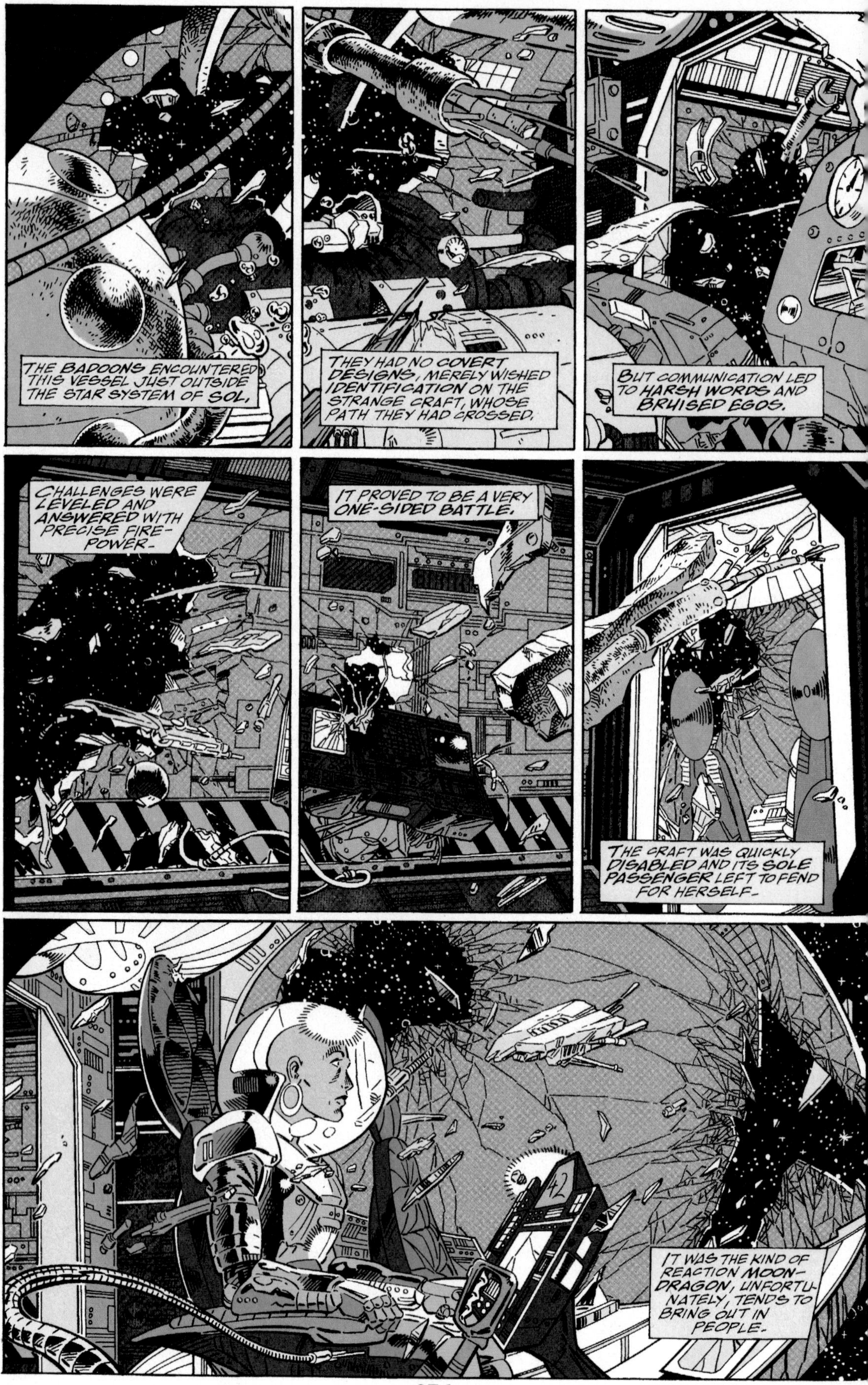
THE BADOONS ENCOUNTERED THIS VESSEL JUST OUTSIDE THE STAR SYSTEM OF SOL,
THEY HAD NO COVERT DESIGNS, MERELY WISHED IDENTIFICATION ON THE STRANGE CRAFT, WHOSE PATH THEY HAD CROSSED.
BUT COMMUNICATION LED TO HARSH WORDS AND BRUISED EGOS.
CHALLENGES WERE LEVELED AND ANSWERED WITH PRECISE FIRE-POWER-
IT PROVED TO BE A VERY ONE-SIDED BATTLE.
THE CRAFT WAS QUICKLY DISABLED AND ITS SOLE PASSENGER LEFT TO FEND FOR HERSELF-
IT WAS THE KIND OF REACTION MOON-DRAGON, UNFORTU-NATELY, TENDS TO BRING OUT IN PEOPLE.

THIS IS QUITE A FIX THAT YOU'RE IN.
WHO?
HOW NICE.
AN UNEXPECTED GUEST.
ADAM WARLOCK, ISN'T IT?
YES.
I'D HEARD YOU'D TAKEN OVER THE JOB OF THE SUPREME BEING OF THIS REALITY.
DIDN'T EXPECT TO MEET YOU ON THIS SIDE OF THE GREAT DIVIDE.
YOU ARE NOT FAR FROM CROSSING OVER.
ONLY 31 SECONDS OF AIR LEFT ACCORDING TO YOUR INSTRUMENT.
SUFFOCATION IS A PARTICULARLY UNPLEASANT WAY TO DIE.
31
HAVE YOU COME TO OFFER ME SOME KIND OF A DEAL?
27
POSSIBLY.
INTERESTED IN A NEW LIFESTYLE?

MAYBE-
MY OLD ONE HASN'T WORKED OUT TOO WELL OF LATE-
IT WOULD REQUIRE SHOULDERING GREAT RESPONSIBILITY AND EARNING MY TRUST-
TRUTHFULLY, I'VE NEVER BEEN VERY GOOD WITH TRUST OR RESPONSI-BILITY-
I KNOW-
BUT I'M WILLING TO GIVE YOU A SECOND CHANCE.
WELL?
4
3
2
1
OXYGEN DEPLETED

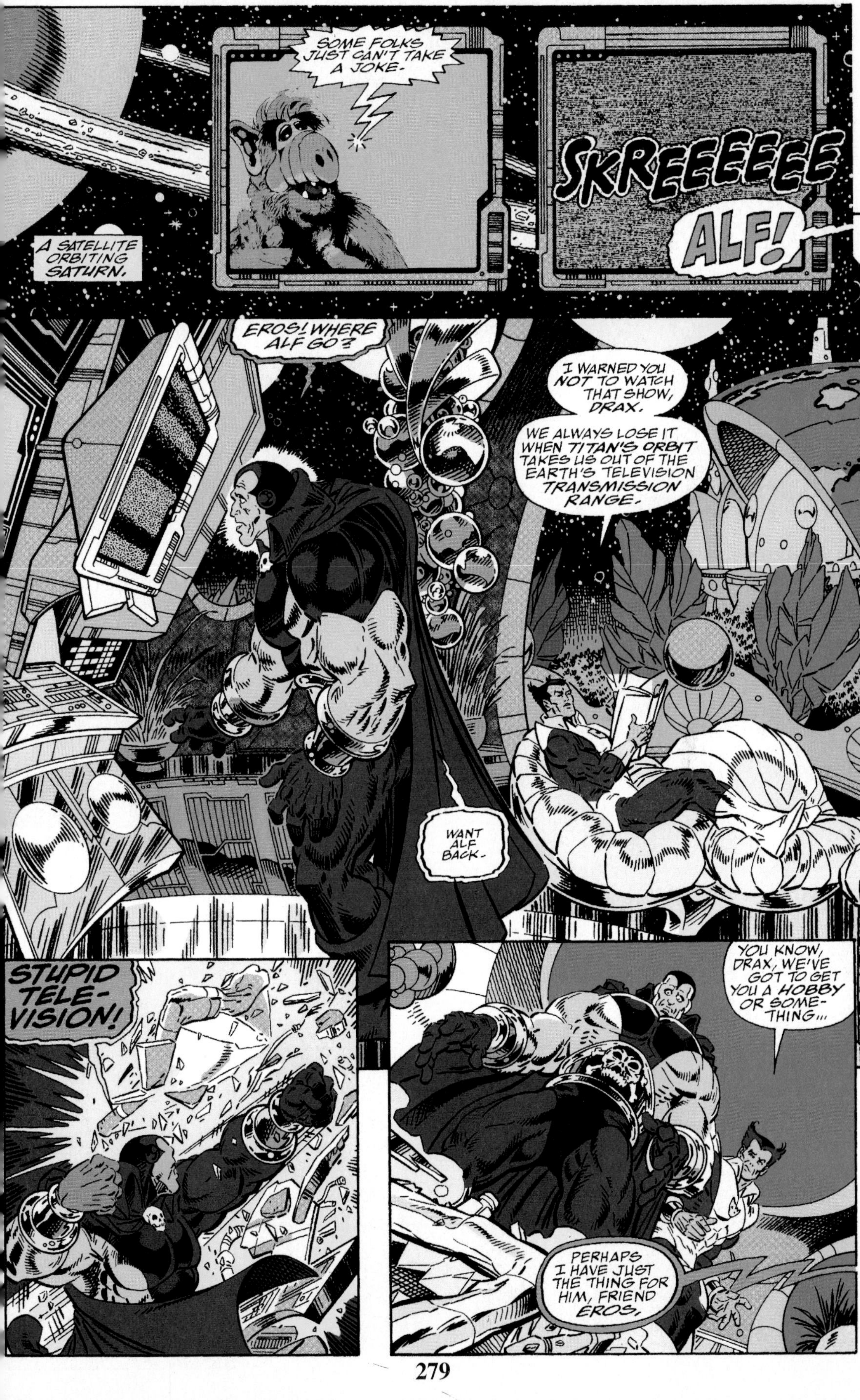
A SATELLITE ORBITING SATURN.
SOME FOLKS JUST CAN'T TAKE A JOKE.
SKREEEEEEE
ALF!
EROS! WHERE ALF GO?
I WARNED YOU NOT TO WATCH THAT SHOW, DRAX.
WE ALWAYS LOSE IT WHEN TITAN'S ORBIT TAKES US OUT OF THE EARTH'S TELEVISION TRANSMISSION RANGE.
WANT ALF BACK.
STUPID TELE-VISION!
YOU KNOW, DRAX, WE'VE GOT TO GET YOU A HOBBY OR SOME-THING...
PERHAPS I HAVE JUST THE THING FOR HIM, FRIEND EROS.

ADAM WARLOCK!
DRAX, DO YOU WISH TO WASTE THE REST OF YOUR DAYS WATCHING CARTOONS?
OR WOULD YOU RATHER HAVE PURPOSE IN YOUR LIFE AGAIN?
LIKE WHEN I WANTED TO KILL THANOS?
YES.
WELL... I DON'T KNOW... MIGHT MISS ALF...
SAY YES, YOU STUPID COUCH POTATO!
YES...
"SO BE IT."

ON AN UNNAMED PLANET IN A FARAWAY STAR SYSTEM...
PIP, HERE COMES ADAM WITH ANOTHER ONE.
HOPE HE'S FRIENDLIER THAN BALDY.
THIS ONE'S A BIG SUCKER. YOU DON'T FIGURE IT'S--
DRAX THE DESTROYER!!
HUH?
I SHOULD HAVE KNOWN THIS WAS A TRAP!
WHY DO I ALWAYS FORGET TO TELL HER ABOUT DRAX?
GODHOOD... WHO NEEDS IT--?

ENOUGH!
DRAX IS NO THREAT TO YOU.
BUT...
I KNOW.
IN HIS LIFE AS ART DOUGLAS, DRAX WAS YOUR FATHER.
HE WAS KILLED IN AN AUTO ACCIDENT WHEN I WAS A CHILD.
THEN WAS RESURRECTED AS THE DESTROYER, AND LATER ON, DURING YOUR PLOT TO CONQUER THE PLANET BA-BANI...
IT WAS AN... ACCIDENT...
...YOU KILLED HIM.
NICE.
MY KIND OF GAL!
LET ME ASSURE YOU THAT THIS DRAX HAS NO VENGEANCE IN HIS HEART.
HE LOOKS DIFFERENT-
BRAIN DAMAGED IN THIS INCARNATION.
PRETTY LADY.
NICE HEAD.
STOP THAT!

DRAX DO SOMETHING WRONG?
NO.
YOU RESPONDED IN THE BEST WAY CONCEIVABLE.
SO WHY HAVE YOU BROUGHT US ALL HERE?
BEEN WONDERING THAT MYSELF.
I THINK I KNOW WHY.
BECAUSE I HAVE AGREED TO RELINQUISH MY OMNIPOTENCE.
I HAVE CHOSEN TO SHARE THIS GREAT POWER.
I PLAN TO SHARE IT WITH YOU.

ADAM, ARE YOU SURE YOU'VE THOUGHT THIS THROUGH THOROUGHLY?
YOU'VE BEEN PRETTY SPACEY SINCE GAINING THE INFINITY GAUNTLET.
DIVINITY HAS CHANGED MY OUTLOOK ON THE UNIVERSE.
I'LL SAY IT HAS.
JUST TAKE A SECOND LOOK AT WHO YOU'RE PLANNING ON SHARING THAT MIGHT WITH.
WHAT'S WRONG WITH THEM?
HAVE YOU LOST YOUR MIND?!
THEY'RE ALL FOUL-UPS!
MY OMNIPOTENCE ASSURES THE INFALLIBILITY OF MY DECISION.
THERE IS NO NEED FOR FURTHER DEBATE.
I GIVE UP! YOU'VE COMPLETELY LOST IT!
DO WHAT YOU WILL.

WITH THE INFINITY GEMS I AM THE MASTER OF ALL TIME, SPACE, POWER, THE MIND AND THE SOUL.
GOD!
EXACTLY.
BUT SUCH POWER IS MORE THAN MY SOUL CAN BEAR.
SUPREMACY IS A MANTLE I WISH TO SHED.
I'LL RELIEVE YOU OF THE BURDEN.
I'M SURE YOU WOULD.
NO ONE INDI-VIDUAL SHOULD HAVE TO SHOULDER SUCH POWER.
THAT IS WHY I BESTOW THE SPACE GEM ON PIP THE TROLL.
WITH IT YOU CAN VIOLATE THE LAWS OF SPACE AS FLAGRANTLY AS YOU DO MAN'S LAWS.
NEATO!

WHY DON'T YOU TRY IT OUT?
HOW DO...
...I MAKE...
...IT WORK?
WHAT?
I KNEW YOU'D BE A NATURAL TELEPORTER, PIP.
ADAM, GIVING THIS LITTLE SCOUNDREL AN INFINITY GEM IS CRAZY!
CRAZY LIKE A FOX.
THIS LITTLE SQUIRT IS ONLY INTELLIGENT ENOUGH TO EXPLOIT THE GEM'S BASEST POTENTIAL.
WHO YOU CALLIN' A SQUIRT?
JUST ENOUGH TO KEEP ANYONE FROM TAKING IT AWAY FROM HIM.
AND SO PROTECTING IT FROM FALLING INTO MORE CAPABLE HANDS.
PRECISELY.
WHICH GEM DO I RECEIVE?
THE MIND GEM.

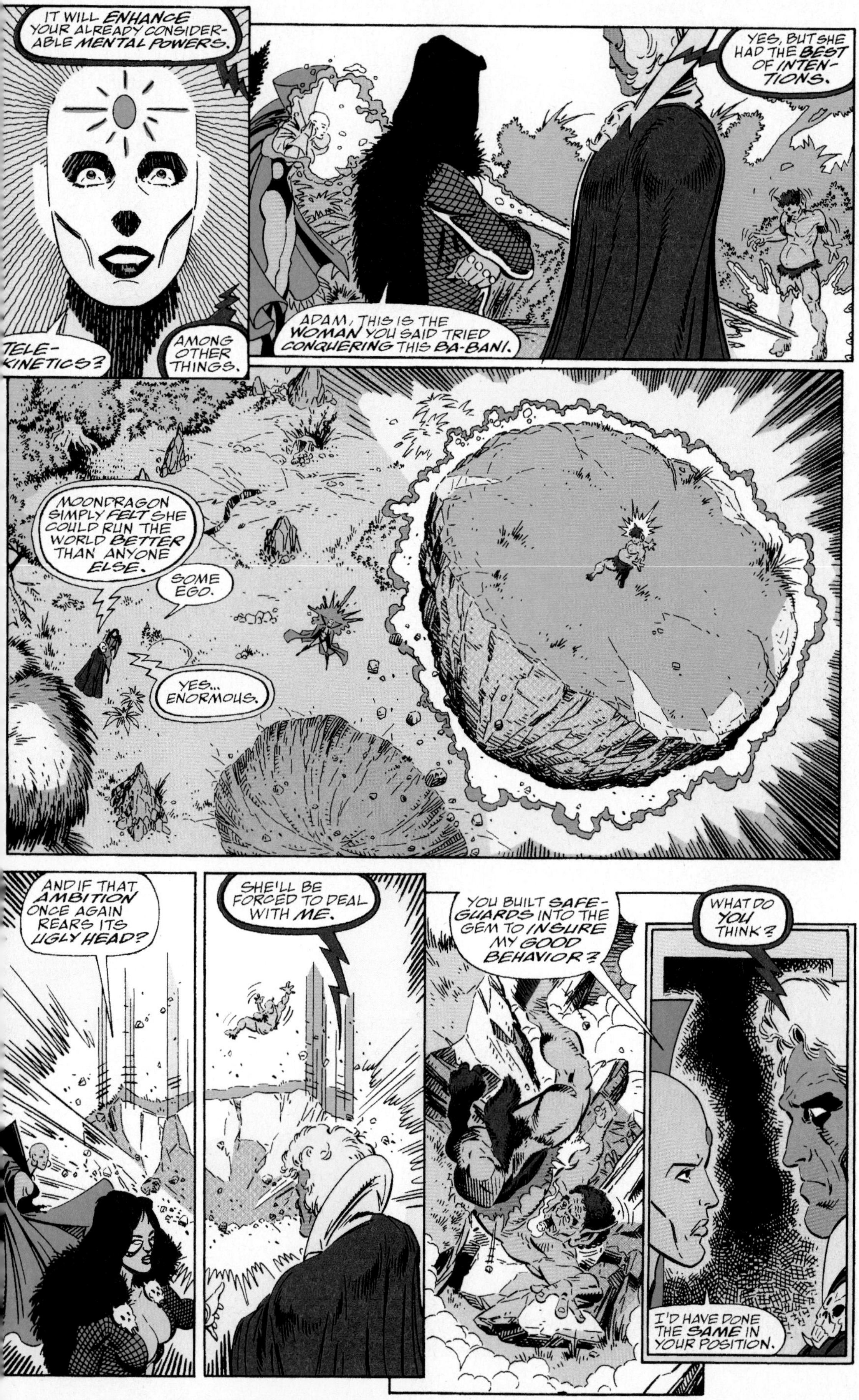
IT WILL ENHANCE YOUR ALREADY CONSIDERABLE MENTAL POWERS.
TELEKINETICS?
AMONG OTHER THINGS.
ADAM, THIS IS THE WOMAN YOU SAID TRIED CONQUERING THIS BA-BANI.
YES, BUT SHE HAD THE BEST OF INTENTIONS.
MOONDRAGON SIMPLY FELT SHE COULD RUN THE WORLD BETTER THAN ANYONE ELSE.
SOME EGO.
YES... ENORMOUS.
AND IF THAT AMBITION ONCE AGAIN REARS ITS UGLY HEAD?
SHE'LL BE FORCED TO DEAL WITH ME.
YOU BUILT SAFEGUARDS INTO THE GEM TO INSURE MY GOOD BEHAVIOR?
WHAT DO YOU THINK?
I'D HAVE DONE THE SAME IN YOUR POSITION.

ANY UNAUTHORIZED USE OF THE GEM ON MY MIND OR PERSON WILL BE CONSIDERED A BREACH OF THE FAITH I HAVE PLACED IN YOU.
AND??
DRAX, I GIVE YOU THE GEM OF POWER.
IT'S ONLY FITTING, SEEING AS HOW YOU ARE ALREADY ALMOST POWER PERSONIFIED.
AND TOO DUMB TO DRAW UPON THE GEM'S MIGHT ON ANYTHING MORE THAN A SUBCONSCIOUS LEVEL.
DUMB?
HAS DRAX MET BALD LADY BEFORE?
SOMETHING FAMILIAR...

I'M SURE DRAX WILL WORK OUT JUST FINE.
WHAT IS THIS THING ON MY HEAD?
JELLY BEAN!!
DRAX! NO!
PLOP
GULLUP
THE GEM WILL BE AS SAFE IN DRAX'S STOMACH AS ANYWHERE...
BUT...
IT'S INDE-STRUCTIBLE AND WON'T DIGEST.
BUT...
DRAX'S PHYSICAL BEING IS UNLIKE MOST CREATURES'.
I'LL EXPLAIN LATER.
TRUST ME, HE WON'T LOSE IT.
PIP, WHERE DID YOUR GEM GO?

A JEWEL ON THE FORE-HEAD AIN'T MY LOOK.
SO WHERE...
BETTER NOT TO ASK.
NOW, GAMORA, MY GIFT TO YOU.
WHICH ONE?
THE TIME GEM!
YOU'VE GOT TO BE KIDDING....
ADAM, I WOULDN'T HAVE THE SLIGHTEST IDEA HOW TO USE THE DANG THING!
I DON'T WANT THIS KIND OF POWER.
I KNOW.
GAMORA, YOU WERE FIRST INTRODUCED TO ME AS THE MOST DANGEROUS WOMAN IN THE UNIVERSE.
IT IS A MOST FITTING TITLE.
THE TIME GEM WILL BE SECURE IN YOUR CUSTODY, EVEN IF YOU CHOOSE NEVER TO UTILIZE ITS MIGHT.
ITS SAFETY IS ALL THAT MATTERS.
WHAT ABOUT THE SOUL GEM?

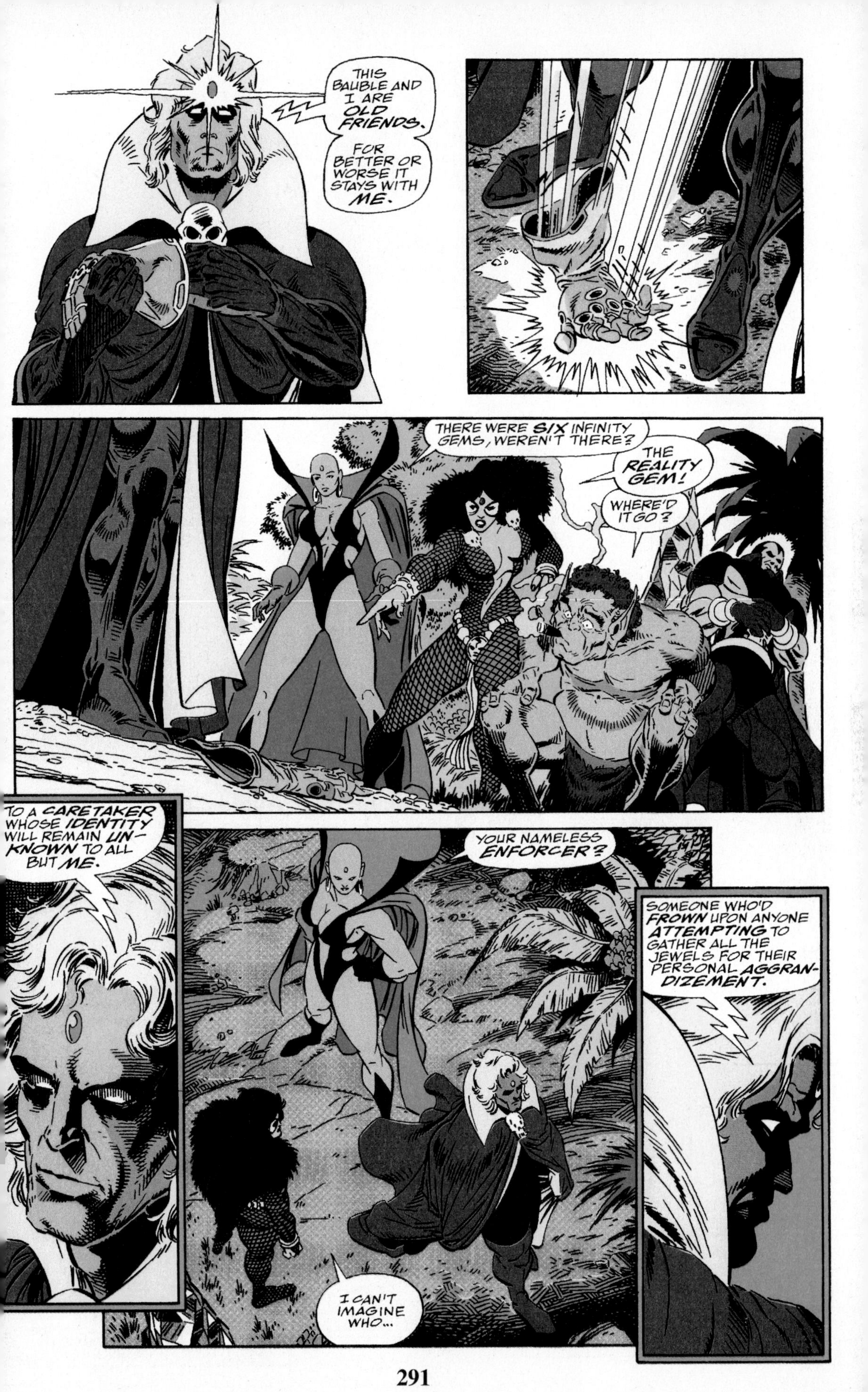

THIS BAUBLE AND I ARE OLD FRIENDS.
FOR BETTER OR WORSE IT STAYS WITH ME.
THERE WERE SIX INFINITY GEMS, WEREN'T THERE?
THE REALITY GEM!
WHERE'D IT GO?
TO A CARETAKER WHOSE IDENTITY WILL REMAIN UNKNOWN TO ALL BUT ME.
YOUR NAMELESS ENFORCER?
SOMEONE WHO'D FROWN UPON ANYONE ATTEMPTING TO GATHER ALL THE JEWELS FOR THEIR PERSONAL AGGRANDIZEMENT.
I CAN'T IMAGINE WHO...

SO WE HAVE TWO BIG BROTHERS KEEPING AN EYE ON US!
SOME-THING LIKE THAT.
BET HE GAVE IT TO THAT DR. STRANGE.
GAVE WHAT?
THAT STINKS!
THINK IT'S A PRETTY CLEVER MOVE, MYSELF.
PURE WARLOCK, ALWAYS THINKING AHEAD.
WHAT'S EVERYONE TALKING ABOUT?
EACH OF YOU CARRIES A GREAT RESPONSIBILITY ON YOUR FOREHEAD.
OR IN YOUR STOMACH.
OR WHEREVER.
MANY WILL COVET THE POWER YOU POSSESS.
THERE WILL BE NO END TO THE SCHEMES THEY'LL EMPLOY TO WREST THE GEMS FROM YOUR GRASP.

CONSTANT VIGILANCE WILL BE YOUR ONLY PROTECTION.
BUT I HAVE FAITH THAT YOU WILL ALL BE STRONG ENOUGH TO LIVE UP TO THE TRUST I HAVE IN YOU.
WE WILL?
BEWARE OF PERSONAL AMBITION BLINDING YOU TO THE DUTY YOU ARE CHARGED WITH.
FOR SOME, THAT WILL PROVE THE GREATEST PERIL.
I HAVE BESTOWED UPON YOU THIS UNIVERSE'S GRANDEST TREASURE, THAT WHICH BINDS IT TOGETHER.
EACH OF YOU IS ENTRUSTED WITH A FACET OF ALL THERE IS.
THE VERY COSMOS DEPENDS ON YOU.
ME?
YOUR TASK IS TO KEEP REALITY FROM TUMBLING INTO THE ABYSS,
FAIL IN THIS DUTY AND ETERNAL NIGHT MIGHT WELL ENSHROUD ALL THE HEAVENS.
FROM THIS MOMENT ON, YOU ARE SOLDIERS OF THE COSMIC GUARD--
MEMBERS OF THE GALACTIC ELITE...

LET THE STARS KNOW YOU TO BE the INFINITY WATCH!

AND NOW IF YOU'LL EXCUSE ME, I MUST BE GOING.
WHAT?!
YOU CAN'T POSSIBLY BE SERIOUS ABOUT LEAVING!
I MOST CERTAINLY AM.
MY PERIOD AS THIS REALITY'S SUPREME BEING HAS BEEN A SHATTERING EXPERIENCE.
I FARED POORLY AS A DIVINE ENTITY.
I AM IN DIRE NEED OF SOLITUDE IN ORDER TO REGENERATE MY SPIRIT AND STRENGTH.
THIS IS HOW IT MUST BE. I AM SORRY.
FAREWELL UNTIL WE MEET AGAIN.

IF NOT WARLOCK, WHO'S GOING TO BE BOSS?
NOT YOU, HIGHPOCKETS. THAT'S FOR SURE.
DRAX NOT TAKING ORDERS FROM A WOMAN OR MIDGET!
MIDGET?!
DRAX LEAVING NOW.
GOOD RIDDANCE.
HATE TO ADMIT IT.
BUT THE BIG GUY'S GOT A POINT.
CATCH YA LATER, GALS!
PiP!
WELL?
I THINK I'LL USE MY NEW POWER TO BUILD A STAR CRAFT.
CAN I DROP YOU SOME-WHERE?
Oh, ADAM. WHAT HAVE YOU DONE?
NEXT THE HIGH EVOLUTIONARY

MARVEL COMICS UK
DEATH'S HEAD II
$1.75 US
$2.15 CAN
1
MARCH
UK 95p
PART ONE OF FOUR
© 1992 Marvel Comics UK Ltd.
DEATH'S HEAD IS COMPLETELY TERMINATED, YES?
THE DEATH OF DEATH'S HEAD

DEATH'S HEAD II #1, published in January 1992, began a limited series starring the freelance peacekeeping agent "upgraded" into a new cyborg body; it was soon followed by an ongoing series. This issue also debuted the "Marvel UK" imprint, which featured several interconnected titles created in the United Kingdom but distributed in the U.S.A.

MARVEL UK COMICS
DEATH'S HEAD II
$1.75 US
$2.15 CAN
1
MARCH
UK 95p
PART ONE OF FOUR
© 1992 Marvel Comics UK Ltd.
WHEN I ABSORB YOUR CONSCIOUSNESS, DEATH'S HEAD... I SHALL BE ALL YOU WERE, AND MORE!
MEET THE NEW DEATH'S HEAD CYBORG

Death's Head II #1 back-cover pinup by Liam Sharp

THE WILD HUNT
PART ONE
MERGERS AND ACQUISITIONS
STORY: DAN ABNETT
PENCILS: LIAM SHARP
INKS: ANDY LANNING AND BAMBOS GEORGIOU
COLORS: HELEN STONE
LETTERS: PERI GODBOLD
EDITOR: STEVE WHITE
EDITOR-IN-CHIEF: PAUL NEARY
TYLER'S WORLD, CANOPUS SYSTEM.
'OLD TYLER'S COME A LONG WAY SINCE I FIRST KNEW HIM. GOT A WORLD NAMED AFTER HIM NOW, YES?
'NOT TO MENTION A FORTRESS DESCRIBED BY THE ARCHITECT AS IMPREGNABLE.
' 'COURSE, ONE GLIMPSE OF A TITANIUM AX AND EVEN THE QUIETEST ARCHITECT WILL TALK HIS HEAD OFF.'

...ESPECIALLY WHEN THE MONEY'S GOOD.
'BESIDES, IN MY BOOK, NOTHING'S IMPREGNABLE...
'HMMM... TYLER'S GOT KRYZOTE MERCENARIES IN FULL ARMOR PATROLLING EVERY INCH OF THE CITADEL...
'...AND THERE I WAS HOPING FOR A CHALLENGE.'

KRYZOTES... PLASTEEL ARMOR, MESON SIDEARMS BUT ABSOLUTELY NO GRASP OF THE WORD 'FUTILE'.
SKAZZZZ
'STILL, I SUPPOSE YOU CAN'T KNOCK THEIR ENTHUSIASM, YES?'
GGK...
CHUD
NOW, ARE YOU OTHERS GOING TO COME QUIETLY?
'OF COURSE NOT.
'BUT I LIKE IT THAT WAY...
NNG...
-IT'LL BE THAT MUCH SWEETER, YES?..
CRAK
SZZZSS
-WHEN I COLLECT ON TYLER.
CHAK

'THEIR WAGE PACKETS MUST BE OUT OF THIS WORLD.
'WILSON TYLER'S ENEMIES ARE WEALTHY TOO. THAT'S WHY I'M HERE. CAN'T PRETEND I'M NOT ENJOYING THIS. BEEN WANTING AN EXCUSE TO GO AFTER TYLER FOR YEARS NOW.
'THREE MILLION WAS A GOOD ENOUGH EXCUSE FOR ME.
'THINK I'LL SHOW TYLER THE CHECK BEFORE I RETIRE HIM.
'THAT WAY, EVEN IF HE GETS TO HEAVEN, HE'LL BE JEALOUS AND WON'T ENJOY IT.
'WHERE ARE YOU, TYLER? YOUR OLD BUDDY'S COME TO VISIT...
'YOUR OLD BUDDY... DEATH'S HEAD.
TYLER!

'PLACE IS SILENT... SILENT AS A GRAVE.
'...OR WORSE.
'MAYBE EVERYBODY ELSE HAS TAKEN THE WEEK OFF, YES?
'NO. STILL HAVE TO BE CAREFUL.
'COULD BE A TRAP...
' IT'S WORSE.'
'SOMEONE'S BEATEN ME TO TYLER...
uh... ngggghh...
'...AND IF THAT WAS AN EXAMPLE OF HIS HANDIWORK...
'SOMETHING TELLS ME I'D BETTER BE CAREFUL, YES?
unghh...
'WAIT, TYLER'S TRYIN' TO SPEAK...

YOU'VE BEEN PAID, HAVEN'T YOU?
-I'LL DOUBLE IT...
-STOP! I'LL PAY ANYTHING!
-NO!
'I GET THE PICTURE... THE GUY'S A BOUNTY HUNTER LIKE ME, YES?
FREEZE HE'S MIN

AAAAGGHHH!
SUBJECT 103 – TYLER, WILSON. INSTINCTS ASSIMILATED.
'INSTINCTS ASSIMILATED'? NOT NORMAL BOUNTY HUNTER JARGON– TYLER WAS MISTAKEN, I THINK...

HOLD IT RIGHT THERE– HAVE THE DROP ON YOU, YES?
MATTER OF FACT– NO... BUT I CAN'T TAKE YOU NOW. I GOT ANOTHER APPOINTMENT FIRST.
TYLER WAS WORTH SEVEN DIGITS TO ME... YOU BEAT ME TO HIM. EXPLAIN MOTIVES, YES?
LIKE I SAID, I HAVE AN APPOINTMENT ...BUT AFTER HIM...
–YOU'RE NEXT!
–BUT RIGHT NOW, I'M OUTTA HERE!
SKKKKTTZZT!
PERSONAL TRANSMAT! HE'S GONE...
...BUT THANKS TO THIS TRACKING BEACON, NOT FORGOTTEN, YES?
GLEEP! GLEEP!

A.I.M.* CENTRAL 2020 A.D.
SKKKTTZZZT!
I DON'T REMEMBER PROGRAMMING YOU FOR HUMOR, MINION.
YOU DIDN'T DOCTOR NECKER.
MISSION ACCOMPLISHED. HUNTING INSTINCT OF SUBJECT 103 TYLER, WILSON : FULLY ASSIMILATED. YOU WANT TO CHECK ME OVER?
CUT THE CHAT AND REPORT TO MEDICAL.
HONEY, I'M HOME.
*A.I.M.-ADVANCED IDEA MECHANICS. -Ed.
LOOKING GOOD, DOCTOR NECKER. ALL SYSTEMS GREEN. SEEMS THE CENTRAL DATA CORE IS ABSORBING THE INSTINCTS BETTER THAN WE'D HOPED.
GIVE IT TO ME STRAIGHT, DOC, HOW LONG HAVE I GOT?
THIS FLIPPANCY ISN'T AMUSING, MINION. YOU'D BETTER GET AFTER THE NEXT SUBJECT.
ANY PROBLEMS WITH TYLER?
NOT REALLY, EXCEPT...
...DEATH'S HEAD WAS THERE.
WHAT?
MINION!
SKKKTZZT!

GAFFNEY! GET A FIX ON HIM WITH THE CONTINUUM TRACKER! SEBBLE! GET ALL THE MEMBERS OF THE EXECUTIVE COMMITTEE READY FOR VIRTUAL CONFERENCE IN TEN MINUTES! PRIORITY!
YES, DOCTOR!
VIRTUAL REALITY CONFERENCE ROOM B, TEN MINUTES LATER.
WILL THE MEETING COME TO ORDER...
A.I.M. EXECUTIVE EXTRAORDINARY GATHERING OF OCTOBER TWELVE 2020. DOCTOR EVELYN NECKER REQUESTING AUDIENCE...
THANK YOU FOR ACCESSING VIRTUALITY SO PROMPTLY. I HAVE A PROGRESS REPORT ON PROJECT MINION.
THE MINION CONSTRUCT HAS NOW ENCODED THE INSTINCTS-
KEEP IT SHORT, NECKER. I HAVE A MEETING IN BEJING IN AN HOUR, AND THEY DON'T HAVE VIRTUALITY YET, SO I'VE GOT TO GO IN PERSON FOR GOD'S SAKE.
GOOD GRIEF! PRIMITIVES!
THE ACQUISITION PROGRAM IS ADVANCING AS PREDICTED. THE CONSTRUCT HAS NOW ENCODED THE INSTINCTS OF ONE HUNDRED AND THREE INDIVIDUALS INTO HIS DATA CORE.
GOOD! THAT MEANS YOU'RE ON SCHEDULE! OVERBUDGET, BUT ON SCHEDULE!

PERHAPS. BY PROGRAMING THE CONSTRUCT TO ARM HIMSELF WITH THE TALENTS OF POWERFUL INDIVIDUALS WE HAVE MADE AN AWESOME FORCE. BUT THERE IS A COMPLICATION...
LIKE WHAT, NECKER?
—ON RETURNING FROM HIS LATEST MISSION, MINION DISPLAYED BEHAVIOR WHICH RAN COUNTER TO HIS PROGRAMING, SUCH AS HUMOR, AND RESISTANCE TO DIRECT COMMANDS.
DOCTOR NECKER, WHEN OUR P.D.C.* UNIT PICKED UP AN UNKNOWN THREAT TO A.I.M. WHICH TOTALLY DEMOLISHES THE ORGANIZATION IN THE NEAR FUTURE, WE AGREED TO FUND YOUR MINION PROJECT FOR OUR DEFENSE... AND NOW YOU'RE SAYING IT ISN'T WORKING?
* PRECOGNITIVE DATA COLLECTION—Ed.
NOT SO, MINION IS ACQUIRING THE INSTINCTS OF THE MOST DEADLY INDIVIDUALS IN THE GALAXY. HE WILL SOON BE READY TO DEFEND A.I.M. AGAINST ANYTHING. I MERELY REQUIRE MORE BACKUP FACILITIES... AND A HIGHER BUDGET.
WE RELUCTANTLY CONCUR, DOCTOR. PLEASE KEEP US UPDATED OF ALL IMPROVEMENTS MADE TO HIS CONDITION.
WHERE IS MINION NOW?
IN THE YEAR 2456 A.D., IN THE ZETA RETICULA QUADRANT, IN PURSUIT OF TARGET 104...
A RATHER LARGE BARBARIAN WARRIOR, NAME OF LEHDROX...

ALTIMA FOUR THREE PARSECS FROM ZETA RETICULA...
PHAEDRA, PHAEDRA... SPARE YOURSELF MORE PAIN AND TELL ME WHAT I WANT TO KNOW. I HAVE TRAVELLED FAR TO BENEFIT FROM YOUR POWER TO FORETELL THE FUTURE AND I WON'T GO AWAY EMPTY-HANDED.
YOU KNOW MY LIMITS, LEHDROX...
...I CANNOT FORESEE FOR THOSE WHO DEMAND IT.
THEN I SHALL NOT DEMAND...
SHLACK!
I SHALL REQUEST... POLITELY...
-TELL ME MY FUTURE! TELL ME WHAT LIES IN STORE FOR ME! I MUST KNOW, MY PRETTY...
SKKKTTTKK!
I MUST KNOW NOW!

ALLOW ME TO ENLIGHTEN YOU, LEHDROX. YOU'RE GOING TO DIE VERY SHORTLY AT THE HANDS OF A CYBORG FROM THE TWENTY-FIRST CENTURY!
EH?
YOU WILL BE DISAPPOINTED, LITTLE ONE.
LEHDROX IS TOO FAST...
THUD
TOO CUNNING...
YOU DON'T NEED TO SELL YOUR TALENTS TO ME, LEHDROX...
FZZAAT
RUMMBLE
THEY'RE THE REASON I'M HERE...
KERRASH
I WANT THEM FOR MYSELF...

LEHDROX..?
NO. I'M AFRAID HE LET THINGS GET ON TOP OF HIM.
RELAX. IT'S LEHDROX I WANTED... MATTER OF FACT, I NEED A COUPLE'A SECS WITH HIS BODY...
-BEFORE HIS INSTINCTS GET TOO RUSTY.
'BUT YOU AND I HAVE SOME UNFINISHED BUSINESS...'
SHAKROOM!
...no.. please...
SHAPOW!
HE IS NOT DEAD...
I AM PICKING UP A GLIMPSE OF THE FUTURE AND I SEE HIM...
-FIGHTING WITH YOU!

SKRUNCH!
UUHHNNN!
...LEHDROX STILL LIVES.
STAY BACK. WELL BACK.
SEEMS YOU'RE PRETTY FREE WITH YOUR GIFT WHEN IT SUITS YOU, PHAEDRA...
...THAT'LL COST YOU DEARLY. LATER.
RIGHT NOW, THOUGH...
...I'M GONNA HAVE MY HANDS FULL!
SKAGGTTTTT

MY, YOU'RE AN UGLY ONE, AIN'T CHA?
MIND IF I MAKE A FEW ALTERATIONS?
CHAKT
SCHAKT
-WHY...
what is the-
SHUT UP.
WORD OF ADVICE, LEHDROX. NEVER TURN YOUR BACK ON A CRANIAL DISRUPTION SYPHON.
AAAAGGHHHHhhh...
SUBJECT 104 LEHDROX, K'VANT. INSTINCTS ASSIMILATED.

I CANNOT CONDONE YOUR METHODS, BUT I THANK YOU FOR MY LIFE.
WHAT, NO GRATEFUL KISS?
I FEEL WE SHALL MEET AGAIN. FAREWELL...
...DEATH'S HEAD
DEATH'S HEAD? DARLING, AS A PRECOG, YOU'RE WAY OUT OF WHACK...
KZ-ZZTTT
SECONDS LATER...
KRAKOOOMM

...MISSED HIM, YES? BUT NOT BY MUCH...
...GOT A FIRM FIX ON HIS TELEPORTER LEADING BACK TO...
GLEEP GLEEP
EARTH... OCTOBER TWELVE 2020.
HERE HE COMES NOW... MINION...
SKKZZZT!
...THAT'S FAR ENOUGH! YOUR DEVIANT BEHAVIOUR CONCERNS ME GREATLY. REPORT FOR A THOROUGH SYSTEMS CHECK!
NO TIME...

...I'VE ABSORBED SUBJECT 104, LEHDROX. CHECK ME OVER QUICKLY SO THAT I CAN MAKE THE NEXT TRIP.
NO GO, MINION. WE'VE SUNK BILLIONS INTO YOUR CREATION TO PROTECT US FROM SOME AS YET UNKNOWN FUTURE THREAT.
WE MUST BE SURE YOU FUNCTION PERFECTLY.
JUST DO IT DOCTOR.
DOCTOR NECKER! WE'RE REGISTERING A MASSIVE POWER SURGE ROOF LEVEL.
TISHHHH!
FOUND YOU, YES?
KRA

...NOW YOU'RE GOING TO PAY IN FULL!
KRA-POW!
NECKER TO ALL SECURITY FIRETEAMS! EMERGENCY IN THE WEAPONS CONSTRUCT CHAMBER! MOVE IT!
YOU CHEATED ME OF TYLER. CAN'T GET NO THREE MILLION NOW, BUT I CAN GET SATISFACTION, YES?
AHHHH... DON'T STRUGGLE. IT'LL BE EASIER FOR YOU...
KIDDING, YES?
DO I LOOK LIKE I'M KIDDING?
AAARRGH!
SKRRANCH
YOU ARE SUBJECT 105, DEATH'S HEAD, AND YOU'VE SAVED ME THE BOTHER OF FINDING YOU!

KRA-CHUNK
I ADMIRE YOUR GUTS, DEATH'S HEAD.
YOU HAVEN'T SEEN THEM.
-YET!
TH
RATCH!
RAAAH!
SKZZZ
SMISSSH!
SKRUNCH

GOOD FIGHT, BUT IT ENDS HERE.
UUUNNFF... NO!
YES!
SUBJECT 105 DEATH'S HEAD...
HIS SYSTEMS ARE OVERLOADING! THERE'S SOMETHING WRONG WITH THAT LAST IMPLANT! I'M LOSING CENTRAL COUNT-ERMAND! DOCTOR NECKER?!
...INSTINCTS ASSIMILATED.
KKZZZMM!
I DON'T... SOMETHING WRONG... AAARRGGHH!
MINION? MINION... ANSWER ME!

I CAN'T... I... HELP ME...
KZZZZTT ...SUBJECT 106. TARGETING LOCKED ON.
MINION? ANSWER ME! WHAT'S GOING ON?
KZZZZTTT!
-I'LL BE BACK. YES?
TELEPORT! HE'S GOING! STOP HIM!
GET A FIX ON HIM! WHERE'S HE GOING?
TIME DILATION READS AS DESTINATION EARTH CIRCA 1992. HE'S GONE AFTER THE LAST TARGET, DOCTOR.
THE COUNCIL'LL STRING ME UP IF WE LOSE HIM. RESET THE TIME JUMP. I'M GOING AFTER HIM.
WHO IS THE LAST TARGET?
ACCORDING TO THIS, SUBJECT 106 IS A HUMAN NAMED...
...REED RICHARDS.
NEXT: THE FANTASTIC 4

THE MARVEL UK UNIVERSE
BEGINS...
PENDRAGON
MOTORMOUTH
DIGITEK
HELL'S ANGE
THE NEW BRITISH MARVEL SUB-UNIVERSE IS ONLY MONTHS AWAY... THE ACTION STARTS HERE...
WARHEADS
SNEAK PREVIEW #1

THE MYS-TECH ORGANISATION

PORLOCK
GRYFFN
RATHCOOLE
CROWE
WYCHWOOD

987 AD... In a cavern beneath *Darkmoor* in Southern England, a bizarre and sinister ritual takes place.

Seven members of an *arcane mystical cult* are gathered to perform a ceremony that will alter the future of the entire world.

Calling upon the druidic powers of the Ancients, the seven mystics attempt to attain immortality. They do this by re-creating a *Ceremony of Incantation* from a partially destroyed document thought to come from ancient Atlantis.

They succeed in manifesting the means to attain *immortality*, but are stunned by the manner in which it is granted to them.

Rather than the spell making them immortal directly, it releases a powerful Demonic Entity who tells them that their incantation has sealed them in a pact with him. They must pay for immortality with *eternal enslavement*.

This consists of fashioning an intricate web of misery, disaster and death which will supply the Entity with a steady feast of lost souls.

1992 AD... A thousand years later, the immortal cult-members, now accomplished *Techno-Wizards*, have become the Board of the evil Multi-National Conglomerate of companies known as MyS -TECH.

But all is not well, for although the Board has prospered beyond imagining from the Entity's gift of immortality, which has allowed them to develop the arts of *Hi-Tech Mysticism*, they are weary of fulfilling the demands of their increasingly greedy master.

They have begun a dangerous program to achieve immortality by their *own* means and then attack and *terminate* the Entity...

HALDANE
TYBURN

Hell's An

Shevaun Haldane is Hell's Angel

Daughter of **MyS-TECH** Board-Member **Ranulph Haldane**, she finds herself suddenly in the position to take over his place on the Board.

As the Chief Researcher for MyS-TECH, and the most accomplished Techno-Wizard on the Board, Ranulph has made sure that his daughter's education in the arcane art of Hi-Tech Mysticism has been complete.

Ranulph, sworn to secrecy, has never told her the details of the MyS-TECH Board's background or operation, but Shevaun has picked up enough to hate all they stand for.

She is aided in her personal struggle against the might of MyS-TECH by **Darkangel**, the Angel of Death. He donates a fragment of the Fabric of the Universe which becomes her costume. She is intrigued to discover that she is now one with the Universe, and begins to learn the extent of her many new powers.

MACNEIL '91

NEXT MONTH!
PREVIEW #2 WILL FEATURE MORE NEW HEROES FROM THE BRITISH MARVEL SUB-UNIVERSE!
- HOW COOL CAN ONE BECOME?
MARVEL COMICS
DEATH'S HEAD II
2
DON'T MISS
THE NEXT GREAT DOUBLE-COVER ISSUE!
- GUEST STARRING THE FANTASTIC FOUR!!
ON SALE IN 30 DAYS!
MARVEL COMICS
DEATH'S HEAD II
2

MARVEL COMICS
IN HER OWN BOOK AT LAST!
SILVER SABLE
& THE WILD PACK
$2.00 US
$2.45 CAN
1
JUNE
£1.00 UK
APPROVED BY THE COMICS CODE AUTHORITY
GUEST-STARRING
the AMAZING SPIDER-MAN!
30TH ANNIVERSARY 1962 1992
THE AMAZING SPIDER-MAN
STEVEN PANOSIAN

SILVER SABLE AND THE WILD PACK #1, published in April 1992, began an ongoing series starring the Symkarian champion and her elite mercenary team.

RELENTLESSLY TRAINED IN MULTIPLE FORMS OF HAND-TO-HAND AND ARMED COMBAT, SILVER SABLE WAS DESTINED TO INHERIT THE COMMAND OF HER FATHER'S PROFESSIONAL SOLDIER UNIT, THE WILDPACK. UNDER THE AUSPICES OF SILVER SABLE INTERNATIONAL, SHE HAS SINCE TRANSFORMED THEM INTO THE ULTIMATE MERCENARY COMBAT FORCE, NOW THE ECONOMIC FOUNDATION OF HER BELOVED HOMELAND, SYMKARIA.

STAN LEE PRESENTS. . . SILVER SABLE & THE WILD PACK

SYMKARIA. A SMALL BALKAN STATE WHOSE ECONOMIC WELL-BEING DEPENDS PRIMARILY ON THE ACTIONS OF ONE WOMAN.
SILVER SABLE.
SHE AND HER ORGANIZATION, SILVER SABLE INTERNATIONAL, ARE THE CORNER-STONE OF THE COUNTRY'S REVENUE.
THEIR BUSINESS IS FAR FROM CONVENTIONAL.
THEY ARE AN UNPARALLELED MER-CENARY COMBAT UNIT, SPECIALIZING IN THE APPREHENSION OF WANT-ED FELONS AND THE RECOVERY OF STOLEN PROPERTY.
PERSONAL STAKES
GREGORY WRIGHT, WRITER STEVEN BUTLER & PENCILER JIM SANDERS III INKER
JOE ROSAS COLORIST
JADE MOEDE LETTERER
CRAIG ANDERSON EDITOR
TOM DeFALCO EDITOR IN CHIEF
SILVER SABLE CREATED BY TOM DeFALCO AND RON FRENZ

THE MERCENARIES IN SABLE'S EMPLOY ARE KNOWN AS THE WILD PACK.
THE SPECTRUM OF CLIENTELE RANGES FROM WEALTHY INDIVIDUALS TO ENTIRE NATIONS.
SILVER SABLE IS A WOMAN WHO DEMANDS NOTHING LESS THAN PERFECTION IN HER OPERATIONS.
SPLOOSH
AND NOTHING PREVENTS HER FROM REACHING HER OBJECTIVES.
THE IMPACT DRIVES THE AIR FROM HIS LUNGS.
AS IT STANDS, HE'LL DROWN IN SECONDS.
HE SHOULD HAVE LEARNED TO DIVE.
IT COULD HAVE SAVED HIS LIFE.

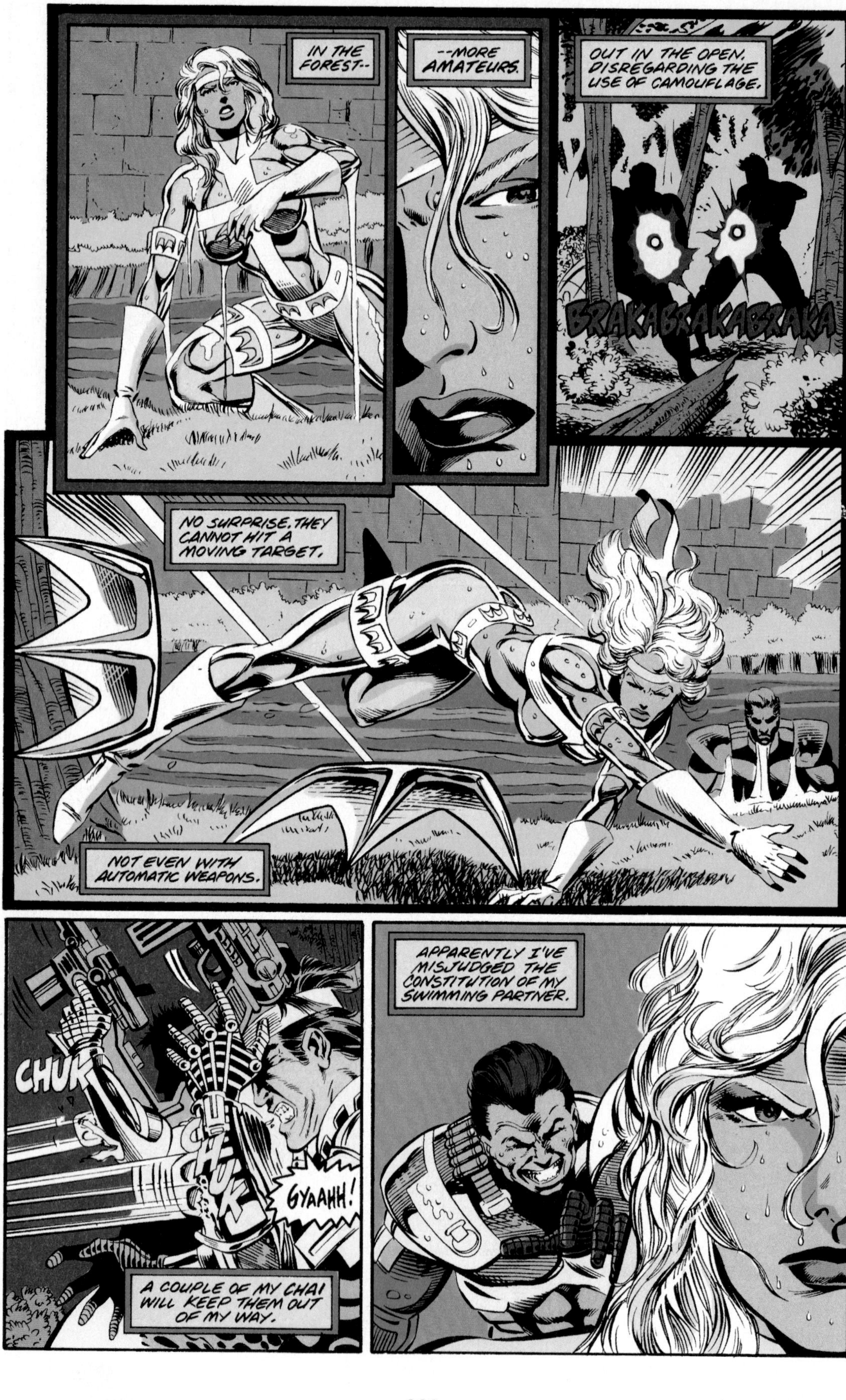
IN THE FOREST--
--MORE AMATEURS.
OUT IN THE OPEN, DISREGARDING THE USE OF CAMOUFLAGE.
BRAKABRAKABRAKA
NO SURPRISE. THEY CANNOT HIT A MOVING TARGET.
NOT EVEN WITH AUTOMATIC WEAPONS.
CHUK
CHUK
CHUK
GYAAHH!
A COUPLE OF MY CHAI WILL KEEP THEM OUT OF MY WAY.
APPARENTLY I'VE MISJUDGED THE CONSTITUTION OF MY SWIMMING PARTNER.

DARLIN', AH'D LIKE A BIT MORE A' YORE--
KRAK
THIS ONE SEEMS TO HAVE A HIGH TOLERANCE FOR PAIN.
THOK
EVERY MAN HAS HIS LIMIT.
AND I'VE NEVER HAD TROUBLE FINDING IT.
SILVER, BABY-- YOU CAN'T GET PAST THREE OF US!
I DETEST UNFOUNDED ARROGANCE--
ARRRHHH!
--AND I DO NOT APPRECIATE BEING CALLED "BABY"!
WHHURGHH!

I BELIEVE I'VE WASTED MORE TIME THAN--
AH'S ALWAYS BEEN PARTIAL TA TACKLIN' A WOMAN FROM BEHIND!
I'M SURE.
I HAD ASSUMED YOUR BRAIN WAS IN YOUR SKULL.
MY MISTAKE.
EEEEEEESHHH!
KRUNCH
I WON'T LET IT HAPPEN AGAIN.
YOU'LL HAVE TO EXCUSE ME--
GUP...
--I HAVE A VICTORY TO CLAIM.
NOT SO FAST, SILVER!
SANDMAN...
...DID YOU REALLY BELIEVE I WOULDN'T FIND A PILE OF SAND A LITTLE UNUSUAL IN A FOREST?
OH. I DIDN'T THINK--

OBVIOUSLY, YOU DIDN'T THINK. LET'S NOT MAKE A HABIT OUT OF IT.
LORNA! UNCLE MORTY!
ZAT VASS DISGRACEFUL! HOW DO ANY OF YOU EXPEKT TO BEKOME HIS VILDPACK?
IT VASN'T EFAN A PROPER EXERCIZE SESSION FOR FRAULEIN SABLE!
YOU HAVE TO SHOUT SO LOUD, LORNA?
ZAY VON'T LISTEN OTHERVISE, MORTY.
PLEASE ACCEPT MY APOLOGIES FOR ZERE DISGRACEFUL PERFORMANCE, FRAULEIN.
I VILL SEND ZEM ALL BACK VERE ZAY CAME--
I WANT TO KEEP THE ONE WITH THE PONYTAIL.
POWELL? NEIN! HE EES SCHWEINHUND! UND VITH HISS BACKGROUND I SHOULD THINK--
HE WITH-STOOD THREE OF MY ATTACKS. HE STAYS.

SUNSET BRINGS THE CLOSE TO ANOTHER DAY OF WORK FOR MOST CITIZENS OF SYMKARIA.
THE SAME IS NOT TRUE FOR THOSE IN THE EMPLOY OF SILVER SABLE.
...ADVICE TO THEM IS TO PAY THE KIDNAPPER'S RANSOM. IT'S FAR LESS THAN MY FEE.
THE "COMPANY'S" OFFER HAS SUBSTANTIALLY INCREASED FOR THE ASSASSINATION OF--
REJECT IT. I'M NOT RUNNING MURDER INC. FOR ANYONE.
AND THE STOLEN IDOLS FROM NORWAY?
AS SOON AS THEY AGREE TO MY ORIGINAL ESTIMATE.
MEXICAN CRUISE LINES HIJACKING?
GIVE THAT ONE TO OUR FRANCHISE IN CANCUN. ANY NEW BUSINESS?
CRANEWOOD SCHOOL FOR GIRLS, IN NORTHAMPTON, LONG ISLAND--
--HYDRA TERRORISTS HAVE SEIZED THE DORMITORY.
SEVERAL WORLDWIDE POLITICAL FIGURES HAVE DAUGHTERS THERE.
I SHOULDN'T BE REMINDING YOU THAT YOUR NIECE, ANNA, IS A STUDENT--
HAS THERE BEEN ANY FINANCIAL OFFERING FOR THIS SITUATION? NO? I'M NOT RUNNING A CHARITY. NEXT.
ANNA IS FAMILY, SO YOU'LL MAKE AN EXCEPTION?
WE ARE DISCUSSING BUSINESS, NOT PERSONAL CONCERNS! NEXT!
BUT THIS IS YOUR OWN BLOOD SILVER!
YOU DON'T EVEN CARE? YOUR FATHER EVEN--
MY FATHER IS DEAD BECAUSE HE CARED!
I'VE LEARNED FROM, AND WILL NOT BE REPEATING HIS MISTAKES!
NEXT!

SSSHHOOOM
NIGHT FALLS AROUND CASTLE SABLE AS A LONE STEALTHCRAFT LAUNCHES INTO THE DARKNESS...
I'M CURSED TO REPEAT MY FATHER'S MISTAKES.
MORTY AND ANNA ARE MY ONLY LIVING RELATIVES.
AND I DO CARE.
MORE THAN I CAN AFFORD TO.
MOTHER DIED TRYING TO KEEP ME FROM FOLLOWING IN FATHERS FOOTSTEPS.
HER DEATH GAVE ME MORE DETERMINATION THAN EVER TO HELP HIM HUNT DOWN NAZI WAR CRIMINALS WITH HIS WILD PACK.
HE TAUGHT ME EVERYTHING HE KNEW.
"NEVER LET IT GET PERSONAL. IT'LL MAKE YOU SLOPPY." HE SAID.
BUT IT WAS ALL PERSONAL.
HE CARED ABOUT ALL OF IT.
THAT'S WHAT KILLED HIM.
TREFKOV HAD WAITED FOR THE SLOPPINESS.
THEN HE VANISHED.
I WILL FIND HIM, AND TAKE MY REVENGE.
BUT NOT TODAY.
TODAY IS FOR ANNA.
SHE WON'T LIKE IT, SANDMAN.
I'M GOIN' AFTER HER, MORTY.
I KNOW IT. BUT SHE GAVE ME A SHOT WHEN I DIDN'T DESERVE ONE.
I GOTTA WATCH HER BACK.

HOURS LATER, CRANEWOOD SCHOOL FOR GIRLS, NORTH-AMPTON, LONG ISLAND.
SILVER SABLE IS NOT THE FIRST TO ARRIVE.
STEALTHCRAFT'S IN CLOAKING MODE.
I SHOULD BE ABLE TO GO IN UNDETECTED.
...DEMANDS FROM HYDRA TERRORISTS ARE REACHING AROUND THE WORLD. THEY ARE REQUIRING THE RE-LEASE OF TWENTY-SEVEN SEPARATE INTERNATIONAL CRIMINALS OF THE VARIOUS STATES...
WBLX
POLICE
PARKER! PETER, THE BUGLE DIDN'T SEND US ALL THE WAY UP HERE TO DAYDREAM!
I WANT YOU TO BE READY FOR--
HUH? OH, SORRY JOY. I'M JUST... UH... TRYING TO SEE THROUGH THIS CROWD--
--I CAN'T GET A CLEAR SHOT FROM HERE... I'M GOING TO TRY FOR A BETTER ANGLE... BYE!
PETER! WAIT, I'LL--
I'LL BE RIGHT BACK. STAY HERE SO I CAN FIND YOU!
I'LL GET ANNA OUT IN RECORD TIME AS LONG AS I DON'T GET ANY INTERFERENCE FROM THE POLICE.

TWO GUARDS.
HEAVILY ARMED.
HE'S SEEN ME.
INCOMING! HEADS UP!
BLAM
I'D HOPED TO DO THIS QUIETLY.
BRAKKA BRAKKA
THOK
WHOOOF!
BRAKKA BRAKKA
A WOMAN?! HAH! SHE WILL BLEED TO DEATH AT OUR FEET!
I'D ALSO HOPED TO ABSTAIN FROM ANY KILLING.
BLAM
SOME THINGS CAN'T BE AVOIDED.

SHOTS! THOSE CAME FROM THE ROOF!
WON'T THESE HYDRA BOZO'S BE SURPRISED TO SEE THEIR FRIENDLY NEIGHBORHOOD--
SPIDER-MAN?
WHAT ARE YOU DOING HERE?
NICE TO SEE YOU, TOO, MS. SABLE.
I DON'T SUPPOSE THAT HYDRA AGENT'S ASLEEP AT YOUR FEET--
SAVE YOUR SPEECHES. I'M IN NO MOOD.
DO YOU HATE ALL MEN, OR JUST ME?
I HEARD THAT. WEB UP THE LIVE ONE AND LEAVE.
I'M GOING IN.
ALONE.
HEY! I'M NOT ONE OF YOUR LACKEYS TO BE ORDERED AROUND!
I'M COMING IN WITH YOU, LIKE IT OR NOT!
NOT.
BUT I'VE NO TIME TO ARGUE.

INSIDE...
THOSE SHOTS CAME FROM THE ROOF.
ANDRE...CHECK IT OUT. AND KEEP CONSTANT CONTACT.
YES, LIEUTENANT.
...LOCAL SWAT TEAMS ARE STANDING READY, WHILE POLICE HELI-COPTERS ARE--
COLA
LET'S SEE WHAT'S HAPPENING AROUND BACK.
HOLMES, YOYO, ANY ACTION ON THE DARK SIDE OF THE MOON?
NEGATIVE.
REGARDLESS, I THINK IT'S TIME WE SHOW THEM WE MEAN BUSINESS.
KILL ONE OF THE GIRLS AND THROW HER OUT THE WINDOW FOR THE POLICE TO SEE.
ANY MORE DELAYING TACTICS ON THEIR PART AND WE DO IT AGAIN.
NO! ANNA, HELP ME!
SARAH!
SLASH
HEARTLESS SWINE... I NEVER SHOULD'VE LEFT SYMKARIA... NEVER!

MEANWHILE...
HALL'S CLEAN. PROCEEDING TO ROOF.
THWIPP
MY, WHAT A BIG GUN YOU HAVE!
?
YOU KNOW WHAT THEY SAY ABOUT THE SIZE OF A MAN'S GUN?
SPIDER-MAN, DON'T--
THE BIGGER THEY ARE... THE HARDER I HIT!
YOU IDIOT!
KRAK
ANDRE--
RAAAGH!
YOU ARE RUINING MY OPERATION.
SORRY. SO SHOOT ME.
DON'T TEMPT ME.
--WHAT'S HAPPENING? ANDRE!!
NOW THEY KNOW WE'RE HERE. WE'VE LOST THE ADVANTAGE.

SOMEWHERE OVER THE ATLANTIC OCEAN, THE CAVALRY RIDES IN A STEALTHCRAFT, MORE THAN SLIGHTLY FASTER THAN HORSES.
YOU KNOW, POWELL, YOU WERE THE ONLY RECRUIT CHOSEN FOR SILVER'S ELITE SQUADRON!
THANKEE, SANDMAN. AH'M SHORE YORE RECOMMENDATION WAS A HELP!
HEY, SILVER SABLE INTERNATIONAL DOES PAY A HEADHUNTERS FEE.
THAT SILVER'S QUITE A SLICE 'A PIE--
AH'M 'A GONNA HAFTA HAVE ME SOME 'A--
YOU TALK LIKE THAT AROUND THE BOSS-LADY AND YOU'LL GET SLICED!
WE'LL SEE.
YOU A BETTIN' MAN?
WHEN THE ODDS ARE STACKED IN MY FAVOR--
--HOW ABOUT $10,000.?
AND I'LL BET WITH THE HOUSE!
YORE ON! FIRST I'LL "TAKE" THE HOUSE, THEN YORE GRAND... Y'HEAH?
NOW, LET'S GIT THEM HYDRA VARMINTS!

ANDRE!
HE'S DOWN--OUR POSITION'S BEEN COMPROMISED.
SPREAD OUT AND BRING ME THE INTRUDER, DEAD!
HOLMES, YOYO--TAKE YOUR SQUADS OUT OF THE DARK SIDE... DO YOU COPY?
AFFIRMATIVE.
YOU LITTLE BOOKWORMS MAY NOT BE GETTING OUT OF HERE ALIVE AFTER ALL...!
YOUR DEATHS WILL PROVE TO THE WORLD THAT HYDRA MUST NOT BE TRIFLED WITH!
YOU ARE NO BETTER THAN HITLER'S GOOSE-STEPPING NAZI PIGS!
YOU ARE WRONG. HYDRA IS FAR SUPERIOR!
WHILE, IN THE HALLWAYS...
SNNAP
EEE!!!!!!
MY TURN. YOU'RE NOT THE ONLY ONE WHO KNOWS AKIDO, HONEY!
VUMP

I CONGRATULATE YOUR KNOWLEDGE.
GUHHHH!
AHHHHH!
KRAKK
KEE-YIAAAH!
"DO SOME RECON OUTSIDE, THAT'LL KEEP YOU OUT OF MY WAY." SHEESH! THAT WOMAN ALWAYS MAKES ME FEEL LIKE SOME RANK AMATEUR!
IF SHE'D TELL ME THE PLAN, I WOULDN'T HAVE TO GUESS!
THE GIRLS MUST BE HELD IN ONE OF THESE ROOMS!
BINGO! AND ONLY THREE BOYS IN GREEN AND YELLOW-- WHAT'S THAT SOUND?
WILD PACK, PREPARE TO DETACH!

UH-OH! I DON'T THINK SILVER SABLE'S GONNA LIKE THIS!
I'LL TAKE THE INDIRECT ROUTE!
SUIT YOURSELF, SANDMAN!
KRA-A-ASH
LOOK! UP IN THE SKY!
WHO ARE THEY?
PETER? WHERE'D HE GO?
IT'S SOME KIND OF PLANE...
BRAKKA BRAKKA
HYDRA IS NOT USUALLY GUILTY OF OVERKILL.
BLAM
THEY WERE EXPECTING A LARGE RESISTANCE.

BLAM
BLAM
BUT THEY DIDN'T EXPECT A COMPETENT OPPONENT.
MISS ME, SUGAH?
BRAMMMM
POWELL?!
WHAT ARE YOU DOING HERE?
SANDMAN FIGGERED YOU MIGHT BE NEEDIN' SOME BACK-UP--
--AN' AH WOULDN'T WANT TA MISS SEEIN' YOU IN--
-GASP --UHHHH-- GASP-
HE THOUGHT WRONG!
SINCE YOU'RE HERE, GET THE REST OF THE WILD PACK AND CLEAN THESE CLOWNS OUT OF HERE!
YOU CAN HANDLE THAT?
OH, YES, MA'AM!
I'VE GOT A HOSTAGE TO RESCUE--
YOU SEND ME ON RECON AND TAKE ALL THE FUN!
THERE ARE PLENTY--
NO, NO, THAT WAS HUMOR, OF WHICH YOU HAVE NO SENSE OF--
BUT-- I FOUND THE GIRLS! C'MON!

WHAT DO YOU MEAN, YOU'RE RETREATING?!
SIR WE'RE UNDER-UHHN! BLAMMBLAMM-ZZHHHHH-
LOOK'S LIKE IT'S YOU WHO WON'T BE GETTING OUT OF HERE ALIVE!
IS... THAT... SO?
PERHAPS YOU'D LIKE TO GRANT A DYING MAN'S LAST WISH, MY LITTLE BEAUTY?
WHILE IN THE HEATING DUCTS...
BEIN' MADE OF SAND SURE SPEEDS UP INFILTRATION!
SABLE'S PACK SEEM TO BE MOPPIN' UP THE PLACE--
BUT WHERE IS SILVER?
I WON'T LET ANYTHING HAPPEN TO HER!

THWAM
YOU GET ONE WARNING-- LET THE GIRL GO NOW OR--
DMITRI?!
WHY IN THE NAME OF GOD ARE YOU ASSOCIATING WITH HYDRA?
SILVER SABLE? I CANNOT IMAGINE WHAT BRINGS YOU HERE!
AUNT SILVER!
WELL, WELL. LET'S JUST SAY IT WAS AN UNBELIEVABLE CAREER OPORTUNITY, AUNT SABLE.
NOW, YOU WOULDN'T KILL A FORMER LOVER WHO HAS YOUR NIECE IN SO PRECARIOUS A POSITION... WOULD YOU?

THREE AGAINST TWO ISN'T VERY SPORTING--
--THANKS FOR VOLUNTEERING TO MAKE THE ODDS EVEN!
THWOK
IT'S OVER, DMITRI. YOU KNOW I CAN PUT THREE BULLETS BETWEEN YOUR EYES BEFORE YOU CAN KILL THE CHILD.
HYDRA FROWNS ON COWARDICE, MY DEAR.
IF I'M TO DIE, THEN YOU'LL BE ACCOMPANYING ME--
--STRAIGHT INTO A COLD PRISON CELL!
WHAT SORT OF--
DISTRACTION LEADS TO DEFEAT. THAT'S ALWAYS BEEN A PROBLEM FOR YOU.
ARRHHH!

LET GO OF ME!
IF YOU'RE IN PAIN 'CAUSE OF A LITTLE GIRL, JUST WAIT TILL I--
NO!
HE BELONGS TO ME!
CHOMP
WE HAVE PERSONAL BUSINESS TO DISCUSS!
UHHHN!
I MIGHT KILL A FORMER LOVER WHO KISSES AND TELLS...
...IF SOMEONE PAID ME ENOUGH!
WE GOT ALL THEM RASCALS ROUNDED UP, SUGAH.
DID AH HEAR YOU RIGHT... YOU... AND A TERRORIST?
AH DO HOPE Y'ALL PRACTICED SAFE--
DON'T SAY IT, POWELL.
I CAN CHANGE MY MIND ABOUT YOU ANYTIME.
THAT'S WHAT AH'M BETTIN' ON.

OUTSIDE, LATER...
LOOKS LIKE WE REALLY CAME THROUGH ON THIS ONE, EH, SILVER? I WAS WORRIED, SO NATURALLY--
SAND-MAN...
OH AUNT SILVER! I WAS SO SCARED!
BUT THEN YOU CAME AND RESCUED ME!
I ABSOLUTELY HATE IT HERE... TAKE ME BACK TO SYMKARIA WITH YOU. TAKE ME BACK--
WHAT?
CEASE THIS UNDIGNIFIED SNIVELING, ANNA.
YOU WILL REMAIN HERE. I'M LAYING OUT THOUSANDS FOR THE FINEST EDUCATION FOR YOU.
YOU WILL DO AS I SAY, WHILE YOU'RE A MINOR, WITHOUT COMPLAINT.
AND YOU--
ME?
YOU AND THOSE WITH YOU WILL NOT ONLY BE DOCKED TWO WEEKS SALARY, BUT FINED AS WELL.
FINED? WHY? WE CAME ALL THE WAY TO--
--WRECKLESSLY ENDANGER YOURSELVES ON AN UNOFFICIALLY SANCTIONED MISSION, WASTE FIGHTER FUEL, AND AMMUNITION--
--AND YOU, SANDMAN, WILL NOW BE DOCKED THREE WEEKS PAY.
CARE TO TRY FOR FURTHER DISCIPLINARY ACTION?
SHEESH!
WELL, C'MON! WE DO HAVE PAYING ASSIGNMENTS WAITING!
NEXT: BIG GUNS PART 1-- GATTLING'S GUNS!

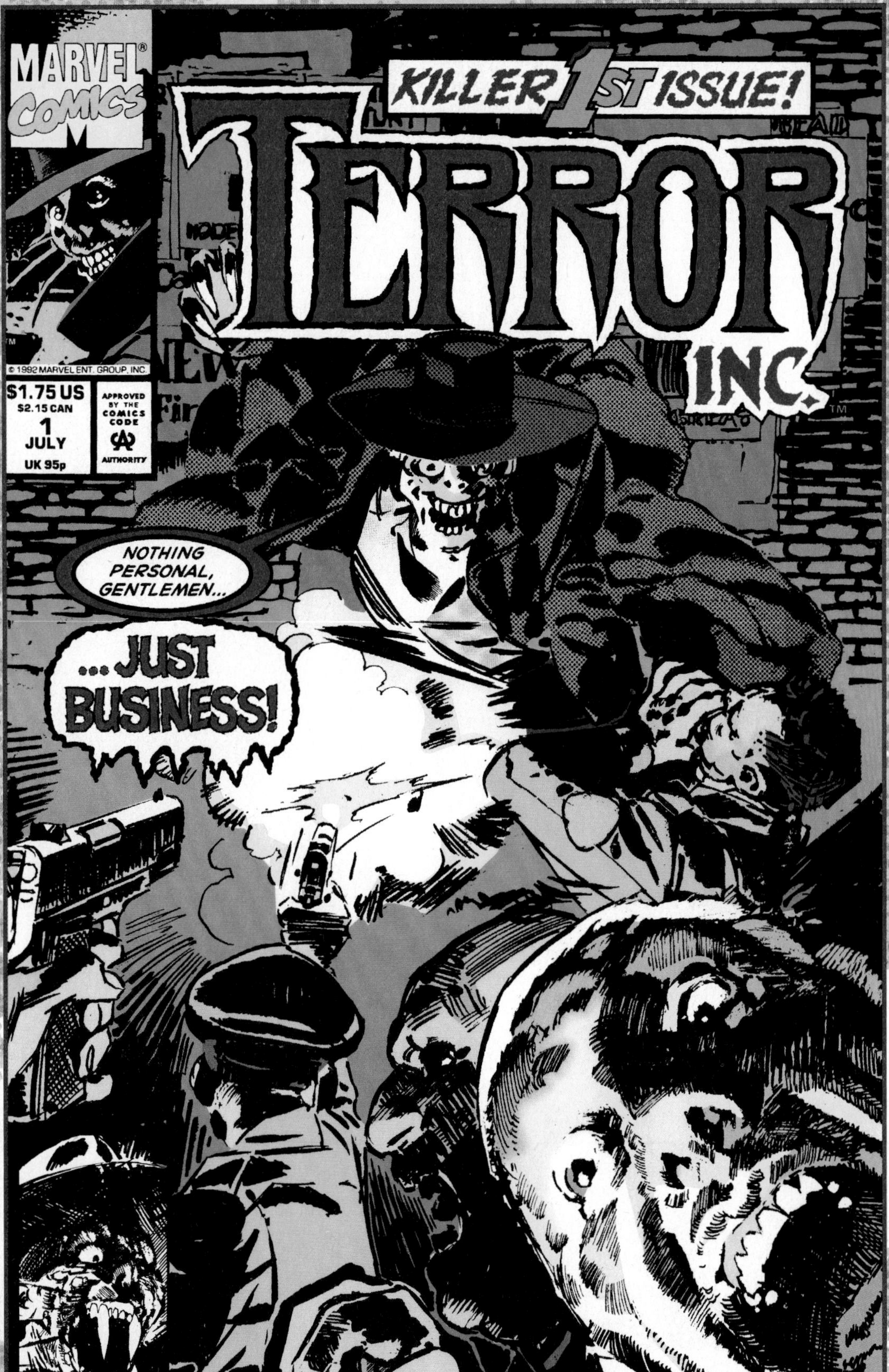
MARVEL COMICS
KILLER 1ST ISSUE!
TERROR INC.
© 1992 MARVEL ENT. GROUP, INC.
$1.75 US
$2.15 CAN
1
JULY
UK 95p
APPROVED BY THE COMICS CODE AUTHORITY
NOTHING PERSONAL, GENTLEMEN...
...JUST BUSINESS!

TERROR INC. #1, published in May 1992, introduced the grotesque limb-stealing mercenary in an ongoing series.

TRADING IN A MACABRE SPECIALTY TO TAKE ON THE TALENTS OF OTHERS' BODY PARTS, HE IS A GRIM ENTREPRENEUR WHO DOES BUSINESS ON THE EDGE OF THE LAW AND THE DARK SIDE OF REALITY. ANTI-HERO AND ROGUE, HE'S AN ARCANE GUN FOR HIRE. STAN LEE PRESENTS:

TERROR INC.
CAVEAT EMPTOR
DRIP
by D.G. CHICHESTER & JORGE ZAFFINO
LETTERER • Gaspar
COLORIST • STEVEN BUCCELLATO
EDITOR • MARCUS McLAURIN
EDITOR IN CHIEF • TOM DeFALCO
SPECIAL THANKS • SVEN LARSEN
CREATED BY D.G. CHICHESTER MARGARET CLARK AND KLAUS JANSON
UNDERSTAND THIS... IT'S NOT THAT I HAD A PROBLEM WITH KILLING ROGER BARBATOS.

DRIP DRIP DRIP
TAP TAP TAP
I'M HURT, TERROR...
...INSULTED REALLY!
YOU'VE SPOILED ME WITH THE ELABORATE, THE IMAGINATIVE--
DRIP
MY DIFFICULTY RESTED IN KEEPING THE CORPULENT TOAD OF A WEAPONS MERCHANT DEAD.
--THE BOMB IN MY BEEMER, STRYCHNINE ON POSTAGE STAMPS, ELECTRIFYING URINALS AT MY FAVORITE RESTAURANTS.
I SHOULD'VE BEEN READY FOR DISAPPOINTMENT WHEN YOU STRAFED ME ON THE YACHT--THAT WAS MUNDANE.
TAP
BUT THIS--SLITTING MY THROAT?--CRUDE!
AND NO MORE EFFECTIVE THAN ANYTHING ELSE.
MY APOLOGIES, BARBATOS...

...DECAPITATION MORE TO YOUR LIKING?
I SUPPOSE YOU THINK THAT'D PUT YOU BACK ON THE CUTTING EDGE, ASSASSIN HA-HA!
STEP BACK SLOW, HANDS IN THE--
BUT WHERE I'M CONCERNED IT'D ONLY BE FURTHER PROOF YOUR PRECIOUS REP'S FAILED YOU AGAIN--
--WHILE THE NEW SECURITY SYSTEM THESE IRRITATING ATTEMPTS ON MY LIFE HAVE FORCED ME TO INSTALL IS AN UNQUALIFIED SUCCESS!
BRATATAT
A BACKWARDS KICK SENDS THE CHAIR WHEELING WILDLY, MOMENTARY DISTRACTION FOR SOME--
GRAAK
--ETERNAL MISDIRECTION FOR OTHERS.
AGGH!
CAN'T SEE! I CAN'T--
BLOOD SPLATTERS, BLINDING, DISORIENTING...
...AND ENABLING AN EARLY WITHDRAWAL FROM TONIGHT'S BAD INVESTMENT.
RB ARMS & MUNITIONS
Roger Barbatos
CEO
FWKAATR

WHERE'S HE ?! WHERE'S HE AT ?!
THERE -- THE DESK!
BUDDA BUDDA
"CAVEAT EMPTOR", I ALWAYS ADVISE MY CLIENTS BEFORE ENTERING INTO A CONTRACT--
I'M TRYING, ROGER-- THE KNOTS, THEY'RE--
GET ME OUT OF THIS, LOLA, GET ME--I WANT THAT MOTHERLESS--!
--"BUYER BEWARE"--
THE LIGHT, HE'S SWINGIN' OFF THE--
JUST SHOOT 'IM, BLOW 'IM AWAY!
--FOR IT IS A MASOCHISTIC FEW WHO APPRECIATE BEING MADE THE TARGET OF MY BRAND OF SALES-MANSHIP.
THOSE S.O.B.'s WHO HIRED YOUR SORRY BACKSIDE, TERROR--
BUT EVEN THE DREAD POTENTIAL OF RICOCHETING VENGEANCE CAN-NOT DISSUADE THOSE ALREADY DRIVEN SO FAR AS TO SEEK--
KRAASH
FWOOM
--TO RISK--
--EMPLOYING MY SELECT SERVICES.
--WHAT'S GONNA BE LEFT OF YOU IS JUST A TASTE OF WHAT THEY'VE GOT COMING!

AS TO THE NATURE OF THAT TRADE, THE CAPITALIST MERCHANDISING OF TERROR--
--MARKETABLE GOODS CHIEFLY BEING THOSE OF SHOCK, INTIMIDATION AND VIOLENCE--
--THIS IS MY BUSINESS.
AND BUSINESS IS GOOD.

PERHAPS NOT AT THIS PARTICULAR MOMENT IN TIME, BUT GENERALLY SPEAKING.
I BRACE MYSELF AGAINST THE IMPACT...
--EVEN AS MY RIGHT ARM COMES OFF JUST BELOW THE SHOULDER, SHEARED THROUGH BY THE RAGGED METAL OF THE CAR ROOF.
WARM, MEATY JELLY THAT WAS MY LEGS STEAMS IN THE CHILL NIGHT, ALREADY STARTING TO CONGEAL OVER MY TORSO.
ROGER, YOUR THROAT...
WHAT ABOUT IT?
HIGH ABOVE, I'M CERTAIN ROGER BARBATOS LOOKS DOWN AT THAT RISING VAPOR AS A SIGN OF MY FIRM'S IMMINENT INSOLVENCY...
GET THE LOBBY GUARDS ON THE HORN, LOLA. TELL THEM TO SCRAPE HIM UP AND BURN IT.
EVERY PIECE, EVERY THING. NOTHING BUT ASHES.

JACK... M-MAYBE WE SHOULD WAIT! THIS GUY, I'VE HEARD STORIES...
YOU MEAN END OF STORY, YA HALF A MARY! THAT FOUNTAIN A' RED WHEN HE HIT WEREN'T NO JELLO, SAMMY!
NOW C'MON, WE GOT A BARBECUE TO LIGHT...
...WHEREAS I SEE THE POTENTIAL FOR CORPORATE EXPANSION.
I'M WAITING...
A PLAYFUL RITUAL OF YOUTH COMES TO MIND, THE SO-CALLED GAME OF "GOT YOUR NOSE!"
SECRETLY TUCKING THUMB BETWEEN FORE AND MIDDLE FINGERS, A SADISTIC UNCLE SNATCHES AT A PREPUBESCENT'S TRUSTING FACE...
PEE-YOO! WHAT A MESS! COME IN HERE, SAMMY, YOU GOTTA SEE--
...THEN PRESENTING A NOW HORRIFIED NEPHEW OR NIECE WITH THE SIGHT OF A DECEITFUL THUMB MASQUERADING AS STOLEN SNOUT.
KLANK
HEY! THIS LITTLE DIRTBAG'S STILL MOVIN' IN HERE!
LET GO A' THAT LIGHT 'FORE I USE IT TO BEAT IN WHAT'S LEFT A' YOUR EFFIN'--
AAA
SHRIIIP
MY VERSION OF THE GAME IS SOMEWHAT MORE ADULT--
--AND ALL TOO REAL.
"GOT YOUR NOSE."
SLTHHPT

HIS ARM JACK'S ARM--!
NOT ANY MORE.
JUST BELOW THE ELBOW OF MY NEW ACQUISITION I FEEL THE SCRAPING OF GENTLE NAILS, A LOVER'S CARESS--
--INTIMATE RECOLLECTION FROM THE HAPLESS JACK'S PERSONAL LIFE.
I DISMISS IT--
--BLOCK IT, BLOCK IT OUT--
HE'S COMIN' FOR ME, SHOOT 'IM, SHOOT IT!
WE'RE GONNA HIT YOU, MOVE OUTTA THE--
--THERE'S NOTHING PERSONAL HERE.
GAAA
NOTHING PERSONAL.
JUST BUSINESS.
THWKT
LOWER LIMBS TREMBLE WITH MEMORIES OF THEIR FORMER OWNER'S EXPERIENCES--
-- SAND SHIFTING UNDERFOOT, A JOGGERS' STRIDE--
BAAM
BLAAM
IT AIN'T HAPPENIN', HE'S NOT STOPPIN'!
HE'S COMIN' IN TOO FAST, TOO--
--GLUK!
--SAMMY LIKED TO RUN, QUICK AND AGILE.
I PUT WHAT WERE HIS TALENTS TO GOOD USE.

HNNGH! HNNGH!
STEIN... STEIN, WHERE ARE YOU? I CAN'T MY GOD I CAN'T...
BARBATOS' INDIFFERENCE TO THE TENETS OF MORTALITY HAS TAXED MY LABORS FOR FAR TOO LONG.
PROFITABILITY IN THIS VENTURE IS ONLY GOING TO BE RESTORED THROUGH THE MISUSE OF INSIDER INFORMATION.
TINGLING IN THE FINGERS OF MY MOST RECENT SUBSIDIARY ALERTS ME TO AN INHERENT MECHANICAL APTITUDE--
--TALENT GAINED IN THE EMPLOY OF ITS FORMER BOSS, NOW PUT TO WORK FOR ME HOT-WIRING MUCH NEEDED TRANSPORTATION.
KRZZK
UNDERNEATH THE COLD PRECISION OF A SKILL WITH MACHINES THERE'S A FLASH OF A FIRM HANDSHAKE...
SCREE
--TOO SUDDEN TO PREPARE AGAINST, TOO FULL OF EMOTION TO ESCAPE--
--A STRONG, PLEASANT CLASP, CONCEIVABLY IN THANKS FOR A JOB WELL DONE ON ANOTHER ENGINE, ANOTHER TIME. WHO CAN SAY?
ONLY A GUARD I'LL NEVER KNOW AS MORE THAN THE STOLEN SENSATION AND EXPERIENCE I LITERALLY HOLD IN ONE HAND.
A MAN WHO CAN PERCHANCE REST EASY WITH THE SORT OF ACCOMPLISHMENT EARNING THAT KIND OF PRESSING OF THE FLESH.
A MAN WHO CAN REST IN PEACE.
...WHILE I'M FORCED TO LIVE WITH WHAT I AM.

"TELLIN' YA, MIKAL--SAN FRANCISCO LOVES YA! DRAKONMEGAS, NUMBER ONE SON OF THE SATANIC THEY'RE CALLIN' YOU!
"AND THE CAREER MOVE FROM LOCAL CELEBRITY TO NATIONAL? THIS CLOSE! SEE HOW FAR APART MY FINGERS ARE! THIS CLOSE!
"MIKAL? MIKAL, ARE YOU LISTENING? MIKAL!"
Cable 47
PAST MYSTERIES
with Mikal Drakonmegas
TALK TO HIM FOR ME, JESSIE? THIS IS SOME OF MY BEST STROKING HERE!
LISTEN TO YOUR WIFE, THEN, IF I'M NOT GOOD ENOUGH--LISTEN TO HER?
MIKAL, C'MON... MAXIMILLIAN CAME ALL THIS WAY JUST TO GO OVER THE DEAL WITH YOU FACE TO FACE. CAN'T YOU... PLEASE?
THEN WILL HE LEAVE? THEN CAN I THINK STRAIGHT?
FINE. OKAY.
OH, JESSIE--KISS-KISS! WHAT WOULD I DO WITHOUT YOU!
THESE ARTIST TYPES--YES, I MEAN YOU, MIKAL!
NOW EVERYTHING'S SET FOR THE BOOK! YOU KNOW HOW MUCH THAT WHITLEY PULLED IN WHEN HE GOT YOKED BY THE ALIENS?
IMAGINE THE ROYALTY FROM A TELL-ALL OF KIDNAPPING AN E.T. OF YOUR OWN! HEAR THEM CASH REGISTERS RING, KA-CHING!

YOU JUST SIGN THE HARPER CONTRACT AND I'LL TAKE CARE OF--
FORGET IT, MAX. NO BOOK. IT'S DEAD.
EXCUSE ME?
MIKAL, THIS IS A DONE DEAL WE'RE TALKING...
YOU KNOW, WINNING THESE MEANT SOMETHING ONCE. OPENING EYES TO THE PERILS AND POTENTIAL OF THE SUPERNATURAL.
MASS MEDIA MADE SENSE TO GET THROUGH TO THE LAYMAN... BACK BEFORE PROFIT BEGAN TO BLUR THE PURITY.
THIS SHOULD BE ABOUT SERIOUS STUDY AND APPRECIATION, MAX, NOT THIS RATINGS SIDE SHOW MY WORK'S BECOME!
AND IF THAT'S NOT BAD ENOUGH, WHAT ABOUT ALL THE SCAM ARTISTS FEEDING OFF THE PUBLIC'S HYPED DESIRE FOR OCCULT MATERIAL?
BUT I CAN FIX IT--STILL! TURN THE TABLES ON THE CON MEN, SHOW UP THEIR SHAMS, CLEAR THE WAY AGAIN FOR SERIOUS ARCANE STUDY!
THEY'LL TEAR YOU APART... THIS ISN'T A FIELD FOR HOLIER-THAN-THOU RIGHTEOUSNESS!
NOW
EVEN UNHOLIER-THAN-THOU!
DRAKONMEGA
New Age Nastiness
I'LL EAT SOME CROW FOR CONTRADICTING SOME OF THE EARLIER STANDS I TOOK MAKING MY POINTS, MAX...
...SMALL PRICE IF I CAN RIGHT SOME OF THE WRONGS I'VE HELPED PERPETRATE!
MIKAL, MIKAL--MIKEY! I'VE SEEN THIS HAPPEN SO MANY TIMES!
TALENTED GUY, DOESN'T THINK HE'S DESERVING THE BUCKS! YOU JUST GIVE YOURSELF A LITTLE TIME, YOU'LL COME TO YOUR SENSES!

SMKRAAK
WHAT IS YOUR PROBLEM!? I DON'T NEED TIME TO COME TO MY SENSES, I HAVE ALREADY!
THAT'S WHY I WANT TO SHIFT GEARS! YOU WORK FOR ME, MAX, DON'T YOU FORGET THAT!
MIKAL! MIKAL, FOR GOD'S SAKE CALM DOWN, MAXIMILLIAN WAS JUST--
NO PROBLEM, NO PROBLEM... YOU'RE THE BOSS, MIKAL, YOU'RE THE TALENT.
I'M JUST THE AGENT, JUST THE PARASITE WITH THE DARK SUNGLASSES AND GOLD CHAINS.
I'M SO SORRY...
DON'T BE, JESSIE, HE'S PERFECTLY WITHIN HIS RIGHTS TO BE A FLAMING--
MAKE THIS WORK FOR ME, MAX--YOU'LL SEE, I'M RIGHT--JUST LET ME DO IT MY--
HOW'D IT GO? LIKE TIANEMEN SQUARE, 'KAY? HE WANTS TO PLAY IT STRAIGHT... uh-huh, NO HYPE!
RATINGS? IN THE TOILET! I KNOW IT'S MY CAREER, TOO! WELL, YEAH, A FEW PROMOTIONAL IDEAS OF MY OWN...
MIKAL, I'VE TOLD YOU I'D SUPPORT YOU IN THIS... CHANGE... BUT NOT IF YOU'RE GOING TO BE RUDE TO OUR FRIENDS!
I CAN UNDERSTAND YOUR BEING NERVOUS ABOUT TRYING SOMETHING NEW, BUT I CAN'T SAY I LIKE WHAT I'M SEEING HERE.
NEITHER CAN I...

"THINK ABOUT THIS CITY, TERROR! 8 MILLION PEOPLE AND STORIES, 8 MILLION GRUDGE MATCHES JUST WAITING TO FORK OVER THE BUCKS TO SOMEONE WHO'LL TAKE CARE OF TWISTING THE KNIFE..."
"I DON'T WORK NEW YORK, ALEXIS, YOU KNOW THAT. HORNHEADED ACROBATS, WISECRACKING ARACHNIDS, FREAKISH FOURSOMES--"
--THE CONCENTRATED LEVEL OF ALTRUISM IS DECIDEDLY NON-CONDUCIVE TO THE GREY AREAS I FREQUENT.
WELL, IF YOU CHANGE YOUR MIND... SAY, CAN YOU? I MEAN, SWITCH YOUR-- FOR ANOTHER-- FORGET I ASKED.
BLEECH-- DO YOU HAVE TO DO THAT HERE?
THE PICTURE NEWSPAPER
THREAT OR MENACE?
ONLY IF YOU WANT RESULTS...
...WASN'T THAT THE SUBTEXT IN YOUR HEARTFELT GREETING OF, "TIME IS MONEY!"? THAT THE CONSORTIUM HIRING ME THROUGH YOU GROW IMPATIENT FOR BARBATOS' DEMISE.
YEAH, BUT... WHADDA YOU HEAR?
A MARITAL ALTERCATION. ACCUSATIONS, DENIALS OF ADULTERY.
I'D PREFER NOT TO... DWELL... ON IT.
ANYWAY, LOOK, A BUNCH A' THIRD WORLD COUNTRIES SICK OF BARBATOS SUPPLYING THEIR ENEMIES-- THEY WANT HIM OUT SO THEY CAN GO BACK TO BEING EVENLY MATCHED.

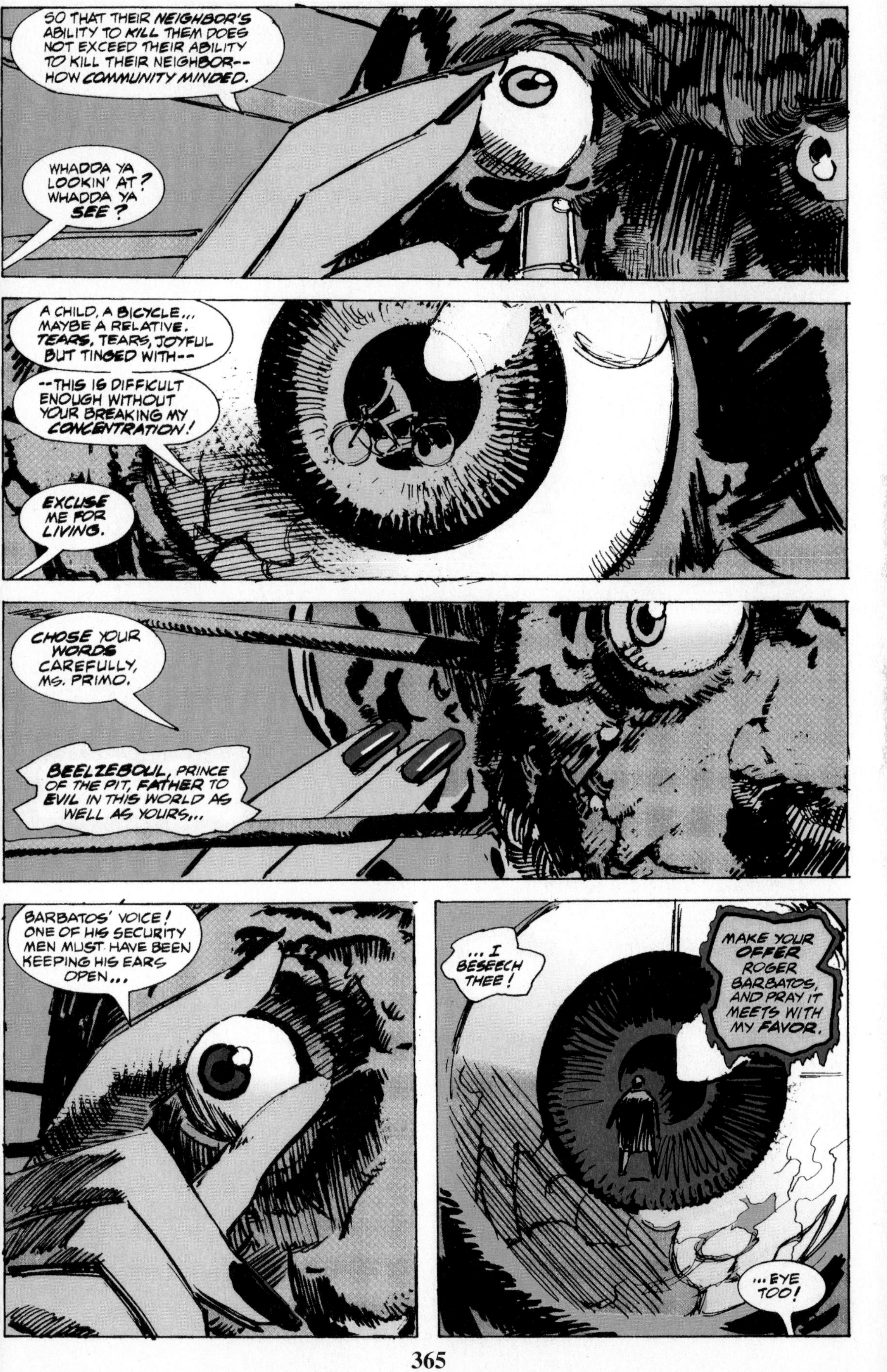
SO THAT THEIR NEIGHBOR'S ABILITY TO KILL THEM DOES NOT EXCEED THEIR ABILITY TO KILL THEIR NEIGHBOR-- HOW COMMUNITY MINDED.
WHADDA YA LOOKIN' AT? WHADDA YA SEE?
A CHILD, A BICYCLE... MAYBE A RELATIVE. TEARS, TEARS, JOYFUL BUT TINGED WITH--
--THIS IS DIFFICULT ENOUGH WITHOUT YOUR BREAKING MY CONCENTRATION!
EXCUSE ME FOR LIVING.
CHOSE YOUR WORDS CAREFULLY, MS. PRIMO.
BEELZEBOUL, PRINCE OF THE PIT, FATHER TO EVIL IN THIS WORLD AS WELL AS YOURS...
BARBATOS' VOICE! ONE OF HIS SECURITY MEN MUST HAVE BEEN KEEPING HIS EARS OPEN...
...I BESEECH THEE!
MAKE YOUR OFFER ROGER BARBATOS, AND PRAY IT MEETS WITH MY FAVOR.
...EYE TOO!

PRAY TO ME.
A STEADY DIET OF DEATH, DESTRUCTION, REAPED FROM THE MUNITIONS I SOW IN YOUR NAME, GREAT ADVERSARY!
IN RETURN, A SMALL BOON... SAFETY FROM THOSE WHO OPPOSE THE DARK WORK I DO FOR YOU!
GRANT ME PROTECTION FROM THEIR VIOLENCE!
WHINING GNAT OF HUMANITY! MY TALONS WERE FORGED TO RIP AND TEAR, NOT SHIELD YOUR WEAK FLESH!
BUT YOU HAVE DEMONSTRATED UNWORTHINESS...
...AND BY THIS PACT YOU MAY UNDO WHATEVER RAVAGES SEIZE YOUR PATHETIC FORM!
BY THIS PACT... BODY AND SOUL...
THE PACT ONLY PROTECTS THE BODY, HUMAN... I ALREADY OWN YOUR SOUL.
LOVE WHAT YOU'VE DONE WITH YOUR NAILS, TERROR!

I WAS MORE CONCERNED WITH ITS ARTISTIC ABILITIES THAN THE AESTHETIC QUALITIES OF ITS CUTICLES.
"IT" GIVE YOU WHAT YOU NEED?
A START. I'VE BEEN TOO CONCERNED WITH CARRYING OUT A CONTRACT--
--WHEN WHAT I REALLY NEED TO DO IS WORK ON BREAKING ONE...
"BUT YOU HATE TRAVELING COMMERCIALLY, TERROR! CRAMPED SEATS, COVERING UP THAT THING YOU CALL A FACE--MAKES YOUR VANITY CRAWL, DOESN'T IT?
"I'D HAVE PAID TO SEE THAT!"
YOUR MALEVOLENT GLEE AT MY PERSONAL HABITS IS NOTED, REKRAB...
...AND WHEN IS THE LAST TIME YOU'VE BEEN OUT OF THIS FIRETRAP YOU OPTIMISTICALLY CALL AN "EMPORIUM"?
PUT THAT-- PUT THAT DOWN! YOU DON'T KNOW WHERE IT'S BEEN!
THE BOX?
YOUR HAND.
I'LL GET TO THE POINT.

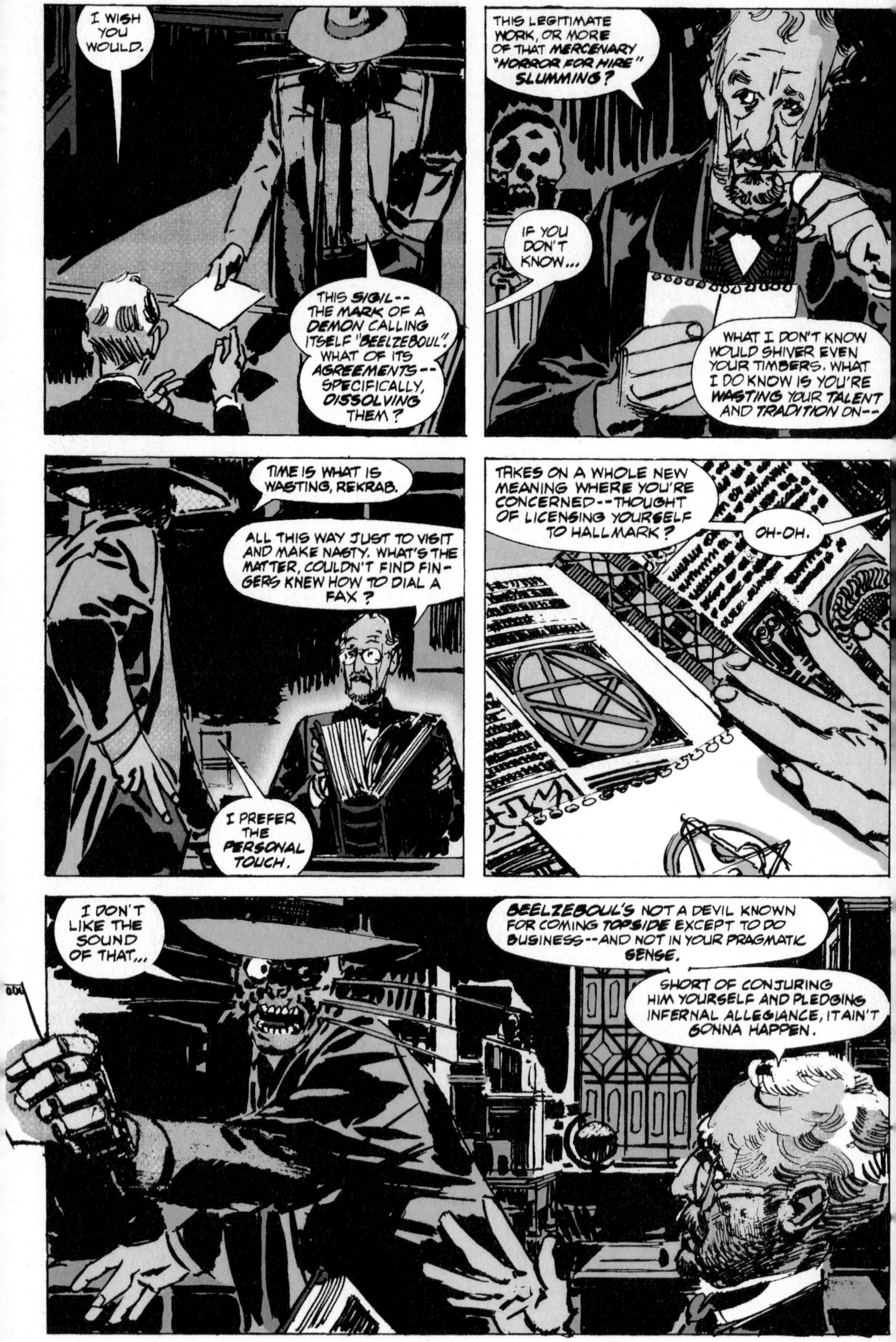
I WISH YOU WOULD.
THIS SIGIL-- THE MARK OF A DEMON CALLING ITSELF "BEELZEBOUL". WHAT OF ITS AGREEMENTS-- SPECIFICALLY, DISSOLVING THEM?
THIS LEGITIMATE WORK, OR MORE OF THAT MERCENARY "HORROR FOR HIRE" SLUMMING?
IF YOU DON'T KNOW...
WHAT I DON'T KNOW WOULD SHIVER EVEN YOUR TIMBERS. WHAT I DO KNOW IS YOU'RE WASTING YOUR TALENT AND TRADITION ON--
TIME IS WHAT IS WASTING, REKRAB.
ALL THIS WAY JUST TO VISIT AND MAKE NASTY. WHAT'S THE MATTER, COULDN'T FIND FINGERS KNEW HOW TO DIAL A FAX?
I PREFER THE PERSONAL TOUCH.
TAKES ON A WHOLE NEW MEANING WHERE YOU'RE CONCERNED--THOUGHT OF LICENSING YOURSELF TO HALLMARK?
OH-OH.
I DON'T LIKE THE SOUND OF THAT...
BEELZEBOUL'S NOT A DEVIL KNOWN FOR COMING TOPSIDE EXCEPT TO DO BUSINESS--AND NOT IN YOUR PRAGMATIC SENSE.
SHORT OF CONJURING HIM YOURSELF AND PLEDGING INFERNAL ALLEGIANCE, IT AIN'T GONNA HAPPEN.

UNLESS... MIKAL DRAGONMEGAS!
A NEW LOW, REKRAB--I'M IMPRESSED. A POP NECROMANCER OF THE SHIRLEY MACLAINE BEST SELLER LIST--BEELZEBOUL IS EVEN NOW PETITIONING HEAVEN FOR ASYLUM.
WHAT'D I TELL YOU ABOUT THIS?
NOW FOLLOW-- BEELZEBOUL CALLS HIMSELF "SATAN" FOR EGO'S SAKE, MOVES ON MANKIND BY SIRING A PREDICTABLY TWISTED HALFBREED NAMED DAIMON HELLSTROM.
COMMON KNOWLEDGE--IN MY CIRCLES, ANYWAY. WHAT'S NOT IS THE WORD DRAKONMEGAS IS HELLSTROM'S HALF BROTHER BY WAY OF DADDY DEAREST.
HELLSTROM BLEW OFF HIS POP, PURGED HIS BIRTHRIGHT, A DERANGED BIT OF BUSINESS CALLED THE DARKSOUL--TRANS-FERRED IT INTO THE BODY OF ONE BAD ATTITUDE SERPENT.
BUT DRAKONMEGAS WAS ILLEGITIMATE--SO IT'S SAID. NEVER GOT HIS WICKED INHERITANCE.
MAYBE THERE'S A WAY OF BRINGING HIM INTO HIS OWN, MAKE HIM A KEY TO DOWN BELOW, CATCH BEELZEBOUL OFF GUARD.
WELL, I ALWAYS DID HAVE A WAY WITH CHILDREN...

RAY MARLIN ROTHERMEL HERE, "THE 13th HOUR"! LOOKING INTO THE DARK AND DEADLY WORLD OF THE PARANORMAL...
NEWS
...AND LOOKING OUT FOR YOU IN THAT FEAR FILLED FORUM, OUR FIRST GUEST, OCCULT ORATOR MIKAL DRAKONMEGAS!
IT'S THE PUBLIC AIRWAVES, MIKEY, START TALKING!
THANKS, RAY!
WITH THE EXTRA-NORMAL, I JUST WANT TO STRESS THAT IT'S NOT ANYONE'S FAULT IF THEY'VE BEEN TAKEN IN BY FRAUD--
--THE ONES AT FAULT ARE THE CON MEN PLAYING ON PEOPLE'S HOPES AND EXPECTATIONS OF THE SUPERNATURAL.
I AGREE COMPLETELY!
ANTONY MANG, MAIN MAN OF THE WACKY AND WICKED TEMPLE OF THE RISEN KING!
TRAINING TO RECOGNIZE THE FRAUDULENT MUST BEGIN EARLY!
OUR CHURCH'S YOUTH GROUP USE THEIR PITCHFORKS TO DIVINE THE TRUE NIGHT SPIRIT FROM THE POOR IMITATION!
I DON'T BELIEVE THIS, I DON'T--
MIKEY, YOUR MIC'S COMIN' LOOSE THERE--

NOW, MIKAL--LET'S TAKE THIS SLOW! A SEGUE--YOU GOTTA BRING YOUR AUDIENCE WITH YOU WHERE YOU WANT TO GO!
7V
NEWS
--EXPERIENCING SOME, uh, TECHNICAL DIFFICULTIES HERE--
YOU COULDN'T LET US TAKE THE HIGH ROAD, COULD YOU, MAX?! YOU HAD TO BOOK ME WITH THAT LUNATIC INSTEAD!
AAARGG
BOTH OF YOU, BOTH OF YOU JUST CALM DOWN.
LISTEN, MAN, YOU WANNA TALK LUNATIC--WE'VE MADE GOOD MONEY TOGETHER, MIKAL, HAD GOOD TIMES, BUT IF YOU'RE--
MIKAL, ARE YOU... ARE YOU OKAY? WHAT'S HAPPENING TO YOU?
WHAT'S HAPPENING IS I'M BEING FORCED INTO PLAYING A PART I DON'T WANT TO, JESSIE, AND NO ONE'S SEEING IT BUT ME!
"WHAT'S HAPPENING IS NO ONE'S OUT THERE WORKING FOR WHO I REALLY AM..."
THE MONKS SAY IT WOULD HAVE DIED WITHOUT THEM, SCALES TURNING BRITTLE AND SHATTERING IN THE SUB-ZERO OF THE HIGH HIMALAYAS.
ZAFFINO
ADURIZ

MERITORIOUS COMPASSION, ALBEIT TAINTED BY A THEOLOGY OF HARNESSING THE HELLISH SERPENT'S DARKSOUL FOR THE SLAUGHTER OF AN UNWORTHY HUMAN RACE.
SO FAR UNSUCCESSFUL, THEY CONTINUE TO ACCEPT PETITIONS FOR MEMBERSHIP IN THEIR MOST UNHOLY ORDER--
--A SCHEMING COLLECTION OF OUTCASTS DRIVEN FROM SOCIETY FOR ABHORRENT BEHAVIOR, DEVIANT PERSONALITY, REPULSIVE APPEARANCE.
NEEDLESS TO SAY, I FIT RIGHT IN.
ONLY THE HIGH FATHER HAS GAINED THE ENLIGHTENMENT TO APPROACH AND TOUCH THE FEROCIOUS BEAST WITHOUT FEAR OF DEATH.
ATTAINING THAT PLATEAU OF ONENESS CAN TAKE YEARS, I'M TOLD-- "A LIFETIME," SOME MONKS WHISPER AS THEY LICK CRACKING LIPS.
HRSSS
MY SCHEDULE DOESN'T ALLOW FOR SUCH A STEEP LEARNING CURVE, BUT I CLAIM AN INTEREST IN TAKING PART IN THEIR RITUALS.

Especially the "taking part" aspect.
HRRSS
HRSSS
HSSSSK
FWRKRAAK
HSSSG

SOME THING DRIPS FROM THE SERPENT'S FANGS, A DIABOLICAL VENOM BLACK AND FOUL AND SHRIEKING OF MADNESS.
THE EARTHLY ESTATE OF A FIEND NAMED BEELZEBOUL WHO, IN PASSING ON FROM THIS REALITY, LEFT A LIVING WILL BEQUEATHING EVERYTHING TO A FIRST BORN NAMED MIKAL DRAKONMEGAS.
A ONCE LIVING WILL--NOW DEAD--I HOLD IN CUNNING HAND.
NATURALLY, I'VE NAMED MYSELF THE EXECUTOR...
NEXT: A BARGAIN YOU WON'T WANT TO MISS--"DEAL WITH THE DEVIL!"

NOVEMBER 1991 (continued)

EADLANDS #1 began an Epic limited ries.

E EVERYMAN was an Epic one-shot.

OK #1 began a limited series reprinting arvel's movie adaptation.

MES BOND JR. #1 began an ongoing series sed on the animated TV characters.

DEBIUS: CHAOS was a magazine-sized Epic t book.

BURBAN NINJA JERSEY SHE-DEVILS was a mor one-shot.

DECEMBER 1991

OST RIDER/WOLVERINE/PUNISHER: ARTS OF DARKNESS was a one-shot.

WER PACK HOLIDAY SPECIAL was a one-ot.

NISHER: AN EYE FOR AN EYE was a reprint e-shot.

ARLOCK AND THE INFINITY WATCH #1 began ongoing series.

FORCE #7 began a sporadic short backup rial starring Garrison Kane.

ARVEL ANNUAL REPORT #1 began a yearly going series of corporate stock reports ne in pseudo-comic style.

JANUARY 1992

EFENDERS OF DYNATRON CITY #1 began a ort ongoing series based on the videogame aracters.

D 'N PLAY #1 began an ongoing series ased on the hip-hop duo.

UNISHER WAR ZONE #1 began an ongoing ries.

UASAR SPECIAL #1 began a limited reprint eries.

FEBRUARY 1992

AGE #1 began an ongoing series.

APTAIN AMERICA #399 began a backup erial starring Diamondback.

EX, LIES AND MUTUAL FUNDS OF THE UPPIES FROM HELL was a humor one-shot.

/CW WORLD CHAMPIONSHIP WRESTLING 1 began an ongoing series based on the restling stars.

DVENTURES OF THE THING #1 began a mited reprint series.

MARCH 1992

ARVEL COMICS PRESENTS #101 began erials starring the Young Gods, Nightcrawler Wolverine, and Dr. Strange & Ghost Rider.

OMAD #1 began an ongoing series.

OXIC CRUSADERS #1 began an ongoing eries based on the animated TV characters.

VARLOCK #1 began a limited reprint series.

IDOL #1 began an Epic limited series.

APRIL 1992

COPS: THE JOB #1 began a limited series.

MOON KNIGHT: DIVIDED WE FALL was a one-shot.

EPIC: AN ANTHOLOGY #1 was an Epic limited series.

ALPHA FLIGHT SPECIAL was a one-shot.

FAREWELL TO WEAPONS was an Epic one-shot reprinting translated Japanese comics.

INFINITY WAR #1 began a limited series.

MOTORMOUTH #1 began an ongoing Marvel UK series.

SAM & MAX: FREELANCE POLICE was an Epic humor one-shot, the sequel to Fishwrap Productions and Comico one-shots.

WARHEADS #1 began an ongoing Marvel UK series.

MAY 1992

THE COMPLETE ALFRED BESTER'S THE STARS MY DESTINATION was a magazine-sized Epic novel adaptation; parts were reprinted from Heavy Metal Magazine.

ORIGINAL GHOST RIDER #1 began an ongoing reprint series.

PENDRAGON #1 began an ongoing Marvel UK series.

HELL'S ANGEL #1 began an ongoing Marvel UK series.

WOLVERINE: SAVE THE TIGER was a reprint one-shot.

MARVEL COMICS PRESENTS #107 began a serial starring Ghost Rider and Werewolf by Night.

JUNE 1992

MARVEL COMICS PRESENTS #108 began a short serial starring Thanos.

AMAZING SPIDER-MAN ANNUAL #26 began short backup serials starring Venom and Cloak & Dagger.

THOR: ALONE AGAINST THE CELESTIALS was a reprint one-shot.

MARVEL COMICS PRESENTS #109 began a serial starring Wolverine and Typhoid Mary.

MARVEL SWIMSUIT SPECIAL #1 began a magazine-sized yearly parody series.

GHOST RIDER/BLAZE: SPIRITS OF VENGEANCE #1 began an ongoing series.

JULY 1992

CAPTAIN AMERICA ANNUAL #11 began a short backup serial starring Kang.

ORIGINAL GHOST RIDER #3 began a new backup serial starring the Phantom Rider.

GHOST RIDER/CABLE: SERVANTS OF THE DEAD was a reprint one-shot.

MORBIUS THE LIVING VAMPIRE #1 began an ongoing series.

SAM & MAX: FREELANCE POLICE SPECIAL COLOR COLLECTION was a colorized reprint one-shot.

CLIVER BARKER'S HELLRAISER SUMMER SPECIAL began a short ongoing series of Hellraiser one-shots.

IRON MAN #284 featured James Rhodes once again adopting the Iron Man identity and taking over the series' lead role.

TEKWORLD #1 began an Epic ongoing series.

AUGUST 1992

AMAZING SPIDER-MAN: SOUL OF THE HUNTER was a one-shot.

MEMORIES was an Epic one-shot reprinting translated Japanese comics.

CABLE: BLOOD & METAL #1 began a limited series.

ONYX OVERLORD #1 began an Epic limited series.

MOON KNIGHT SPECIAL was a one-shot.

PUNISHER/CAPTAIN AMERICA: BLOOD & GLORY #1 began a limited series.

TED MCKEEVER'S METROPOL: A.D. #1 began an Epic limited series.

BLOODLINES: A TALE FROM THE HEART OF AFRICA was an Epic one-shot.

FISH POLICE #1 began a short ongoing series reprinting the Fishwrap Productions and Comico series.

MARVEL COMICS PRESENTS #113 began serials starring Giant-Man and Ghost Rider & Iron Fist.

ALIEN LEGION: GRIMROD was an Epic one-shot.

THE 'NAM #73 began a backup serial starring Sgt. Polkow.

SEPTEMBER 1992

PUNISHER: BACK TO SCHOOL SPECIAL began a short yearly ongoing series.

KNIGHTS OF PENDRAGON #5 changed the series' title from Pendragon.

SLAPSTICK #1 began a limited series.

SWEET XVI: BACK TO SCHOOL SPECIAL was a one-shot.

X-MEN ADVENTURES #1 began an ongoing series adapting the animated TV show.

MOTORMOUTH AND KILLPOWER #6 changed the series' title from Motormouth.

SOVIET SUPER-SOLDIERS was a one-shot.

SPIDER-MAN: THE TRIAL OF VENOM was a giveaway one-shot sponsored by UNICEF.

MARVEL COMICS
FROM THE PAGES OF THE NEW WARRIORS!
NIGHT THRASHER
FOUR CONTROL
© 1992 MARVEL ENT. GROUP, INC.
$2.00 US
$2.45 CAN
1
OCT
APPROVED BY THE COMICS CODE AUTHORITY
Part 1 of 4
IN HIS OWN LIMITED SERIES AT LAST!
BAGLEY/HO

NIGHT THRASHER: FOUR CONTROL #1, published in August 1992, began a limited series starring the New Warriors' armored leader. It was soon followed by an ongoing series.

HIS PARENTS WERE KILLED WHEN HE WAS A CHILD. HE WAS RAISED TO BE A WALKING WEAPON IN THE WAR AGAINST CRIME. HE LEARNED HIS ENTIRE LIFE WAS A LIE. TO REDISCOVER HIMSELF, DWAYNE TAYLOR WILL FIGHT WITHOUT THE VERY TEAM HE ORGANIZED, THE NEW WARRIORS — FIGHT FOR HIS PAST — AND HIS FUTURE! STAN LEE PRESENTS. . NIGHT THRASHER!

SO AS I PATROL HELL'S KITCHEN, LOOKING FOR A REASON TO TEST OUT THE IMPROVE-MENTS ON MY ARMOR, WHAT AM I SUPPOSED TO THINK--
--WHEN I SEE A LONE GANG MEMBER RUNNING FROM A SMALL MOB ?
I'VE RECENTLY LEARNED THAT THE TRUTH, IN MANY CASES, IS A LIE.
I THINK, THAT WITH THE RECENT GANG SKIRMISHES ACROSS THE CITY--
--THAT SOME-ONE ENCROACHED ON SOMEONE ELSE'S TERRITORY.
NO RIGHT, NO WRONG. EVERYTHING'S A MURKY GREY AREA AND MY LIFE'S TAKEN A SWAN DIVE RIGHT INTO THAT HOLE.
THE RUNNER IS FROM THE POISON MEMORIES, A CHINATOWN GANG. THE OTHERS, I'M NOT SURE ABOUT.

FOR ALL I KNOW THEY HAVE EVERY REASON IN THE WORLD TO CRACK THE MEM'S HEAD IN.
IN TOO MANY WAYS, THESE GANGS REMIND ME OF MYSELF--
PHHH PHHH PHHH
HEY-- WHAT THE--?!
SPHOOOOPH
--THEY ONLY KNOW ONE WAY TO GET THINGS DONE--
IS IT TEAR GAS?
NO, MAN-- IT'S JUST-- SMOKE--!

--THE NIGHT THRASHER WAY--
--THE HARD WAY!!
CONTROL
ONE
RENGTH
NIGHT THRASHER CREATED BY TOM DEFALCO & RON FRENZ
FABIAN NICIEZA WRITER
DAVE HOOVER ARTIST
CHRIS ELIOPOULOS LETTERER
BRAD VANCATA COLORIST
DANNY FINGEROTH EDITOR
TOM DeFALCO ED. IN CHIEF

NNFFGH
ONE DOWN. ARMOR'S RUNNING SMOOTHLY.
HEY!
A DOUBLE-TRUNCHEON LAUNCH TAKES OUT TWO MORE.
PHWOOP
PHWOOP
KCHAK
LET THEM GO. I NEEDED THE WORKOUT MORE THAN I NEEDED TO STOP WHAT-EVER IT IS THEY WERE DOING. SPEAK-ING OF WHICH...
WHY WERE THEY AFTER YOU?
WHAT DIFFERENCE DOES WHY MAKE? IT'S ALL ABOUT HATE, RIGHT? ABOUT WHO'S STRONG-ER, RIGHT?
SO WHAT DO I DO, BUST HIM FOR HAVING AN ATTITUDE?
ESPECIALLY WHEN I'M NOT SURE WHETHER HE'S RIGHT OR NOT?

MORNING. MT. SINAI HOSPITAL...
DON'T TRY TO TALK--
--IT'S A MIRACLE YOU'RE EVEN ALIVE AFTER TRYING TO KILL YOURSELF!
--HAD-- SOME-- HELB--
MYSTICAL HELP. FROM TAI. MY GRANDMOTHER. I KNOW.
FUNNY, SHE SAVED YOUR LIFE JUST SO SHE COULD TRY TO TAKE OURS.
BUT SHE'S DEAD NOW.*
*SEE NEW WARRIORS #18-25 FOR DETAILS. --DANNY
--SO WHEN YOU GO INTO SURGERY TOMORROW, IT'S UP TO YOU AND THE DOCTORS, CHORD.
--SILOU--EDDE-- YOU CAN CALL ME--FAHDDER...
I--KNOW--!
IT'S HARD--
--TO FIND OUT YOU HAVE A FATHER-- AFTER THINKING YOU DIDN'T FOR YOUR ENTIRE LIFE--
AFTER THE SURGERY-- AS YOU GET BETTER-- THEN WE'LL WORK ON TRYING TO BE A FATHER AND DAUGHTER.
THIL-- IF I DON' MAYG ID--

DON'T TALK LIKE THAT, CHORD, YOU'LL BE--
LITHEN-- BLEASE--IN AMBROTHE BUILDING--
-- A GOMPUDER FILE--
A COMPUTER FILE? WHAT ABOUT IT?
INTHIDE UDILIDIES FOLDER--MARGGED-- CONDROL--
OBEN ID-- HELB DWAYNE-- KEEP DAYLOR FOUNDA-SHUN--
I DON'T UNDER--
MISS SILHOUETTE, I HAVE TO CHECK HIS CHARTS.
BUT THE OTHER NURSE JUST--
MMRRGHH!
THIL-- NO-- STOB--
HAVE A NICE SLEEP.

KRASSHHK
OH, REAL SUBTLE, BOYS!
NO ONE SAID ANYTHING ABOUT BEIN' QUIET, VU THI.
'SIDE, THE POISON MEMORIES ALWAYS LIKE TO LEAVE THEIR MARK!
THREEK
--STOB--
THIS GUY'S PATHETIC! YOU SURE HE'S THE ONE?
--UHHNNGH--
ABSOLUTELY, NGUYEN. THAT OLD MAN IS GONNA MAKE US ALL A LOT OF MONEY!
THEN WE'RE SET TO ROLL
SAY GOOD-BYE TO THE PRETTY GIRL.
G'BYE, PRETTY GIRL.

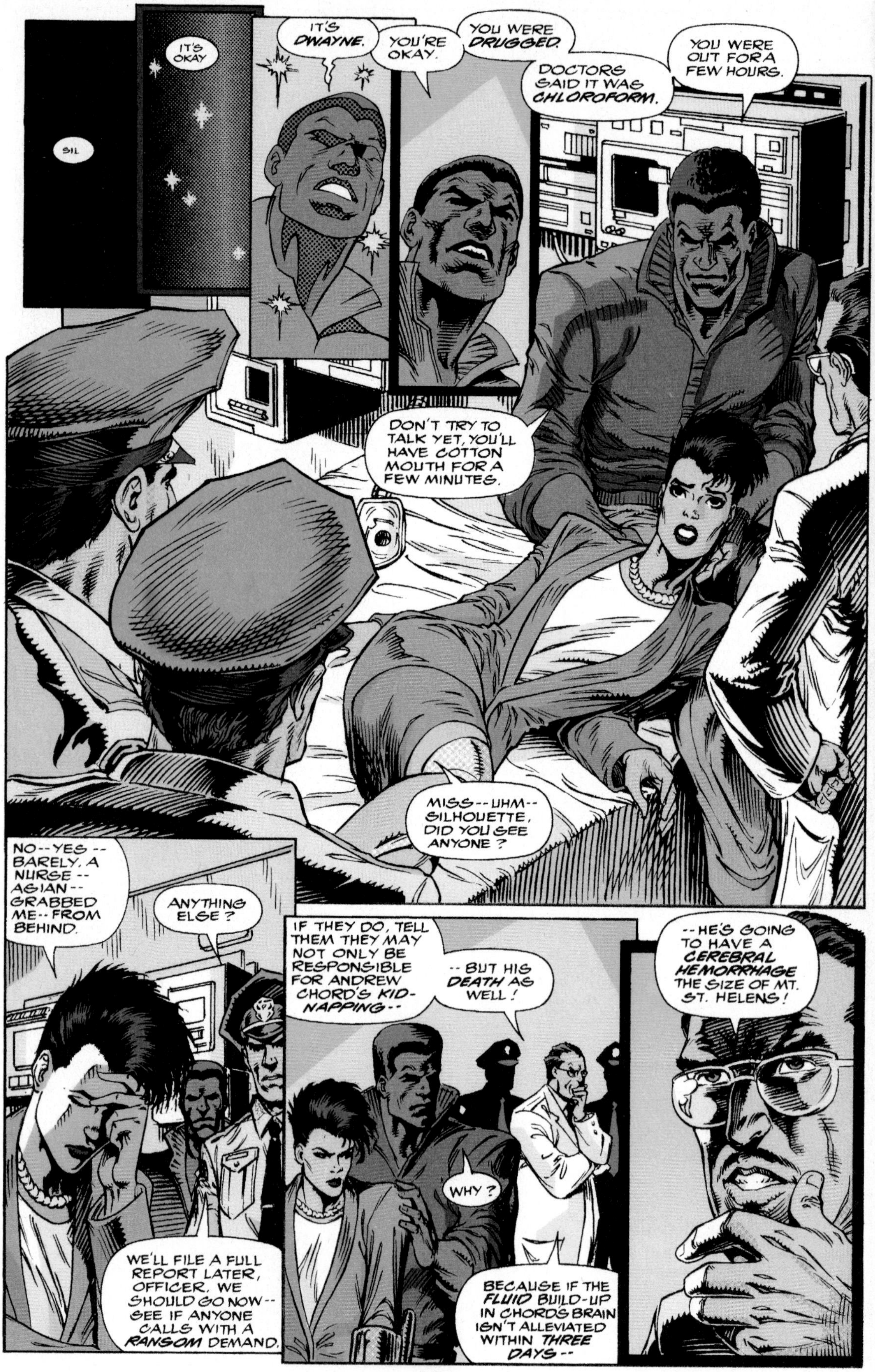

SIL
IT'S OKAY
IT'S DWAYNE.
YOU'RE OKAY.
YOU WERE DRUGGED.
DOCTORS SAID IT WAS CHLOROFORM.
YOU WERE OUT FOR A FEW HOURS.
DON'T TRY TO TALK YET, YOU'LL HAVE COTTON MOUTH FOR A FEW MINUTES.
MISS--UHM--SILHOUETTE, DID YOU SEE ANYONE ?
NO--YES--BARELY. A NURSE--ASIAN--GRABBED ME--FROM BEHIND.
ANYTHING ELSE ?
WE'LL FILE A FULL REPORT LATER, OFFICER. WE SHOULD GO NOW--SEE IF ANYONE CALLS WITH A RANSOM DEMAND.
IF THEY DO, TELL THEM THEY MAY NOT ONLY BE RESPONSIBLE FOR ANDREW CHORD'S KID-NAPPING--
--BUT HIS DEATH AS WELL !
WHY ?
BECAUSE IF THE FLUID BUILD-UP IN CHORDS BRAIN ISN'T ALLEVIATED WITHIN THREE DAYS--
--HE'S GOING TO HAVE A CEREBRAL HEMORRHAGE THE SIZE OF MT. ST. HELENS !

ONE HOUR LATER, AT THE AMBROSE BUILDING PENTHOUSE HOME OF DWAYNE TAYLOR...
ARE YOU SURE HE SAID IT WAS IN HIS UTILITIES FOLDER?
POSITIVE. MARKED "CONTROL." THAT'S WHAT CHORD TOLD ME ABOUT BEFORE WE WERE ATTACKED.
DID HE TELL YOU WHAT WAS IN THE FILE?
NO, BUT I HAVE TO ASSUME IT'S IMPORTANT--
--OR ELSE HE WOULD HAVE WAITED UNTIL AFTER HIS SURGERY TO MENTION IT.
WHY WON'T THE SYSTEM ACCESS THE FILE?
WHAT'S THIS?
Hello, Dwayne. It's your father, Daryl, here.
WHAT'S GOING ON?
If you are reading this, there is trouble with the foundation. In order to surmount trouble, what is the one thing I always told you to have?
WHAT DOES THIS MEAN?
I DON'T KNOW.
WHAT DID YOUR FATHER TELL YOU? LOVE? HOPE?
I DON'T REMEMBER...

...TAI TOOK SO MUCH FROM ME-- MY MEMORIES-- MY PAST-- WAIT-- WAIT--
STREN--
TOK TOK
STRENGTH?
TOK TOK
TOK TOK
THE FILE'S OPENING!
Taylor Foundation®
Management Paralysis Control Document
File Section 32.G
Registered with the N.Y. State Business Affairs officer; June 6, 1977. Notary Seal 66Y.344 Hector Colinado, Esq. presiding.
This document states, that in the event of a hostile corporate shareholder situation, control of the existing parameters of the Taylor Foundation be maintained within the
IT'S A LEGAL FAIL-SAFE TO PREVENT ME FROM LOSING THE TAYLOR FOUNDATION!
IT SAYS THAT IN THE EVENT OF A HOSTILE TAKEOVER, I CAN KEEP THE FOUNDATION BY HAVING SOMEONE ON THE EXECUTIVE BOARD SIGN THIS DOCUMENT.
SOMEONE KNEW ABOUT YOUR FATHER'S FAIL-SAFE!
THEY KIDNAPPED CHORD BECAUSE THEY WERE PLANNING A CORPORATE RAID AGAINST ME?
AND THEY KNEW HE WOULD SIGN THE DOCUMENT FOR YOU! BUT WHO ON THE BOARD WOULD DO THIS?
THERE ARE THREE MEMBERS ON THE BOARD BESIDES TAI, CHORD AND MYSELF.
TREVOR MADSDEN. EVE MAGDALENE. GAI NO DON.
I HAVE TO FIND ALL THREE OF THEM AND SEE IF THEY'RE RESPONSIBLE FOR THIS WITHIN THE NEXT THREE DAYS--
--OR NOT ONLY WILL I LOSE MY FATHER'S FOUNDATION--
--I'LL LOSE CHORD AS WELL!

BZZT
MR. TAYLOR, THIS IS JEFFREY IN THE LOBBY--
--THERE'S A FATHER MICHAEL JANES HERE TO SEE YOU.
REALLY?
LOUSY TIMING. SEND HIM UP, JEFFREY.
HAVEN'T SEEN JANES SINCE I SAVED HIM FROM A MIS-GUIDED ASSASSINATION ATTEMPT BY A MAN CALLED THE BENGAL.*
SILHOUETTE-- DWAYNE-- YOU'RE BOTH LOOKING WELL.
*NW'S #7-9. --DANNY
FATHER--IT'S GOOD TO SEE YOU AGAIN. HOW HAVE YOU BEEN?
TROUBLED.
THE MONTHS I'VE SPENT TRYING TO HEAL THE EMOTIONAL WOUNDS VIET-NAM LEFT IN BOTH MY-SELF AND THE BENGAL--
--HAVE PROVEN FRUITLESS.
I NEED YOU TO STOP HIM-- BEFORE HE TRIES TO KILL AGAIN!
BEFORE HE TRIES TO KILL SOMEONE YOU KNOW, DWAYNE!
ME?
THIS PHOTO WAS TAKEN IN 1965.
IT IS OF A NORTH VIETNAMESE GENERAL NAMED LI PAN. HE WAS A BUTCHER OF THOUSANDS.
THAT LOOKS LIKE--THAT COULDN'T BE RIGHT--
--IS THE MAN IN THAT PHOTO GAI NO DON?!

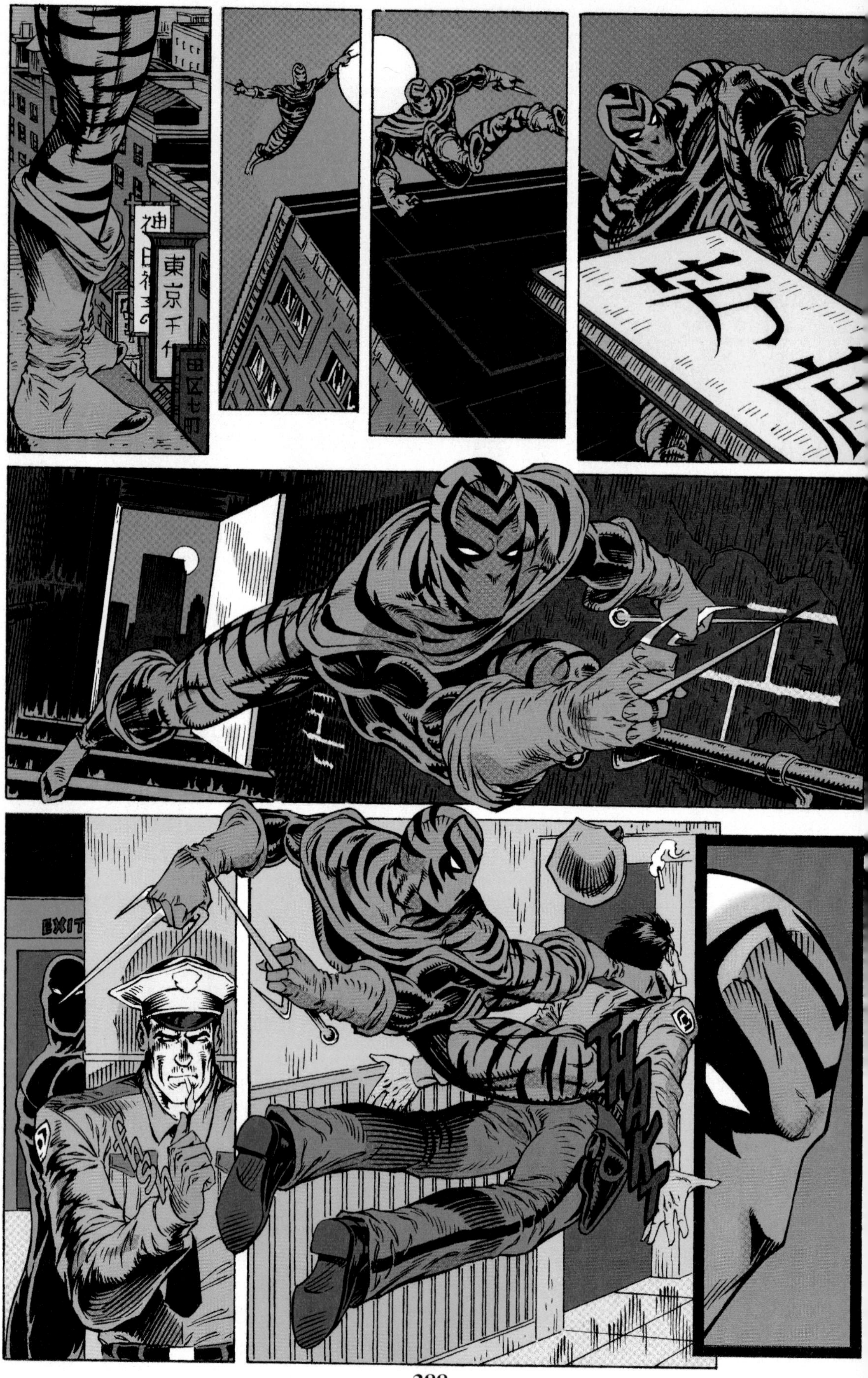

神
東京千
田区七町
EXIT
THAKK

SEE THAT METS GAME LAST NIGHT?
SHREKT
SHREKKT
LI PAN -- DEED DE JUNGLE BREAT?
I WOULD IMAGINE, YOUNG MAN, THAT IF YOU WISH TO OPERATE IN THIS COUNTRY...
...YOU COULD AT LEAST LEARN ITS LANGUAGE.
DEED DE JUNGLE BREAT?
"DID THE JUNGLE BREATHE?"
YOU WONDER IF I WAS RESPONSIBLE FOR THE SLAUGHTER OF YOUR FAMILY'S VILLAGE IN SOUTH VIETNAM?
WHAT DIFFERENCE DOES IT MAKE ANYMORE?

BENGAL-- STOP RIGHT THERE!
PLEASE--IT DOESN'T HAVE TO BE THIS WAY.
DON'T MAKE ANOTHER MOVE! GAI NO DON IS NOT THE MAN YOU WANT!
HE ADMIT-- DE JUNGLE BREAT.
NO!
AAAGH!
KCHASH
HE PREFERRED ESCAPE OVER CONFRONTATION.
MY THANKS TO YOUR EMPLOYER--MR. TAYLOR-- FOR HAVING PROVIDED ME YOUR SERVICES, NIGHT THRASHER.

YOU'RE ON THE TAYLOR FOUNDATION EXECUTIVE BOARD.
IT WOULDN'T BE IN MR. TAYLOR'S BEST INTEREST TO FIND OUT YOU WERE A BARBARIC WAR GENERAL.
THE BACKGROUND CHECK I DID ON YOU CONFIRMS YOU ARE WHAT YOU SAY--A KOREAN BUSINESSMAN.
THAT'S WHY I PROTECTED YOU FROM THE BENGAL.
NOW DO SOMETHING FOR MY EMPLOYER. WHAT DO YOU KNOW OF ANDREW CHORD'S KIDNAPPING?
WHAT DO I KNOW? EVERYTHING. NOTHING.
I KNOW OF THE FOUR CORNERS OF LIFE WHICH NEED TO BE UNDERSTOOD IN ORDER TO BE CONTROLLED.
CONTROL OF CHORD MEANS CONTROL OF THE TAYLOR FOUNDATION.
CONTROL OF TF MEANS CONTROL OVER HUGE SUMS OF MONEY.
CONTROL OVER THAT MONEY AFFORDS SOMEONE THE POWER NEEDED TO INFLUENCE WORLD EVENTS.
CONTROL OVER THAT POWER PROVIDES STRENGTH FROM WHICH INFLUENTIAL DECISIONS CAN BE MADE.
CONTROL OVER STRENGTH PROVIDES AN ACCESS TO HELP OR HINDER THE PATH OF OTHERS.
SO DO YOU THINK YOU ASK A SIMPLE QUESTION WHEN YOU ASK ME ABOUT THE KIDNAPPING OF ANDREW CHORD?

I ONLY EXPECT A SIMPLE ANSWER-- NOT RIDDLES--ARE YOU INVOLVED IN CHORD'S KIDNAPPING?!
NO.
AS FOR MY RIDDLES--THEY WILL ONLY HELP YOU MASTER THE DISCIPLINES WHICH WILL CONTROL THE DESTINY OF YOUR OWN LIFE.
DO YOU WANT THAT?
IT'S ALL I'VE EVER WANTED...
BUT CAN I BELIEVE ANYTHING THIS MAN SAYS TO ME? WILL HE HELP ME FIND THE CONTROL I NEED?
THE PATH TO CHORD LIES IN A CORNER YOU FOLDED YESTERDAY THROUGH STRENGTH.
"IT'S ALL ABOUT WHO'S STRONGER." THE MEM SAID THAT LAST NIGHT. SIL SAID THE NURSE WAS ASIAN. IS IT HATE OR LOGIC WHICH LEADS ME TO THE ANSWER?
THE POISON MEMORIES!
FIND THEM AND YOU WILL FIND CHORD.
HOW?
BECAUSE THE MEMORIES WORK FOR A LOS ANGELES BASED CRIMELORD NAMED LOTUS. SHE, IN TURN, HAS BEEN HIRED BY A HONG KONG BUSINESSMAN NAMED--
TREVOR MADSDEN--!
WE HIT CHINATOWN LIKE A COLD WIND. I DON'T KNOW IF I'M BEING PLAYED FOR A PAWN, BUT I ONLY HAVE ONE WAY TO FIND OUT...

IT SHOULDN'T TAKE US LONG TO SCARF UP SOME INFORMATION ON A GANG AS PERVASIVE AS THE MEMORIES ARE.
SKASH
GET HIM!
HE'S TOO FAST!
I'M ON HIM!
KRAKT
SHVIK
UMMPH
SHTHAK

WHADDYOU WANT, HUH?!
WHAT?!
LI PAN. GAI NO DON. DEED DE JUNGLE BREAT?
THPP
I TOLD YOU THE TRUTH! DON IS NOT THE ONE!
FWIPP

DON'T DO THIS, BENGAL!
SFCHING
SFCHING
SFCHING
DON'T MAKE ME FIGHT YOU AGAIN.
I KNOW HOW THE PAST CAN BURY YOU--!
YOU HAVE TO RISE ABOVE IT!
YOU HAVE TO, OR THE PAST WILL KILL YOU--

--WAY BEFORE YOU GET THE CHANCE TO KILL IT!
NO.
EH--?
YOU ARE NOT GOING ANYWHERE.
THUK
NOT UNTIL WE FIND OUT WHAT YOUR ASSOCIATION WITH GAI NO DON IS.
SHK
WHAT IS IT THAT YOU WANT, BENGAL? REVENGE?
AGAINST WHAT-- GHOSTS?
IS BLOOD GOING TO BE THE GLUE WHICH PUTS THE PIECES OF YOUR LIFE BACK TOGETHER AGAIN?

THE MAN YOU HUNTED EARLIER IS NAMED GAI NO DON!
HE IMMIGRATED INTO THE UNITED STATES FROM SOUTH KOREA IN 1968!
HE IS A LEGITIMATE BUSINESSMAN! HE IS NOT A NORTH VIETNAMESE ARMY GENERAL!
DO YOU UNDERSTAND?
ASK THE POISON MEMORIES--WOULD THEY WORK FOR AN NVA GENERAL?
WE'RE A SOUTH VIETNAMESE ASSOCIATION!
THE NVA RAPED OUR PEOPLE--OUR LAND--WE'D NEVER WORK WITH THEM!
ENOUGH?
NIGHT TAH-SHER--DEED YOUR JUNGLE BREAT?
TAI'S BLOOD. BLOOD I SPILLED TO PUT THE SHATTERED PIECES OF MY OWN PAST TOGETHER.
HE KNOWS. HE SMELLS IT ON ME. SMELLS THE BLOOD.
THE BLOOD THAT'S ON MY HANDS.

YESTERDAY, YOU TOLD ME LIFE WAS ALL ABOUT ANGER AND HATRED.
WHY?
HOW OLD ARE YOU-- EIGHTEEN?
IS HATING SOME-ONE ELSE'S HERITAGE THE ONLY WAY YOU CAN IDENTIFY WITH YOUR OWN?
WHAT WOULD YOU KNOW ABOUT IT?
I KNOW HOW IMPORTANT A PAST IS--BE-CAUSE I DON'T HAVE ONE!
AND YOU'RE TRYING TO TAKE AWAY WHAT LITTLE OF IT I HAVE!
THE MAN NAMED CHORD-- WHERE IS HE?
STOP--HE WAS SENT TO SAN FRANCISCO!
KIMEI-- HE WOULDN'T'VE HURT ME--HE AIN'T STRONG ENOUGH!
IT DOESN'T TAKE STRENGTH TO HURT PEOPLE LIKE YOU--IT TAKES STRENGTH NOT TO!
AND WHAT WILL IT TAKE TO PUT TOGETHER MY FRACTURED LIFE THIS TIME?
HOW FAR AM I WILLING TO GO?
AS FAR AS SAN FRANCISCO, AT LEAST--AND A MEETING WITH THIS CRIME-LORD, LOTUS...
...AND THEN-- AS FAR AS IT TAKES TO GET CHORD BACK!
NEXT: THE MOST-DEMANDED LIMITED SERIES OF THE YEAR CONTINUES!

NIGHT THRASHER
FOUR CONTROL™

danny fingeroth EDITOR **eric fein** ASSISTANT EDITOR

c/o MARVEL COMICS—387 PARK AVENUE SOUTH—NEW YORK, NEW YORK—10016

ATTENTION CORRESPONDENTS: ALL LETTERS TO BE CONSIDERED FOR PUBLICATION MUST INCLUDE YOUR NAME AND ADDRESS THOUGH WE WILL WITHHOLD THAT INFO BY REQUEST!

Welcome to the NIGHT THRASHER: 'OUR CONTROL Limited Series. If you're a egular reader of the NEW WARRIORS title, ve hope that you're as excited reading this xtension of the WARRIORS family as we re bringing it to you.

If you are a new reader coming into this itle without having read about Thrash in the Varriors, well, *shame on you* for missing ut on the niftiest comic this side of – well, he niftiest comic book *period*!

To be fair, let's bring our new readers up o date on Thrash – who is he, where does e come from and how did he get to be vhere he is?

The character of NIGHT THRASHER, and he team he organized, the NEW VARRIORS, resulted as the brainchild of om DeFalco and Ron Frenz, who eveloped his background and designed his riginal armor.

The character, since the very first issue of IEW WARRIORS, has been developed nder the guiding hand of Fabian Nicieza nd Mark Bagley.

Dwayne Taylor is the orphaned son of aryl and Melody Taylor. His parents, who ad forged an international organization for ro-social activities and charitable deeds, alled the Taylor Foundation, were nurdered under mysterious circumstances vhen Dwayne was a child.

Raised by his father's business partner, Andrew Chord, and their elderly house-keeper, Tai, Dwayne was brought up to elieve strongly in the values of justice, law nd order.

To that end, he dedicated his young life to ighting crime and never allowing the ragedy which happened to him to befall nyone else. With Chord's help and nstruction, Dwayne honed his body and nind into a fighting machine. An armor was hen developed for him which he could use o wage his one-man war against all forms f crime.

Dwayne quickly learned that more could be accomplished with a group of like-minded individuals, and to that end, he recruited and funded the New Warriors.

It was that easy.

And that complicated.

In recent months (NEW WARRIORS #18-#25), Thrash has learned that most everything he believed or was told about himself was a carefully orchestrated lie.

In reality, *all* of the events which led to Dwayne's forming of the Warriors were based on manipulation conducted by Tai.

For her own purposes, she had coerced Chord into killing Dwayne's parents, just like she convinced Chord to train Dwayne and to organize the Warriors.

Why did she do all this? Whew, it sure is complicated. Hmm... in a nutshell, she needed super-powered youths to serve as sacrifices in her deluded quest for ultimate power. We *told* you it was complicated!

Forced to choose between the lives of his friends or that of Tai, Thrash killed the woman who raised him and freed the Warriors from her trap.

Which sort of brings us to the beginning of this series. Because of Tai's death and Chord's incapacitation, the Taylor Foundation is in disarray. In order to save his father's dream -- the last tangible link Dwayne has to his dead parents – Dwayne must wrest control of the Taylor Foundation from those who are trying to steal it from him, while also trying to find the kidnapped Chord in time to save his life!

This series will show different sides of both Thrash and Dwayne Taylor. It isn't called "Four Control" for nothing! Thrash must learn to control the four key aspects of his life – or *lose* control of everything that matters to him. You'll see Dwayne act as a businessman as well as a crime fighter. You'll also see the parameters of his nifty new armor (thanks to Fabe and Mark for that one) unleashed in full-on, body-slamming action!

We'll also see the return of some familiar faces (starting with this issue's return of the BENGAL – a character WARRIORS readers have *demanded* return since his first appearance in NW's #7-#9, and then Gideon's appearance in issue #3), as well as some fresh new ones (check out next issue's debut of TANTRUM).

We'd also like to do something rather nifty for a Limited Series – we'd like to run *your* comments on the title as we go along. In order to do that, you'll have to respond very quickly to each issue as it comes out. We hope to be able to include comments from you, the reader, by issue #3. It'll be a tight squeeze, but we'll give it a shot!

As for the future of NIGHT THRASHER as anything *more* than a Limited Series? Well, let's just say that it's up to you!

Let us know if you want to see more solo Thrash in the future. Tell your friends to check Thrash out. Once everyone finds out how cool he is, then we'll get the hint and maybe we'll see a monthly NIGHT THRASHER series by next year!

Oh, by the way, check out NEW WARRIORS #27, on sale now! It's our obligatory INFINITY WARS tie-in, but it's also way cool! Where else can you see RAGE battle his evil side, EN-RAGE-D? Or SPEEDBALL fight BLACKBALL?

And on sale in three weeks is NEW WARRIORS #28, featuring the return of the SEA URCHIN, the introduction of a new nasty named CARDINAL -- and the titanic Marvel debut of TURBO! All in one issue! Sheesh!

And hey, while you're still reading all of this rambling-on, check out the cover to NIGHT THRASHER #2! The gentleman's name is TANTRUM and he is one wacky, out-of-control assassin for hire. You'll be meeting him the same time Thrash does, and that'll be in thirty days!

Be there! Aloha!

BAGLEY+HOOVER

RISE OF THE
MIDNIGHT SONS
MARVEL® COMICS
DARKHOLD
© 1992 MARVEL ENT. GROUP, INC.
$2.75 US
$3.30 CAN
1
OCT
UK £1.85
APPROVED BY THE COMICS CODE AUTHORITY
Part 4 of 6

DARKHOLD: PAGES FROM THE BOOK OF SINS #1, published in August 1992, introduced Vicki Montesi and the Darkhold Redeemers in an ongoing series.

For eons, the walls between our earth and the supernatural realms have held fast ... until now. Now those walls are weakening, and LILITH, Queen of Evil, Mother of Demons, has risen from her slumber to shatter the walls and free her hellish spawn. Only the strangest of alliances can drive her back ... a union of old enemies and new heroes, in a battle forever to be remembered as the ...

RISE OF THE MIDNIGHT SONS™

DARKHOLD #1
PART 4

Writer: CHRISTIAN COOPER
Penciler: RICHARD CASE
Inker: MARK McKENNA
Colorist: GLYNIS OLIVER
Letterer: PHIL FELIX
Editor: BOBBIE CHASE
Managing Editor: KELLY CORVESE
Editor In Chief: TOM DEFALCO

GHOST RIDER #28 Part 1
SPIRITS OF VENGEANCE #1 Part 2
MORBIUS #1 Part 3
NIGHTSTALKERS #1 Part 5
GHOST RIDER #31 Part 6

YOU REALLY OUGHT TO TAKE A LOOK AT WHAT'S INSIDE. YOU'RE GONNA LOVE IT.
AW, C'MON. YOU KNOW YOU'RE DYING TO OPEN IT.
TRUST ME. YOU'RE GONNA LOVE THIS STUFF.

NEW YORK...
...HANG ON A SEC, DOCTOR...
I'LL BE RIGHT WITH YOU, FELLA.
LOOK, DOC, THIS ARGUING IS AGGRAVATING MY ULCER. IF IT WORKED FOR KENNY ROGERS, IT'LL WORK FOR ME... GOOD. LIPOSUCTION ON THURS-DAY. I'LL SEE YOU THEN.
WHAT THE DEVIL'S GOING ON AROUND HERE?! HOW'D YOU GET PAST MY SECRETARY?!
REALLY, MR. WALSH, IF YOU'LL JUST READ THIS...
I DON'T HANDLE FREAK ACTS.
TAKE IT TO VAUDE-VILLE.
HEH. YOU'RE A FUNNY MAN, MR. WALSH...
...BUT AS YOU CAN SEE, THIS IS ABOUT YOU, NOT ME.
DONALD J. WALSH
KEEP THOSE HITS COMING, MR. WALSH.
I'LL GIVE YOU A HIT, YOU LITTLE--
HMPH. PROBABLY THAT BIMBO ZEPHYR'S LATEST ATTEMPT TO SERVE ME WITH DIVORCE PAPERS...
THE EXCLUSIVE NORTH SHORE OF LONG ISLAND, A FEW HOURS LATER...
ZEFF?
ZEFF, HONEY, ARE YOU HOME?

WHAT'S THIS--A SICK LOVE LETTER FROM ONE OF YOUR FLOOZIES? YOU SCUM! I'LL KILL YOU--THIS TIME I MEAN IT!
SO WHY'S YOUR HAND SHAKING?
SHUT UP, DONNY! OR SO HELP ME...
I'LL MAKE IT EASY FOR YOU.
WH-WHAT?
I CAN'T LIVE WITH MY-SELF ANY-MORE. GOOD-BYE, ZEFF.
WAIT--
BUT--
I--
BLAM
OOPS.
OMIGOD...
I NEED YOU, ZEFF...
PLEASE... NEED TO TOUCH YOU, TASTE YOU...
...INSIDE AND OUT.
OH.
OH, YES.
LOVELY.
GRMMMNNRMPH!

"VICKI?
"YO! EARTH TO VICKI MONTESI!"
ROME.
I'VE HEARD OF SPACING OUT, VICKI, BUT IN MID-SENTENCE...?
SORRY. GUESS I'M NOT FEELING SO WELL.
NASH, DON'T YOU THINK SPAGHETTI LOOKS KIND OF... Y'KNOW, GROSS?
NO. STOP CHANGING THE SUBJECT.
YOU'VE BEEN ZONING OUT A LOT LATELY.
WELL... I HAVEN'T BEEN GETTING MUCH SLEEP.
NO KIDDING. YOU'RE A SLAVE TO THAT HOSPITAL. I HARDLY SEE YOU AT HOME ANYMORE.
THE FIRST YEAR OUT OF MED SCHOOL'S THE ROUGHEST.
BUT I DIDN'T KNOW YOU CARED.
OH! I'M CUT! I BLEED! I MUST HIE ME TO THE LADIES' ROOM TO TEND MY WOUND!
RIGHT. TEND TO YOUR BLADDER, MORE LIKE.
WHAT IS WRONG WITH ME? THESE MENTAL LAPSES ARE GETTING SCARY. MAYBE I SHOULD--
AW, CRUD.
< WELL, WELL, WELL. IF IT ISN'T THE LITTLE MONGREL! >*
* TRANSLATED FROM THE ITALIAN.

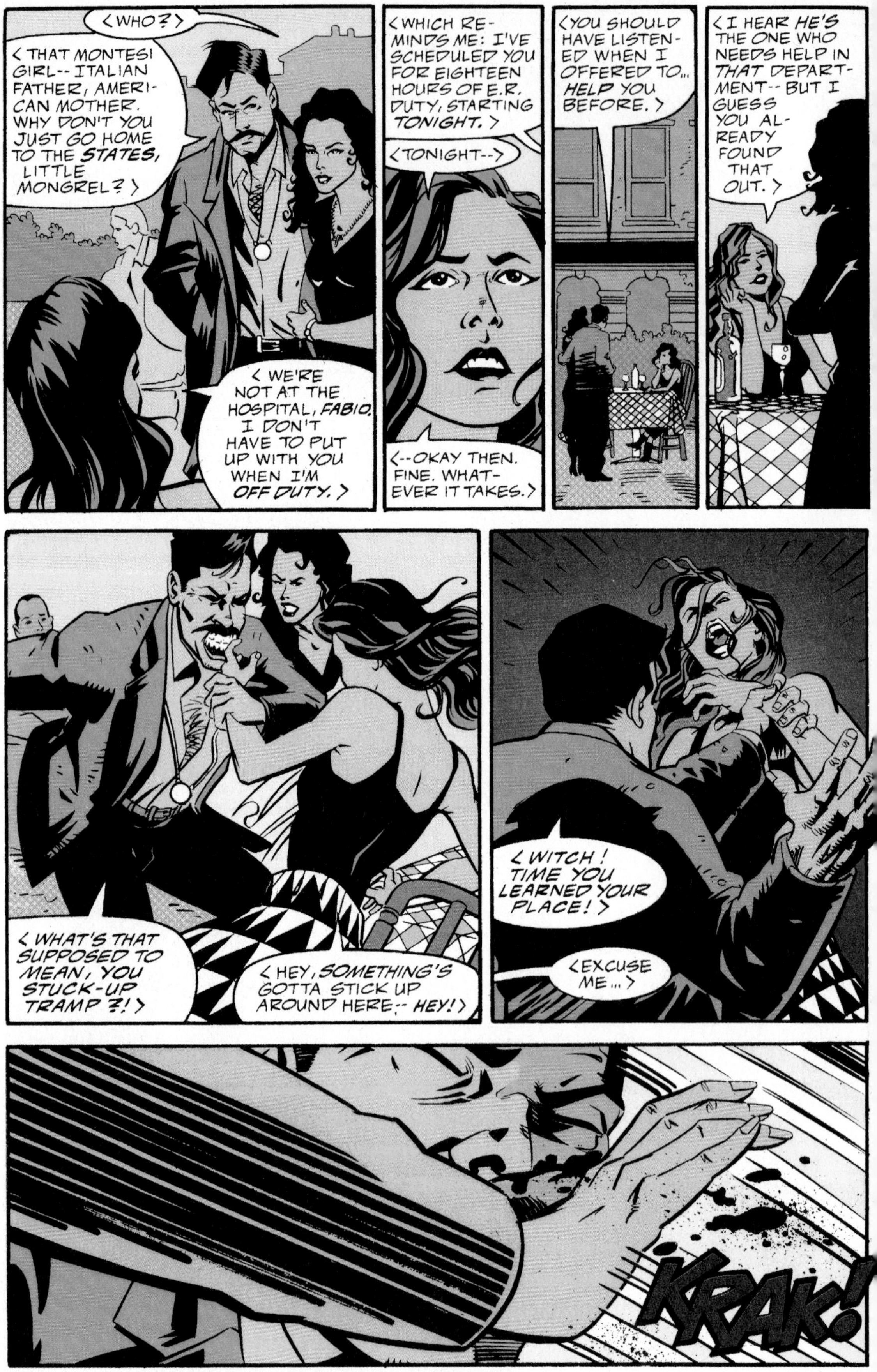

<WHO?>
<THAT MONTESI GIRL-- ITALIAN FATHER, AMERICAN MOTHER. WHY DON'T YOU JUST GO HOME TO THE STATES, LITTLE MONGREL?>
<WE'RE NOT AT THE HOSPITAL, FABIO. I DON'T HAVE TO PUT UP WITH YOU WHEN I'M OFF DUTY.>
<WHICH REMINDS ME: I'VE SCHEDULED YOU FOR EIGHTEEN HOURS OF E.R. DUTY, STARTING TONIGHT.>
<TONIGHT-->
<--OKAY THEN. FINE. WHATEVER IT TAKES.>
<YOU SHOULD HAVE LISTENED WHEN I OFFERED TO... HELP YOU BEFORE.>
<I HEAR HE'S THE ONE WHO NEEDS HELP IN THAT DEPARTMENT-- BUT I GUESS YOU ALREADY FOUND THAT OUT.>
<WHAT'S THAT SUPPOSED TO MEAN, YOU STUCK-UP TRAMP?!>
<HEY, SOMETHING'S GOTTA STICK UP AROUND HERE-- HEY!>
<WITCH! TIME YOU LEARNED YOUR PLACE!>
<EXCUSE ME...>
KRAK!

<...BUT THAT'S MY ROOMMATE YOU'RE MAN-HANDLING!>
POLIZIA! POLIZIA!
WHO WAS THAT LOSER?
MY SUPERVISOR.
OH.
MY LIFE'S GONNA BE A NIGHTMARE FROM NOW ON...
--AND I DON'T CARE! THAT WAS GREAT! WE SHOULD BUST HEADS MORE OFTEN!
"WE"? I'M THE BLACK BELT, REMEMBER?
WELL, IF YOU'D TEACH ME A MOVE OR TWO...
I'VE TRIED!
UH-OH--MY KEYS! I MUST HAVE LOST THEM IN THE SCUFFLE!
S'OKAY--I'VE GOT MINE.
YOU DO?
I KNOW--I NEVER HAVE MY KEYS WITH ME, AND YOU NEVER LOSE YOURS!
GUESS IT'S JUST GONNA BE ONE OF THEM DAYS, SWEETHEART!
CLICK!

BOOM!
NASH! UUNNNNNNNNNNGH
WHERE AM I?
WHO--?
PLEASE...
YOU MUST UNDERSTAND...
I ONLY WANT TO TOUCH YOU... KNOW YOUR WARM, LIVING FLESH...
KEEP AWAY!

NO!
EASY, VICKI. IT'S DR. DIFINIZIO. THERE WAS A BOMB BLAST...
... BUT YOU'RE SAFE NOW, IN ST. ANTHONY'S HOSPITAL. YOU'VE BEEN OUT FOR THREE DAYS...
...THIS IS FATHER VITTORIO, FROM THE VATICAN-- OUT OF CLERICAL GARB AT THE MOMENT--
I KNOW WHO HE IS, LORENZO. IS HE HERE TO GIVE ME LAST RITES?
HARDLY. BESIDES SOME MINOR HEAD TRAUMA, YOU'RE FINE.
GOOD. THEN GET HIM OUT OF HERE.
VICKI...
YOU DON'T GET IT, LORENZO. FATHER VITTORIO IS MY FATHER. LITERALLY.
OH, HE'LL SPOUT SOME MUMBO-JUMBO ABOUT SPECIAL RULES THAT LET PRIESTS IN OUR FAMILY MARRY. MY MOM BOUGHT IT... I DON'T.
YOU SHOULD. OUR FAMILY'S SPECIAL STATUS IS WHY EVIL FORCES HAVE TARGETTED YOU. FOR AFTER I'M GONE, YOU WILL BE THE LAST MONTESI.
BUT, FATHER, WHY WOULD SOMEONE WANT TO DESTROY THE MONTESIS?
"BECAUSE OF THE DUTY WE'VE BORNE FOR GENERATIONS"-- HERE IT COMES, LORENZO...
WE MONTESIS ARE INCORRUPTIBLE, AND SO IT FELL ON US TO SAFEGUARD THE WORLD...
...FROM AN ANCIENT COMPENDIUM OF ALL THE VILEST, DARKEST SORCERIES... A WRETCHED TOME SO FOUL IT EARNED THE TITLE THE BOOK OF SINS--
--THE DARKHOLD.
MORE MUMBO-JUMBO.

ASSUMING SUCH A BOOK EXISTS, WHY NOT BURN IT?
ITS PAGES ARE INDESTRUCTIBLE.
OF COURSE.
THOUGH AN AMERICAN CURRENTLY KEEPS THE BOOK, SOMEDAY IT WILL RETURN TO OUR HANDS. YOU, VICTORIA, MUST BE READY TO TAKE UP THE BURDEN.
DON'T COUNT ON IT.
WHY? WHY MUST YOU ALWAYS DEFY ME?
LET'S SEE... ONE: THERE'S ALL YOUR RESENTMENT BECAUSE I WASN'T BORN A BOY TO CARRY ON YOUR PRECIOUS TRADITIONS... TWO: THERE'S ALL THE NEGLECT OF ME AND MOM AS YOU BURIED YOURSELF IN YOUR OCCULT LIBRARY...
...ARE YOU GETTING ALL THIS? THREE: THAT WHOLE STORY'S THE BIGGEST CROCK I EVER...
...EVER HEARD...
VICKI? VICKI, WHAT'S WRONG?
WHAT'S THE MATTER WITH HER, DOCTOR?

I'M... FINE. JUST TIRED, I GUESS. WHO'S THE STRONG, SILENT TYPE?
THIS IS SPECIAL AGENT SAM BUCHANAN, FROM INTERPOL.
HE DOESN'T SPEAK?
NOT AS MUCH AS YOU DO.
CUTE. I CAN'T HELP YOU, SPECIAL AGENT BUCHANAN. ALL I REMEMBER IS A FLASH OF LIGHT JUST AS NASH--
OH, GOD-- NASH. TELL ME, LORENZO. IS SHE... DEAD?
VICKI... HER MIND IS INTACT. BUT HER BODY...
LET'S JUST SAY SHE WON'T BE PRACTICING KARATE ANYMORE.
YOU...! GET OUT, ALL OF YOU!
YOU TWO ARE BEST PALS, EH?
REAL CHUMMY.
LOOK, MS. MONTESI, I DON'T BUY THAT MYSTICAL CRUD ONE BIT...
...BUT SOMEBODY DOES, AND THEY'RE WILLING TO KILL YOU FOR IT.
INTERPOL HAS ASSIGNED ME TO PROTECT YOU, AT THE VATICAN'S REQUEST. I GO WHERE YOU GO, UNTIL THE DANGER'S PAST. THOSE ARE MY ORDERS.
HERE ARE NEW ONES: I WON'T HAVE ANYTHING TO DO WITH MY FATHER OR HIS CONSPIRACY THEORIES, SO STAY AWAY-- OR I'LL MAKE MYSELF SICK. UNDERSTOOD?
NOW I KNOW HOW YOU SURVIVED THAT BLAST...
...YOU'RE TOO HARDHEADED FOR ANY PERMANENT DAMAGE.

MEANWHILE, IN NEW YORK...
GOLDEN PLAZA
PARDON ME, MA'AM, BUT...
...AREN'T YOU PROFESSOR LOUISE HASTINGS?
GOOD GOD --ANOTHER ONE.
SEE HERE, CHAP--I CAN'T TALK TO THE PRESS ABOUT THE WALSH MURDER CASE.
I'M NOT A REPORTER.
NO? YOU LOOK LIKE ONE--UNKEMPT, AS IF YOU HAVEN'T BATHED IN A WEEK.
ER... I'VE BEEN ON THE ROAD...
THE NAME'S JOHN BLAZE.
NGO'S PIZZA
WHEN I READ YOU WERE CONSULTING ON THE WALSH CASE, SAW YOUR PHOTO IN THE PAPERS...
...I KNEW I HAD TO FIND YOU.
UH-OH--HE'S DAFT.
ACTUALLY, THE ONE YOU SHOULD REALLY TALK TO...
...IS HIM.
ZARATHOS UNBOUND!

...A WOMAN NAMED LILITH.
WE HAVE ALREADY TURNED BACK HER FORCES ONCE...
WE THINK YOU AND CERTAIN OTHERS MAY BE HER NEXT TARGETS. IF SO...
I DO NOT KNOW THIS "ZARATHOS." I AM CALLED THE GHOST RIDER.
YOUR FACE, AND THOSE OF OTHERS WE HAVE YET TO FIND, WERE REVEALED TO ME IN A VISION.
THE VISION WARNED OF A WOMAN WHO WILL OVER-RUN THE WORLD WITH HER DEMONIC CHILDREN...

"...YOU'RE ALL IN TERRIBLE DANGER!"
GOD, I HATE THE GRAVEYARD SHIFT. JUST MAKING MY ROUNDS GIVES ME THE CREEPS.
WHO LEFT THAT WINDOW OPEN? THE NIGHTS ARE TOO COOL...
AT LEAST VICKI'S SLEEPING SOUNDLY...
POOR THING. A PATIENT IN HER OWN HOSPITAL. LIFE'S FULL OF--
VICTORIA
!?!

THAT STUFFED BEAR WON'T FOOL THE NURSES FOR LONG...
...BUT I HAD TO GET OUT OF THE HOSPITAL. EVER SINCE MY HEAD INJURY, IMAGES HAVE CRAMMED MY MIND, FORCING ME TO SEEK OUT... WHAT? WHERE?
AND WHY DO I HAVE THE FEELING I'M BEING FOLLOWED?
LISTEN TO ME. MY FATHER REALLY HAS ME SPOOKED.
WHEREVER I'M GOING, I'LL NEED MONEY. MY CREDIT CARDS WERE TRASHED IN THE BLAST...
I'LL TRY SOFIA. SHE'S ALWAYS GOT LIRA TO SPARE.
BREEP BREEP BREEP
C'MON, SOFE, ANSWER THE... PHONE...
SKRASH!
NO!
THINK FAST, MONTESI!
WHAK
Telefono
Telefono
I DID IT! I'M SAFE!

Telefono
Telefono
HUH?!
BLAM!
BUCHANAN! BUT HOW--?
BEEN TAILING YOU SINCE THE HOSPITAL.
MIND TELLING ME WHO THESE GOONS ARE?
THEY MUST BE DARKHOLDERS-- A SECRET CULT RUN BY POWER SEEKERS WHO WORSHIP THAT BOOK. MY FATHER ALWAYS TALKED ABOUT THEM, BUT I NEVER BELIEVED--
BELIEVE IT.
I'M SORRY, MS. MONTESI--
I CAN'T STOP THEM. I'M NOT GOING TO DIE TRYING.
--BUT I'M NO FOOL. I KNOW THE ODDS.
IT'S THE WOMAN YOU WANT, RIGHT? SO TAKE HER.
WHAT?!

BLAM
BLAM
BLAM
A SECOND GUN--HIDDEN UP HIS SLEEVE!
SAPS! GET DOWN, MONTESI!
HOW DO YOU USE THIS THING?!
BLAM BLAM
BLAM
CLICK!
OH.
YOUR FRIENDS ARE DOWN-- AND A GINSU AGAINST A GUN--
CLICK!
NO! OUT OF AMMO--!
YO! HANDKERCHIEF-HEAD!
KRAK!

NICE MOVE.
LEARNED IT FROM A FRIEND.
WE'D BETTER GET TO AN EMBASSY. LOCAL POLICE MAY BE COMPROMISED.
I'VE GOT A BETTER IDEA. WE'RE GOING TO... NEW YORK--AFTER I HELP THESE VERMIN.
WHAT?! THEY JUST TRIED TO KILL YOU!
I'M A DOCTOR. THEY MAY BE THE VERY ONES WHO BLEW UP NASH, BUT I'M STILL OBLIGATED TO HELP THEM.
MONTESI, WE'VE GOT TO MOVE. THERE COULD BE MORE ASSASSINS.
BESIDES, THE AUTHORITIES WILL BE HERE SOON. THEY'LL SEE TO THE INJURED. WE'RE GOING TO AN EMBASSY NOW.
NO. NEW YORK.
THERE'S NO TIME FOR THIS!
LOOK, I CAN'T EXPLAIN IT, I JUST KNOW ALL THE ANSWERS ARE IN NEW YORK. BESIDES, WHO'LL LOOK FOR US THERE?
AND WHAT SAFER PLACE IN ROME THAN AN AIRPORT, WITH ITS HIGH SECURITY?
MAYBE...
LET ME PUT IT THIS WAY: NEW YORK, OR I KEEP PLAYING DOCTOR.
NEW YORK IT IS.
GENTLEMEN, AS YOU CAN SEE THROUGH THIS GIFTED CHILD'S EYES...
...YOUR MEN HAVE FAILED AGAIN.

AND WHAT INTEREST OF YOURS, LILITH, WHETHER THE GIRL LIVES OR DIES?
SHE THREATENS THE DARKHOLD...
...THE BOOK THAT CAN RETURN CHTHON'S CHILDREN FROM EXILE...
...THAT I MAY LOVE THEM AS MY OWN!
I DON'T TRUST HER!
SILENCE! MY MASK PRESIDES!
AND WE DARKHOLDERS HAVE NOTHING TO LOSE FROM A TEMPORARY ALLIANCE.
THESE MEN ARE NOW YOURS.
BUT WHAT WILL YOU DO WITH THEM THAT WE HAVEN'T?
RE-SHAPE THEM.
TAKE THEM, DOC!
BUT REALLY, MY CHILD-- TRY NOT TO MAKE SUCH A MESS THIS TIME.
AAIIEEEE
THEY'LL BE FASTER, STRONGER. AND ONCE THEY'VE KILLED MONTESI...
...WE'LL SEE WHAT PLANS I HAVE FOR THIS LITTLE CULT.

LONG ISLAND.
THIS IS IN-SANE. WE TRAVEL HALFWAY 'ROUND THE WORLD TO NEW YORK, TREK OUT TO THE SUBURBS--
WALSH
EP OUT CRIME SCENE
--TO A CRIME SCENE? ARE YOU SURE ABOUT THIS INSTINCT OF YOURS?
NO. BUT I HAVE TO SEE THIS THROUGH.
HOLD IT. THIS PADLOCK'S ALREADY OPEN, AND THE TAPE'S BEEN BROKEN.
RIME SCENE
SOMEONE'S HERE.
WE'LL GO IN THE BACK...
AND KEEP IT QUIET...

LOOK!
A BLACK ENVELOPE?
PUT THAT DOWN THIS INSTANT!

FREEZE, LADY!
SEE HERE, YOU BLOODY COWBOY...
VICKI?
LOUISE!
YOU'RE ALIVE! WHEN I HEARD ABOUT THE BLAST... BUT WHAT ARE YOU DOING HERE?
WHAT I WAS ABOUT TO ASK YOU.
YOU KNOW HER, EH?
AGENT BUCHANAN, MEET LOUISE HASTINGS-- PROFESSOR OF ARCHAE-OLOGY AT OXFORD, OCCULT EXPERT...
...AND THE ONLY FRIEND OF MY FATHER'S I EVER LOVED.
HOW CONVENIENT THAT SHE JUST HAPPENS TO BE HERE.
ACTUALLY, THE POLICE FLEW ME HERE TO HELP WITH THE CASE...
...WHEN THEY FOUND THIS ANCIENT PARCHMENT AT THE MURDER SITE!
IN A BLACK ENVELOPE.
WHAT IS IT?
THE GREATEST FIND OF THE CENTURY--A PAGE OF THE DARKHOLD!
WHATEVER BROUGHT YOU HERE, IT CAN'T BE COINCIDENCE. YOU'RE A MONTESI, AND THAT MAKES ME CERTAIN --
--THIS IS ONE OF THE FABLED LOST PAGES OF THE BOOK OF SINS!

OH NO, NOT AGAIN. I'LL DO MY SLEUTHING IN THE REAL WORLD, THANK YOU.
AS I WAS SAYING... THIS IS OF VAST SIGNIFICANCE. THERE ARE LEGENDS ABOUT THE DARKHOLD IN EVERY CULTURE...
...ABOUT HOW IT WAS AUTHORED BY CHTHON--A FOUL, INCOMPREHENSIBLE BEING, GREATEST OF THE ELDER GODS--
--SO HIS--ITS--POWER WOULD ENDURE AND ONE DAY SUMMON IT HOME FROM EXILE.
MY FATHER NEVER MENTIONED THAT PART...
...IT DOESN'T SQUARE WITH CATHOLIC DOCTRINE.
BUT THEN, MY FATHER ALWAYS SAID THE BOOK IS CURRENTLY IN THE COLLECTION OF A MR. WEIRD--
STRANGE--AND HE CLAIMS TO BE A DOCTOR, THOUGH FROM WHAT I'VE READ, HE'S JUST A CRACKPOT. HE'S GOT THE BOOK...
...BUT IN MEDIEVAL DAYS, THE PAGES WERE SCATTERED TO BREAK THE BOOK'S POWER. LATER, MOST WERE RE-COLLECTED. BUT SOME REMAINED LOST...
...UNTIL NOW.
I'VE TRANSLATED THIS PAGE...
PLOP!
...IT DESCRIBES A SPELL FOR IMMORTALITY...
...BUT AS A SWARM OF WORMS!

MAKE ME FEEL ALIVE!
BLAM!
MMMPH!
BUCHANAN!
AND YOU-- Ohhhh.
oooh.
UNIQUE. I MUST HAVE MORE...
PLEASE. HELP ME.
...WHEN I'M DONE HERE,
HONESTLY, OLD WOMAN.
KLIK!
DID YOU THINK THE LIGHTS WOULD HURT ME?
NO--

--THEY WILL!
WE GOT YOUR SIGNAL, PROF! BUT WHAT--
YEEESH! IS THAT ONE OF LILITH'S?
SKRAASH!
WHAT-EVER IT IS, IT MUST BE STOPPED!
SQUIISH!
BOOM!
AAIIEEEEE!
LET'S SEE WHAT MY HELLFIRE SHOTGUN WILL DO!

YOU'LL ALL PAY FOR THIS!
GAK! GAK!
BOOM!
GET THESE THINGS OFFA ME!
HAH! THIS TIME YOUR BLAST HAD NO EFFECT!
HE'S ESCAPING!
NO.
CIAO!
NO!
GLUG GLUG
YOU SON-UVA--
GLUG GLUG GLUG
I'VE STILL GOT ENOUGH OF YOU TO SQUISH!
WAIT!
I'VE GOT A BETTER IDEA...

NOW THAT WE ALL KNOW WHO WE ARE...
...IF NOT WHAT WE ARE...
...SHALL WE GET ON WITH IT, EH?
AND SOON, IN MANHATTAN'S GOLDEN PLAZA HOTEL...
YOU HEARD THE MAN, WALSH...
FORM UP...
PICKLES
...OR BLAZE PULLS THE TRIGGER!
WAIT!
The Golden Plaza Hotel
I'LL TELL YOU EVERY-THING!
"I LIVED LIFE AT 120 M.P.H....
"WORKED HARD, PLAYED HARDER, BROKE IN SOME NEW TALENT...
"IT TAKES ITS TOLL.
"WHAT I'D GIVE TO BEAT THE RAVAGES OF TIME...
"THEN CAME THAT MISERABLE DWARF...
"COULDN'T READ A WORD OF WHAT WAS INSIDE, AND YET...
ENAMORATH! EMMORETH! BA'AL SET ELIANATH!

"GOD KNOWS WHAT I SAID.
"NO. NOT GOD.
"A VISION ROSE FROM THE PAGE...
"CALLED ITSELF 'THE OTHER'...
"...OFFERED ME IMMORTALITY. I ACCEPTED...
"...NOT KNOWING I'D SPEND ETERNITY...
"...AS A ROTTING PILE OF WORMS PASSING FOR HUMAN.
"ME, A GLUTTON FOR LIFE, DOOMED TO FEEL DECAY...
...EXCEPT WHEN TASTING THE LIVING WARMTH OF OTHERS.
BELIEVE ME, I CAN'T BE KILLED.
TO-GETHER, THE WORMS ARE IN-VULNER-ABLE...
SEPAR-ATELY, YOU'D HAVE TO KILL EACH ONE...
"IF EVEN ONE SURVIVED..."
THESE CHAMELEON WOR ARE A STROKE OF LUCK THEY KEEP OUR TAR-GETS SO BUSY...
...WHEN WE STRIKE, THEY'LL NEVER KNOW WHAT HIT THEM !

AS DAWN BREAKS...
VICKI'S FINALLY GETTING SOME SLEEP.
WHERE'S THE PROF?
"GOING FOR A STROLL," SHE TOLD ME--
"--BUT WHAT'S SHE REALLY UP TO?"
GOT IT!
BACK TO THE HOTEL QUICK, OLD GIRL--
EEEEEEE
--AND PUT THE PLAN INTO MOTION!

VICKI, WHAT--GOOD LORD!
SO MANY?
THEY'RE MULTIPLYING! SOON THERE'LL BE ENOUGH FOR TWO WALSHES!
THEY MUST HAVE HOMED IN ON THE OTHERS TO FIND US!
WORMS YOU TOLD US TO KEEP!
NO TIME TO ARGUE--
TCHINK!
--JUST ACT!
THANKS! BUT WHAT NOW?
NO TIME TO EXPLAIN-- JUST RUN FOR THE PARK!
AND BLAZE, BUCHANAN-- NO GUN-FIRE!

YOU DON'T UNDERSTAND! I MUST HAVE YOU!
NO OTHER SENSATION EVEN COMES CLOSE!
STUFF IT!
SMASH
C'MON, YOU PILE OF ROT!
GOT TO TIME THIS JUST RIGHT...
YESSS, TAUNT ME! IT WILL MAKE YOUR FLESH THAT MUCH SWEETER!
...NOW!
WALK
SPLOOSH!

NICE TRY, WOMAN!
BLAST! BUYS ME TIME, THOUGH...
...TO REACH THE PARK!
WE'RE HERE, MS. MONTESI.
GREAT...
...NOW WHAT?
NOW, YOU DIE!
LILITH!

I'VE GOT A CLEAR SHOT--
NO, SAM-- NO SHOT AT ALL!
I KNEW IT! YOU--
JUST SHUT UP, WATCH-- AND PRAY.
RUN, VICKI! KEEP GOING!
HOW CAN THIS BE? THEY STAND BEFORE MY STRONGEST BLOWS!
BRAK
TELL ME ABOUT IT!

WHEN YOU'VE GOT A FREE MOMENT, GHOST RIDER--!
VROOOM
KROM!
THANK YOU, BIKE! AND NOW--
NO WONDER THEY'RE TOUGH! THEY'RE NOT HUMAN!
FORGET THE BIKERS! GET THE WOMAN!
NO!

UUNGH!
YES! SHE'S OURS!
I TOLD YOU I'D HAVE YOU, WOMAN!
BUT NOW--
WE'LL HAVE TWO TIMES THE FUN!
NOT HUMAN? THEN I'LL HOLD BACK NO LONGER!
TOO LATE, FALSE DEMON!
TOO LATE!

"THE BIRDS!"
WAIT--LOOK! THE BIRDS!
NO! STOP THEM!
DON'T LET THEM--
NOOOOOOOOOOO

NO GUNS-- OF COURSE. SHOTS WOULD HAVE SCARED AWAY THE BIRDS.
SORRY, SAM, THERE JUST WASN'T TIME TO EXPLAIN.
THEN THERE'S JUST ONE BIT OF BUSINESS LEFT--
BOOM
MOTHER-- LOOK OUT!
AIIIIEEEE!
YOU, BLAZE, AND YOU, GHOST RIDER--AND YOU SELF-APPOINTED DARKHOLD RE-DEEMERS--YOU'LL ALL PAY--!
NOT JUST WITH YOUR LIVES--
--BUT WITH YOUR VERY SOULS!
WAIT FOR...
...MEEEE!
UH-OH.

SHE WON'T GET FAR.
FOR NOW, AT LEAST, THE THREAT TO YOU FROM LILITH IS PAST.
STILL, YOU AND BLAZE MUST CONTINUE TO FIGHT HER--
--WHILE I FIGHT THE DARKHOLD.
BUT WITH WALSH GONE, THAT DANGER'S OVER!
THAT PARTICULAR MENACE IS GONE--BUT IF THAT DARKHOLD PAGE TURNED UP AFTER ALL THOSE CENTURIES, WHY NOT OTHERS?
ONE HAS. I HAD ANOTHER VISION WHILE I SLEPT.
YOU'RE NOT GOING AFTER THEM ALONE-- I'M PROTECTING YOU, REMEMBER?
AND I WOULDN'T MISS THIS CHANCE FOR FIRSTHAND OCCULT RESEARCH FOR THE WORLD!
OH, PLEASE--CAN WE DROP THIS HOCUS-POCUS STUFF?
I DON'T UNDERSTAND THESE HORRORS--I'M STILL NOT SURE I BE-LIEVE IN THEM--BUT I KNOW I'VE GOT TO STOP THEM.
THEY HAVEN'T NOTICED ME! I'M FREE! FREEEEEEE--EEEEE
FIE...
...I REALLY MUST WATCH WHERE I STEP.
SPLORSH!
MORE IMPOR-TANTLY, I MUST WATCH THIS MONTESI...
...VERY CLOSELY, ME-THINKS!

ELSEWHERE...
BLAST! THESE THINGS NEVER WORK WHEN YOU NEED 'EM!
CLICK FZZ CLICK FZZ CLICK FZZ
ALLOW ME...
CLICK-- FWOOSH!
UH... YOU'RE MY PAROLE OFFICER, RIGHT?
LIBRARY OF CONGRESS
NOT QUITE...
BUT I DO HAVE SOMETHING THAT COULD TAKE YOUR CAREER IN A WHOLE NEW DIRECTION...
3:18:54
CAUTION:
KEROSENE
THE MIDNIGHT SONS SAGA CONTINUES NEXT MONTH IN THE PREMIERE OF THE LAST NEW BOOK: DON'T MISS
NIGHTSTALKERS
TO BE CONTINUED...

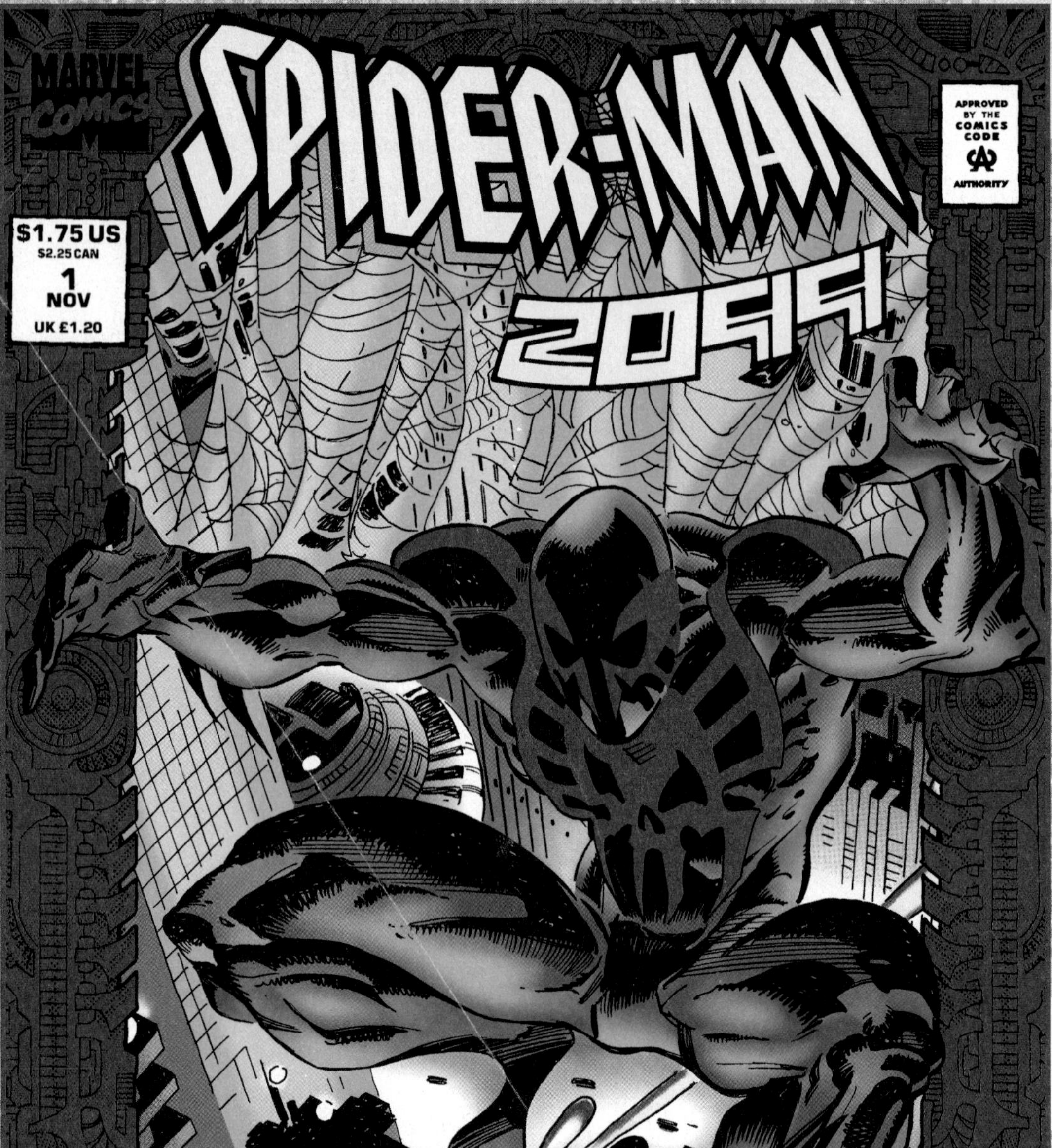
MARVEL COMICS
SPIDER-MAN
2099
APPROVED BY THE COMICS CODE AUTHORITY
$1.75 US
$2.25 CAN
1
NOV
UK £1.20
2099
LEONARDI
WILLIAMSON

SPIDER-MAN 2099 #1, published in September 1992, introduced the Spider-Man of the future in an ongoing series. It also debuted the "2099" imprint, which featured several interconnected titles all set in the same alternate future.

NEW YORK...
IN THE YEAR 2099.
WE'RE GONNA GET CAUGHT.
- NO LEADS IN
MANY THINGS HAVE CHANGED.
NAPITKA!
ALCHEMAX MYSTERY EXPLOSIO
WE'RE NOT GONNA GET CAUGHT.
I'M TELLING YA, THE FLYBOYS NEVER COME UP THIS HIGH.
THEY DON'T LIKE THE CROSSWINDS. JUST A BUNCHA STONELESS...
HEY!!
WHAT THE SHOCK IS THAT?!
ON THE OTHER HAND, THERE ARE SOME THINGS...

...THAT REMAIN DEPRESSINGLY THE SAME.
HALT!
AS AUTHORIZED REPRESENTATIVES OF THE PUBLIC EYE, WE'RE ORDERING YOU TO HALT!
GET THOSE IDIOT KIDS OUT OF THE WAY!
YOU BRATS IN THE WHISPER 3000-- VACATE THIS AREA IMMEDIATELY!
ALL SUCH VEHICLES ARE FORBIDDEN IN THE INNER CITY! YOUR REGISTRATION HAS BEEN NOTED! RETURN HOME AT ONCE, WHERE YOUR VEHICLE WILL BE CONFISCATED!
MOVE!!
PETER DAVID WRITER
RICK LEONARDI PENCILER
AL WILLIAMSON INKER
RICK PARKER LETTERER
STEVE BUCCELLATO COLORIST
JOEY CAVALIERI EDITOR
TOM DEFALCO, EDITOR IN CHIEF
Begin the Future History of...

STAN LEE PRESENTS
SPIDER-MAN
2099

THIS IS YOUR FINAL WARNING! SURRENDER INSTANTLY OR WE WILL USE DEADLY FORCE!
WHAT THE BLAZES--!
HOW DOES HE MOVE THAT FAST?!
10
WE'RE HERE TO ARREST HIM, NOT ADMIRE HIM!
HE WENT BETWEEN THOSE BUILDINGS! MALIK, WITH ME! THE REST OF YOU, CUT HIM OFF FROM THE OTHER SIDE!
OKAY, MALIK, PROCEED WITH CAUTION. ALCHEMAX WANTS HIM ALIVE IF AT ALL POSSIBLE.
I BET THEY DO, SARGE, AND I WANT ME ALIVE IF AT ALL POSSIBLE.
CAN THE JOKES, MALIK. WATCH THE DRAFTS-- THEY'RE REALLY NASTY UP HERE.
NOW WHERE DID HE GO?
SARGE! ABOVE YOU!

TARGET ACQUIRED! ALL UNITS, CONVERGE ON MY SIGNAL!
THERE HE GOES! ON MARK, AND--
FIRE!
THOSE WERE WARNING SHOTS! DON'T MAKE US HURT YOU!
CHOOM
CHOOM
SWING AROUND! MALIK, BRING IT AROUND!
WHAT'S HE DOING?! HE'S IN FREEFALL!
HE'LL KILL HIMSELF!

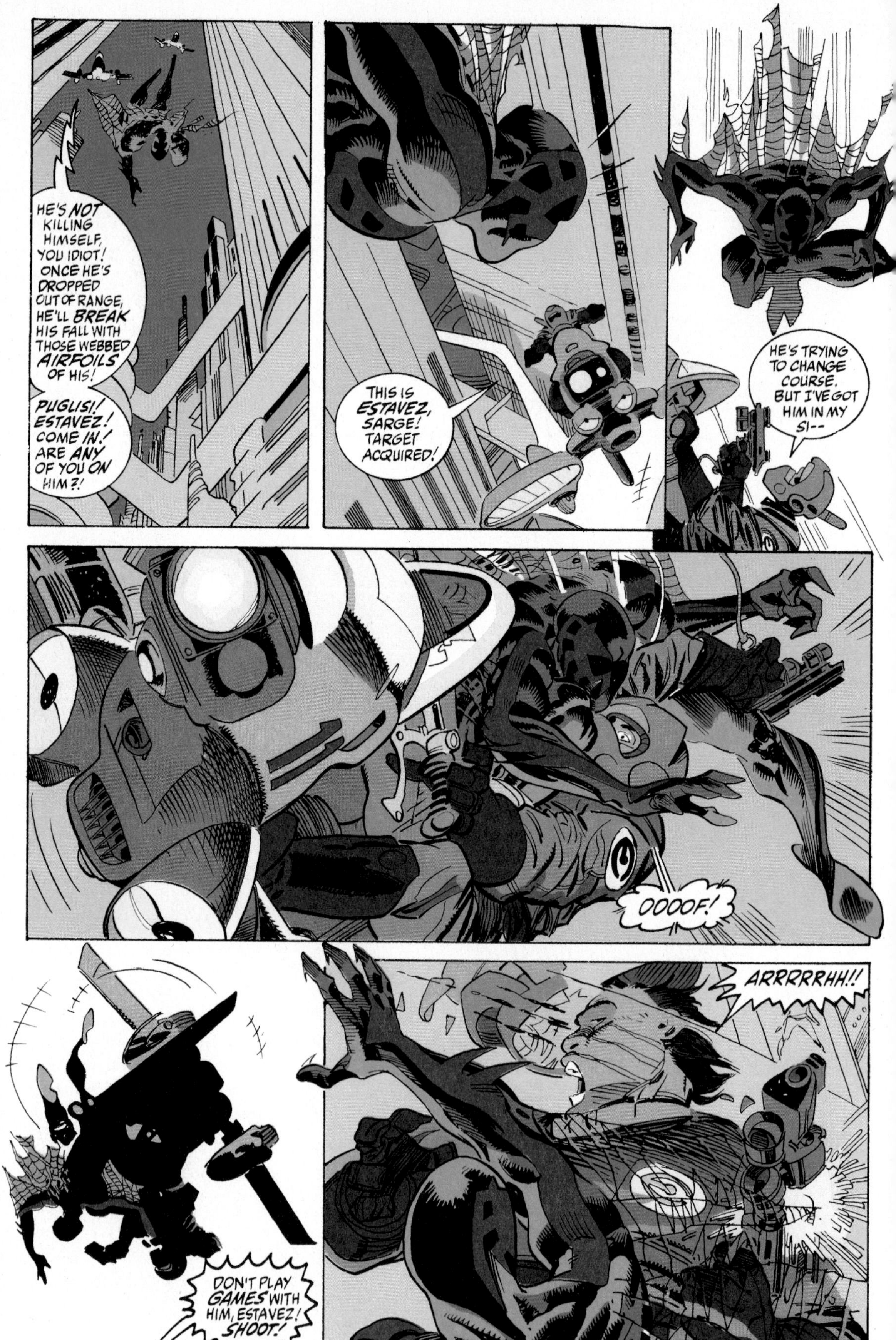
HE'S NOT KILLING HIMSELF, YOU IDIOT! ONCE HE'S DROPPED OUT OF RANGE, HE'LL BREAK HIS FALL WITH THOSE WEBBED AIRFOILS OF HIS!
PUGLISI! ESTAVEZ! COME IN! ARE ANY OF YOU ON HIM?!
THIS IS ESTAVEZ, SARGE! TARGET ACQUIRED!
HE'S TRYING TO CHANGE COURSE, BUT I'VE GOT HIM IN MY SI--
OOOOF!
DON'T PLAY GAMES WITH HIM, ESTAVEZ! SHOOT!
ARRRRRHH!!

EVERYONE OUT OF THE WAY!
MY FACE! I'M BLEEDING TO DEATH!! YOU CUT MY FACE! YOU TRIED TO KILL ME! YOU--
JUST SHUT UP WOULD YA, PLEASE?
TME
DID YOU SEE IT?
NEVER SAW A FLYBOY CRASH BEFORE.
PUBLIC EYE GOT A BLACK EYE, IF Y'ASK--
ALCHEMAX
WHOA! CHECK IT!
IT'S ESTAVEZ, AWRIGHT! GET HIM TO THE NEAREST DOCS IN A BOX!
WHERE'D HE GO, ESTY?
THAT WAY, SOMEWHERE. I DUNNO.
OKAY, MEN. PROCEED WITH CAUTION. HE COULD BE...
ANYWHERE.
AW, SHOCK.

BABYLON TOWERS.
A SUBSIDIARY OF ALCHEMAX.
AHH!
LIGHTS TO ONE QUARTER!
HUNH.
BETTER.
MUCH BETTER.
GOOD EVENING, MIGUEL.
THE TIME IS 0133 HOURS.
OUTDOOR TEMPERATURE IS 54° AIR IS PARTLY BREATHABLE. FORECAST FOR THE NEXT TWO DAYS IS OCCASIONAL CLOUDINESS WITH A 50% CHANCE OF RAIN.
FIFTY PERCENT. THAT MEANS MAYBE IT'LL RAIN, MAYBE IT WON'T.
YOUR PERSONAL BIO READINGS INDICATE ACCELERATED HEART-BEAT AND PULSE ABOVE THE NORM. YOU'VE BEEN EXERTING YOURSELF.
TELL ME ABOUT IT.

YOU HAVE SIX MESSAGES PENDING, MIGUEL. WOULD YOU LIKE TO SEE THEM?
SURE, LYLA.
MIKE. I STRONGLY SUGGEST YOU COME TO ME SO THAT WE CAN WORK SOMETHING OUT.
YOU NEED THE DRUG. YOU KNOW IT, AND I KNOW IT.
TYLER, THERE'S A TRAIN LEAVING AT 0830, BE UNDER IT.
THE SOONER WE CAN COME TO AN ACCORD, THE BETTER IT WILL BE FOR ALL OF US.
TYLER STONE, HUMANITARIAN. NEXT, LYLA.
MIGUEL, IT'S GABE.
YEAH, I KNOW IT'S YOU, GABE. HOLOS, REMEMBER?
LOOK, AVOIDING ME ISN'T GOING TO MAKE THINGS BETTER.
I STAND BY WHAT I SAID BEFORE. THE WHOLE CORPORATE RAIDER PROGRAM IS A NASTY PIECE OF WORK. AND YOU'RE A NASTY PART OF IT.
BUT I STILL LOVE YA, MAN. I--
DUMP IT AND MOVE ON, LYLA.

MIGUEL? ARE YOU THERE? C'MON, HONEY. PICK UP.
NO?
LOOK... MIG... I...
I'M REALLY FRIGHTENED FOR YOU.
THE OTHER DAY, WHEN YOU WERE STRUNG OUT ON THE DRUGS... I'VE NEVER BEEN SO SCARED...
AND NOW IT'S... IT'S LIKE YOU VANISHED OFF THE FACE OF THE EARTH.
MIGUEL, I'M YOUR FIANCÉE DON'T LEAVE ME HANGING AFTER--
DUMP IT.
THE REMAINING THREE ARE ALSO FROM DANA.
DUMP 'EM ALL.
MIGUEL, YOUR PRESENT BEHAVIOR IS NOT WITHIN NORMAL PROGRAMMING PARAMETERS. YOU'VE DIVERTED FROM YOUR STANDARD PATTERN OF DOMESTIC ARRIVAL ACTIVITIES.
YOU'VE MADE NO ENTRIES IN YOUR PERSONAL JOURNAL FOR FIVE DAYS. YOU--
MY JOURNAL?
MY JOURNAL, HUH?
ALL RIGHT, LYLA. JOURNAL MODE, THEN.
TAKE THIS DOWN.

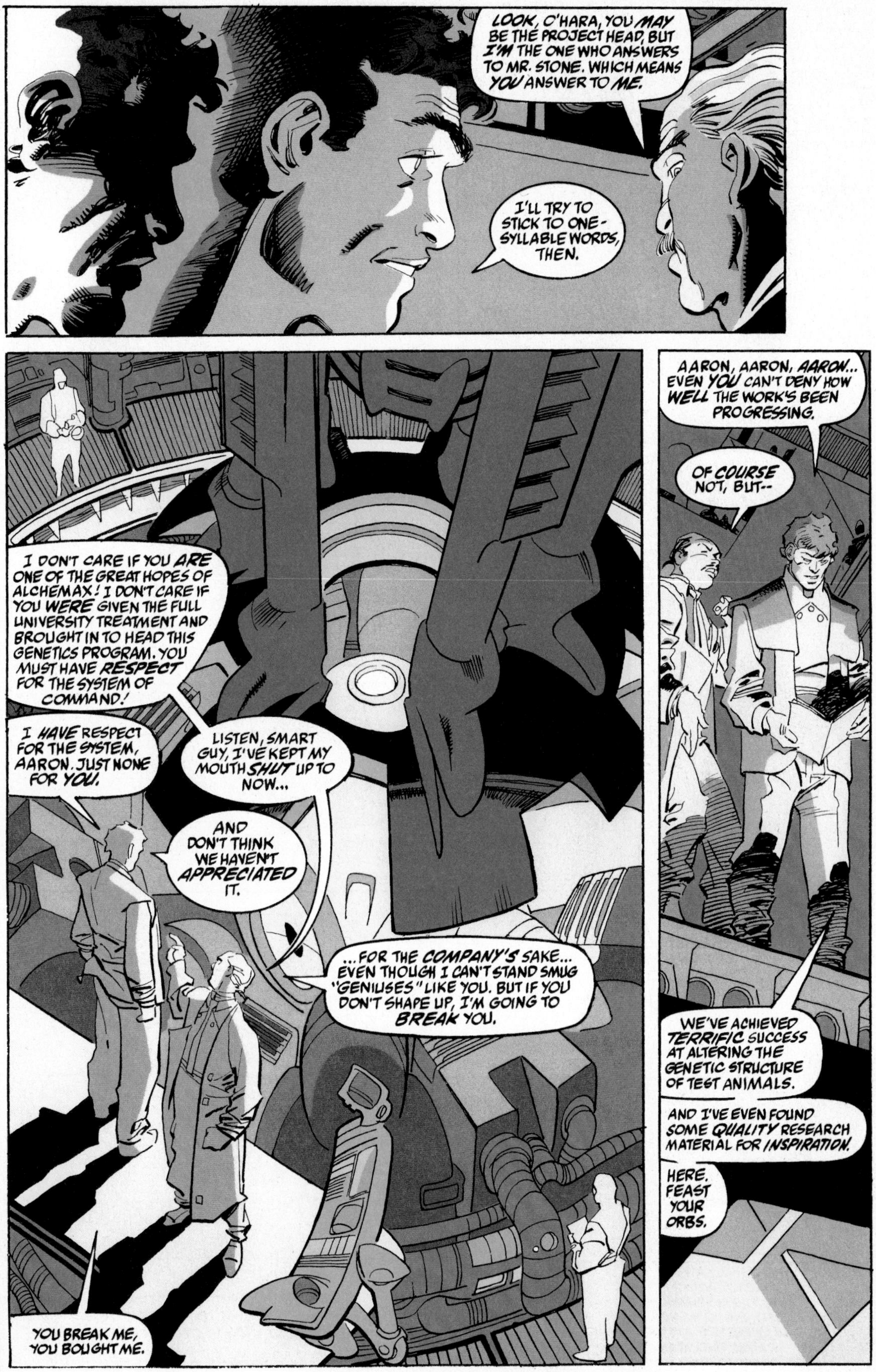
LOOK, O'HARA, YOU MAY BE THE PROJECT HEAD, BUT I'M THE ONE WHO ANSWERS TO MR. STONE. WHICH MEANS YOU ANSWER TO ME.
I'LL TRY TO STICK TO ONE-SYLLABLE WORDS, THEN.
I DON'T CARE IF YOU ARE ONE OF THE GREAT HOPES OF ALCHEMAX! I DON'T CARE IF YOU WERE GIVEN THE FULL UNIVERSITY TREATMENT AND BROUGHT IN TO HEAD THIS GENETICS PROGRAM. YOU MUST HAVE RESPECT FOR THE SYSTEM OF COMMAND!
I HAVE RESPECT FOR THE SYSTEM, AARON. JUST NONE FOR YOU.
LISTEN, SMART GUY, I'VE KEPT MY MOUTH SHUT UP TO NOW...
AND DON'T THINK WE HAVEN'T APPRECIATED IT.
...FOR THE COMPANY'S SAKE... EVEN THOUGH I CAN'T STAND SMUG "GENIUSES" LIKE YOU. BUT IF YOU DON'T SHAPE UP, I'M GOING TO BREAK YOU.
YOU BREAK ME, YOU BOUGHT ME.
AARON, AARON, AARON... EVEN YOU CAN'T DENY HOW WELL THE WORK'S BEEN PROGRESSING.
OF COURSE NOT, BUT--
WE'VE ACHIEVED TERRIFIC SUCCESS AT ALTERING THE GENETIC STRUCTURE OF TEST ANIMALS.
AND I'VE EVEN FOUND SOME QUALITY RESEARCH MATERIAL FOR INSPIRATION.
HERE. FEAST YOUR ORBS.

HIS NAME WAS SPIDER-MAN. ONE OF THE PREMIER BOYS FROM THE OLD HEROIC AGE, 'ROUND THE TURN OF THE CENTURY.
PROPORTIONATE STRENGTH OF A SPIDER.
WHAT DO YOU MEAN, "PROPORTIONATE?"
IT MEANS HE DIDN'T GET A SWELLED HEAD ABOUT IT.
YOU WANT AN IDEAL CORPORATE RAIDER? IMAGINE ONE THAT COULD SCALE WALLS, JUMP 50 FEET. STRONG, AGILE.
THAT'S THE DIRECTION WE'RE GOING. WE JUST CAN'T GO TOO QUICKLY. OTHERWISE...
OTHERWISE WHAT?
OTHERWISE WE'D LOSE YOU. SO WE'RE TAKING IT NICE AND SLOW, SO THAT YOU CAN FOLLOW ALONG.
ENJOY THE BOOK. IT HAS LOTS OF PICTURES.
ALL RIGHT, YOU LITTLE--
GENTLEMEN, I COULDN'T HELP BUT OVER-HEAR...
MR. STONE! NOT LONG ENOUGH NO SEE.
BUT AARON HERE IS CORRECT. ALCHEMAX WANTS RESULTS.
ALCHEMAX CAN'T WANT ANYTHING, TY. IT'S A CORPORATION, A LEGAL "THING." ONLY HUMANS CAN HAVE HUMAN DESIRES. AND HUMANS HAVE TO BE AWARE THAT RECKLESS TESTING ON HUMAN SUBJECTS WOULD BE--
MIKE, IF MY FATHER WERE ALIVE TODAY, YOU KNOW WHAT HE'D SAY?
"HELP, HELP, GET ME OUT OF THIS COFFIN?"
HE'D SAY CAUTION IS THE FIRST REFUGE OF THE COWARD.
AND HE'D SAY THAT BECAUSE--
HE LOVES THE SOUND OF HIS OWN VOICE?
BECAUSE IT WOULD BE TRUE. WHICH IS WHY WE'VE BROUGHT IN MR. SIMS HERE.
MIND TELLING ME WHAT SORT OF WARPED JOKE THIS IS?
NO JOKE. RATHER THAN FACE AGING 40 YEARS AS HIS PUNISH-MENT, MR. SIMS HAS VOLUNTEERED FOR THE RAIDER PROGRAM.
THIS IS CRAZY. WE'RE NOT READY FOR HUMANS YET. MR. SIMS, IT'S FAR TOO DANGEROUS.
LOOK, DOC-- I WANT TO DO THIS. I REALLY, REALLY DON'T WANT THEM TO MAKE A DODDERING OLD MAN OUTTA ME. I GOT A CHANCE HERE TO GET MY SENTENCE COM-MUTED.
JUST... DO THE BEST JOB YA CAN FOR ME, OKAY?

NICE HOW YOU STOOD UP TO Mr. STONE, GENIUS-BOY.
IF I WALK, STONE WOULD GO AHEAD WITHOUT ME. THEN SIMS' LIFE IS IN YOUR HANDS, AARON. THAT PUTS HIS CHANCES SOMEWHERE BETWEEN ZERO AND NONE.
I'M HIS ONLY SHOT.
Mr. SIMS, CAN YOU HEAR ME?
Y... YEAH.
WHAT WE'RE TRYING TO DO IS TINKER WITH YOUR GENETIC STRUCTURE. WE HAVE A VARIETY OF DIFFERENT IMPRINTS WE COULD BE USING.
AT THE MOMENT, I'M TRYING SOMETHING SIMPLE...SOMETHING THAT WOULD, IDEALLY, GIVE YOU AUGMENTED STRENGTH.
WHAT ABOUT THAT SPIDER-IMPRINT PROGRAM YOU WERE TALKING ABOUT?
ONE STEP AT A TIME, AARON. I DON'T WANT TO TRY AND TOTALLY RE-WRITE THE MAN'S GENETIC MAKE-UP.
WE COULD END UP WITH A HIDEOUS, MUTATED FREAK.
OR EVEN WORSE... YOU.
ALL RIGHT, GENTLEMEN, LET'S BRING IT TO FULL POWER.
LIKE THE DESIGN OF THE TRANSFORMATION CHAMBER, AARON?
GOT IT OFF AN OLD HOLO... "THE FLY."
YOU'D LIKE IT.
IT'S ABOUT SOMEONE WHO TURNS INTO A TOTALLY DISGUSTING CREEP. I BET YOU COULD RELATE TO IT.
YOU CAN'T FOOL ME, O'HARA. YOU'RE KEEPING UP THE FLIP RE-MARKS, BUT YOU'RE TERRIFIED YOU'RE GOING TO FALL FLAT ON YOUR FACE THIS TIME.
WELL, YA GOT ME, AARON. HERE I AM, SCARED ABOUT A HUMAN LIFE AT RISK. WHAT COULD I HAVE BEEN THINKING?
OKAY, MEN. OPEN HER UP.
MR. SIMS? STILL WITH US?
NOW YOU'LL PROBABLY FEEL A FAIRLY SHARP TINGLING. THAT SHOULD PASS IN A COUPLE OF--

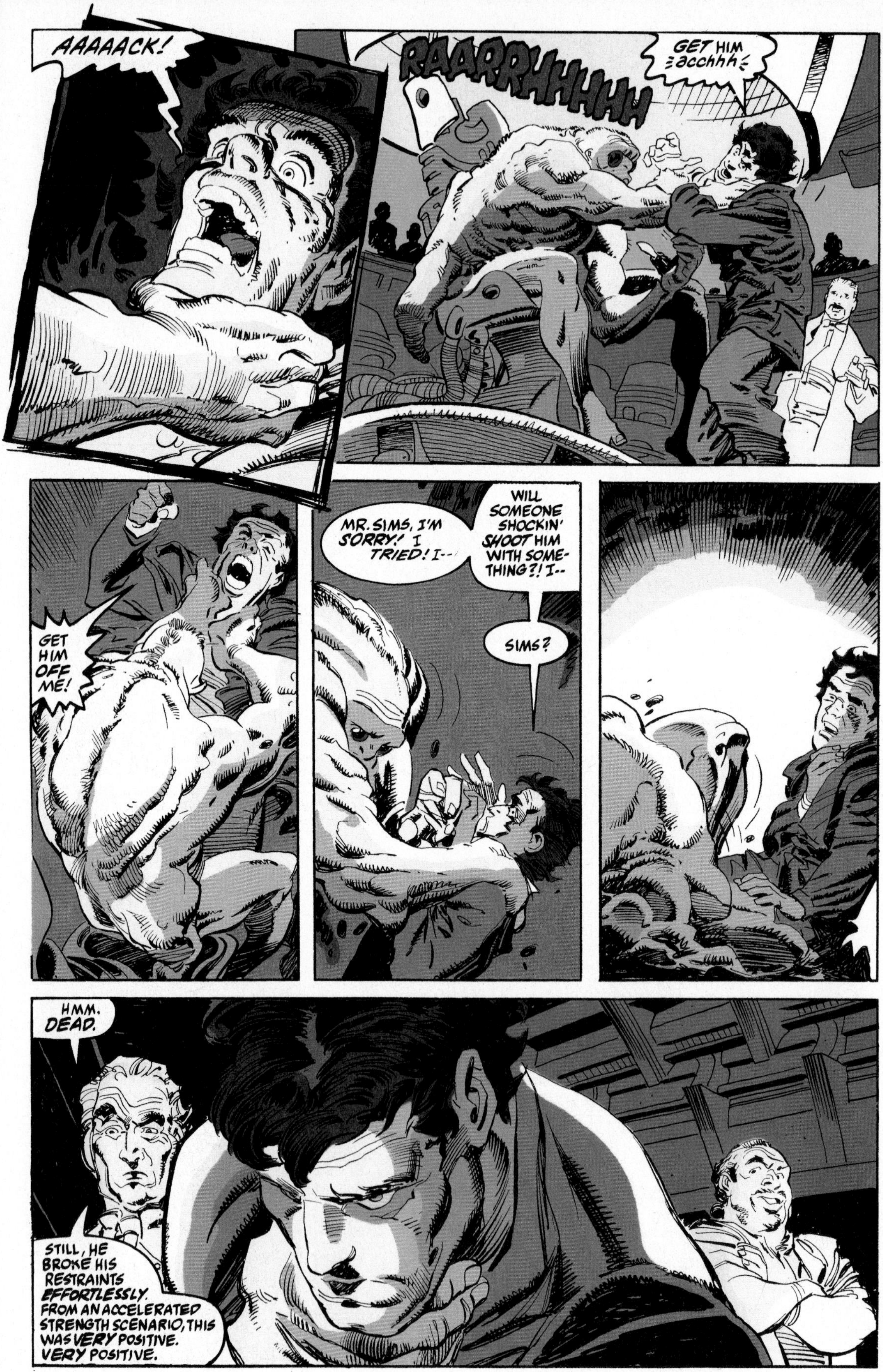
AAAAACK!
RAARRHHHHHH
GET HIM ≡acchhh≡
GET HIM OFF ME!
MR. SIMS, I'M SORRY! I TRIED! I--
WILL SOMEONE SHOCKIN' SHOOT HIM WITH SOMETHING?! I--
SIMS?
HMM. DEAD.
STILL, HE BROKE HIS RESTRAINTS EFFORTLESSLY. FROM AN ACCELERATED STRENGTH SCENARIO, THIS WAS VERY POSITIVE. VERY POSITIVE.

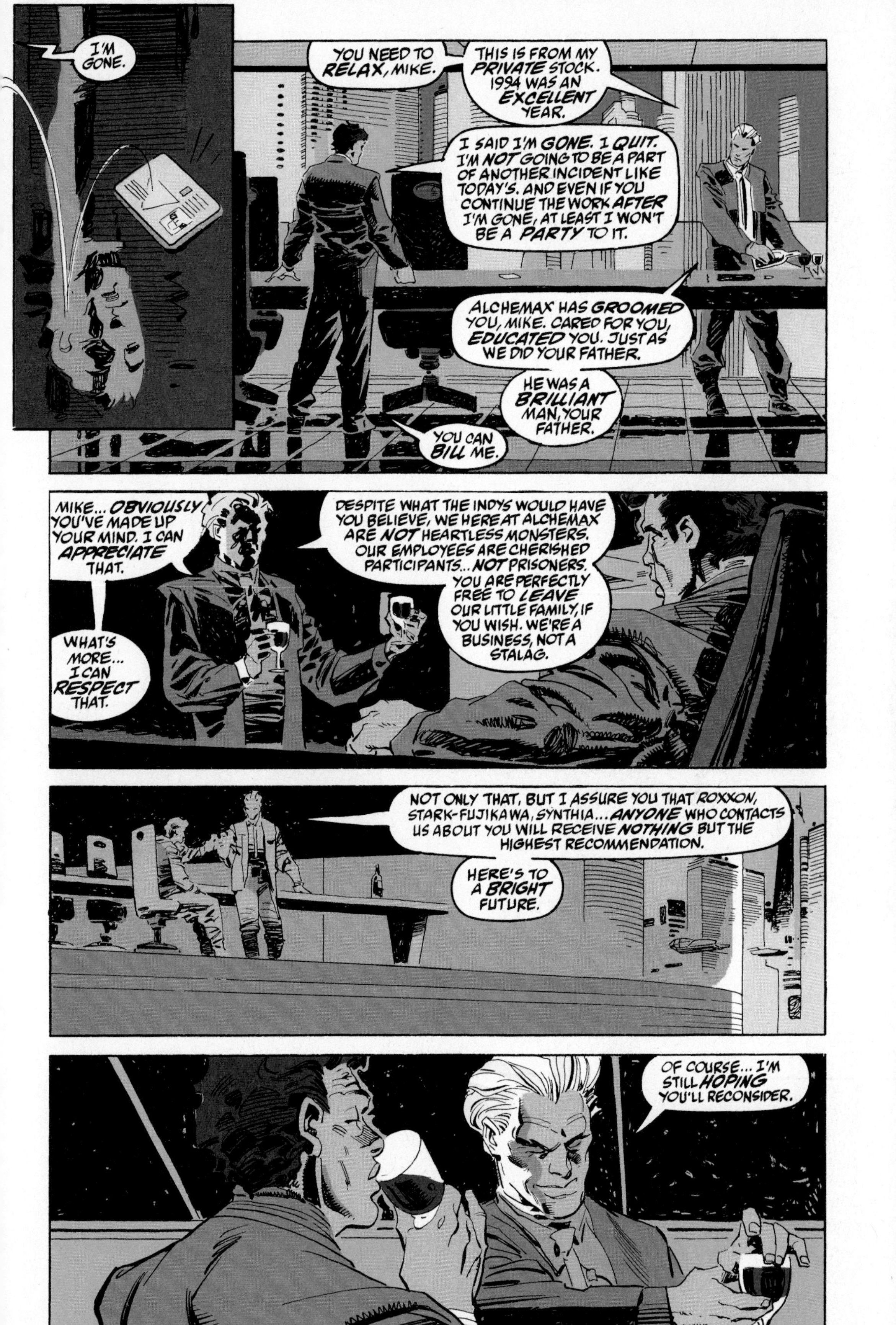
I'M GONE.
YOU NEED TO RELAX, MIKE.
THIS IS FROM MY PRIVATE STOCK. 1994 WAS AN EXCELLENT YEAR.
I SAID I'M GONE. I QUIT. I'M NOT GOING TO BE A PART OF ANOTHER INCIDENT LIKE TODAY'S. AND EVEN IF YOU CONTINUE THE WORK AFTER I'M GONE, AT LEAST I WON'T BE A PARTY TO IT.
ALCHEMAX HAS GROOMED YOU, MIKE. CARED FOR YOU, EDUCATED YOU. JUST AS WE DID YOUR FATHER.
HE WAS A BRILLIANT MAN, YOUR FATHER.
YOU CAN BILL ME.
MIKE... OBVIOUSLY YOU'VE MADE UP YOUR MIND. I CAN APPRECIATE THAT.
WHAT'S MORE... I CAN RESPECT THAT.
DESPITE WHAT THE INDYS WOULD HAVE YOU BELIEVE, WE HERE AT ALCHEMAX ARE NOT HEARTLESS MONSTERS. OUR EMPLOYEES ARE CHERISHED PARTICIPANTS... NOT PRISONERS.
YOU ARE PERFECTLY FREE TO LEAVE OUR LITTLE FAMILY, IF YOU WISH. WE'RE A BUSINESS, NOT A STALAG.
NOT ONLY THAT, BUT I ASSURE YOU THAT ROXXON, STARK-FUJIKAWA, SYNTHIA... ANYONE WHO CONTACTS US ABOUT YOU WILL RECEIVE NOTHING BUT THE HIGHEST RECOMMENDATION.
HERE'S TO A BRIGHT FUTURE.
OF COURSE... I'M STILL HOPING YOU'LL RECONSIDER.

TY, DID WE JUST HAVE SYNAPTIC MELTDOWN IN THE LAST FEW MINUTES?
I'M LEAVING, REMEMBER? VAPOR. POOF. AND Y'KNOW, NOW THAT I'VE MADE THE DECISION...
I FEEL MORE RELAXED THAN EVER.
YES, THAT WOULD PROBABLY BE BECAUSE OF MY PARTING GIFT. THE RAPTURE.
WH-WHAT?
THE RAPTURE, IN THE WINE YOU JUST DRANK. I'M SURE YOU'RE FAMILIAR WITH IT.
A VERY HIGH-POWERED, MIND-EXPANDING HALLUCINOGEN. PERFECTLY LEGAL, OF COURSE. A NUMBER OF ALCHEMAX EMPLOYEES ARE ALREADY USERS...
BUT MY RECORDS INDICATE YOU'D NEVER AVAILED YOURSELF OF IT. I THOUGHT MAYBE THE PROHIBITIVE EXPENSE HAD MADE YOU HESITATE, SO CONSIDER THIS A PRESENT.
YOU... CREEPING PIECE OF...
NOW THAT I THINK OF IT... PERHAPS YOU'VE PASSED ON IT BECAUSE RAPTURE IS SO ADDICTIVE. ONCE IT'S IN YOUR SYSTEM, YOU NEED IT THE WAY YOU NEED OXYGEN TO BREATHE. WITHOUT RAPTURE, YOU'LL DIE.
YOU WANT TO HIT ME, DON'T YOU? I WOULDN'T. I THINK YOU'LL WANT ME TO REMAIN KINDLY DISPOSED TOWARDS YOU...
ESPECIALLY SINCE ALCHEMAX IS THE ONLY AUTHORIZED RAPTURE DISTRIBUTOR. THAT'S PROBABLY ANOTHER REASON IT HELD NO APPEAL FOR YOU. YOU BEING SUCH AN INDEPENDENT SORT, MIKE... YOU'D NEVER WANT TO GIVE UP YOUR ABILITY TO JUST WALK OUT.
YOU CAN STILL WALK AWAY, MIKE. BUT YOU WON'T LIKE THE CONSEQUENCES.
I'LL HAVE A CAR BRING YOU HOME. GET SOME REST... AND ENJOY THE RAPTURE. IF YOU FIGHT IT, IT CAN BE QUITE NASTY, SO I'D JUST GIVE IN IF I WERE YOU.
AND MIKE... HERE'S HOPING YOU CHOOSE TO BE A MEMBER OF THE ALCHEMAX FAMILY FOR SOME TIME TO COME.

ONE TWO THREE FOUR
COME ON DANA, DO SOME MORE
DON'T SLOW DOWN, DON'T TAKE RESTS
THIS WILL HELP TO FIRM YOUR--
UHHHHH....
MIGUEL! WHAT'S WRONG, LOVER? YOU'RE HOME EARLY!
ARE YOU SICK? SHOULD I--
FREEZE PROGRAM!
GET AWAY!
URRKKHHH!

AWW, SHOCK, DANA!
I... I DIDN'T REALIZE IT WAS--
I THOUGHT YOU WERE A--
JUST... JUST KEEP AWAY FROM ME.
HONEY, I SWEAR, I--
AW, MAN, YOUR FACE. I... I FEEL LIKE DIRT.
GOOD!
WHY DID YOU--?
IT'S THE RAPTURE. I WAS FIGHTING IT... SEEING MONSTERS EVERYWHERE. I--
RAPTURE?! SINCE WHEN DO YOU DROP RAPTURE?
SINCE TYLER STONE DECIDED TO SLIP ME SOME AS INCENTIVE FOR ME TO STAY.
YOU WERE QUITTING ALCHEMAX?
I... I WAS. BUT NOW...
I MEAN, THE EFFECTS HAVE FINALLY PASSED. BUT I CAN FEEL IT GNAWING AT ME. I'LL NEED IT AGAIN, SOON... BUT THEN ALCHEMAX HAS MY BUTT IN A PERMANENT SLING.
LISTEN. I HAVE FRIENDS. EVEN IF YOU QUIT ALCHEMAX, I CAN PROBABLY GET RAPTURE THROUGH BLACK MARKET--
YOU WANT ME TO BE A LOUSY DRUG ADDICT MY WHOLE LIFE?!
I WANT YOU NOT TO HURT! THAT'S ALL!
THAT'S ALL.

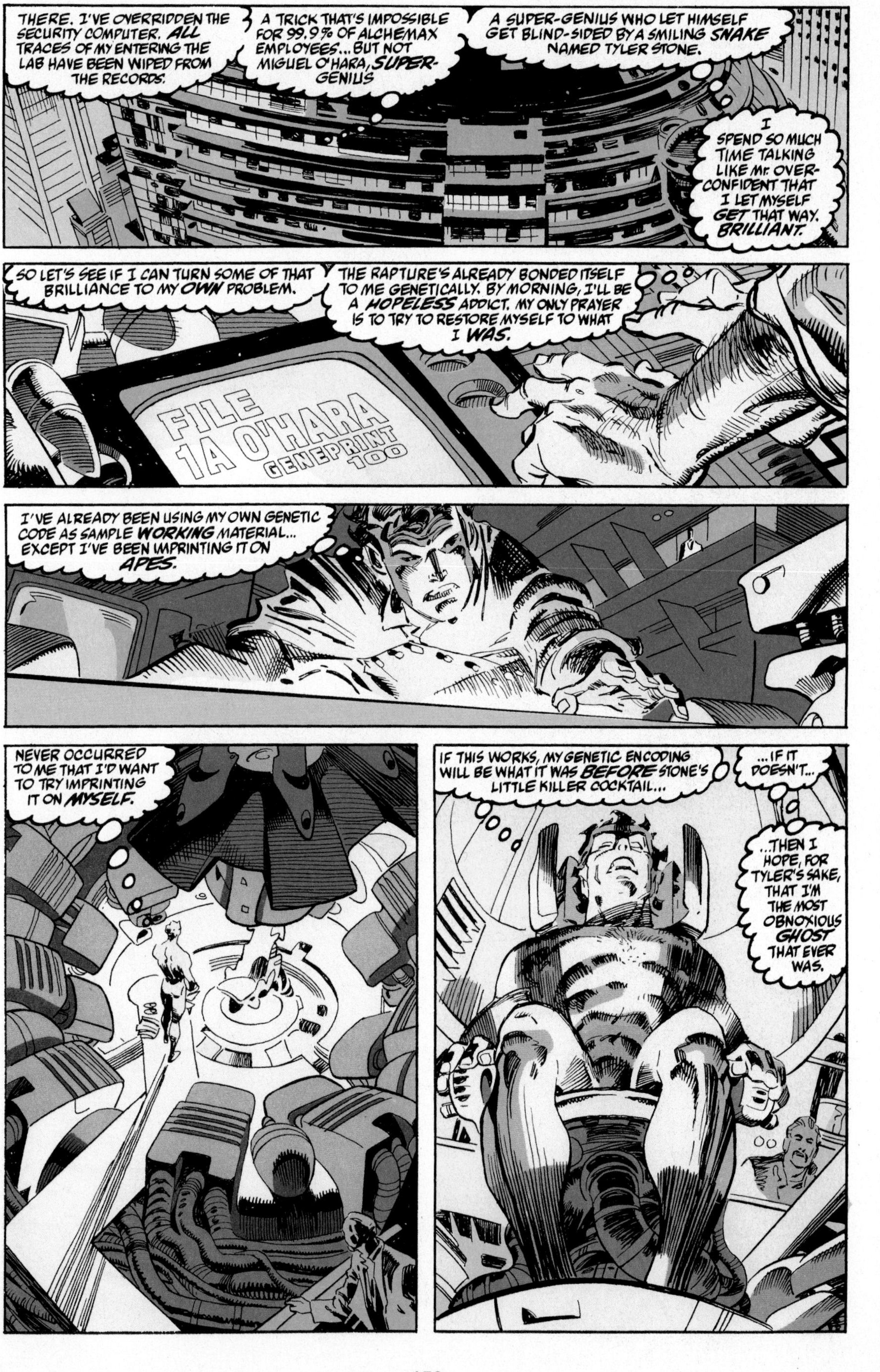
THERE. I'VE OVERRIDDEN THE SECURITY COMPUTER. ALL TRACES OF MY ENTERING THE LAB HAVE BEEN WIPED FROM THE RECORDS.
A TRICK THAT'S IMPOSSIBLE FOR 99.9% OF ALCHEMAX EMPLOYEES... BUT NOT MIGUEL O'HARA, SUPER-GENIUS
A SUPER-GENIUS WHO LET HIMSELF GET BLIND-SIDED BY A SMILING SNAKE NAMED TYLER STONE.
I SPEND SO MUCH TIME TALKING LIKE Mr. OVER-CONFIDENT THAT I LET MYSELF GET THAT WAY. BRILLIANT.
SO LET'S SEE IF I CAN TURN SOME OF THAT BRILLIANCE TO MY OWN PROBLEM.
THE RAPTURE'S ALREADY BONDED ITSELF TO ME GENETICALLY. BY MORNING, I'LL BE A HOPELESS ADDICT. MY ONLY PRAYER IS TO TRY TO RESTORE MYSELF TO WHAT I WAS.
FILE 1A O'HARA GENEPRINT 100
I'VE ALREADY BEEN USING MY OWN GENETIC CODE AS SAMPLE WORKING MATERIAL... EXCEPT I'VE BEEN IMPRINTING IT ON APES.
NEVER OCCURRED TO ME THAT I'D WANT TO TRY IMPRINTING IT ON MYSELF.
IF THIS WORKS, MY GENETIC ENCODING WILL BE WHAT IT WAS BEFORE STONE'S LITTLE KILLER COCKTAIL...
...IF IT DOESN'T...
...THEN I HOPE, FOR TYLER'S SAKE, THAT I'M THE MOST OBNOXIOUS GHOST THAT EVER WAS.

MIGUEL O'HARA, WORKING OVER-TIME.
FILE 1A O'HARA 50
FILE 47-A SPIDER 50
MY PUMPING UP THE LEVELS OF EVERY BLASTED PIECE OF EQUIPMENT IN THE IMPRINT SEQUENCE.
WHAT'S THIS BUTTON DO? POOR, DUMB OLD AARON DELGATO WOULDN'T UNDERSTAND YOUR GREAT CONCEPTS, WOULD I, O'HARA?
A PITY IF SOME-THING WENT WRONG... SOMETHING LIKE... SAY...
DOESN'T MUCH MATTER WHEN I'M IN THE DRIVER'S SEAT, THOUGH, DOES IT?!
WARNING. EQUIPMENT IS EXCEEDING RECOMMENDED SAFETY LEVELS. AUTOMATIC SHUTDOWN IN T MINUS 5 SECONDS...
WARNING
EXCEEDING RECOMMENDED SAFETY LIMITS
OVERRIDE IN EFFECT FILES MERGING
OVERRIDE! REPEAT, MANUAL OVERRIDE!
AAAARRRRHHHHA

HAAH! HOW DID YOU LIKE THAT, Mr. GENIUS! Mr. SMART-MOUTH WISE-CRACKER! HOW DID--!
HUH?
I DON'T BELIEVE IT! STILL ALIVE--AND UNHARMED!
BUT HE DOESN'T KNOW I OVER-LOADED THE CIRCUITRY. I CAN USE THAT.
LATE NIGHT MAD-SCIENTIST THEATRICS, O'HARA? YOU'VE JUST BLOWN IT BIG TIME, BOY.
WHEN I TELL MR. STONE HOW YOU WRECKED THE EQUIPMENT IN SOME TEMPERAMENTAL TAN-TRUM, THAT'S GOING TO FINISH YOU.
THEN I'LL BE BACK IN CHARGE, DOING THINGS THE WAY THEY SHOULD BE...
TURN AROUND WHEN I SPEAK TO YOU, BOY! BEFORE I KICK YOUR BUTT FROM HERE TO--
--TO--

Next:
NOTHING
VENTURED

ARACHNOPHILIA

JOEY CAVALIERI
EDITOR
SARRA MOSSOFF
ASSISTANT EDITOR

c/o MARVEL COMICS GROUP
387 PARK AVENUE SOUTH
NEW YORK, NEW YORK 10016

ATTENTION CORRESPONDENTS: ALL LETTERS TO BE CONSIDERED FOR PUBLICATION MUST INCLUDE YOUR NAME AND ADDRESS THOUGH WE WILL WITHHOLD THAT INFO BY REQUEST

OUT OF MY HEAD

"Editing a science-fiction magazine is very much like walking a narrow and treacherous path atop a wall dividing two sheer precipices. At their foot, on the one side, lurks a pack of horrendously articulate and ferocious fans, waiting to snap and snarl at every slightest deviation from what each of them considers the classic norm.

"On the other, coiled and hissing, the science experts lie in wait, striking at every possible technical flaw the editor allows in print.

"If the wall falls away, the editor lands in both abysses to be torn apart in a savage tug-of-war."

Wish I'd said that.

You've guessed that wasn't *my* voice. It's part of an editorial from the August 1951 issue of a pulp called *Thrilling Wonder Stories.*

Sam Merwin, who wrote it, got it exactly right.

In our case, it was a question of how far we (that's the editorial "we") could "deviate from the classic norm." Creating a "first issue" of *any* Spider-Man title is a tough act to follow. But do we try to duplicate the Spider-Man whose adventures we know and follow avidly? Or strive to break new ground as we tell stories about the next century?

And what about that next century? How close is it to the Marvel Universe we're familiar with? How closely should it adhere to our expectations of the world of tomorrow? And above all, why did Marvel entrust its vision of the next hundred years to an editor who can't see far enough ahead to decide what's for lunch?

It's like stage fright. Imagine getting pushed out there *knowing* that for as many members of the audience you will please, that's as many as you'll tick off.

Well, the worst stage fright can be defeated by a good script, cast and crew. Here's ours:

If you're gonna write about science-fictional super heroes, get a guy who makes the *Times* best-seller list writing about 'em. A guy like PETER DAVID, for example.

RICK LEONARDI depicts the future so well, I'm beginning to suspect he has a time machine in his basement. AL WILLIAMSON has a list of credits longer than this editorial, and his favorite character of all time is probably Flash Gordon. So that counts as credentials.

We can't stray too far from home base, given that we've got a guy named Peter writing this book, and a guy named Parker lettering it. RICK PARKER, that is. And STEVE BUCCELLATO is considered like unto a demi-god in the coloring community. The competition points to the work of logo designer KEN LOPEZ when they want something done Marvel-style. Also, thanks to M. KRAIGER for designing the heading above, and ED LAZELLARI, DAN CARR, FRANK PERCY and JOHNNY GREENE for executing it so well. Nice job, guys.

We promise plenty of "thrilling wonder stories." It's now up to you "horrendously articulate and ferocious fans," to let us know how we're doing!

Enough already, Joey!

Let's give them a glimpse of what's ahead for 2099!

LYLA! OPEN THE WINDOW!
THE WINDOWS DON'T OPEN, MIGUEL. THEY'RE SEALED FOR YOUR PROTECTION.
MIGUEL... I'M CONCERNED ABOUT YOUR SAFETY.
ALL RIGHT, THE UPDRAFTS SHOULD CATCH THE LIGHT BYTE CLOTH RIGHT ABOUT...
NOW!
I SAID...
RIGHT ABOUT...
NOW!
I SAID...

Here's a page from Spidey 2099 #2 – exciting stuff!

And be sure not to miss the next book in our new series – RAVAGE 2099 → on sale next month!
Sarra

MARVEL COMICS
RAVAGE
2099

All six parts of the "Rise of the Midnight Sons" crossover were bagged with sections of an interlocking poster by Andy & Adam Kubert.